SDN: Software Defined Networks

Thomas D. Nadeau and Ken Gray

O'REILLY®

Beijing · Cambridge · Farnham · Köln · Sebastopol · Tokyo

SDN: Software Defined Networks

by Thomas D. Nadeau and Ken Gray

Published by O'Reilly Media, Inc., 1005 Gravenstein Highway North, Sebastopol, CA 95472.

O'Reilly books may be purchased for educational, business, or sales promotional use. Online editions are also available for most titles (*http://my.safaribooksonline.com*). For more information, contact our corporate/institutional sales department: 800-998-9938 or *corporate@oreilly.com*.

Editors: Mike Loukides and Meghan Blanchette	**Indexer:** Judith McConville
Production Editor: Kristen Borg	**Cover Designer:** Karen Montgomery
Copyeditor: Jasmine Kwityn	**Interior Designer:** David Futato
Proofreader: Amanda Kersey	**Illustrator:** Rebecca Demarest and Kara Ebrahim

August 2013:   First Edition

Revision History for the First Edition:

2013-08-07:   First release

See *http://oreilly.com/catalog/errata.csp?isbn=9781449342302* for release details.

ISBN: 978-1-449-34230-2

[LSI]

Table of Contents

Foreword by David Meyer

Although the ideas underlying software-defined networking (SDN) have only recently come into the public consciousness, a few of us who are active in the research, operator, and vendor communities immediately saw the applicability of SDN-like techniques to data center and service provider environments (and beyond). In addition to the explosion of innovative thinking going on in the research community, we also saw SDN as a programmatic way to optimize, monetize, and scale networks of all kinds.

In 2011, the first organization dedicated to the growth and success of SDN began with the Open Networking Foundation (ONF). Among its stated missions was to evolve the OpenFlow protocol from its academic roots to a commercially viable substrate for building networks and networking products. Within two years, the ONF's membership had grown to approximately 100 entities, representing the diverse interest and expectations for SDN. Against this backdrop, many of us were looking at the wider implications of the ideas underlying SDN, and in the process, generalized SDN to include not only OpenFlow but other forms of network programmability as well.

Early on in this process, both Tom Nadeau and Ken Gray realized that SDN was really about general network programmability and the associated interfaces, protocols, data models, and APIs. Using this insight, they helped to organize the SDN Birds of a Feather session at IETF 82, in Taipei, to investigate this more general SDN model. At that meeting, Tom presented a framework for software-defined networks that envisioned SDN as a generalized mechanism for network programmability. This work encouraged the community to take a more general view of SDN and eventually led to the formation of the Interface to the Routing System Working Group in the IETF.

Since that time, in addition to their many contributions to Internet technologies, Tom and Ken have become well-respected senior members of the SDN community. They are active participants in the core SDN industry activities and develop products for the SDN market. Some of the key industry activities that Tom and Ken drive include the ONF, IETF, ETSI, industry events such as SDN Summit 2012/2013, as well as open source consortia such as the Open Daylight Project. This book draws on their deep understanding and experience in the field and offers a unique perspective on SDN. It will help you understand not only the technology but also how it is being developed, standardized, and deployed.

Tom and Ken are eminently qualified to give you a lucid understanding of the technology and the common-sense use and deployment of network programmability techniques. In particular, their book is an excellent and practical introduction to the fundamentals of SDN and is filled with innumerable anecdotes explaining the ideas and the background behind the development of SDN. So if you are interested in writing SDN applications, building SDN capable networks, or just understanding what SDN is, this book is for you!

—David Meyer
CTO and Chief Scientist, Brocade Communications

Foreword by David Ward

Technological shifts that affect how developers and engineers build and design their business architectures are monumental. These shifts are not applicable to Moore's law and tend to be transformations that affect not only the IT landscape but the business landscape as well. These shifts tend to occur every 8 to 10 years and have a long-lasting impact on how people build, consume, and distribute technologies. They also force people to frame their business opportunities in new ways.

In 1996, Gartner coined the term "service-oriented architecture." By 2000, it had taken center stage with the core purpose of allowing for the easy cooperation of a large number of computers connected over a network to exchange information via services without human interaction. There was no need to make underlying changes to the program or application itself. Essentially, it took on the same role as a single operating system on one machine and applied it to the entire infrastructure of servers, allowing for more usable, flexible, and scalable applications and services to be built, tested, deployed, and managed. It introduced web services as the de facto way to make functional building blocks accessible over standard Internet protocols independent of platforms and languages—allowing for faster and easier development, testing, deployment, and manageability of IT infrastructures. SOA drastically changed the way developers, their managers, and the business looked at technology.

When you look at software-defined networking, you see similarities. The network is the cornerstone of IT in that it can enable new architectures that in turn create new business opportunities. In essence, it allows IT to become more relevant than ever and the enabler of new business. The network is now the largest business enabler if architected and utilized in the correct way—allowing for the network, server, and storage to be tied together to enable the principles of SOA to be executed at the network layer. SDN and APIs to the network change the accessibility to programming intent and receiving state from the network and services, thus overcoming the traditional view that the network has to be built and run by magicians. However, when SOA principles become applied to the networking layer, the network becomes more accessible, programmable, and flexible, allowing organizations to actually shift IT at the speed that the business moves, all while adding increased value to the business in new ways.

But what is a software-defined network? There are many camps that have varying definitions. When broken down into simple terms, it needs to be looked at as an approach or architecture to not only simplify your network but also to make it more reactive to the requirements of workloads and services placed in the network. IT infrastructure needs to move at the speed of business opportunities and must enable new ways to do business quickly, flexibly, and faster than before. A pragmatic definition is this: SDN functionally enables the network to be accessed by operators programmatically, allowing for automated management and orchestration techniques; application of configuration policy across multiple routers, switches, and servers; and the decoupling of the application that performs these operations from the network device's operating system.

As SDN becomes increasingly the buzzword of multiple industries, it's worthwhile to take a look at why SDN came about. Historically, network configuration state has remained largely static, unchanged, and commonly untouchable. Manual configuration and CLI-based configuration on a device-by-device basis was the norm, and network management constituted the basic "screen scraping" or use of Expect scripts as a way to solve manageability problems and core scalability issues (cut-and-paste methodology). The highest end of programmatic interfaces included XML interfaces and onboard Perl, Tk/Tcl, and Expect. However, when you're dealing with multiple routers, switches, and servers working as a system (and services that are routing traffic across multiple domains with different users, permissions, and policies), control and management state needs to be applied across the network as an operation. Element-by-element management simply doesn't provide enough flexibility and agility or the notion of dynamic or ephemeral data (configuration and state not persistently held in the config file). But as service-oriented architecture principles started to shift southbound down the stack and the realization of their application at the networking layer was recognized, new architectures—coupled with advancements in networking—allowed for software-defined networking to emerge and users to realize the power that the network was capable of in new ways.

Yes, it's true that there is a history of protocol interfaces to routers, switches, servers, gateways, and so on. Decades of deployment of the current Internet that program dynamic data associated with subscribers, sessions, and applications does currently exist and is widely deployed. These protocol servers (e.g., Radius, Diameter, PCMM, COPS, 3GPP) all could be considered early forms of SDN, so why aren't they? What's a bit different now is that one major functionality of the SDN architecture is the ability to write applications on top of a platform that customizes data from different sources or data bases into one network-wide operation.

SDN is also an architecture that allows for a centrally managed and distributed control, management, and data plane, where policy that dictates the forwarding rules is centralized, while the actual forwarding rule processing is distributed among multiple devices. In this model, application policy calculation (e.g., QoS, access control lists, and tunnel creation) happens locally in real time and the quality, security, and monitoring of policies are managed centrally and then pushed to the switching/routing nodes. This allows for more flexibility, control, and scalability of the network itself, and the use of templates, variables, multiple databases of users, and policies all working in combination to derive or compile the desired configuration and state to be downloaded to the routers and switches. What's key to understand is that SDN doesn't replace the control plane on the router or switch. It augments them. How? By having a view of the entire network all at once versus only from one position in the topology (e.g., the router or switch). The marriage of dynamic routing and signaling and a centralized view is incredibly powerful. It enables the fastest possible protection in the event of a failure, the greatest resiliency, and the ability to place services into a network in one command. The two technologies working together are really a major step forward that wasn't previously in our toolbox.

There are a few variations on the SDN theme and some oft spoken components to be considered. OpenFlow is one, which architecturally separates the control and management planes from the data plane on the networking device. This allows for a centralized controller to manage the flows in the forwarding nodes. However, OpenFlow is only one protocol and one element of SDN. There are many other protocols now. Some examples include I2RS, PCE-P, BGP-LS, FORCES, OMI, and NetConf/Yang. All of these are also open standards. What's important to remember is that SDN is not a protocol; it's an operational and programming architecture.

What do we get from SDN? The architecture brings the network and networking data closer to the application layer and the applications closer to the networking layer. As practiced in SOA, no longer is there the need for a human element or scripting languages to act as humans to distribute data and information bidirectionally because APIs and tooling now have evolved in a way that this can be delivered in a secure and scalable way via open interfaces and interoperability. The data in the network (e.g., stats, state, subscriber info, service state, security, peering, etc.) can be analyzed and used by an application to create policy intent and program the network into a new configuration. It can be programmed this way persistently or only ephemerally.

Programmability (i.e., the ability to access the network via APIs and open interfaces) is central to SDN. The notion of removing the control and management planes to an off-switch/router application connected to the networking device by SDN protocols is equally important. This off-box application is really what software developers would call a "platform," as it has its own set of APIs, logic, and the ability for an application to make requests to the network, receive events, and speak the SDN protocols. What's key here is that programmers don't need to know the SDN protocols because they write to the controller's APIs. Programmers don't need to know the different configuration syntax or semantics of different networking devices because they program to a set of APIs on the controller that can speak to many different devices. Different vendors, eras of equipment, and classes of equipment (e.g., transport, simple switches, wireless base stations, subscriber termination gateways, peering routers, core routers, and servers) all are on the trajectory to be able to be programmed by the SDN protocols that plug into the bottom of the controller. The programmer only uses the APIs on the top of the controller to automate, orchestrate, and operate the network. This doesn't necessarily mean there is a grand unification theory of controllers and one to serve all layers and functions of networking, but what it does mean is that the network now has been abstracted and is being programmed off box. Thus, when integrated into an IaaS (Infrastructure as a Service) layer in a stack, OSS, or IT system, the network is being automated and orchestrated as fast as users log onto the net and as fast as workloads are being spun up on servers.

The use of new tooling practices typically utilized by system administrators and new available to network operators are related to the whole SDN movement. Tools such as Puppet, Chef, CFEngine, and others are being used to automate and orchestrate the network in new ways as plug-ins can now be created to utilize the network data via the open interfaces of the network. Controller APIs also allow for easier and faster ways to build and apply policy across the network in multiple languages and with integration into existing tools such as IDEs (NetBeans, Eclipse, et al.). This allows for a better user experience for network engineers versus the traditionally used CLI model.

Before we dig into examples, it's important to understand what SDN actually solves and why there is a shift to this particular architecture. As networks evolve and new services are deployed, it's critical to implement new ways for users to more easily provision and orchestrate network resources in real time. By implementing this, cost can be reduced by the automation of moving resources around faster and more reliably, and by allowing the network to respond directly to a request from an application (versus the intervention by a human). This allows for operators to use programmatic (scalable) control versus manual to create and apply these services in a way that is simpler than a command-line interface. Additionally, it enables the ability to utilize new resources from the network (user data, traffic path information, etc.) and create new types of applications that can control policy for the network in a scalable fashion. It also allows for the optimization of infrastructure, services, and applications by allowing for new network data and capabilities to be extended and applied into the aforementioned architecture, creating new ways to not only optimize existing applications but also to insert new services or offerings that can provide a better user experience or create a new offering or advanced feature that could be monetized.

As SDN evolves, it's important to look at some implementations to understand why it's so critical for multiple industries (e.g., video delivery, user services and mobile, cable and broadband, security, and provider edge) to embrace. Where SDN reaches its potential, however, is when you look at it for not just programming the network functions and scaling those across your infrastructure, but also for actually tying server, storage, and the network together for new use cases. In this case, systems can actually interact with each other, allowing for more infrastructure flexibility, whether physical, virtual, or hybrid.

Traffic policy and rerouting based on network conditions and/or regulation shifts are also common applications, as are the insertion of new services or data into applications that may be able to more clearly prioritize bandwidth for a user that pays a premium amount for faster connection speeds. When you apply SDN and a centralized management plane that is separate from the data plane, you can more quickly make decisions on where data traffic can be rerouted, as this can occur programmatically with software interfaces (APIs), versus on-the-box CLI methodology.

One advanced use case is the hybrid cloud. In this case, an application may run in a private cloud or data center yet utilize the public cloud when the demand for computing capacity spikes or cost can be reduced. Historically, cloud bursting was typically used only in environments with non-mission critical applications or services, but with the network tie-in and software principles applied, the use case shifts. Applications now remain in compliance with the IT organizations' policies and regulations. The application can also retain its dependency model if it is reliant on different data or information that it typically has on premises versus off, or in the public cloud environment. It also allows for the application to run across different platforms regardless of where the application was built.

As we look at SDN, we must also consider Network Functions Virtualization and how this ties into the broader infrastructure and virtualization picture. The transition from physical to virtual is one that is leading many of these changes in the industry. By tying the hardware (physical) to software (virtual), including network, server, and storage, there's the opportunity to virtualize network services and have them orchestrated as fast as any other workload. Tie this via programmatic interfaces to the WAN, and you can absolutely guarantee service delivery. SDN coupled with NFV is a pivotal architectural shift in both computing and networking. This shift is marked by dynamic changes to infrastructure to closely match customer demand, analytics to assist in predicting performance requirements, and a set of management and orchestration tools that allow network functions and applications to scale up, down, and out with greater speed and less manual intervention. This change affects how we build cloud platforms for applications and at the most basic level must provide the tools and techniques that allow the network to respond to changing workload requirements as quickly as the platforms that leverage them. It also allows workload requirements to include network requirements and have them satisfied.

It's important to note that not all networks are the same, and that's why it's critical to understand the importance of the underlying infrastructure when abstracting control from the network—either from physical or virtual devices. Network Functions Virtualization is simply the addition of virtual or off-premises devices to augment traditional infrastructure. However, the tie to both the on- and off-premises offerings must be considered when running applications and services to ensure a seamless experience not just for the organization running the applications or services but also for the consumer of the services (whether they be enterprise and in-house users or external customers).

So why should you care? From a technical perspective, SDN allows for more flexibility and agility as well as options for your infrastructure. By allowing data to be controlled centrally and tied into not just the network, but also the storage and server, you get a more cohesive view on performance, speed, traffic optimization, and service guarantees. With programmatic interfaces (APIs) that can be exposed in multiple languages and utilized with tools, your operators and administrators can more quickly respond to the demand of the business side of the house or external customer needs. They can now apply policies for other development organizations in-house to allow them network data to more effectively spin up server farms or even build applications with network intelligence built in for faster, better performing applications. By allowing for the data to be exposed in a secure and scalable way, the entire IT organization benefits, and with faster development and deployment cycles and easier delivery of new services, so too does the business. The promise that SOA gave developers—write once, run anywhere —can now be fully realized with the underlying network's ability to distribute information across the enterprise, access, WAN, and data center (both physical and virtual). This allows for applications to break free from the boundaries of the OSS and management platforms that had previously limited their ability to run in different environments.

The IT industry is going through a massive shift that will revolutionize the way users build, test, deploy, and monetize their applications. With SDN, the network is now closer to applications (and vice versa), allowing for a new breed of smarter, faster, and better performing applications. It enables the network to be automated in new ways, providing more flexibility and scalability for users, and unleashes the potential for business cost savings and revenue-generating opportunities. It's a new era in networking and the IT industry overall, and it will be a game-changing one. Check out this book—it's required reading.

—David Ward
CTO, Cisco Systems

Preface

The first question most readers of an O'Reilly book might ask is about the choice of the cover animal. In this case, "why a duck?" Well, for the record, our first choice was a unicorn decked out in glitter and a rainbow sash.

That response always gets a laugh (we are sure you just giggled a little), but it also brings to the surface a common perception of software-defined networks among many experienced network professionals. Although we think there is some truth to this perception, there is certainly more meat than myth to this unicorn.

So, starting over, the better answer to that first question is that the movement of a duck[1] is not just what one sees on the water; most of the action is under the water, which

---

1. The real answer is that one of the authors has a fondness for ducks, as he raises Muscovy Ducks on his family farm.

you can't easily see. Under the waterline, some very muscular feet are paddling away to move that duck along. In many ways, this is analogous to the progress of software-defined networks.

The surface view of SDN might lead the casual observer to conclude a few things. First, defining what SDN is, or might be, is something many organizations are frantically trying to do in order to resuscitate their business plans or revive their standards-developing organizations (SDOs). Second, that SDN is all about the active rebranding of existing products to be this mythical thing that they are not. Many have claimed that products they built four or five years ago were the origins of SDN, and therefore everything they have done since is SDN, too.

Along these lines, the branding of seemingly everything anew as SDN and the expected hyperbole of the startup community that SDN has been spawning for the past three or four years have also contributed negatively toward this end.

If observers are predisposed by their respective network religions and politics to dismiss SDN, it may seem like SDN is an idea adrift.

Now go ahead and arm yourself with a quick pointer to the Gartner hype-cycle.[2] We understand that perspective and can see where that cycle predicts things are at.

Some of these same aspects of the present SDN movement made us lobby *hard* for the glitter-horned unicorn just to make a point—that we see things *differently*.

For more than two years, our involvement in various customer meetings, forums, consortia, and SDOs discussing the topic, as well as our work with many of the startups, converts, and early adopters in the SDN space, leads us to believe that something worth noting *is* going on *under* the waterline. This is where much of the real work is going on to push the SDN effort forward toward a goal of what we think is optimal operational efficiency and flexibility for networks and applications that utilize those networks.

There is real evidence that SDN has finally started a *new* dialogue about network programmability, control models, the modernization of application interfaces to the network, and true openness around these things.

In that light, SDN is not constrained to a single network domain such as the data center —although it is true that the tidal wave of manageable network endpoints hatched via virtualization is a prime mover of SDN at present. SDN is also not constrained to a single customer type (e.g., research/education), a single application (e.g., data center orchestration), or even a single protocol/architecture (e.g., OpenFlow). Nor is SDN constrained to a single architectural model (e.g., the canonical model of a centralized controller and a group of droid switches). We hope you see that in this book.

---

2. *http://www.gartner.com/technology/research/methodologies/hype-cycle.jsp*

At the time of writing of the first edition of this book, both Thomas Nadeau and Ken Gray work at Juniper Networks in the Platform Systems Division Chief Technologist's Office. We both also have extensive experience that spans roles both with other vendors, such as Cisco Systems, and service providers, such as BT and Bell Atlantic (now Verizon). We have tried our best to be inclusive of everyone that is relevant in the SDN space without being encyclopedic on the topic still providing enough breadth of material to cover the space. In some cases, we have relied on references or examples that came from our experiences with our most recent employer (Juniper Networks) in the text, only because they are either part of a larger survey or because alternative examples on the topic are net yet freely available for us to divulge. We hope the reader finds any bias to be accidental and not distracting or overwhelming. If this can be corrected or enhanced in a subsequent revision, we will do so. We both agree that there are likely to be many updates to this text going forward, given how young SDN still is and how rapidly it continues to evolve.

Finally, we hope the reader finds the depth and breadth of information presented herein to be interesting and informative, while at the same time evocative. We give our opinions about topics, but only after presenting the material and its pros and cons in as unbiased a manner as possible.

We do hope you find unicorns, fairy dust, and especially lots of paddling feet in this book.

Assumptions

SDN is a new approach to the current world of networking, but it is still networking. As you get into this book, we're assuming a certain level of networking knowledge. You don't have to be an engineer, but knowing how networking principles work—and frankly, don't work—will aid your comprehension of the text.

You should be familiar with the following terms/concepts:

OSI model
> The Open Systems Interconnection (OSI) model defines seven different layers of technology: physical, data link, network, transport, session, presentation, and application. This model allows network engineers and network vendors to easily discuss and apply technology to a specific OSI level. This segmentation lets engineers divide the overall problem of getting one application to talk to another into discrete parts and more manageable sections. Each level has certain attributes that describe it and each level interacts with its neighboring levels in a very well-defined manner. Knowledge of the layers above layer 7 is not mandatory, but understanding that interoperability is not always about electrons and photons will help.

Switches

These devices operate at layer 2 of the OSI model and use logical local addressing to move frames across a network. Devices in this category include Ethernet in all its variations, VLANs, aggregates, and redundancies.

Routers

These devices operate at layer 3 of the OSI model and connect IP subnets to each other. Routers move packets across a network in a hop-by-hop fashion.

Ethernet

These broadcast domains connect multiple hosts together on a common infrastructure. Hosts communicate with each other using layer 2 media access control (MAC) addresses.

IP addressing and subnetting

Hosts using IP to communicate with each other use 32-bit addresses. Humans often use a dotted decimal format to represent this address. This address notation includes a network portion and a host portion, which is normally displayed as 192.168.1.1/24.

TCP and UDP

These layer 4 protocols define methods for communicating between hosts. The Transmission Control Protocol (TCP) provides for connection-oriented communications, whereas the User Datagram Protocol (UDP) uses a connectionless paradigm. Other benefits of using TCP include flow control, windowing/buffering, and explicit acknowledgments.

ICMP

Network engineers use this protocol to troubleshoot and operate a network, as it is the core protocol used (on some platforms) by the ping and traceroute programs. In addition, the Internet Control Message Protocol (ICMP) is used to signal error and other messages between hosts in an IP-based network.

Data center

A facility used to house computer systems and associated components, such as telecommunications and storage systems. It generally includes redundant or backup power supplies, redundant data communications connections, environmental controls (e.g., air conditioning and fire suppression), and security devices. Large data centers are industrial-scale operations that use as much electricity as a small town.

MPLS

Multiprotocol Label Switching (MPLS) is a mechanism in high-performance networks that directs data from one network node to the next based on short path labels rather than long network addresses, avoiding complex lookups in a routing table. The labels identify virtual links (*paths*) between distant nodes rather than endpoints. MPLS can encapsulate packets of various network protocols. MPLS supports a range of access technologies.

Northbound interface
An interface that conceptualizes the lower-level details (e.g., data or functions) used by, or in, the component. It is used to interface with higher-level layers using the southbound interface of the higher-level component(s). In architectural overview, the northbound interface is normally drawn at the top of the component it is defined in, hence the name northbound interface. Examples of a northbound interface are JSON or Thrift.

Southbound interface
An interface that conceptualizes the opposite of a northbound interface. The southbound interface is normally drawn at the bottom of an architectural diagram. Examples of southbound interfaces include I2RS, NETCONF, or a command-line interface.

Network topology
The arrangement of the various elements (links, nodes, interfaces, hosts, etc.) of a computer network. Essentially, it is the topological structure of a network and may be depicted physically or logically. *Physical topology* refers to the placement of the network's various components, including device location and cable installation, while *logical topology* shows how data flows within a network, regardless of its physical design. Distances between nodes, physical interconnections, transmission rates, and/or signal types may differ between two networks, yet their topologies may be identical.

Application programming interfaces
A specification of how some software components should interact with each other. In practice, an API is usually a library that includes specification for variables, routines, object classes, and data structures. An API specification can take many forms, including an international standard (e.g., POSIX), vendor documentation (e.g., the JunOS SDK), or the libraries of a programming language.

What's in This Book?

Chapter 1, Introduction
This chapter introduces and frames the conversation this book engages in around the concepts of SDN, where they came from, and why they are important to discuss.

Chapter 2, Centralized and Distributed Control and Data Planes
SDN is often framed as a decision between a distributed/consensus or centralized network control-plane model for future network architectures. In this chapter, we visit the fundamentals of distributed and central control, how the data plane is

generated in both, past history with both models,[3] some assumed functionality in the present distributed/consensus model that we may expect to translate into any substitute, and the merits of these models.

Chapter 3, OpenFlow

OpenFlow has been marketed either as equivalent to SDN (i.e., OpenFlow is SDN) or a critical component of SDN, depending on the whim of the marketing of the Open Networking Foundation. It can certainly be credited with sparking the discussion of the centralized control model. In this chapter, we visit the current state of the OpenFlow model.

Chapter 4, SDN Controllers

For some, the discussion of SDN technology is all about the management of network state, and that is the role of the SDN controller. In this chapter, we survey the controllers available (both open source and commercial), their structure and capabilities, and then compare them to an idealized model (that is developed in Chapter 9).

Chapter 5, Network Programmability

This chapter introduces network programmability as one of the key tenets of SDN. It first describes the problem of *the network divide* that essentially boils down to older management interfaces and paradigms keeping applications at arm's length from the network. In the chapter, we show why this is a bad thing and how it can be rectified using modern programmatic interfaces. This chapter firmly sets the tone for what concrete changes are happening in the real world of applications and network devices that are following the SDN paradigm shift.

Chapter 6, Data Center Concepts and Constructs

This chapter introduces the reader to the notion of the modern data center through an initial exploration of the historical evolution of the desktop-centric world of the late 1990s to the highly distributed world we live in today, in which applications—as well as the actual pieces that make up applications—are distributed across multiple data centers. Multitenancy is introduced as a key driver for virtualization in the data center, as well as other techniques around virtualization. Finally, we explain why these things form some of the keys to the SDN approach and why they are driving much of the SDN movement.

Chapter 7, Network Function Virtualization

In this chapter, we build on some of the SDN concepts that were introduced earlier, such as programmability, controllers, virtualization, and data center concepts. The chapter explores one of the cutting-edge areas for SDN, which takes key concepts and components and puts them together in such a way that not only allows one to

---

3. Yes, we have had centralized control models in the past!

virtualize services, but also to connect those instances together in new and interesting ways.

Chapter 8, Network Topology and Topological Information Abstraction

This chapter introduces the reader to the notion of network topology, not only as it exists today but also how it has evolved over time. We discuss why network topology—its discovery, ongoing maintenance, as well as an application's interaction with it—is critical to many of the SDN concepts, including NFV. We discuss a number of ways in which this nut has been partially cracked and how more recently, the IETF's I2RS effort may have finally cracked it for good.

Chapter 9, Building an SDN Framework

This chapter describes an idealized SDN framework for SDN controllers, applications, and ecosystems. This concept is quite important in that it forms the architectural basis for *all* of the SDN controller offerings available today and also shows a glimpse of where they can or are going in terms of their evolution. In the chapter, we present the various incarnations and evolutions of such a framework over time and ultimately land on the one that now forms the Open Daylight Consortium's approach. This approach to an idealized framework is the best that we reckon exists today both because it is technically sound and pragmatic, and also because it very closely resembles the one that we embarked on ourselves after quite a lot of trial and error.

Chapter 10, Use Cases for Bandwidth Scheduling, Manipulation, and Calendaring

This chapter presents the reader with a number of use cases that fall under the areas of bandwidth scheduling, manipulation, and bandwidth calendaring. We demonstrate use cases that we have actually constructed in the lab as proof-of-concept trials, as well as those that others have instrumented in their own lab environments. These proof-of-concept approaches have funneled their way into some production applications, so while they may be toy examples, they do have real-world applicability.

Chapter 11, Use Cases for Data Center Overlays, Big Data, and Network Function Virtualization

This chapter shows some use cases that fall under the areas of data centers. Specifically, we show some interesting use cases around data center overlays, and network function virtualization. We also show how big data can play a role in driving some SDN concepts.

Chapter 12, Use Cases for Input Traffic Monitoring, Classification, and Triggered Actions

This chapter presents the reader with some use cases in the input traffic/triggered actions category. These uses cases concern themselves with the general action of receiving some traffic at the edge of the network and then taking some action. The action might be preprogrammed via a centralized controller, or a device might need to ask a controller what to do once certain traffic is encountered. Here we present two use cases to demonstrate these concepts. First, we show how we built a proof of concept that effectively replaced the Network Access Control (NAC) protocol and its moving parts with an OpenFlow controller and some real routers. This solved a real problem at a large enterprise that could not have been easily solved otherwise. We also show a case of how a virtual firewall can be used to detect and trigger certain actions based on controller interaction.

Chapter 13, Final Thoughts and Conclusions
This chapter brings the book into the present tense—re-emphasizing some of our fundamental opinions on the current state of SDN (as of this writing) and providing a few final observations on the topic.

Conventions Used in This Book

The following typographical conventions are used in this book:

Italic
Indicates new terms, URLs, email addresses, filenames, file extensions, pathnames, directories, and Unix utilities.

`Constant width`
Indicates commands, options, switches, variables, attributes, keys, functions, types, classes, namespaces, methods, modules, properties, parameters, values, objects, events, event handlers, XML tags, HTML tags, macros, the contents of files, and the output from commands.

`Constant width bold`
Shows commands and other text that should be typed literally by the user, as well as important lines of code.

`Constant width italic`
Shows text that should be replaced with user-supplied values.

 This icon signifies a tip, suggestion, or general note.

 This icon indicates a warning or caution.

Using Code Examples

Supplemental material (code examples, exercises, etc.) is available for download at *http://oreil.ly/SDN_1e*. This page hosts a *.txt* file of the complete configurations used in Chapter 10's use case. You may download the configurations for use in your own lab.

This book is here to help you get your job done. In general, if this book includes code examples, you may use the code in your programs and documentation. You do not need to contact us for permission unless you're reproducing a significant portion of the code. For example, writing a program that uses several chunks of code from this book does not require permission. Selling or distributing a CD-ROM of examples from O'Reilly books does require permission. Answering a question by citing this book and quoting example code does not require permission. Incorporating a significant amount of example code from this book into your product's documentation does require permission.

We appreciate, but do not require, attribution. An attribution usually includes the title, author, publisher, and ISBN, for example: "*SDN: Software-Defined Networks* by Thomas D. Nadeau and Ken Gray. Copyright 2013 Thomas D. Nadeau and Ken Gray, 978-1-449-34230-2."

If you feel your use of code examples falls outside fair use or the permission given above, feel free to contact us at *permissions@oreilly.com*.

Safari® Books Online

 Safari Books Online (*www.safaribooksonline.com*) is an on-demand digital library that delivers expert content in both book and video form from the world's leading authors in technology and business.

Technology professionals, software developers, web designers, and business and creative professionals use Safari Books Online as their primary resource for research, problem solving, learning, and certification training.

Safari Books Online offers a range of product mixes and pricing programs for organizations, government agencies, and individuals. Subscribers have access to thousands of books, training videos, and prepublication manuscripts in one fully searchable database from publishers like O'Reilly Media, Prentice Hall Professional, Addison-Wesley Professional, Microsoft Press, Sams, Que, Peachpit Press, Focal Press, Cisco Press, John Wiley & Sons, Syngress, Morgan Kaufmann, IBM Redbooks, Packt, Adobe Press, FT Press, Apress, Manning, New Riders, McGraw-Hill, Jones & Bartlett, Course Technology, and dozens more. For more information about Safari Books Online, please visit us online.

How to Contact Us

Please address comments and questions concerning this book to the publisher:

O'Reilly Media, Inc.
1005 Gravenstein Highway North
Sebastopol, CA 95472
800-998-9938 (in the United States or Canada)
707-829-0515 (international or local)
707-829-0104 (fax)

We have a web page for this book, where we list errata, examples, and any additional information. You can access this page at *http://oreil.ly/SDN_1e*. The authors also have created a blog and discussion forum about SDN and network programmability at *http://sdnprogrammability.net*.

To comment or ask technical questions about this book, send email to *bookques tions@oreilly.com*.

For more information about our books, courses, conferences, and news, see our website at *http://www.oreilly.com*.

Find us on Facebook: *http://facebook.com/oreilly*

Follow us on Twitter: *http://twitter.com/oreillymedia*

Watch us on YouTube: *http://www.youtube.com/oreillymedia*

Acknowledgments from Thomas Nadeau

I would like to first thank my wonderful wife, Katie, and two sons, Thomas Peter and Henry Clifford. I can't imagine being happy without you guys. Life is a journey, and I am glad you guys are walking the road with me. I would also like to thank my parents, Clement and Janina. Without your support and encouragement, I would likely have never made it as an engineer—or at least without Dad's instruction at a young age, I wouldn't be so adept at soldering now. Thank you to my many colleagues present and past who pushed me to stretch my imagination in the area of SDN. These folks include but are not limited to David Ward, Dave Meyer, Jan Medved, Jim Guichard, Ping Pan, Alia Atlas, Michael Beesley, Benson Scliesser, Chris Liljenstolpe, Dan Backman, Nils Swart, and Michael Bushong. Also, I will never forget how George Swallow took me on as his young Padawan and gave me the Jedi training that helped me be where I am today. Without that, I would likely not have achieved the accomplishments I have in the networking industry. There are many others from my journey at Cisco, CA, and my current employer, Juniper Networks, who are too numerous to mention. I would like to thank the larger SDN community, including those at Stanford, who were truly on to something in the early days of this work, and my colleagues at the IETF, ONF, and Open Daylight Project. Thank you to Meghan Blanchette and the rest of the staff at O'Reilly. And, of course, Patrick Ames, our editor who held the course when we strayed and helped us express the best, most articulate message we could convey.

Last, but surely not least, I would like to give my heartfelt thanks to Ken Gray, my coauthor on this book. Without you grabbing the other oar of this boat, I am not sure I would have been able to row it myself to the end. Your contributions truly enhanced this book beyond anything I would have imagined myself.

Acknowledgments from Ken Gray

I would like to thank my amazing wife, Leslie. You patiently supported me through this project and all that went with it and provided much needed balance and sanity.

For my children, Lilly and Zane, I hope my daring to write this first book may provide inspiration for you to start your own great work (whatever it may be).

The space here can't contain the list of customers, colleagues, and friends whose conversations over the last two years have shaped my views on this topic.

It's no coincidence that my acknowledgments list of colleagues, standards bodies, and (of course) those who assisted in this publication would look exactly like that of my coauthor. I would particularly like to reiterate the thanks to my past Juniper Networks colleagues (many now with SDN startups) who got started in SDN with both of us over two years ago, when the word that described SDN theorists and strategists was not "visionary," and who helped shape my views. And, if another redundancy can be spared, I'd extend a special thanks to a present Juniper colleague, Benson Schliesser, for the same reasons.

I'd finally like to give great thanks to my coauthor, Thomas Nadeau. We share a common view on this topic that we developed from two different but complementary perspectives. Putting those two views together, first in our numerous public engagements over the past year and finally in print, has been a great experience for me, has helped me personally refine the way I talk about SDN, and hopefully has resulted in a great book.

CHAPTER 1

Introduction

Up until a few years ago, storage, computing, and network resources were intentionally kept physically and operationally separate from one another. Even the systems used to manage those resources were separated—often physically. Applications that interacted with any of these resources, such as an operational monitoring system, were also kept at arm's length significantly involved access policies, systems, and access procedures all in the name of security. This is the way IT departments liked it. It was really only after the introduction of (and demand for) inexpensive computing power, storage, and networking in data center environments that organizations were forced to bring these different elements together. It was a paradigm shift that also brought applications that manage and operate these resources much, much closer than ever before.

Data centers were originally designed to physically separate traditional computing elements (e.g., PC servers), their associated storage, and the networks that interconnected them with client users. The computing power that existed in these types of data centers became focused on specific server functionality—running applications such as mail servers, database servers, or other such widely used functionality in order to serve desktop clients. Previously, those functions—which were executed on the often thousands (or more) of desktops within an enterprise organization—were handled by departmental servers that provided services dedicated only to local use. As time went on, the departmental servers migrated into the data center for a variety of reasons—first and foremost, to facilitate ease of management, and second, to enable sharing among the enterprise's users.

It was around 10 years ago that an interesting transformation took place. A company called VMware had invented an interesting technology that allowed a host operating system such as one of the popular Linux distributions to execute one or more client operating systems (e.g., Windows). What VMware did was to create a small program that created a virtual environment that synthesized a real computing environment (e.g., virtual NIC, BIOS, sound adapter, and video). It then marshaled real resources between the virtual machines. This supervisory program was called a *hypervisor*.

Originally, VMware was designed for engineers who wanted to run Linux for most of their computing needs and Windows (which was the corporate norm at the time) only for those situations that required that specific OS environment to execute. When they were finished, they would simply close Windows as if it were another program, and continue on with Linux. This had the interesting effect of allowing a user to treat the client operating system as if it were just a program consisting of a file (albeit large) that existed on her hard disk. That file could be manipulated as any other file could be (i.e., it could be moved or copied to other machines and executed there as if it were running on the machine on which it was originally installed). Even more interestingly, the operating system could be paused without it knowing, essentially causing it to enter into a state of suspended animation.

With the advent of operating system virtualization, the servers that typically ran a single, dedicated operating system, such as Microsoft Windows Server, and the applications specifically tailored for that operating system could now be viewed as a ubiquitous computing and storage platform. With further advances and increases in memory, computing, and storage, data center compute servers were increasingly capable of executing a variety of operating systems simultaneously in a virtual environment. VMware expanded its single-host version to a more data-center-friendly environment that was capable of executing and controlling many hundreds or thousands of virtual machines from a single console. Operating systems such as Windows Server that previously occupied an entire "bare metal" machine were now executed as virtual machines, each running whatever applications client users demanded. The only difference was that each was executing in its own self-contained environment that could be paused, relocated, cloned, or copied (i.e., as a backup). Thus began the age of *elastic computing*.

Within the elastic computing environment, operations departments were able to move servers to any physical data center location simply by pausing a virtual machine and copying a file. They could even spin up new virtual machines simply by cloning the same file and telling the hypervisor to execute it as a new instance. This flexibility allowed network operators to start optimizing the data center resource location and thus utilization based on metrics such as power and cooling. By packing together all active machines, an operator could turn down cooling in another part of a data center by sleeping or idling entire banks or rows of physical machines, thus optimizing the cooling load on a data center. Similarly, an operator could move or dynamically expand computing, storage, or network resources by geographical demand.

As with all advances in technology, this newly discovered flexibility in operational deployment of computing, storage, and networking resources brought about a new problem: one not only of operational efficiency both in terms of maximizing the utilization of storage and computing power, but also in terms of power and cooling. As mentioned earlier, network operators began to realize that computing power demand in general increased over time. To keep up with this demand, IT departments (which typically budget on a yearly basis) would order all the equipment they predicted would be needed for the following year. However, once this equipment arrived and was placed in racks, it would consume power, cooling, and space resources—even if it was not yet used! This was the dilemma discovered first at Amazon. At the time, Amazon's business was growing at the rate of a "hockey stick" graph—doubling every six to nine months. As a result, growth had to stay ahead of demand for its computing services, which served its retail ordering, stock, and warehouse management systems, as well as internal IT systems. As a result, Amazon's IT department was forced to order large quantities of storage, network, and computing resources in advance, but faced the dilemma of having that equipment sit idle until the demand caught up with those resources. Amazon Web Services (AWS) was invented as a way to commercialize this unused resource pool so that it would be utilized at a rate closer to 100%. When internal resources needed more resources, AWS would simply push off retail users, and when it was not, retail compute users could use up the unused resources. Some call this elastic computing services, but this book calls it *hyper virtualization*.

It was only then that companies like Amazon and Rackspace, which were buying storage and computing in huge quantities for pricing efficiency, realized they were not efficiently utilizing all of their computing and storage and could resell their spare computing power and storage to external users in an effort to recoup some of their capital investments. This gave rise to a multitenant data center. This of course created a new problem, which was how to separate thousands of potential tenants, whose resources needed to be spread arbitrarily across different physical data centers' virtual machines.

Another way to understand this dilemma is to note that during the move to hyper virtualized environments, execution environments were generally run by a single enterprise or organization. That is, they typically owned and operated all of the computing and storage (although some rented co-location space) as if they were a single, flat local area network (LAN) interconnecting a large number of virtual or physical machines and network attached storage. (The exception was in financial institutions where regulatory requirements mandated separation.) However, the number of departments in these cases was relatively small—fewer than 100—and so this was easily solved using existing tools such as layer 2 or layer 3 MPLS VPNs. In both cases, though, the network components that linked all of the computing and storage resources up until that point were rather simplistic; it was generally a flat Ethernet LAN that connected all of the physical and virtual machines. Most of these environments assigned IP addresses to all of the devices (virtual or physical) in the network from a single network (perhaps with IP subnets), as a single enterprise owned the machines and needed access to them. This also meant that it was generally not a problem moving virtual machines between different data centers located within that enterprise because, again, they all fell within the same routed domain and could reach one another regardless of physical location.

In a multitenant data center, computing, storage, and network resources can be offered in slices that are independent or isolated from one another. It is, in fact, critical that they are kept separate. This posed some interesting challenges that were not present in the single tenant data center environment of the past. Keep in mind that their environment allowed for the execution of any number of operating systems and applications on top of those operating systems, but each needed a unique network address if it was to be accessed by its owner or other external users such as customer. In the past, addresses could be assigned from a single, internal block of possibly private addresses and routed internally easily. Now, however, you needed to assign unique addresses that are externally routable and accessible. Furthermore, consider that each virtual machine in question had a unique layer 2 address as well. When a router delivers a packet, it ultimately has to deliver a packet using Ethernet (not just IP). This is generally not an issue until you consider virtual machine mobility (*VM mobility*). In these cases, virtual machines are relocated for power, cooling, or computing compacting reasons. In here lies the rub because physical relocation means physical address relocation. It also possibly means changes to layer 3 routing in order to ensure packets previously destined for that machine in its original location can now be changed to its new location.

At the same time data centers were evolving, network equipment seemed to stand still in terms of innovations beyond feeds and speeds. That is, beyond the steady increase in switch fabric capacities and interface speeds, data communications had not evolved much since the advent of IP, MPLS, and mobile technologies. IP and MPLS allowed a network operator to create networks and virtual network overlays on top of those base networks much in the way that data center operators were able to create virtual machines to run over physical ones with the advent of computing virtualization. Network virtualization was generally referred to as *virtual private networks* (VPN) and came in a number of flavors, including point-to-point (e.g., a personal VPN as you might run on your laptop and connect to your corporate network); layer 3 (virtualizing an IP or routed network in cases such as to allow a network operator to securely host enterprise in a manner that isolated their traffic from other enterprise); and layer 2 VPNs (switched network virtualization that isolates similarly to a layer 3 VPN except that the addresses used are Ethernet).

Commercial routers and switches typically come with management interfaces that allow a network operator to configure and otherwise manage these devices. Some examples of management interfaces include command line interfaces, XML/Netconf, graphical user interfaces (GUIs), and the Simple Network Management Protocol (SNMP). These options provide an interface that allows an operator suitable access to a device's capabilities, but they still often hide the lowest levels of details from the operator. For example, network operators can program static routes or other static forwarding entries, but those ultimately are requests that are passed through the device's operating system. This is generally not a problem until one wants to program using syntax or semantics of functionality that exists in a device. If someone wishes to experiment with some new routing protocol, they cannot on a device where the firmware has not been written to support that protocol. In such cases, it was common for a customer to make a feature enhancement request of a device vendor, and then typically wait some amount of time (several years was not out of the ordinary).

At the same time, the concept of a distributed (at least logically) control plane came back onto the scene. A network device is comprised of a data plane that is often a switch fabric connecting the various network ports on a device and a control plane that is the brains of a device. For example, routing protocols that are used to construct loop-free paths within a network are most often implemented in a distributed manner. That is, each device in the network has a control plane that implements the protocol. These communicate with each other to coordinate network path construction. However, in a centralized control plane paradigm, one single (or at least logical) control plane would exist. This über brain would push commands to each device, thus commanding it to manipulate its physical switching and routing hardware. It is important to note that although the hardware that executed data planes of devices remained quite specialized, and thus expensive, the control plane continued to gravitate toward less and less expensive, general-purpose computing, such as those central processing units produced by Intel.

All of these aforementioned concepts are important, as they created the nucleus of motivation for what has evolved into what today is called *software-defined networking* (SDN). Early proponents of SDN saw that network device vendors were not meeting their needs, particularly in the feature development and innovation spaces. High-end routing and switching equipment was also viewed as being highly overpriced for at least the control plane components of their devices. At the same time, they saw the cost of raw, elastic computing power diminishing rapidly to the point where having thousands of processors at one's disposal was a reality. It was then that they realized that this processing power could possibly be harnessed to run a logically centralized control plane and potentially even use inexpensive, commodity-priced switching hardware. A few engineers from Stanford University created a protocol called OpenFlow that could be implemented in just such a configuration. OpenFlow was architected for a number of devices containing only data planes to respond to commands sent to them from a (logically) centralized controller that housed the single control plane for that network. The controller was responsible for maintaining all of the network paths, as well as programming each of the network devices it controlled. The commands and responses to those commands are described in the OpenFlow protocol. It is worth noting that the Open Networking Foundation (ONF) commercially supported the SDN effort and today remains its central standardization authority and marketing organization. Based on this basic architecture just described, one can now imagine how quickly and easily it was to devise a new networking protocol by simply implementing it within a data center on commodity priced hardware. Even better, one could implement it in an elastic computing environment in a virtual machine.

A slightly different view of SDN is what some in the industry refer to as *software-driven networks*, as opposed to software-defined networks. This play on words is not meant to completely confuse the reader, but instead highlight a difference in philosophy of approaches. In the software-driven approach, one views OpenFlow and that architecture as a distinct subset of functionality that is possible. Rather than viewing the network as being comprised of logically centralized control planes with brainless network devices, one views the world as more of a hybrid of the old and the new. More to the point, the reality is that it is unrealistic to think that existing networks are going to be dismantled wholesale to make way for a new world proposed by the ONF and software-defined networks. It is also unrealistic to discard all of the advances in network technology that exist today and are responsible for things like the Internet. Instead, there is more likely a hybrid approach whereby some portion of networks are operated by a logically centralized controller, while other parts would be run by the more traditional distributed control plane. This would also imply that those two worlds would need to interwork with each other.

It is interesting to observe that at least one of the major parts of what SDN and OpenFlow proponents are trying to achieve is greater and more flexible network device programmability. This does not necessarily have anything to do with the location of the network control and data planes; however, it is concerned with how they are programmed. Do not forget that one of the motivations for creating SDN and OpenFlow was the flexibility of *how* one could program a network device, not just *where* it is programmed. If one observes what is happening in the SDN architecture just described, both of those questions are solved. The question is whether or not the programmability aspect is the most optimal choice.

To address this, individuals representing Juniper, Cisco, Level3, and other vendors and service providers have recently spearheaded an effort around network programmability called the Interface to the Routing System (I2RS). A number of folks from these sources have contributed to several IETF drafts, including the primary requirements and framework drafts to which Alia Atlas, David Ward, and Tom have been primary contributors. In the near future, at least a dozen drafts around this topic should appear online. Clearly there is great interest in this effort. The basic idea around I2RS is to create a protocol and components to act as a means of programming a network device's routing information base (RIB) using a fast path protocol that allows for a quick cut-through of provisioning operations in order to allow for real-time interaction with the RIB and the RIB manager that controls it. Previously, the only access one had to the RIB was via the device's configuration system (in Juniper's case, Netconf or SNMP).

The key to understanding I2RS is that it is most definitely *not* just another provisioning protocol; that's because there are a number of other key concepts that comprise an entire solution to the overarching problem of speeding up the feedback loop between network elements, network programming, state and statistical gathering, and post-processing analytics. Today, this loop is painfully slow. Those involved in I2RS believe the key to the future of programmable networks lies within optimizing this loop.

To this end, I2RS provides varying levels of abstraction in terms of programmability of network paths, policies, and port configuration, but in all cases has the advantage of allowing for adult supervision of said programming as a means of checking the commands prior to committing them. For example, some protocols exist today for programming at the hardware abstraction layer (HAL), which is far too granular or detailed for the network's efficiency and in fact places undue burden on its operational systems. Another example is providing operational support systems (OSS) applications quick and optimal access to the RIB in order to quickly program changes and then witness the results, only to be able to quickly reprogram in order to optimize the network's behavior. One key aspect around all of these examples is that the discourse between the applications and the RIB occur via the RIB manager. This is important, as many operators would like to preserve their operational and workflow investment in routing protocol intelligence that exists in device operating systems such as Junos or IOS-XR while leveraging this new and useful programmability paradigm to allow additional levels of optimization in their networks.

I2RS also lends itself well to a growing desire to logically centralize routing and path decisions and programmability. The protocol has requirements to run on a device or outside of a device. In this way, distributed controller functionality is embraced in cases where it is desired; however, in cases where more classic distributed control is desired, we are able to support those as well.

Finally, another key subcomponent of I2RS is normalized and abstracted topology. Defining a common and extensible object model will represent this topology. The service also allows for multiple abstractions of topological representation to be exposed. A key aspect of this model is that nonrouters (or routing protocol speakers) can more easily manipulate and change the RIB state going forward. Today, nonrouters have a major difficulty getting at this information at best. Going forward, components of a network management/OSS, analytics, or other applications that we cannot yet envision will be able to interact quickly and efficiently with routing state and network topology.

So, to culminate these thoughts, it is appropriate that we define SDN for what we think it is and will become:

Software-defined networks (SDN): an architectural approach that optimizes and simplifies network operations by more closely binding the interaction (i.e., provisioning, messaging, and alarming) among applications and network services and devices, whether they be real or virtualized. It often is achieved by employing a point of logically centralized network control—which is often realized as an SDN controller—which then orchestrates, mediates, and facilitates communication between applications wishing to interact with network elements and network elements wishing to convey information to those applications. The controller then exposes and abstracts network functions and operations via modern, application-friendly and bidirectional programmatic interfaces.

So, as you can see, software-defined, software-driven, and programmable networks come with a rich and complex set of historical lineage, challenges, and a variety of solutions to those problems. It is the success of the technologies that preceded software-defined, software-driven, and programmable networks that makes advancing technology based on those things possible. The fact of the matter is that most of the world's networks—including the Internet—operate on the basis of IP, BGP, MPLS, and Ethernet. Virtualization technology today is based on the technologies started by VMware years ago and continues to be the basis on which it and other products are based. Network attached storage enjoys a similarly rich history.

I2RS has a similar future ahead of it insofar as solving the problems of network, compute, and storage virtualization as well as those of the programmability, accessibility, location, and relocation of the applications that execute within these hyper virtualized environments.

Although SDN controllers continue to rule the roost when it comes to press, many other advances have taken place just in the time we have been writing this book. One very interesting and bright one is the Open Daylight Project. Open Daylight's mission is to facilitate a community-led, industry-supported open source framework, including code and architecture, to accelerate and advance a common, robust software-defined networking platform. To this end, Open Daylight is hosted under the Linux Foundation's umbrella and will facilitate a truly game changing, and potentially field-leveling effort around SDN controllers. This effort will also spur innovation where we think it matters most in this space: *applications*. While we have seen many advances in controllers over the past few years, controllers really represent the foundational infrastructure for SDN-enabled applications. In that vein, the industry has struggled to design and develop controllers over the past few years while mostly ignoring applications. We think that SDN is really about operational optimization and efficiency at the end of the day, and the best way to achieve this is through quickly checking off that infrastructure and allowing the industry to focus on innovating in the application and device layers of the SDN architecture.

This book focuses on the network aspects of software-defined, software-driven, and programmable networks while giving sufficient coverage to the virtualization, location, and programming of storage, network, and compute aspects of the equation. It is the goal of this book to explore the details and motivations around the advances in network technology that gave rise to and support of hyper virtualization of network, storage, and computing resources that are now considered to be part of SDN.

CHAPTER 2

Centralized and Distributed Control and Data Planes

One of the tenets expressed early in the introduction of SDN is the *potential* advantage in the separation of a network device's control and data planes. This separation affords a network operator certain advantages in terms of centralized or semi-centralized programmatic control. It also has a potential economic advantage based on the ability to consolidate in one or a few places what is often a considerably complex piece of software to configure and control onto less expensive, so-called commodity hardware.

Introduction

The separation of the control and data planes is indeed one of the fundamental tenets of SDN—and one of its more controversial, too. Although it's not a new concept, the contemporary way of thinking has some interesting twists on an old idea: how far away the control plane can be located from the data plane, how many instances are needed to exist to satisfy resiliency and high-availability requirements, and whether or not 100% of the control plane can be, in fact, relocated further away than a few inches are all intensely debated. The way we like to approach these ideas is to think of them as a continuum of possibilities stretching between the simplest, being the canonical *fully distributed* control plane, to the *semi-* or *logically* centralized control plane, to finally the *strictly* centralized control plane. Figure 2-1 illustrates the spectrum of options available to the network operator, as well as some of the pros and cons of each approach.

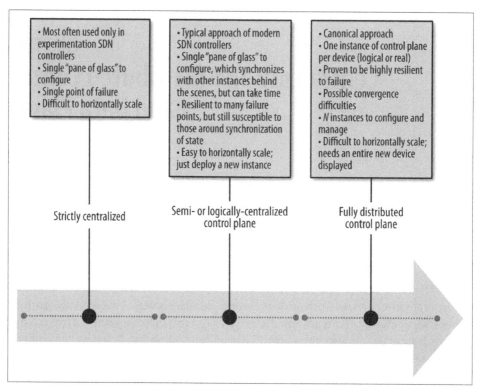

Figure 2-1. Spectrum of control and data plane distribution options

Evolution versus Revolution

At one end of the spectrum of answers to the question of where to put the control plane lies the *revolutionary* proponents, who propose a clean slate approach in which the control plane of a network is completely centralized. In most cases, this extreme approach has been tempered to be, in reality, a logically centralized approach due to either scale or high availability requirements that make a strictly centralized approach difficult. In this model, no control plane functions effectively exist at a device; instead, a device is a dumb (albeit fast) switching device under the *total* control of the remotely located, centralized control plane. We shall explore this in detail later in the chapter and show why it generally applies best to newly deployed networks rather than existing ones.

Toward the middle of the spectrum, the *evolutionary* proponents see domains within the general definition of networks in which a centralized control paradigm provides *some* new capabilities, but does *not* replace every capability nor does it completely remove the control plane from the device. Instead, this paradigm typically works in conjunction with a distributed control plane in some fashion, meaning that the device retains some classical control plane functions (e.g., ARP processing or MAC address learning), while allowing a centralized controller to manipulate other areas of functionality more convenient for that operational paradigm. This view is often characterized as the hybrid operation or as part of the underlay/overlay concept in which the distributed control plane provides the underlay and the centralized control plane provides a logical overlay that utilizes the underlay as a network transport.

Finally, at the other end of the spectrum is the classic use of control planes: completely distributed. In this model, every device runs a complete instance of a control plane in addition to at least one data plane. Also in this model, each independent control plane must cooperate with the other control planes in order to support a cohesive and operational network. The approach obviously presents nothing new and is neither revolutionary nor evolutionary.

This chapter will not present the reader with a comprehensive discussion of control/data plane design or development, as this could be the topic of an entire book. Therefore, we will discuss general concepts as they pertain to the SDN space and refer the reader to other references, when possible, for further detailed investigation.[1] Instead, we will explore each of the places on the spectrum of control plane distribution and operation that were just introduced. These will include some past and present examples of centralization of control, hybrid, and fully distributed operation.

What Do They Do?

Let's first discuss the fundamental components and behaviors of control and data planes, why they differ, and how they might be implemented.

The Control Plane

At a very high level, the control plane establishes the local data set used to create the forwarding table entries, which are in turn used by the data plane to forward traffic between ingress and egress ports on a device.[2] The data set used to store the network topology is called the routing information base (RIB). The RIB is often kept consistent (i.e., loop-free) through the exchange of information between other instances of control planes within the network. Forwarding table entries are commonly called the forwarding information base (FIB) and are often mirrored between the control and data planes of a typical device. The FIB is programmed once the RIB is deemed consistent and stable. To perform this task, the control entity/program has to develop a view of the network

---

1. As part of its evolution, the Open Networking Foundation has alternately bound the definition of SDN to OpenFlow tightly (i.e., OpenFlow = SDN) and loosely (i.e., OpenFlow is a critical component of SDN). Regardless, it's undeniable that the existence of OpenFlow and the active marketing of the ONF triggered the market/public discussion and interest in SDN.

2. The management plane is responsible for element configuration that may affect local forwarding decisions (forwarding features) like access control lists (ACLs) or policy-based routing (PBR).

topology that satisfies certain constraints. This view of the network can be programmed manually, learned through observation, or built from pieces of information gathered through discourse with other instances of control planes, which can be through the use of one or many routing protocols, manual programming, or a combination of both.

The mechanics of the control and data planes is demonstrated in Figure 2-2, which represents a network of interconnected switches. At the top of the figure, a network of switches is shown, with an expansion of the details of the control and data planes of two of those switches (noted as A and B). In the figure, packets are received by switch A on the leftmost control plane and ultimately forwarded to switch B on the righthand side of the figure. Inside each expansion, note that the control and data planes are separated, with the control plane executing on its own processor/card and the data plane executing on a separate one. Both are contained within a single chassis. We will discuss this and other variations on this theme of physical location of the control and data planes later in the chapter. In the figure, packets are received on the input ports of the line card where the data plane resides. If, for example, a packet is received that comes from an unknown MAC address, it is punted or redirected (4) to the control plane of the device, where it is learned, processed, and later forwarded onward. This same treatment is given to control traffic such as routing protocol messages (e.g., OSPF link-state advertisements). Once a packet has been delivered to the control plane, the information contained therein is processed and possibly results in an alteration of the RIB as well as the transmission of additional messages to its peers, alerting them of this update (i.e., a new route is learned). When the RIB becomes stable, the FIB is updated in both the control plane and the data plane. Subsequently, forwarding will be updated and reflect these changes. However, in this case, because the packet received was one of an unlearned MAC address, the control plane returns the packet (C) to the data plane (2), which forwards the packet accordingly (3). If additional FIB programming is needed, this also takes place in the (C) step, which would be the case for now the MAC addresses source has been learned. The same algorithm for packet processing happens in the next switch to the right.

The history of the Internet maps roughly to the evolution of control schemes for managing reachability information, protocols for the distribution of reachability information, and the algorithmic generation of optimized paths in the face of several challenges. In the case of the latter, this includes an increasing growth of the information base used (i.e., route table size growth) and how to manage it. Not doing so could result in the possibility of a great deal of instability in the physical network. This in turn may lead to high rates of change in the network or even nonoperation. Another challenge to overcome as the size of routing information grows is the diffusion of responsibility for advertising reachability to parts of the destination/target data, not only between local instances of the data plane but also across administrative boundaries.

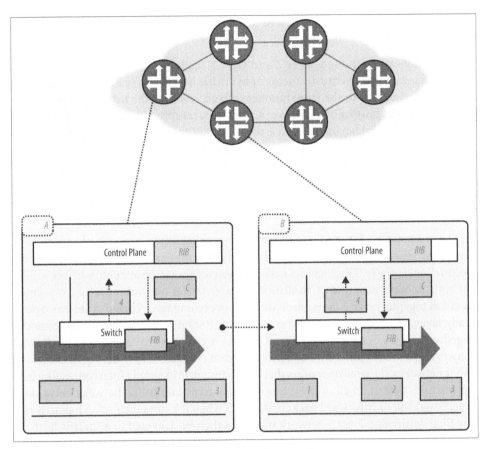

Figure 2-2. Control and data planes of a typical network

In reality, the control plane for the Internet that was just discussed is some combination of layer 2 or layer 3 control planes. As such, it should be no surprise then that the same progression and evolution has taken place for both layer 2 and layer 3 networks and the protocols that made up these control planes. In fact, the progression of the Internet happened *because* these protocols evolved both in terms of functionality and hardware vendors learned how to implement them in highly scalable and highly available ways.

A layer 2 control plane focuses on hardware or physical layer addresses such as IEEE MAC addresses. A layer 3 control plane is built to facilitate network layer addresses such as those of the IP protocol. In a layer 2 network, the behaviors around learning MAC addresses, the mechanisms used to guarantee an acyclic graph (familiar to most readers through the Spanning Tree Protocol), and flooding of BUM (broadcast, unicast unknown, and multicast) traffic create their own scalability challenges and also reveal their scalability limitations. There have been several iterations or generations of standards-based layer 2 control protocols whose goals were to address these and other issues. Most notably, these included SPB/802.1aq from the IEEE and TRILL from the IETF.

As a generalization, though, layer 2 and layer 3 scaling concerns and their resulting control plane designs eventually merge or hybridize because layer 2 networks ultimately do not scale well due to the large numbers of end hosts. At the heart of these issues is dealing with end hosts moving between networks, resulting in a massive churn of forwarding tables—and having to update them quickly enough to not disrupt traffic flow. In a layer 2 network, forwarding focuses on the reachability of MAC addresses. Thus, layer 2 networks primarily deal with the storage of MAC addresses for forwarding purposes. Since the MAC addresses of hosts can be enormous in a large enterprise network, the management of these addresses is difficult. Worse, imagine managing all of the MAC addresses across multiple enterprises or the Internet!

In a layer 3 network, forwarding focuses on the reachability of network addresses. Layer 3 network reachability information primarily concerns itself with the reachability of a destination IP prefix. This includes network prefixes across a number of address families for both unicast and multicast. In all modern cases, layer 3 networking is used to segment or stitch together layer 2 domains in order to overcome layer 2 scale problems. Specifically, layer 2 bridges that represent some sets of IP subnetworks are typically connected together with a layer 3 router. Layer 3 routers are connected together to form larger networks—or really different subnetwork address ranges. Larger networks connect to other networks via *gateway* routers that often specialize in simply interconnecting large networks. However, in all of these cases, the router routes traffic between networks at layer 3 and will only forward packets at layer 2 when it knows the packet has arrived at the final destination layer 3 network that must then be delivered to a specific host.

Some notable blurring of these lines occurs with the Multiprotocol Label Switching (MPLS) protocol, the Ethernet Virtual Private Network (EVPN) protocol, and the Locator/ID Separation Protocol (LISP). The MPLS protocol—really a suite of protocols—was formed on the basis of combining the best parts of layer 2 forwarding (or switching) with the best parts of layer 3 IP routing to form a technology that shares the extremely fast-packet forwarding that ATM invented with the very flexible and complex path signaling techniques adopted from the IP world. The EVPN protocol is an attempt to solve the layer 2 networking scale problems that were just described by effectively tunneling distant layer 2 bridges together over an MPLS (or GRE) infrastructure—only then is layer 2 addressing and reachability information exchanged over these tunnels and thus does not contaminate (or affect) the scale of the underlying layer 3 networks. Reachability information between distant bridges is exchanged as data inside a new BGP address family, again not contaminating the underlying network. There are also other optimizations that limit the amount of layer 2 addresses that are exchanged over the tunnels, again optimizing the level of interaction between bridges. This is a design that minimizes the need for broadcast and multicast. The other hybrid worth mentioning is LISP (see RFC 4984). At its heart, LISP attempts to solve some of the shortcomings of the general distributed control plane model as applied to multihoming, adding new addressing domains and separating the site address from the provider in a new map and encapsulation control and forwarding protocol.

At a slightly lower level, there are adjunct control processes particular to certain network types that are used to augment the knowledge of the greater control plane. The services provided by these processes include verification/notification of link availability or quality information, neighbor discovery, and address resolution.

Because some of these services have very tight performance loops (for short event detection times), they are almost invariably local to the data plane (e.g., OAM)—regardless of the strategy chosen for the control plane. This is depicted in Figure 2-3 by showing the various routing protocols as well as RIB-to-FIB control that comprises the heart of the control plane. Note that we do not stipulate where the control and data planes reside, only that the data plane resides on the line card (shown in Figure 2-3 in the LC box), and the control plane is situated on the route processor (denoted by the RP box).

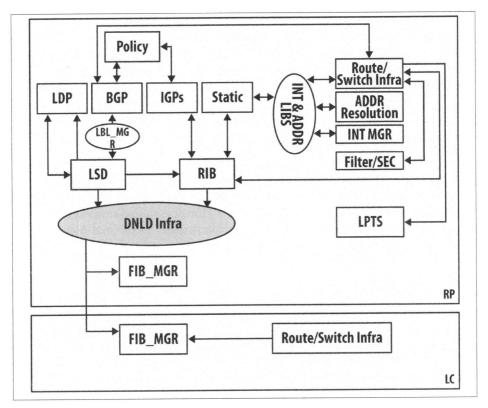

Figure 2-3. Control and data planes of a typical network device

Data Plane

The data plane handles incoming datagrams (on the wire, fiber, or in wireless media) through a series of link-level operations that collect the datagram and perform basic sanity checks. A well-formed (i.e., correct) datagram[3] is processed in the data plane by performing lookups in the FIB table (or tables, in some implementations) that are programmed earlier by the control plane. This is sometimes referred to as the *fast path* for packet processing because it needs no further interrogation other than identifying the packet's destination using the preprogrammed FIB. The one exception to this processing is when packets cannot be matched to those rules, such as when an unknown destination is detected, and these packets are sent to the route processor where the control plane can further process them using the RIB. It is important to understand that FIB tables could reside in a number of forwarding targets—software, hardware-accelerated software (GPU/CPU, as exemplified by Intel or ARM), commodity silicon (NPU, as exemplified by Broadcom, Intel, or Marvell, in the Ethernet switch market), FPGA and specialized silicon (ASICs like the Juniper Trio), or any combination[4]—depending on the network element design.

The *software path* in this exposition is exemplified by CPU-driven forwarding of the modern dedicated network element (e.g., router or switch), which trades off a processor intensive lookup (whether this is in the kernel or user space is a vendor-specific design decision bound by the characteristics and infrastructure of the host operating system) for the seemingly limitless table storage of processor memory. Its hypervisor-based switch or bridge counterpart of the modern compute environment has many of the optimizations (and some of the limitations) of hardware forwarding models.

Historically, lookups in hardware tables have proven to result in much higher packet forwarding performance and therefore have dominated network element designs, particularly for higher bandwidth network elements. However, recent advances in the I/O processing of generic processors, spurred on by the growth and innovation in cloud computing, are giving purpose-built designs, particularly in the mid-to-low performance ranges, quite a run for the money.

---

3. Some implementations do additional sanity checks beyond proper sizing, alignment, encapsulation rule adherence, and checksum verification. In particular, once a datagram "type" has been identified, additional "bogon" rules may be applied to check for specific violations for the type.

4. It is not uncommon for hardware platforms to have an "overflow" table design where failed lookups or lookups requiring more information in the "fast path"/hardware (normally due to resource constraints in either number of entries or width of entry) are subsequently reattempted against a table maintained in software— a "slow" path lookup.

Nor is it uncommon to combine both commodity silicon and ASICs to perform layer 2-based functions in front of layer 3-based functions—without having consolidated them into a single chip.

The differences in hardware forwarding designs are spread across a variety of factors, including (board and rack) space, budget, power utilization, and throughput[5] target requirements. These can lead to differences in the type (speed, width, size, and location) of memory as well as a budget of operation (number, sequence, or type of operations performed on the packet) to maintain forwarding at line rate (i.e., close to the maximum signaled or theoretical throughput for an interface) for a specific target packet size (or blend). Ultimately, this leads to differences in forwarding feature support and forwarding scale (e.g., number of forwarding entries, number of tables) among the designs.

The typical actions resulting from the data plane forwarding lookup are *forward* (and in special cases such as multicast, *replicate*), *drop*, *re-mark*, *count*, and *queue*. Some of these actions may be combined or chained together. In some cases, the forward decision returns a local port, indicating the traffic is destined for a locally running process such as OSPF or BGP[6]. These datagrams take what is referred to as the punt path whereby they leave the hardware-forwarding path and are forwarded to the route processor using an internal communications channel. This path is generally a relatively low-throughput path, as it is not designed for high-throughput packet forwarding of normal traffic; however, some designs simply add an additional path to the internal switching fabric for this purpose, which can result in near-line rate forwarding within the box.

In addition to the forwarding decision, the data plane may implement some small services/features commonly referred to as forwarding features (exemplified by Access Control Lists and QoS/Policy). In some systems, these features use their own discrete tables, while others perform as extensions to the forwarding tables (increasing entry width). Additionally, different designs can implement different features and forwarding operation order (Figure 2-4). Some ordering may make some feature operations exclusive of others.

With these features, you can (to a small degree) locally alter or preempt the outcome of the forwarding lookup. For example:

- An access control list entry may specify a drop action for a specific matching flow (note that in the ACL, a wider set of parameters may be involved in the forwarding decision). In its absence, there may have been a legitimate forwarding entry and thus the packet would NOT be dropped.

- A QOS policy can ultimately map a flow to a queue on egress or remark its TOS/COS to normalize service with policies across the network. And, like the ACL,

---

5. There are many (cascading) factors in ASIC design in particular that ultimately tie into yield/cost from the process and die size and flowing down into logic placement/routing, timing and clock frequency (which may have bearing on the eventual wear of parts), and table sharing—in addition to the power, thermal, and size considerations.

6. There are many examples here, including the aforementioned OAM, BFD, RSTP, and LACP.

it may mark the packet to be dropped (shaped) regardless of the existing forwarding entry for the destination/flow.

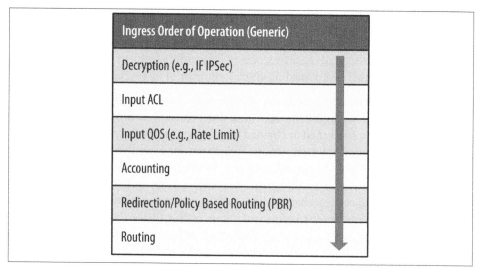

Figure 2-4. Generic example of ingress feature application on a traditional router/ switch.

These forwarding features overlap the definition of services in Chapter 7. Arguably, a data plane and control plane component of these services exists, and their definition seems to diverge cleanly when we begin to discuss session management, proxy, and large-scale transforms of the datagram header. As part of the forwarding operation, the data plane elements have to do some level of datagram header rewrite.

Moving Information Between Planes

The internal function of larger, multislot/multicard (chassis-based) distributed for-warding systems of today mimic some of the behaviors of the logically centralized but physically distributed control mechanisms of SDN. Particularly those aspects of the distribution of tables and their instantiation in hardware are of interest here. An ex-amination of the inner workings of a typical distributed switch reveals a number of functions and behaviors that mimic those of an externalized control plane. For example, in systems where the control plane resides on an independent processor/line card and data planes exist on other, independent line cards, certain behaviors around the com-munication between these elements must exist for the system to be resilient and fault tolerant. It is worth investigating whether or not all of these are needed if the control plane is removed from the chassis and relocated further away (i.e., logically or strictly centralized).

Let's first begin with the concept of basic packet forwarding. When the data plane is instructed by the control plane to forward packets, does the data plane listen? And does it listen for *each and every* packet it receives? More specifically, are there ways in which traffic can be black holed[7] (i.e., dropped without any indication in hardware-based forwarding systems that are addressed in different vendor's implementations)? This is a question that one should ask that is independent of whether or not the control entity/program is centralized, semi-centralized, or otherwise synchronized with other elements in a distributed control network. In these systems, mechanisms for detecting forwarding table distribution errors can be embedded in the data (e.g., table versioning) or in the transfer mechanism (e.g., signing the table with some form of hash or cookie generated from its contents). Such mechanisms ensure that the distributed software versions of the table are synchronized and correct once programmed. Similarly, verification routines between the software version of the table and the hardware version are implemented in the memory driver software (specific to the forwarding hardware).

Some vendors have implemented routines to verify hardware entries *post facto*—after the control plane programs the data plane—checking for soft errors in the forwarding chip and ancillary memories. In these cases, there are associated routines to mark bad blocks, move entries, and references. In general, these hardware verification routines are expensive, so they are often implemented as a background (a.k.a. scavenger) processes. To this end, both the transfer and memory write routines are also optimized to reduce transaction overhead, commonly by batching and bulking techniques.

Some multislot/multicard systems do two-stage lookups wherein the first stage at ingress simply identifies the outgoing slot/card on which a secondary lookup is performed. Depending on how it's implemented, two-stage lookups can enable an optimization that allows a phenomenon called localization to reduce the egress FIB size. In these cases, scenarios around two-stage asynchronous loss may occur that require some attention and are in fact difficult to detect until they fail. These have relevance to SDN forwarding control.

---

7. A black hole occurs when there is a discrepancy between the control-process-generated version of the forwarding table(s), which are normally maintained in DRAM in most equipment (commonly referred to as a software-based forwarding table) and either the software-based tables on peer (or slave) processors in the same system or the hardware-based forwarding entries created from those software tables. The latter will normally require some sort of transform or "packing" when written to specialized hardware associated memories and can be exposed by driver-level errors in the transform or write as well as soft errors in the memories themselves that can lead to incomplete or incorrect entries (and ultimately, a drop of the datagram). Some "black hole" problems can also result from inefficient/unsynchronized table updating algorithms on systems that create the forwarding entries by combining information from separate tables (e.g., when the hardware address of a next hop to a destination is not populated in an adjacency table but a route using that next hop populates the route table, leading to an "unresolvable" forwarding entry).

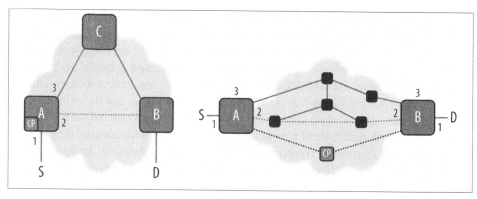

Figure 2-5. Two-stage asynchronous loss

The left side of Figure 2-5 shows a multislot router/switch that does a two-stage lookup. When link A-B comes up, the resulting FIB ingress lookup on card 1 changes from card 3 to card 2. *If* the update to card 2 happens after 1 and 3, then the secondary lookup (on egress) will fail. Similarly, in an SDN environment (shown in the cloud on the right side), if the tunnel connecting A and B changes from interface 3 (respectively) to interface 2 on these systems (due to an administrative or network event)—then the mapping of flows from 1–3 to 1–2 on these elements has to be synchronized by the application on the SDN controller (CP).

These mitigation techniques/optimizations are mentioned for the purpose of further discussions when we talk about consistency in the context of centralizing the control plane.

Why Can Separation Be Important?

The separation of the control and data planes is *not* a new concept. For example, any multislot router/switch built in the last 10 years or so has its control plane (i.e., its brain) executing on a dedicated processor/card (often two for redundancy) and the switching functions of the data plane executing independently on one or more line cards, each of which has a dedicated processor and/or packet processor. Figure 2-6 illustrates this by showing the route processor engine (denoted as the route processor box in Figure 2-6).

In Figure 2-6, the data plane is implemented in the lower box, which would be a separate line card with dedicated port processing ASICs connected to the ingress and egress ports on the line card (i.e., Ethernet interfaces). Under normal operation, the ports in Figure 2-6 have forwarding tables that dictate how they process inbound-to-outbound interface switching. These tables are populated and managed by the route processor's CPU/control plane program or programs. When control plane messages or unknown packets are received on these interfaces, they are generally pushed up to the route processor for further processing. Think of the route processor and line cards as being connected over a small but high-speed, internal network because in reality this is in fact how modern switches are built.

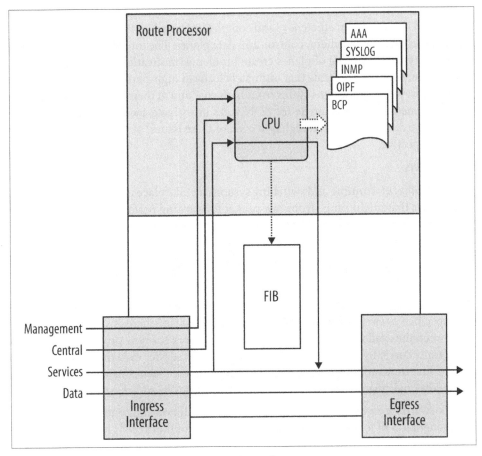

Figure 2-6. Control and data plane example implementation

In addition to this, some protocols are actually designed with this architecture in mind to optimize and enhance their behavior. For example, the Multiprotocol Label Switching (MPLS) protocol carries control traffic using the IP protocol suite, which ideally would be implemented on a dedicated route processor engine running a general-purpose CPU, while leveraging a fixed label-based switching paradigm that is best suited to more simplified yet far higher-performance packet processor engine on a different line card.

Until the discussion of SDN and its separation of the control and data planes at distances greater than say a meter (i.e., within a single chassis or a directly tethered multichassis system), the control planes and data planes described in the previous section were distributed but built and managed as a tightly integrated (and relatively closely located) package of hardware and software. In addition to those components and *a lot* of internal infrastructure that was largely hidden from the external observer of those systems, the resulting packaging of these components led to the proliferation of purpose-driven network elements. These elements were often built on the same hardware family base and varied in throughput efficiency (and complexity) based on the emphasis on balance between service, management, control, and data planes. The interdependencies created by this very tight coupling of planes create problems (motivation) that revolve around innovation, stability, and scale that ultimately leads to high-performance in all of these areas. However, these designs suffer from high cost due to their enormous complexity, which is one motivational angle for SDN. Let's investigate each of these components because the discussion should highlight each of these issues, or benefits, depending on your perspective.

Scale matters

The scalability of a routing and switching system can take place in myriad ways, coupled with issues that might range from raw packet forwarding performance to power consumption, just to name a few. Ultimately, these scaling issues revolve around a number of trade-offs that tug between cost and performance:

- The service cards are limited to a certain amount of subscriber/flow/service state that they can support for a particular generation of the card. Further, because service cards (particularly those that use special embedded CPUs) have to use a vendor-specific system interconnection and switching fabric,[8] there is a significant lag between the availability of a new family of processors (or new processors within the family currently employed on the card) and a new service card that takes advantage of that innovation. The bottom line here is that it takes considerable time to do additional custom design. This unfortunately leads to added system cost.

- Forwarding cards could support a certain scale of forwarding entries for a particular generation of forwarding chip design, but some of these cards have separate, local slave or peer processors to the control processor on the control board, and these in turn have local processing limitations of their own—for example, running flow sampling on the forwarding card CPU in some designs could drive the local CPU utilization up and consume the CPU processing budget for the system.

---

8. The term "fabric" is used generically, as there are numerous technologies available to interconnect the blades/boards/cards of a multiboard network element.

- The control card[9] memories can handle a certain route scale or other state and have processing limitations based on the generation of the CPU complex on the card, but this memory is also used to store control protocol state and management such as BFD or SNMP. Another fundamental limitation to these designs is that that this memory is, generally speaking, the fastest money can buy and thus the most expensive.

Evolution

So in the past, the network operator had to follow a hardware upgrade path to solve the scale or processing related problems of the control plane. While doing this, the operator had to keep an eye on the forwarding card scale as well as the price-to-performance numbers to pick just the right time to participate in an upgrade. Though it is more pertinent to the separation of the control plane discussion, in the highly specialized platform solutions, they might have to balance the ratio of service cards to forwarding cards, which could significantly reduce the overall forwarding potential of the device (giving up forwarding slots for service slots). One way equipment vendors tried to help this situation was by separating the control and data planes apart so that they could evolve and scale independently—or at least much better than if they were combined.

The SDN-driven twist on the typical equipment evolution is that while there may still exist a cycle of growth/scale and upgrade in the control (and service) plane to accommodate scale, this is much easier to pursue in a COTS compute environment. This is particularly true given the innovations in this environment being driven by cloud computing. Further, dissecting the control plane from the management processes further provides some level of scale impact isolation[10] by running those user-level processes on COTS hardware within the router/switch, or even remotely.

Hardware forwarding components will still follow an upgrade cycle of their own to deal with forwarding scale regardless of the control plane (i.e., route processor) configuration. Upgrades due to bandwidth/throughput demands of a forwarding platform are part of a normal aggregation scheme, where great parts of the lower speed forwarding components are typically repositioned at layers closer to the edges of the network (this is potentially a more likely scenario as their function becomes more generic). Figure 2-7 illustrates this.

---

9. Depending on the type of device (router or switch), this would be more commonly referred to as a route processor or supervisor (different vendors have different names). On a device that was not based on a multislot chassis design, this could be just a control processor on a daughter card (or even integrated into a single board design).

10. Operating system design for network elements has evolved a view that management processes can be decoupled from but still provide services to the control processes (routing/forwarding), potentially on a pubsub basis. This isolates tasks like inventory management, environmental management, lower-level logging, alarm handling, and other chassis management tasks from the control process while keeping them aware of forwarding related events (like the restart of one of the forwarding cards).

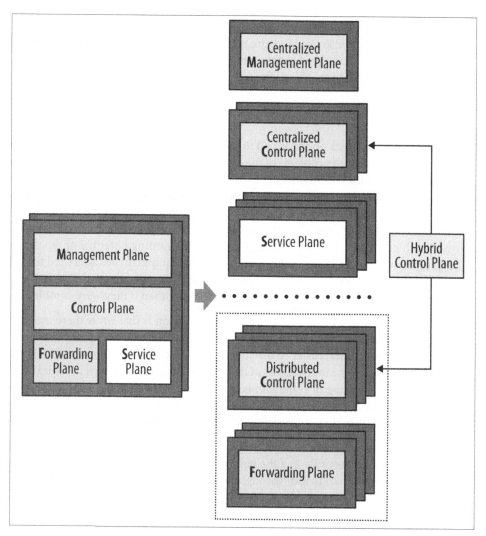

Figure 2-7. Separating the integrated management, control, service, and forwarding planes so that they can scale independently

Cost

For such an attention-getting word, there is less to say about cost than other motivators. Cost has capital (CAPEX) and operational (OPEX) components. Cost is driven by its companions: scale (a CAPEX driver), complexity, and stability (OPEX drivers). Let's start with the obvious statement about CAPEX—for many customers (particularly service providers or large enterprises with data center operations), the cost of processing power is very cheap on generic compute (COTS) in comparison to the cost of processing in their network elements. The integration costs associated with the integrated service and control cards drive some of this cost differential. Admittedly, some of this cost differential is also driven by a margin expectation of the vendor for the operating system (those control, management, and service processes), which are not always licensed separately. It's a way to recover their investment in their intellectual property and fund ongoing maintenance and development.

This is a subtle point for the conversation going forward. While SDN will definitely reduce the hardware integration component of this cost, the component that is the vendor's intellectual property (control or service) may be repriced to what the vendor perceives as its true value (to be tested by the market). Additionally, an integration cost will remain in the software components.[11]

Innovation

An argument can be made that there are innovation benefits from the separation of the control and data planes (the argument is stronger when considering the separation of the service plane as well). Theoretically, separation can benefit the consumer by changing the software release model in a way that enables innovations in either plane to proceed independently from each other (as compared to the current model in which innovations in either plane are gated by the build cycle of the multipurpose integrated monolith).

More relevant to the control/data separation would be the ability to support the introduction of new hardware in the forwarding plane without having to iterate the control plane (for example, the physical handling of the device would be innovation in the data plane component via new drivers).

Stability

The truth is that when we talk about the separation of these planes in an SDN context, there will probably be some subcomponents of the control plane that cannot be centralized and that there will be a local agent (perhaps more than one) that accepts forwarding modifications and/or aggregates management information back to the central control point. In spite of these realities, by separating the control and data planes, the forwarding elements may become more stable by virtue of having a smaller and less volatile codebase. The premise that a smaller codebase is generally more stable is fairly common these days. For example, a related (and popular) SDN benefit claim comes from the clean slate proposition, which posits that the gradual development of features in areas like Multiprotocol Label Switching (MPLS) followed a meandering path of feature upgrades that naturally bloats the code bases of existing implementations. This bloat leads to implementations that are overly complex and ultimately fragile. The claim

---

11. While the expectation is for a loose coupling of components and open standards enabling a high degree of confidence in interoperability/substitutability, there will probably be some combination compatibility management for new features and support that were more or less guaranteed in the integrated packaging.

is that the implementation of the same functionality using centralized label distribution to emulate the functionality of the distributed LDP or RSVP and a centralized knowledge of network topology could be done with a codebase at least an order of magnitude smaller than currently available commercial codebases.[12] The natural claim is that in a highly prescriptive and centralized control system, the network behavior can approach that of completely static forwarding, which is arguably stable.

Complexity and its resulting fragility

The question of how many control planes and where these control planes are located directly impacts the scale, performance, and resiliency—or lack thereof, which we refer to as *fragility*—of a network. Specifically, network operators plan on deploying enough devices within a network to handle some percentage of peak demand. When the utilization approaches this, new devices must be deployed to satisfy the demand. In traditional routing and switching systems, it's important to understand how much localized forwarding throughput demand can be satisfied without increasing the number of managed devices and their resulting control protocol entities in the network. Note from our discussion that the general paradigm of switch and router design is to use a firmly distributed control plane model, and that generally means that for each device deployed, a control plane instance will be brought up to control the data plane within that chassis. The question then is this: how does this additional control plane impact the scale of the overall network control plane for such things as network convergence (i.e., the time it takes for the entirety of running control planes to achieve and agreed upon a loop-free state of the network)? The answer is that it *does* impact the resiliency and performance of the overall system, and the greater the number of control planes, the potential at least exists for additional fragility in the system. It does also increase the *anti-fragility* of the system if tuned properly, however, in that it creates a system that eventually becomes consistent regardless of the conditions. Simply put, the number of protocol speakers in distributed or eventual consistency control models can create management and operations complexity.

Initially, an effort to curtail the growth of control planes was addressed by creating small clusters of systems from stand-alone elements. Each element of the cluster was bonded by a common inter-chassis data and control fabric that was commonly implemented as a small, dedicated switched Ethernet network. The multichassis system took this concept a step further by providing an interconnecting fabric between the shelves and thus behaved as a single logical system, controlled by a single control plane. Connectivity between the shelves was, however, implemented through external (network) ports, and the centralized control plane uses multiple virtual control plane instances—one per shelf. It was also managed as such in that it revealed a single IP address to the network

---

12. The Stanford document reference is available online (*http://bit.ly/17Tykj0*). Although this study advocates aspects of SDN outside the discussion in this chapter, part of its root premise is that smaller codebases are generally more stable.

operator, giving them one logical entity to manage. Figure 2-8 demonstrates both approaches.

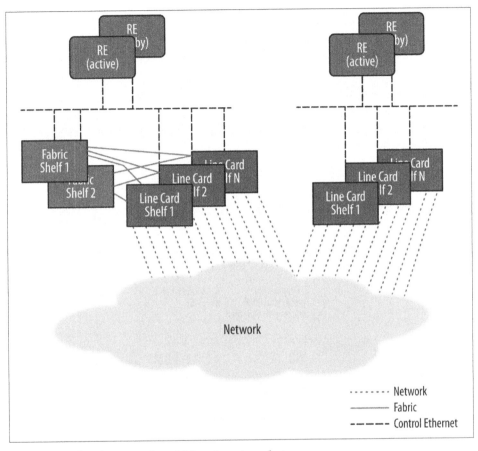

Figure 2-8. The cluster and multichassis system designs

In Figure 2-8's cluster and multichassis system designs, an external control plane constructed of an interconnecting Control Ethernet network (implemented via redundant Ethernet switches) allows the flow of external control protocol packets forwarding table updates and infrastructure management messaging between processors on the line card (port) shelves and the control processors (e.g., route engine).

Two strategies have evolved to address the control of these systems: distributing processing across the control points in the chassis (process placement) to more fully utilize the processing power (and spread the scale), or centralizing the processing on an outboard control system (that is wired into the control fabric of the system). The latter strategy potentially moves the scale point to one more modular and technologically faster moving device (these are commonly a packaged switch and compute device, without a requirement for a specific form or carrier card fabrication or a proprietary fabric interface).

You should note that this latter view of multichassis or cluster systems approaches some of the characteristics of SDN (centralization and more independent scaling of the control plane), albeit without solving the programmability/flexibility problems of the control plane.

There is also the potential to reduce the number and interaction of protocols required to create forwarding state in the elements. Figure 2-9 shows the process interaction in an IGP/BGP/MPLS network to learn/advertise prefixes and label bindings to populate forwarding in the data plane.

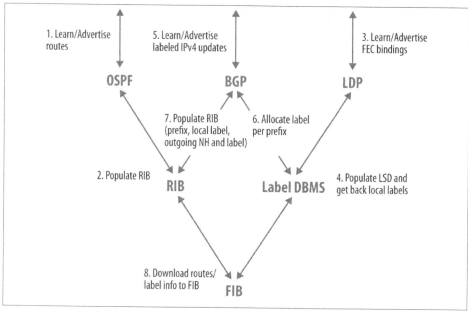

Figure 2-9. Process interaction in an IGP/BGP/MPLS network

Distributed Control Planes

The control paradigm that has evolved with the Internet, which is our ultimate network scale problem to date, is a distributed, eventual consensus model. In this model, the individual elements or their proxies participate together to distribute reachability information in order to develop a localized view of a consistent, loop-free network. We label the model as one of *eventual consensus* because of the propagation delays of reachability updates, inherent in the distributed control plane model in anything beyond a small home network, forms a fairly complex network graph. By design, the model is of intermittent nonsynchronization that could lead to less optimal forwarding paths but (hopefully) avoiding or limiting transient cycles otherwise known as *micro-loops* in the overall path. Figure 2-10 illustrates this concept.

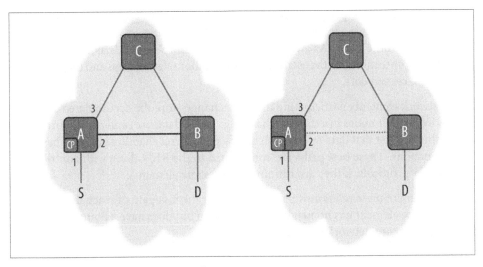

Figure 2-10. Eventual consistency of routing state

Observe the network on the left represented by the cloud and three nodes (A, B, and C). At time = 0, the network state is inconsistent and exhibiting a looping network. In this case, packets could cycle if transmitted, as the forwarding at nodes A and B are allowing traffic to flow between them. However, at time = 1, represented by the cloud on the right of the figure, the link between nodes A and B is broken. This represents the eventual consistency concept whereby the network, for a fraction of a second in time, could remain unstable until the routing message updates are exchanged between the nodes in the network.

IP and MPLS

IP and MPLS forwarding are examples of a distributed control model. In these forwarding paradigms, routes and reachability information is exchanged that later results in data plane paths being programmed to realize those paths. Books have already been written on the operation of IGPs, as well as numerous, freely available IETF drafts and standards, so we will not go into the specifics of these models. However, a hasty generalization will allow a discussion of some of the relative merits/limitations of this particular model and hence a better understanding of some of the SDN concepts around distribution of the control and data planes.

Creating the IP Underlay

The foundation of the current IP control plane paradigm is to use an IGP. This normally is in the form of a link-state protocol such as OSPF or ISIS. The IGP is used to establish reachability between a connected, acyclic graph of IP forwarding elements.

Once configured, IGP protocols establish relationships with appropriately configured neighbors and manage control protocol sessions that exchange reachability information (i.e., NLRI or route state). As awareness of infrastructure security has evolved, so have the built-in protections for the establishing of neighbor relationships and the acceptance of protocol related data.

The network elements participating in this exchange store the accumulated advertisements from other nodes in a state database (e.g., OSPF database) and run a shortest path algorithm against that data to establish a self-centered reachability graph of best paths to destinations. These best paths are contributed to the RIB (along with contributions from other protocols, if they are running on the same element).

The loss/gain of these relationships (neighbors) or the loss/gain of reachability on links on which the element has no neighbor relationship but does have a bound reachability advertisement are network events.

These events use a distributed flooding algorithm within the protocol definition to propagate, such that all elements speaking a particular control protocol in the domain that remain connected to each other (directly or indirectly) eventually see and process the event.

Scale of the control plane state in such networks is addressed both in physical and logical design, using the tools of recursion, summarization, route filtering, and compartmentalization (physical/logical). To handle the general scale problem arising from the number of IGP neighbors supported—the number of events that can be processed, the size of the link state database or other state structure and/or other related entities—the elements can be divided physically/logically into areas or other IGP hierarchies. At area boundaries, the operator has the controls to summarize (if possible) reachability information from other areas or leak specific information across the area borders.

To advertise reachability across administrative boundaries or to carry reachability data sets[13]—notably, different address families that represent further abstractions like virtual private networks across a network without carrying it in the IGP—the IP control paradigm typically uses the border gateway protocol (BGP). Like the IGP component of the control plane, a peering relationship between these neighbors, akin to that of the IGP, results in an exchange of all or any subsets of the neighbor's BGP data store. This occurs because reachability information is partitioned into various address families.

---

13. BGP has evolved into a very extensible database and database exchange protocol.

This information is made more accessible and scalable in both the control and data plane through *recursion*. Recursion allows the network control plane to distribute information with different attributes specific to different protocols that link through a series of shared keys, as shown in Figure 2-11. For example, this optimization allows the representation of a large number of BGP NLRI through a single IP destination address in the IGP data set (or a set if the operator uses control plane protocol features that allow multiple best paths to the destination, and/or has multiple equal cost paths to the advertising entity). The BGP information becomes information associated with leaves off our acyclic IGP graph when the control plane builds the entries for the data plane (FIB).

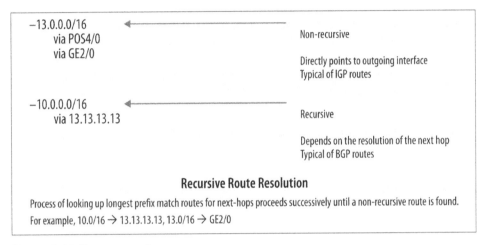

Figure 2-11. Route recursion

In the data plane, this recursion ultimately resolves the BGP prefix via the IGP "next hop" to a pointer to a fully qualified adjacency for the layer 2 components of a forwarding entry. This forwarding entry ultimately represents a destination MAC entry for the next router/switch interface in the path.

At these external boundaries, the operator has some additional control over summarization and advertisement of control state through the use of various policy tools. In the IP model, a certain amount of additional, localized control over which data in the control plane data set is selected for forwarding in the data plane is enabled through both standardized and proprietary[14] behaviors that allow local policies to govern the preference of learned reachability.

For example, these tools can indirectly affect the preferences of neighbors for a particular route state through local redistribution of a static route entry into a dynamic routing

---

14. There is RFC 1104 Models of Policy Based Routing.

protocol or by manipulating attributes of a prefix before re-advertisement.[15] A non-redistributed static route can affect local decisions if there is no existing route in the RIB of greater length or higher administrative preference. Preference for a prefix in each protocol table is controlled by the rules of that protocol and in the RIB by administrative preference between the different protocols' tables, but ultimately forwarding decisions in the FIB will be made on a longest match of a destination prefix. Admittedly, the combination of IGP/BGP recursion and the use of policy tools can become complex, but this is how control planes are administered in the real world.

Like any configuration atom in modern routers/switches, these configuration changes that could affect outcomes in the control and data plane can be administered centrally and pushed to the distributed elements. This mechanism is plagued by some of the fundamental problems that drive SDN's popularity. That is, one very pragmatic feature of an SDN controller is one of a provisioning agent, a control point that facilitates slow configuration commit times and inconsistency in CLI semantics and data models between vendors. Ultimately, it is this slowness of operation that inhibits the programmatic control of network elements and is one of the enhancements that SDN brings to the table.

To many network operators, control is about the flexibility to affect the outcomes of forwarding decisions and the ability to do this simply (and *programmatically*!). For example, this includes making the network more elastic and efficient based on additional knowledge or demands that we have above and beyond the algorithmic determination of "best." Both static routes and route policies also have limited scalability in most implementations.

Convergence Time

The FIB (or the data plane forwarding state entries) in the IP model has undergone years of optimization of both structure and traversal (lookup) algorithm. In this model, convergence and load balancing are as important focal points for network operators/designers as aforementioned black holes. Convergence is the time it takes from when a network element introduces a change in reachability of a destination due to a network event to when this change is seen and instantiated by all other relevant network elements. One of the components of convergence that might be obvious to the reader is the propagation delay of a specific update. This is normally a function of the average distance from the site of first change measured in the number of intervening nodes that have to re-flood/re-advertise the update. The remaining components of convergence focus on the processing of the update locally, such as updating the RIB and instantiation in the data plane which includes updating the FIB.

---

15. Arguably, this treatment is more specifically applicable to BGP.

To optimize convergence processing at the protocol level, as well as the propagation/flooding mechanism, each protocol has a different internal timer that is used to generate various types of events for that protocol. This includes, for example, the generation of "hello" messages to neighbors. At one point, part of the arcana of IP networking was in the knowledge of the optimal settings for a protocol's timers in a specific network design. Today, much of this has been internalized as defaults for the various protocols in most popular implementations. Of particular interest is how this is done for BGP, which moves large volumes of data to many peers. To this end, different vendors have message update packing, update prioritization, peer update grouping, and other internal optimizations to reduce redundant update generation processing, increase the speed of convergence at the routing or control plane level, and increase update transmission efficiency.

To optimize the updates to the FIB, different vendors have developed table organization strategies and event-driven reaction strategies for key components of the recursive nature of the FIB (e.g., the BGP next hop). These optimizations minimize the number and type of changes to the FIB that happen in response to a network event and thus minimize convergence.[16] These optimizations make it possible to perform anywhere from several thousand to greater than 10,000 updates per second[17] on some types of hardware.

Load Balancing

Load balancing in distributed IP forwarding evolved from packet-by-packet processing to hashes of increasingly greater parts of the IP header. This occurred as a reaction to the extent to which more and more individual flows began to be represented by gateway devices, such as those used for voice and other media[18]. Load balancing is normally applied to equal cost paths or bundled point-to-point circuits, although there are non-equal-cost variants for certain purposes. The actual efficiency of a load balancing algorithm is bounded by both the computation algorithm itself, as well as the potential imbalances in flow size an implementation might encounter. These can result in bin-packing efficiency problems that ultimately lead to limitations in the number of equal cost paths or bundle members supported by the implementation.

---

16. Examples include Next Hop Tracking and Protocol Independent Convergence.

17. Drawn from RIB/FIB update optimization studies on different Tier 1 Service Provider networks. Results vary by vendor and are dependent on prefix distribution and failure scenarios. One such study in 2010, shows a range of overall convergence times between 7 and 0.7 seconds for ~14,000 prefixes (depending on the percentage of IGP prefixes, particularly /32 prefix mask length—and assuming a constant raw RIB/FIB prefix update time of less than 300usec per /32 prefix).

18. Some current vendor implementations are capable of a 7-tuple load balancing hash.

High Availability

High Availability in the distributed IP context is provided through several mechanisms:

- Redundancy at the network level (the "two of everything" approach, where redundant routers/switches and redundant paths in the network design allow for the failure of a link or element).

- Redundancy at the element level using redundant route processors/switch control modules. The redundant processors can work in either a stateless active/standby mode (which normally implies an interruption in forwarding if there is no alternative path) or through stateful mirroring of control process data (e.g., nonstop routing).

Creating the MPLS Overlay

In terms of a discussion of SDN, MPLS is an addition to the packet header—an encapsulation that allows the operator of an IP network to create overlays or logical tunnels on the IP network (the underlay), as shown in Figure 2-12.

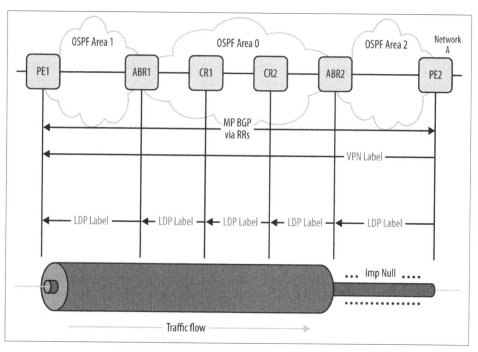

Figure 2-12. An MPLS VPN (VRF label distribution via route reflection) over an OSPF multiarea underlay

The label itself is 24 bits, which means there are 1,048,575 labels (the labels 0 through 15 are reserved), as shown in Figure 2-13.

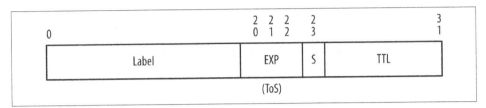

Figure 2-13. MPLS label

Labels can be stacked in a LIFO (last in, first out) order. The stacking of labels allows for the creation of multiple services or tunnels across a network. These were precursors to today's network overlays.

- A single label can enable an expedited lookup in the label table versus the IP forwarding table.
- Two labels create an abstraction that enables isolation, like that of the VPN where the external label expedites forwarding to an element with multiple virtual instances (VRFs) whose discriminator is the inner label[19], as shown in Figure 2-14.
- Three or four labels create abstractions that enable the same forwarding through an intervening tunnel (unprotected or protected), like VPNs constructed over traffic engineering tunnels (with or without fast reroute protection).

Like the IGP, many books have been written about the operation of MPLS, so we will not attempt to explain it all, but again, a general description will help with our SDN discussion going forward.

---

19. An MPLS VPN can be created using MPLS labels inside GRE encapsulation (if the transiting network doesn't support MPLS label switching—essentially replacing the outer or IGP label). There have been recent proposals to support similar functionality via MPLS in VxLAN encapsulation.

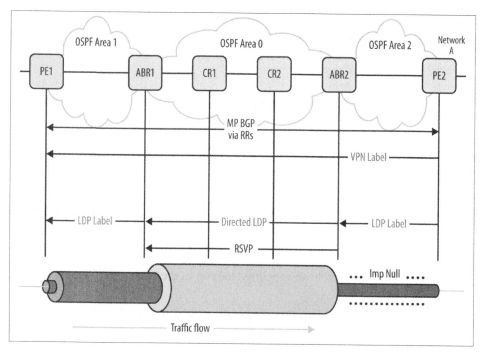

Figure 2-14. An MPLS VPN (VRF label distribution via route reflection) over an MPLS TE core (all over an OSPF underlay)

The main aspects of MPLS operation involve label allocation, address binding, and label distribution—all of which are controlled by configuration:

- The label distribution protocols can be LDP, RSVP (and BGP for the labeled unicast address family). These control protocols have neighbor/session forming behaviors and information exchange.

- Label allocation is normally dynamic, but label scale can be controlled somewhat in some vendor implementations particularly in the context of VPNs by per-VRF allocation or per-prefix/per-platform allocation. The assignment of these labels can be ordered (but this is not a requirement).

- Label distribution can be downstream on-demand (e.g., RSVP for traffic engineering[20]) or downstream unsolicited which is the default behavior of LDP.

Like the IGP, certain aspects of MPLS control plane behavior can be controlled by global and local configuration with the same limitations listed previously. This includes the ability to filter label advertisements, control label retention policy, control label range

---

20. Downstream-on-demand is also a feature of "seamless MPLS" implementation.

and the use and distribution of reserved labels. The network element can perform label actions that include push, pop, swap, multiple push, and swap-and-push (in addition to forward). Historically, not all network elements were capable of performing all of these actions, nor were they capable of adequately supporting deeper label stacks.

When MPLS is deployed, the forwarding behavior of the data plane changes from longest destination prefix match to a match of the topmost label on the label stack. However, the forwarding path will still follow the acyclic graph computed for the destination prefix. While this leads to a more expeditious lookup, it adds complexity by maintaining additional tables and references between the IP forwarding table and the label table. MPLS also adds to the overall complexity of the distributed IP control paradigm.

The specific application of MPLS traffic-engineered tunnels allows the operator to control the path of tunnels and thus exploit areas of the network not used for ordinary destination prefix-based forwarding. These MPLS tunnels are loaded based on the next hop address of a class of prefixes, called a Forwarding Equivalence Class (FEC). A FEC can also be a set of policies that specifically identify specific flows or quality of service characteristics of the flows such as those used by policy-based routing.

Like the IP IGP, MPLS has been enhanced over time, particularly in the area of multipath load balancing through innovations like the creation of sub-LSPs and entropy labels.

Replication

Both IP and MPLS distributed control apply equally to unicast and multicast, though they both require unique protocols and data structures for multicast replication. Multicast replication has a fairly long history in IP-only networks, starting with DVMRP, then MOSPF, and evolving to PIM. In MPLS networks, there have been recent developments around multicast in the VPN context (MVPN). Like their unicast relatives, the multicast control protocols optimize around scale, convergence, and stability, as well as strive to avoid black holes and cycle/loops. In the case of MVPN, there are additional concerns about balancing multicast state in the network with the burden of replicating packets on elements at the edge of the network.

Again, like the unicast protocols, these protocols allow a certain amount of configuration-driven control, which suffers from the same limitations of unicast IP protocols and MPLS configuration-based control.

Centralized Control Planes

The concept of a centralized control plane isn't unique to the SDN movement. In fact, the distributed model of control exists in part because the characteristics available in more recently developed databases didn't exist. Thus, it was difficult to achieve reliable synchronization required for high availability and guaranteed consistency between two or more control points.

The primary advantage of a centralized control plane is the view of the network it can provide to an application and the simplification of programmatic control. To achieve an end-to-end change in a large network, the application no longer has to know of or directly touch the individual elements, but interacts instead with a few control points that take care of these details. While they are not SDN solutions, there are some current and historic models of partial or total centralization, notably the route server in the IP domain and the ATM switch controller.[21]

There is also a famous attempt to productize what many consider a forbearer of modern SDN[22] via Ipsilon Networks. Their solution had an ATM component, though the value proposition was actually deterministic routing using a combination of IP and ATM,[23] which was subsequently marginalized by the introduction of tag switching and ultimately MPLS.

It should also be mentioned that the IETF has attempted to tackle some aspects of what are now considered SDN. These included the separation of control/data planes through both ForCES (RFC 3746) and Generalized Switch Management Protocol (GSMP—RFC 3292). The latter dates to February 2002!

Logical Versus Literal

To discuss a centralized control plane, it is necessary to separate the logical from the literal.

Factors such as the following make literal centralization of control extremely difficult and perhaps undesirable:

Scale
> A central controller will support a control session with each managed device. As the scale and volatility of the network increases, updates to an individual element require increases in per-session I/O and processing. Additional features such as collecting analytics through the channel or performing other management tasks, presents an additional burden. At some point, it makes sense to divide the burden into more manageable pieces.

---

21. Other examples include SS7 in voice networks and control of media gateways in VoIP.

22. While the Ipsilon solution didn't provide an open programmable interface, it did provide a level of network flexibility to the operator.

23. Ipsilon has (at least) two interesting IETF RFCs on this topic RFC 1953 and RFC 1954.

High Availability

Even if the control session scale burden can be handled by a single controller, that controller becomes a single point of failure that would result in the entire network failing. Even if the entire network is configured to operate "headless" for a significant period, at some point other network failures or changes will need interaction with the controller. If the controller has not been restored by then, this will be a problem. The simplest high availability strategy would allow for an active/standby combination of controllers.

Geography

Within a data center, almost everything managed is relatively close even if your data center is many city blocks or many stories tall. Once the controller and controlled element are separated by a metro, state, or national network, transmission delay can begin to affect the efficiency of operation.[24] Greater geographies also increase the risk of partition (separating the controller from the element).[25]

Given these factors, a logically centralized but physically distributed control plane seems to make more sense. The embrace of this concept is also the embrace of a federation protocol of some kind to synchronize state among the physically distributed controllers.

ATM/LANE

Asynchronous Transfer Mode (ATM) is a connection-oriented cell switching and multiplexing technology (standardized through the ITU-T). Like the previously described IP and MPLS environments, a general (nonexhaustive) description of the protocol is provided (focusing on those parts relevant to the discussion of SDN).

Most of ATM's function was originally statically provisioned, supporting two types of services; static circuits (permanent virtual circuits) and the later developed dynamic circuits (switched virtual circuits). SVCs are dynamically set up (and torn down) using a signaling protocol between the endpoints and the switches on a well-known channel (VPI/VCI pair).

Using a subnet-able NSAP-based addressing scheme for the endpoints (independent of higher layer protocols), ATM call control (circuit setup was patterned on telephony call setup) or routing was based on source/destination NSAP, traffic and required QoS (virtual circuits could be Variable Bit Rate or Committed Bit Rate depending on the manipulation of QoS attributes[26]).

---

24. This is even more important if the state updates require acknowledgement—which they should!

25. Once the controller and controlled are not co-resident, the "backhoe factor" is introduced along with concerns about SRLG (shared risk link groups) and other physical hazards.

26. Peak Information Rate, Committed Information Rate and Burst Size and Excess Burst Size.

Many networks later moved on to use something like the dynamic distributed routing protocols of the IP environment (the ATM Forum standard, PNNI) for the distribution of NSAP VPI/VCI mapping.

LAN emulation (LANE) emerged as an ATM Forum-defined specification that makes an ATM network appear (to higher layers) much like an Ethernet (or Token Ring) network—providing the same MAC-layer service interface. This interface manifested differently in an ATM host than at the demarcation points where a true layer 2 device (e.g., an Ethernet switch with an ATM NIC) interfaced with an ATM switch.

The most important point about the LANE protocol itself was that it creates an overlay on the ATM switching underlay and was transparent to the switches.

To create this overlay, some ATM-connected, role-specific servers were required and offered through one or more controllers. This is illustrated in Figure 2-15. The required servers were the LES, the LEC, and the BUS:

- The LES (LAN Emulation Server) provided a MAC registration and control server (one per emulated LAN) to LAN Emulation Clients (LEC)—essentially, the role of ARP server for the ELAN (LE-ARP). The LEC was the protocol interface on the host (or element) between the MAC and higher layer protocols.

- The LES was paired with a BUS. The BUS (Broadcast and Unknown Server) was a multicast server that handled BUM traffic for a specific ELAN.

- The LECS (LAN Emulation Client Server) maintained a domain-wide database of LEC/ELAN mappings was a query point for this level of resolution (providing the ATM address of the LES serving a specific ELAN).

- The LECS addresses were manually configured on the ATM switches and discovered (by end stations) through either ILMI, a well-known ATM NSAP address for the LECS or a connection on a well-known channel (VPI/VCI pair). The clients connect to the servers via bidirectional control-direct (LES) and configuration-direct (LECS) VCC. The clients connect to the BUS as a leaf of a point-to-multipoint VCC.

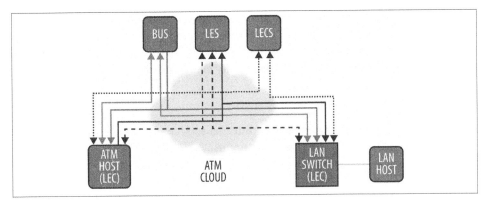

Figure 2-15. LANE clients and servers

In Chapter 6, there should be striking resemblances between some of these overlay fundamentals and some of the more modern underpinnings of data center orchestration.

Though ATM has faded in its role in data networking, some of the first commercially visible work in high availability and state maintenance in a controller/client environment occurred in LANE. In fact, in version 1.0 of LANE, there was no redundancy at all.

Later, SSRP evolved to provides a mechanism for the LECS to establish a logical/physical hierarchy (priorities drive the creation of a VCC tree between LECS) that allows the switch to provide multiple LECS addresses to the original LEC discovery mechanism with a local switch. The LECS hierarchy allows just one primary to respond to the LEC queries and the others to serve as a backup (that sense primary failure through the loss of a VCC from the primary).

SSRP also allows for redundancy of LES/BUS pairs in an ELAN using a priority mechanism (again, VCC connectivity to the LECS is a used as a liveliness test for a pair).

This redundancy scheme added significant overhead to the network (a large number of VCCs used solely for control), and the onus was on a network administrator to keep all the LECS databases in sync—manually![27]

From an SDN perspective then, ATM switching had static and dynamic controls (the former was centrally administered through a proprietary management interface) that created an underlay. Control was not programmatic (vendors provided a proprietary

---

27. The LES/BUS works with dynamic state, and there was a "relearning" period when the LEC shifted from a primary pair to a secondary (the Cisco FSSRP protocol attempted to work around the LEC disruption problem, in exchange for more VCC scale and complexity). In some implementations, the user was required to maintain the ordering of the LECS table on all the ATM switches.

provisioning system as part of an overall management system with no real external API). LANE provides a specific type of logical overlay, supported by multiple servers (or controller-like functionality). These server functions also did not have a programmatic interface and had rudimentary high-availability characteristics.

Route Servers

The route server evolved as a means for Internet service providers to handle the scale of peers and policies at external peering points. A slightly different mechanism (the route reflector) was standardized for this purpose for internal peers.

A route server is an eBGP-based control point (normally on a shared segment that appears to all parties as a separate autonomous system) that receives control state updates (NLRI) from each participant, applies filters and policies to those updates, calculates best path based on the resulting data (which could be different than normal BGP best path based on this intermediary policy step), and creates a per-participant RIB (that is returned to the participant)[28] and shown in Figure 2-16. The route server is transparent as far as attributes like AS path. Each participant needs only a single BGP session for the exchange.

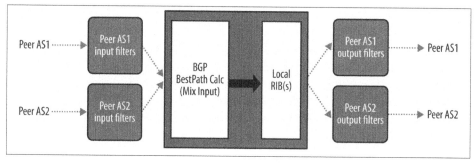

Figure 2-16. Route server architecture

The route server can interface to a routing registry.[29] The registry is a distributed store of route objects (ASN, policies, prefixes, authentication info) that provides a toolset that can enable automatic provisioning of both stand-alone peers (edge routers) and route servers, as shown in Figure 2-17.

---

28. Notable examples include Quagga (*http://www.nongnu.org/quagga/*) (a fork of GNU Zebra) and BIRD (*http://bird.network.cz/*).

29. The RIPE IRR (*http://www.irr.net*) is an example of such a registry.

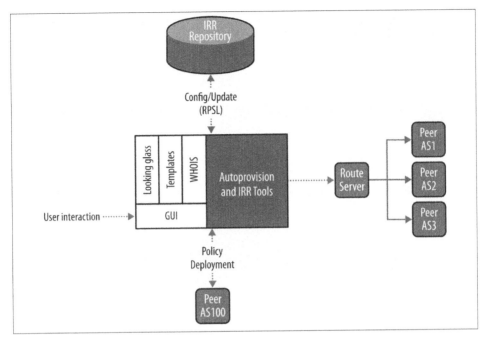

Figure 2-17. IIR and route server interconnection

A route reflector provides a similar service to internal peers, though it is a more transparent service (as the term "reflector" implies) with some limited intermediary policy insertion and a stricter set of defined behaviors.[30]

A good example of its use is the VPN service-specific reflector that removes the need for all VPN edge routers (the customer facing Provider Edge router) from having to form and maintain a complete mesh of BGP sessions to exchange NLRI for the VPN address families, shown in Figure 2-18. Route reflectors support high availability (clusters) and hierarchical distribution.

---

30. As route reflector usage has grown in importance in service provider networks, some ability to alter the defined/standardized behaviors of the reflector have emerged (e.g., the ability to advertise more than one best path to a client and the ability to advertise next-hop-self).

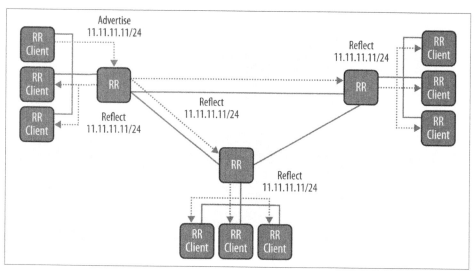

Figure 2-18. Route reflection of prefix 11.11.11.11/24 from one client across a hierarchy of reflectors to all clients

Both of these devices offer a centralized point of control from which a provider could potentially inject route state. Many service providers use such control points with their own scripted/automated interfaces to provision VPN services, mitigate DDOS attacks (injecting black-hole or attractor routes), and perform other tasks.

Because these devices communicate via a standard control protocol (BGP) that provides for both inter- and intra-domain information exchange, they are easily federated and synchronized to enable geographic distribution.

From an SDN perspective, the main problem with the BGP-based control point today is a lack of standardized programmability. Some would argue that RPSL (Route Policy Specification Language) *is* a standard for expressing/programming BGP policy in a route server. However, this is not a complete/adequate solution (missing a standard API, transaction orientation) for a generalized BGP control point like a route reflector. Some ISP's use in-house developed tools that process RPSL database files directly and help in the automation of their BGP controls.

Conclusions

The distributed control plane and its eventual consensus model have evolved over time to try and satisfy not only the continual scale/growth of the Internet in general, but to address the concerns of network operators around consistency (black-hole and loop avoidance) and fast convergence.

In this paradigm, the fundamental concept of an underlay and overlay abstraction gained widespread acceptance (exemplified by IP forwarding and the overlay abstraction of MPLS).

The chief weaknesses of the distributed control model are in the areas of network flexibility and user control (there is not enough granular control over the consensus path selection to provide sufficient flexibility), programmability (there are no standard API to inject state or extract information and most automation is either vendor dependent or heavily embedded with knowledge of vendor configuration/operation command semantics), as well as the high degree of integration of its control, data, service, and management planes (driving a scale upgrade cycle and other dependencies). Elements in this model have only recently begun to experiment with the externalizing the control plane so that the route processor can run on more scalable (and easily upgradeable) compute platforms (that are not bound by the drag introduced in creating specific carriers and fabric interfaces for an in-shelf processor).

It could be argued that the recursion through and interaction of the IGP/BGP/MPLS paradigm introduce a good deal of complexity and overhead. However, models are also evolving a number of integrated convergence, high-availability, and black-hole avoidance mechanisms that providers find desirable.

Centralizing the control plane in a logically centralized but physically distributed model makes sense from scale, high-availability, and geographical perspectives.

SDN advocates can learn from historical attempts at centralization. Two examples are provided; ATM LANE (which is truly historical) and the route server (still used in the IP forwarding domain).

The LANE system of servers provided the first glimpses into the complexities of high availability in a centralized model. Their high-availability model lacked synchronization and often required the user to manually maintain the LECS database in a specific order. These models significantly increased the scale of the control plane infrastructure (in the form of a very large VCC fan out between servers and elements).

The more modern route server and route reflector provide a centralized control point[31] for an otherwise distributed IP control plane.

Both of these central control points reduce the scale of the distributed control infrastructure. The route server provides programmability, but not in a standardized fashion, and doesn't introduce any more flexibility or granularity of control. The same can be said for the route reflector, though many service providers use automation on top of the route reflector to influence forwarding in their networks. Though the route server

---

31. These control points are considered the "opportunity point" for SDN development (to be discussed in Chapter 4).

has specific applications layered on top of its database (e.g., WHOIS), it doesn't directly provide additional application services to programmers (e.g., topology).

OpenFlow (and its accompanying SDO, the ONF) is credited with starting the discussion of SDN and providing the first vestige of modern SDN control: a centralized point of control, a northbound API that exposes topology, path computation, and provisioning services to an application above the controller), as well as a standardized southbound protocol for instantiating forwarding state on a multivendor infrastructure.

Unfortunately, the OpenFlow architecture does not provide a standardized northbound API (yet), nor does it provide a standardized east-west state distribution protocol that allows both application portability and controller vendor interoperability. Standardization may progress through the newly spawned Architecture Working Group.

OpenFlow provides a great deal of flow/traffic control for those platforms that can exploit the full set of OpenFlow primitives. The ONF has spawned a working group to address the description/discovery of the capabilities of vendor hardware implementations as they apply to the use of the primitive set to implement well-known network application models.

Even though there are questions about the level of abstraction implemented by Open-Flow and whether its eventual API represents a complete SDN API, there is interest in its application, and ongoing efforts around hybrid operation may make it easier to integrate its capability for matching/qualifying traffic in traditional/distributed networks or at the borders between OpenFlow domains and native domains.

CHAPTER 3

OpenFlow

Introduction

Chapter 2 reviewed the control and data planes. In this chapter, a lot of our focus will be on the continuously evolving OpenFlow proposal and protocols, viewed by many as the progenitor of the clean slate theory and instigator of the SDN discussion, but we will also discuss, in general terms, how SDN controllers can implement a network's control plane, and in doing so, potentially reshape the landscape of an operator's network.

OpenFlow was originally imagined and implemented as part of network research at Stanford University. Its original focus was to allow the creation of experimental protocols on campus networks that could be used for research and experimentation. Prior to that, universities had to create their own experimentation platforms from scratch. What evolved from this initial kernel of an idea was a view that OpenFlow could replace the functionality of layer 2 and layer 3 protocols completely in commercial switches and routers. This approach is commonly referred to as the *clean slate proposition*.

In 2011, a nonprofit consortium called the Open Networking Foundation (ONF) was formed by a group of service providers[1] to commercialize, standardize, and promote the use of OpenFlow in production networks. The ONF is a new type of Standards Development Organization in that it has a very active marketing department that is used to promote the OpenFlow protocol and other SDN-related efforts. The organization hosts an annual conference called the Open Networking Summit as part of these efforts.

---

1. There are currently 90+ members of the ONF, including academic and government institutions, enterprises, service providers, software companies, and equipment manufacturers.

In the larger picture, the ONF has to be credited with bringing attention to the phenomenon of software-defined networks.

The key components of the OpenFlow model, as shown in Figure 3-1, have become at least part of the common definition of SDN, mainly:

- Separation of the control and data planes (in the case of the ONF, the control plane is managed on a logically centralized controller system).
- Using a standardized protocol between controller and an agent on the network element for instantiating state (in the case of OpenFlow, forwarding state).
- Providing network programmability from a centralized view via a modern, extensible API.

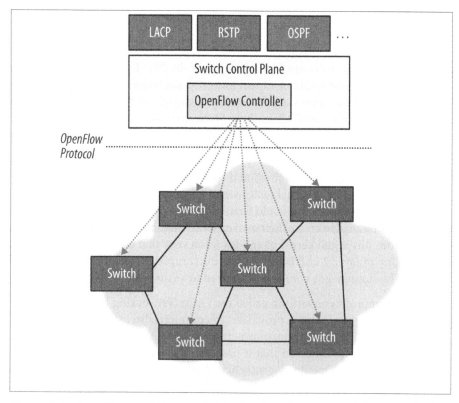

Figure 3-1. OpenFlow architecture (with the view that some of the control plane apps will ride on TOP of the controller—emulating the behavior of traditional control plane apps)

OpenFlow is a set of protocols and an API, not a product per se or even a single feature of a product. Put another way, the controller does nothing without an application program (possibly more than one) giving instructions on which flows go on which elements (for their own reasons).

The OpenFlow protocols are currently divided in two parts:

- A wire protocol (currently version 1.3.x) for establishing a control session, defining a message structure for exchanging flow modifications (flowmods) and collecting statistics, and defining the fundamental structure of a switch (ports and tables). Version 1.1 added the ability to support multiple tables, stored action execution, and metadata passing—ultimately creating logical pipeline processing within a switch for handling flows.
- A configuration and management protocol, of-config (currently version 1.1) based on NETCONF (using Yang data models) to allocate physical switch ports to a particular controller, define high availability (active/standby) and behaviors on controller connection failure. Though OpenFlow can configure the basic operation of OpenFlow command/control it cannot (yet) boot or maintain (manage in an FCAPS context) an element.

In 2012, the ONF moved from "plugfests" to test interoperability and compliance, to a more formalized test (outsourced to Indiana University). This was driven by the complexity of the post-OpenFlow wire version 1.0 primitive set.

While the ONF has discussed establishing a reference implementation, as of this writing, this has not happened (there *are* many open source controller implementations).

OpenFlow protocols don't directly provide the network slicing (an attractive feature that enables the ability to divide an element into separately controlled groups of ports or a network into separate administrative domains). However, tools like FlowVisor[2] (which acts as a transparent proxy between multiple controllers and elements) and specific vendor implementations (agents that enable the creation of multiple virtual switches with separate controller sessions) make this possible.

---

2. FlowVisor (*https://openflow.stanford.edu/display/DOCS/Flowvisor*) will introduce some intermediary delay since it has to handle packets between the switch and controller.

Wire Protocol

So, where does OpenFlow go that we haven't been before?

First, it introduces the concept of substituting ephemeral state (flow entries are not stored in permanent storage on the network element) for the rigid and unstandardized semantics of various vendors' protocol configuration.[3] Ephemeral state also bypasses the slower configuration commit models of past attempts at network automation.

For most network engineers, the ultimate result of such configuration is to create forwarding state (albeit distributed and learned in a distributed control environment). In fact, for many, the test of proper configuration is to verify forwarding state (looking at routing, forwarding, or bridging tables). Of course, this shifts some of the management burden to the controller(s)—at least the maintenance of this state (if we want to be proactive and always have certain forwarding rules in the forwarding table) versus the distributed management of configuration stanzas on the network elements.[4]

Second, in an OpenFlow flow entry, the entire packet header (at least the layer 2 and layer 3 fields) are available for match and modify actions, as shown in Figure 3-2. Many of the field matches can be masked[5]. These have evolved over the different releases of OpenFlow[6]. Figure 3-2 illustrates the complexity of implementing the L2+L3+ACL forwarding functionality (with next hop abstraction for fast convergence) can be. The combination of primitives supported from table to table leads to a very broad combination of contingencies to support.

---

3. The ability to create ephemeral state in combination with programmatic control may only be a temporary advantage of OpenFlow, as there are proposals to add this functionality existing programmatic methods (like NETCONF).

4. This is not a unique proposition in that PCRF/PCEF/PCC systems (with associated Diameter interactions) have done this in the past in mobile networks on a per-subscriber basis. Standards organizations have been working on a clear definition and standardized processing of the interchanged messages and vendor interoperability between components of the overall system. There is no doubt that the mobile policy systems could evolve into SDN systems and have SDN characteristics. When this happens, the primary distinctions between them and OpenFlow may be flexibility (simplicity, though objective, may also be appropriate).

5. The type of match supported (contiguous or offset based) is another platform-dependent capability.

6. Unfortunately, backward compatibility was broken between version 1.2 and prior versions when a TLV structure was added to ofp_match (and match fields were reorganized). In fact, version 1.2 was considered non-implementable because of the number and types of changes (though there was an open source agent that finally did come out in 2012). There were changes to the HELLO handshake to do version discovery, and incompatible switch versions fail to form sessions with the controller.

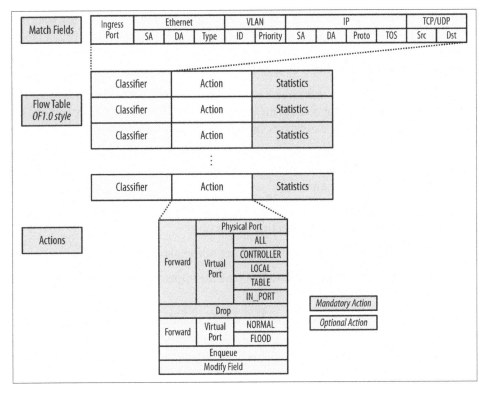

Match Fields	Ingress Port	Ethernet			VLAN		IP				TCP/UDP	
		SA	DA	Type	ID	Priority	SA	DA	Proto	TOS	Src	Dst

Figure 3-2. OpenFlow (wire) version 1.0 primitives

This is a striking difference in breadth of operator control when compared with the distributed IP/MPLS model (OpenFlow has an 11-tuple match space). A short list of possibilities includes:

- Because of the masking capability in the match instructions, the network could emulate IP destination forwarding behavior.

- At both layer 2 and layer 3, the network can exhibit source/destination routing behavior.

- There is no standardized equivalent (at present) to the packet matching strengths of OpenFlow, making it a very strong substitute for Policy Based Routing or other match/forward mechanisms in the distributed control environment.

Finally, there is the promise of the modify action. The original concept was that the switch (via an application running above the switch) could be made to behave like a service appliance, performing services like NAT or firewall). Whether or not this is realizable in hardware-based forwarding systems, this capability is highly dependent on vendor implementation (instructions supported, their ordering, and the budgeted number of operations to maintain line rate performance)[7]. However, with the label manipulation actions added to version 1.3 of the wire protocol, it is possible that an OpenFlow controlled element could easily emulate integrated platform behaviors like an MPLS LSR (or other traditional distributed platform functions).

The OpenFlow protocol is extensible through an EXPERIMENTER extension (which can be public or private) for control messages, flow match fields, meter operation, statistics, and vendor-specific extensions (which can be public or private).

Table entries can be prioritized (in case of overlapping entries) and have a timed expiry (saving clean-up operation in some cases, and setting a drop dead efficacy for flows in one of the controller loss scenarios).

OpenFlow supports PHYSICAL, LOGICAL, and RESERVED port types. These ports are used as ingress, egress, or bidirectional structures.

The RESERVED ports IN_PORT and ANY are self-explanatory.

TABLE was required to create a multitable pipeline (OpenFlow supports up to 255 untyped tables with arbitrary GoTo ordering).

The remaining RESERVED ports enable important (and interesting) behaviors[8]:

LOCAL
> An egress-only port, this logical port allows OpenFlow applications access ports (and thus processes) of the element host OS.

NORMAL
> An egress-only port, this logical port allows the switch to function like a traditional Ethernet switch (with associated flooding/learning behaviors). According to the protocol functional specification, this port is only supported by a Hybrid switch.[9]

FLOOD
> An egress-only port, this logical port uses the replication engine of the network element to send the packet out all standard (nonreserved) ports. FLOOD differs from ALL (another reserved port) in that ALL includes the ingress port. FLOOD leverages the element packet replication engine.

---

7. A later use case explores creating such an application above the controller or virtualizing it in a virtual service path.

8. CONTROLLER is the only required reserved port in this particular set (the others are optional). The other ports are ANY, IN_PORT, ALL, and TABLE, which are all required. The combinations listed here are interesting for their potential interactions in a hybrid.

9. The original definition of a "hybrid" was a switch that would behave both as an OpenFlow switch and a layer 2 switch (for the ports in the OpenFlow domain).

CONTROLLER
>   Allows the flow rule to forward packets (over the control channel) from data path
>   to the controller (and the reverse). This enables PACKET_IN and PACKET_OUT
>   behavior.

The forwarding paradigm offers two modes: proactive (pre-provisioned) and reactive (data-plane driven). In the proactive mode, the control program places forwarding entries ahead of demand. If the flow does not match an existing entry, the operator has two (global) options—to drop the flow or to use the PACKET_IN option to make a decision to create a flow entry that accommodates the packet (with either a positive/forward or negative/disposition)—in the reactive mode.

The control channel was originally specified as a symmetric TCP session (potentially secured by TLS). This channel is used to configure, manage (place flows, collect events, and statistics) and provide the path for packets from the switch to and from the controller/applications.

Statistics support covers flow, aggregate, table, port, queue, and vendor-specific counters.

In version 1.3 of the protocol, multiple auxiliary connections are allowed (TCP, UDP, TLS, or DTLS) that are capable of handling any OpenFlow message type or subtype. There is no guarantee of ordering on the UDP and DTLS channels, and behavioral guidelines are set in the specification to make sure that packet-specific operations are symmetric (to avoid ordering problems at the controller).[10]

OpenFlow supports the BARRIER message to create a pacing mechanism (creating atomicity or flow control) for cases where there may be dependencies between subsequent messages (the given example is a PACKET_OUT operation that requires a flow to first be placed to match the packet that enables forwarding).

Replication

OpenFlow provides several mechanisms for packet replication.

The ANY and FLOOD reserved virtual ports are used primarily for emulating/supporting the behaviors of existing protocols (e.g., LLDP, used to collect topology for the controller, often uses FLOOD as its output port).

Group tables allow the grouping of ports into an output port set to support multicasting, multipath, indirection, and fast-failover. Each group table is essentially a list of action buckets (where ostensibly one of the actions is output, and an egress port is indicated). There are four group table types, but only two are required:

---

10. There is a rather complete commentary regarding these changes to the protocol, particularly the change of the protocol from a session-based channel to UDP in a JIRA ticket filed by David Ward.

All
>Used for multicast all action buckets in the list have to be executed[11]

Indirect
>Used to simulate the next hop convergence behavior in IP forwarding for faster convergence

Action lists in the Apply action (the Apply action was a singleton in OpenFlow version 1.0) allow successive replications by creating using a list of output/port actions.

FAWG (Forwarding Abstraction Workgroup)

The model for an OpenFlow switch (Figure 3-3) works well on a software-based switch (eminently flexible in scale and packet manipulation characteristics) or a hardware-forwarding entity that conforms to some simplifying assumptions (e.g., large, wide, deep, and multi-entrant memories like a TCAM). But because not all devices are built this way, there's a great deal of variation in the support of all the packet manipulations enabled by the set of OpenFlow primitives, multiple tables, and other aspects that give OpenFlow its full breadth and power.

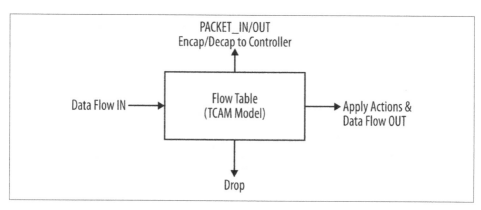

Figure 3-3. The OpenFlow 1.0 forwarding model (very simple shared table model)

In general, the potential combinatorial complexity of OpenFlow version 1.1 (see Figure 3-4) and beyond do not work well on ASIC-based forwarders. For this reason, the level of abstraction chosen for OpenFlow has come into question, as has its applicability for ALL applications.

---

11. The specification claims the "all" group type is usable for multipath, but this is not multipath in the IP forwarding sense, as the packet IS replicated to both paths. This behavior is more aligned with live/live video feeds or other types of multipathing that require rectification at an end node.

While this is a commonly held belief, an interview of Martin Casado (OpenFlow creator) is often cited in the more general argument about abstraction level.[12]

In full context of the interview, Martin cites a role for OpenFlow in Traffic Engineering applications, makes comments on the current limitations of implementing OpenFlow on existing ASICs (to the general point), and then makes a specific comment on the applicability of OpenFlow for Network Virtualization: "I think OpenFlow is too low-level for this.")[13]

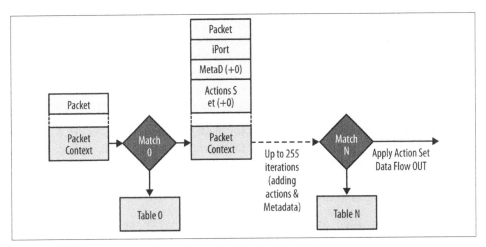

Figure 3-4. The post OpenFlow pipeline model in version 1.1 and beyond (very complex —combinations complexity $O(n!^* a(2^l))$ paths where n = number of tables, a = number of actions and l = width of match fields)

The protocol had limited capability detection in earlier versions, which was refactored in version 1.3 to support some primordial table capability description (adding match type for each match field—e.g., exact match, wildcard, and LPM).

The following shortcomings were cited for the existing abstraction[14]:

- Information loss
- Information leakage
- Weak control plane to data plane abstraction

---

12. *http://searchnetworking.techtarget.com/news/2240174517/Why-Nicira-abandoned-OpenFlow-hardware-control* (Subscription required to read full article.)

13. This expression of OpenFlow complexity courtesy of David Meyer.

14. *FPMODs and Table Typing Where To From Here?* (David Meyer/Curt Beckmann) ONF TAG-CoC 07/17/12.

- Combinatorial state explosion
- Data-plane-driven control events
- Weak indirection infrastructure
- Time-sensitive periodic messaging
- Multiple control engines
- Weak extensibility
- Missing primitives

A separate workgroup, FAWG, is attempting a first-generation, negotiated switch model through table type patterns (TTPs).[15] FAWG has developed a process of building, identifying (uniquely), and sharing TTPs. The negotiation algorithm (built on a Yang model) and messaging to establish an agreed TTP between controller and switch is also being developed (a potential addition to of-config version 1.4).

A TTP model is a predefined switch behavior model (e.g., HVPLS_over_TE forwarder and L2+L3+ACL) represented by certain table profiles (match/mask and action) and table interconnections (a logical pipeline that embodies a personality). These profiles may differ based on the element's role in the service flow (e.g., for the HVPLS forwarder, whether the element is head-end, mid-point, or egress).

Early model contributions suggest further extensions may be required to achieve TTP in OpenFlow version 1.3.x.

If FAWG is successful, it may be possible for applications above the controller to be aware of element capabilities, at least from a behavior profile perspective.

Here is a simple example of the need for TTP (or FPMOD).[16]

Hardware tables can be shared when they contain similar data and have low key diversity (e.g., a logical table with two views; MAC forwarding and MAC Learning). This table could be implemented many different ways, including as a single hardware table. An OpenFlow controller implementing MAC learning/bridging will have to have a separate table for MAC learning and a different table for MAC bridging (a limitation in expression in OpenFlow). There is no way today to tie these two potentially differing views together. In this simple example shown in Figure 3-5, there could arise timing scenarios

---

15. A more complex solution was proposed (under the title Forwarding Plane Models - FPMOD) by the Open-Flow Future Discussion Group but was tabled for the simpler table type profile model being developed in FAWG (suggested by the TAG). This solution is less a set of models and more an extensible set of primitives that are mapped at the switch Hardware Abstraction Layer coding time instead of at the controller (of course, based on a negotiated model of behavior, but not necessarily a static predefined model limited to a pipeline description).

16. This example also comes from the Meyer/Beckman reference cited earlier in this chapter.

where synchronization of table of flow mods from the two separate OpenFlow table entities may be necessary (i.e., you can't do forwarding *before* learning).

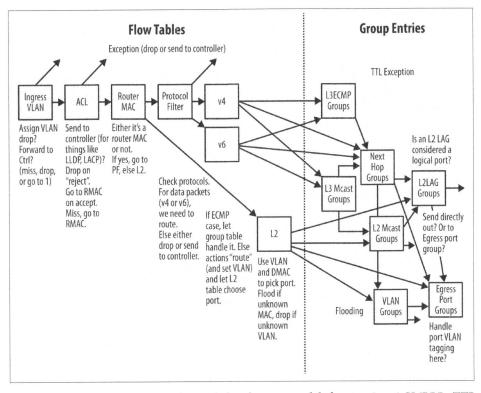

Figure 3-5. Example of complexity behind TTP model for L2+L3+ACL/PBR TTP (source: D. Meyer and C. Beckmann of Brocade)

In Figure 3-5's case, IPv4 and IPv6 tables point to group tables to emulate the use of the next hop abstraction in traditional FIBs (for faster convergence).

Config and Extensibility

The of-config protocol was originally designed to set OpenFlow related information on the network element (of-config 1.0). The protocol is structured around XML schemas, Yang data models, and the NETCONF protocol for delivery.

Proposals to extend of-config can come from within the Config-Mgmt Working Group or from other groups (e.g., FAWG, Transport[17]).

---

17. Much of optical switch configuration is static and persistent, so some of the extensions required may be better suited to of-config.

As of version 1.1 of of-config, the standard decouples itself from any assumptions that an operator would run FlowVisor (or a similar, external slicing proxy) to achieve multiple virtual switch abstractions in a physical switch. This changes the working model to one in which the physical switch can have multiple internal logical switches, as illustrated in Figure 3-6.

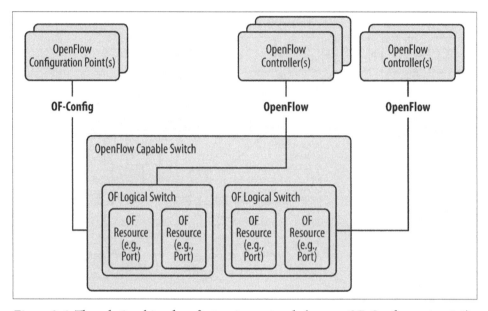

Figure 3-6. The relationship of config to wire protocols (source: OF-Config version 1.1)

Using of-config version 1.1, in addition to controllers, certificates, ports, queues, and switch capabilities operators can configure some logical tunnel types (IP-in-GRE, NV-GRE, VX-LAN). This extension requires the support of the creation of logical ports on the switch.

Proposals exist to expand of-config further in the areas of bootstrapping and to expand the abilities of the of-config protocol in version 1.2 (see Figure 3-7) to support even more switch/native functionality (e.g., the ability to configure a local/native OAM protocol daemon has been proposed as an extension).

OF-Config v1.0	OF-Config v1.1	OF-Config v1.2 (proposed)
Based on OpenFlow v1.2 • assigning controllers to logical switches • retrieving assignment of resources to logical switches • configuring some properties of ports and queues	**Based on OpenFlow v1.3** • aded controller certificates and resource type "table" • retrieving logical switch capabilities signed to controller • configuring of tunnel endpoints	**Based on OpenFlow v1.4 (proposed)** • retrieving capable switch capabilities, configuring logical switch capabilities • assigning resources to logical switches • simple topology detection • event notification

Figure 3-7. Capability progression of OF-Config

By extending of-config into native components, the ONF may have inadvertently broached the topic of hybrid operation and may also have created some standards-related confusion[18].

One of the slated items for the Architecture group to study is a potential merge of the wire and configuration protocols. The Architecture group is not chartered to produce any protcols or specifications as its output, so that would have to be done at a future time by a different group.

The use of NETCONF may also be expanded in call home scenarios (i.e., switch-initiated connections), but the designation of BEEP (specified for NETCONF connections of this type in of-config) to a historical protocol may require some changes in the specification or cooperative work with the IETF.

The Extensibility Working Group exists to vet proposed extensions to the wire protocol to add new functionality to OpenFlow (see Figure 3-8 for the general progression of the protocol).

---

18. Because of-config uses NETCONF/Yang, the working group is establishing their own Yang data models for these entities (tunnels, OAM). From an SDO perspective, this may not be a good model going forward.

OF v1.1	OF v1.2	OF v1.3
MPLS • Multi-label support • Match on MPLS label, traffic class • Actions to set MPLS label, traffic class • Actions to decrement, set, copy-inward, copy-outward TTL • Actions to push, pop MPLS shim headers **VLAN and QinQ** • Supports multiple levels of VLAN tagging • Actions to set VLAN ID, priority • Actions push, pop VLAN headers **Groups** Group properties: Group ID, Type (all, select, indirect, fast-fallover), Counters	**IPv6** • Match on IPv6 source and destination address (prefix/ arbitrary bitmask, IPv6 flow lael, IP protocol, IP DSCP, IP ECN) • Match on ICMPv6 type, code, ND target, ND source, and destination link layer • Actions to set IPv6 fields (same field as match fields above) • Actions to set, decrement, copy-out, copy-in TTL	**Per flow meters** • Meter properties: Meter ID, Flags (bps, pps, burst size, stats), Counters (packets, bytes, duration), list of meter bands • Meter band properties: Type (drop, DSCP re-mark, experimenter), Rate, Burst size, Counters (packets, bytes) • Special meters (slowpath, to-controller, and all-flows) **PBB**

Figure 3-8. The progression of enhancements to the OpenFlow pipeline from OF v1.1 through OF v1.3

In April 2012, when OpenFlow wire protocol version 1.3 was released, the ONF decided to slow down extensibility releases until there was a higher adoption rate of that version and to allow for interim bug-fix releases (e.g., allowing a 1.3.1 release to fix minor things in 1.3).[19]

---

19. Later, the ONF moved to require new extensibility and config-management suggestions to be implemented as prototypes using the extension parts of the protocol as a working proof of concept (somewhat like other SDO's requirements for working code to accompany a standard).

The major extension candidates for the OpenFlow wire protocol version 1.4 come from a newly formed Transport Discussion Group,[20] whose focus is on an interface between OpenFlow and optical transport network management systems to create a standard, multivendor transport network control (i.e., provisioning) environment.[21]

Look for full coverage of OpenFlow version 1.4 enhancements in a future edition of this book.

The first efforts at the integration of transport and OpenFlow demonstrated capability by abstracting the optical network into an understandable switch model for OpenFlow —an abstract view to create a virtual overlay.

The architecture of the currently proposed transport solution(s) coming out of the discussion group will combine the equipment level information models (i.e., OTN-NE, Ethernet NE, and MPLS-TP NE) and network level information models (MTOSI, MTNM) in combination with an OpenFlow driven control plane—a direct control alternative.[22]

Even in the direct control scenario, questions remain about various hybrid control plane scenarios. This is the case over whether or not there will be a combination of traditional EMS/NMS protocols and OpenFlow-driven control on the same transport network. This is illustrated in Figure 3-9.

---

20. A proposal to extend the wire protocol to support optical circuit switching (EXT-154). This extension deals with simple wavelength tuning and further definitions of a port.

21. There is some merit to the claim that GMPLS was supposed to provide this standardization but that the definitions, interpretations, and thus the implementations of GMPLS are inconsistent enough to void a guarantee of multivendor interoperability.

22. The solution will either allow direct control of the elements or leverage the proxy slicing functionality of a FlowVisor-like layer and introduce the concept of a client controller for each virtual slice of the optical/ transport network (to fit the business applications common or projected in the transport environment).

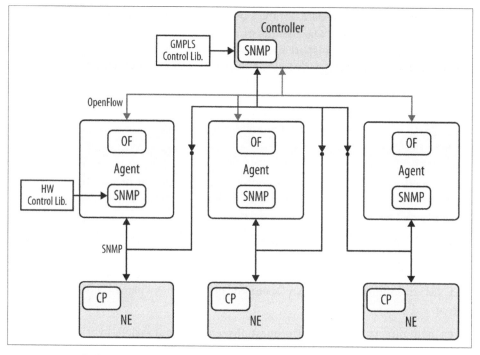

Figure 3-9. A hybrid control environment for a transport network that includes Open-Flow control

Architecture

While OpenFlow provides a standardized southbound (controller to element agent) protocol for instantiating flows, there is no standard for either the northbound (application facing) API or the east/west API.

The east/west state distribution on most available controllers is based on a database distribution model, which allows federation of a single vendor's controllers but doesn't allow an interoperable state exchange.

The Architecture Working Group is attempting to address this at least indirectly—defining for SDN a general SDN architecture. The ONF has a history of marrying the definition of SDN and OpenFlow. Without these standardized interfaces, the question arises whether the ONF definition of SDN implies openness.

Most OpenFlow controllers (Figure 3-10) provide a basic set of application services: path computation, topology (determined through LLDP, which limits topology to layer 2), and provisioning. To support of-config, they need to support a NETCONF driver.

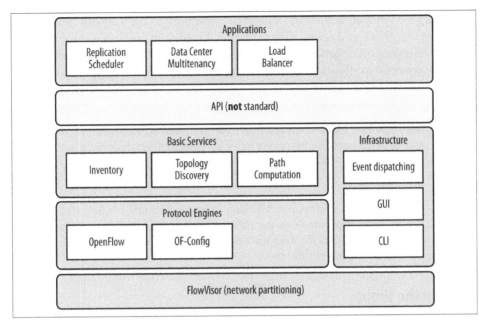

Figure 3-10. OpenFlow controller components (FlowVisor and the applications are separate entities)

The ongoing questions about SDN architecture and OpenFlow are around whether the types of application services provided by an OpenFlow controller (and the network layer at which OpenFlow operates) are sufficient for all potential SDN applications.[23]

Research into macro topics around the OpenFlow model (e.g., troubleshooting, the expression of higher level policies with OpenFlow semantics, and the need for a verification layer between controllers and elements) are being conducted in many academic and research facilities, but specifically at the Open Network Research Center (ONRC) (*http://onrc.net/*).

Hybrid Approaches

The ONF did spawn a Hybrid Working Group. The group proposed architectures for a Ships in the Night (SIN) model of operation and an Integrated Hybrid model. The board only accepted the recommendations of the SIN model.

The Integrated Hybrid model spawned a series of questions around security and the inadvertent creation of a hybrid network.

---

23. There has been an ongoing debate as to whether OpenFlow *is* SDN (*http://gigaom.com/2013/01/30/sdn-is-not-openflow-but-openflow-is-a-real-disruption/*).

Assuming a controlled demarcation point is introduced in the network element (between the OpenFlow and native control planes), the security questions revolve around how the reserved ports (particularly CONTROLLER, NORMAL, FLOOD, and LOCAL) could be exploited to allow access to native daemons on the hybrid (applications on the controller or OpenFlow ports spoofing IGP peers and other protocol sessions to insert or derive state) or the native network.

The security perimeter expands in the case of an unintended connection that creates a hybrid network. This occurs when one end of an external/non-loopback network link is connected to an OpenFlow domain and the other end to a native domain.

 A newly forming Security Working Group could address hybrid security concerns, which at the time of this writing didn't encompass enough material for a separate discussion. Look for more on this in future editions of this book.

Ships in the Night

The Ships in the Night proposition assumes that a port (physical or logical) can only be used for OpenFlow or native, but not both (see Figure 3-11). The focus of SIN was on:

- Bounding the allocated resources of the OpenFlow process and such that they couldn't impede the operation of the native side (and the reverse). Suggestions included the use of modern process level segregation in the native host OS (or by virtualization).

- Avoiding the need to synchronize state or event notifications between the control planes.

- Strict rules for the processing of flows that included the use of the LOCAL, NORMAL, and FLOOD reserved ports (with explicit caveats[25]).

SIN expands the preceding ONF definition of hybrid (as reflected in the definition of NORMAL).

The SIN model allowed port segregation by logical port or VLAN and recommended the use of MSTP for spanning tree in such an environment (a step that is actually necessary for certain types of integrated hybrids).

Lastly, SIN pointed out the ambiguities in the interactions of the reserved ports and the looseness of the port delegation model as potential areas of improvement for a SIN hybrid.

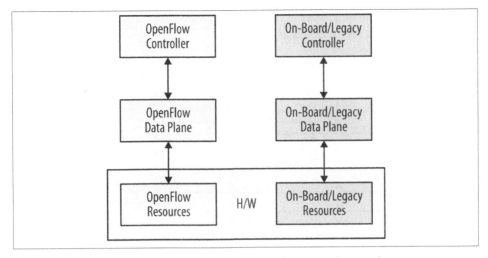

Figure 3-11. SIN architecture (source: ONF Hybrid SIN WorkGroup)

Dual Function Switches

The recommendations of the Hybrid Working Group's Integrated Architecture white paper were rejected by the ONF. The board later recommended the formation of a Migration Working Group to assist OpenFlow adopters in the deployment of OpenFlow network architecture without a transitory period through hybrid use. However, demand for integrated hybrids still remains, and the newly formed Migration Working Group may address hybrid devices and hybrid networks.[24]

One of the existing/deployed models of integration is to integrate the OpenFlow domain with the native domain at the control level (e.g., RouteFlow (*https://sites.google.com/site/routeflow/*)). Unlike the integrated hybrid, this purposely builds a hybrid network (see Figure 3-12).

The general concept behind this approach is to run a routing stack on a virtual host and bind the virtual ports on the hypervisor vswitch in that host to physical ports on associated OpenFlow switches. Through these ports, the virtual router forms IGP and/or BGP adjacencies with the native network at appropriate physical boundary points by enabling the appropriate protocol flows in the flow tables of the boundary switches. The virtual router then advertises the prefixes assigned to the OpenFlow domain through appropriate boundary points (appearing to the native network as if they were learned through an adjacent peer). Additionally, (by using internal logic and policies) the virtual router creates flow rules in the OpenFlow domain that direct traffic toward destination

---

24. For those that desire a hybrid network, a hybrid-network design proposal (the Panopticon hybrid) with a structure similar to a Data Center overlay model (using pseudowires for the overlay) was presented at ONS 2013 (*http://www.opennetsummit.org/pdf/2013/research_track/poster_papers/final/ons2013-final22.pdf*).

prefixes learned from neighbors in this exchange using flow rules that ultimately point to appropriate ports on the boundary switch.

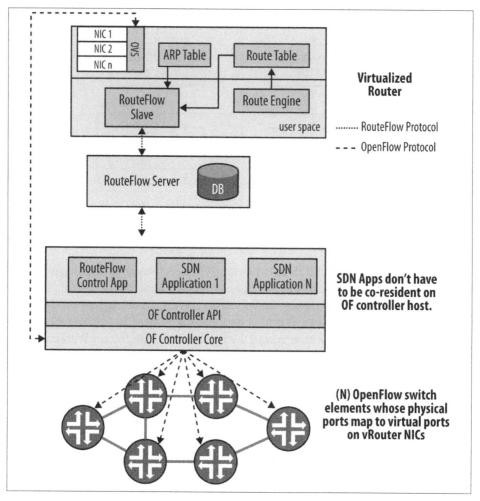

Figure 3-12. RouteFlow architecture (source: http://cpqd.github.io/RouteFlow/)

One potential drawback of this hybrid design is that flow management and packet I/O take place serially on a common TCP session, which brings the design back around to the problems that needed to be addressed in the traditional distributed control plane: blocking, control packet I/O, latency, queue management, and hardware programming speed. Some of these problems may be ameliorated by the use of alternative control channels (proposed in OpenFlow 1.3), as these ideas progress and mature in the Open-Flow wire protocol.

The tools we have at hand to form an integrated hybrid connection (in the OpenFlow protocol and the native protocols on the same device) are tables and interfaces.

A table-based solution could be crafted that uses the GoToTable semantics of OpenFlow to do a secondary lookup in a native table. Today, OpenFlow has no knowledge of tables other than its own and no way to acquire this knowledge. A solution could be crafted that allows the discovery of native tables during session initialization. The problems with this solution are as follows:

- The table namespace in OpenFlow is too narrow for VRF table names in native domains.
- There can be a great deal of dynamic table creation on the native side, particularly on a provider edge or data center gateway device that would need to be updated to the controller (restarting the session could be onerous and dynamic discovery requires even more standardization effort).
- The native domain could have more than 64 tables on certain devices.
- Though a GoToTable solution would be elegant (incorporating all our assumptions for transparency above), it seems like a complicated and impactful route.

There currently are unofficial, interface-based solutions to achieve bidirectional flow between domains. The most common is to insert a layer 3 forwarding artifact in the OpenFlow switch domain. That artifact can then be leveraged through a combination of NORMAL behavior, DHCP, and ARP, such that end stations can discover a forwarding gateway device in an OpenFlow domain. While this works, it is far from robust. The NORMAL logical port is an egress-only port on the OpenFlow side, so flowmods to control the traffic in the reverse direction are not possible. Further, some administrators/operators do not like to use the NORMAL construct for security reasons.

It is possible to create rules directly cross-connecting a layer 3 artifact with OpenFlow controlled ports to allow ingress and egress rules, if we move forward with some extension to the interface definition that allows us to tag the interface as a layer 3 forwarder or native port (the semantics are our least concern). For example, in the Junos OS (Juniper Networks), there is a construct called a logical tunnel (see Figure 3-13). This construct can have one end in the OpenFlow domain and one in any routing domain on the native side. For an operator, this provides a scalable, transparent hybrid solution, but the only tag the operator can hang on the port (to discover its dual nature) is its name (which is unfortunately unique to Juniper Networks).

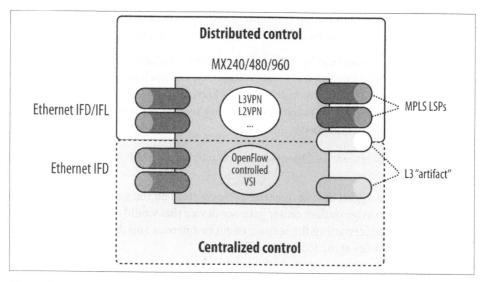

Figure 3-13. Juniper Networks' integrated hybrid proposal (source: Juniper Networks)

An interface-based solution would then require the following:

- At minimum, an extension to port description to tag it as a native artifact (an access point between domains). Other additional attributes may indicate the nature of the domains (e.g., IP/MPLS) and the routing-instances that they host. These attributes can be exchanged with the vendor agent during port-status message or in Features-reply message, as part of port-info. (These are proposed extensions to the OpenFlow standard.)

- The vendor agent should implement any MAC-related functionality required for bidirectional traffic flow (e.g., auto-associate the MAC of the artifact with any prefixes assigned to or point to the artifact in the native table).

- The vendor agent should support OpenFlow-ARP-related functionality so that devices in the OpenFlow domain can discover the MAC of the artifact.

- The native port can be implemented as an internal loopback port (preferable) or as an external loopback (i.e., a symmetric solution is preferred over an asymmetric solution).

- It will be preferable if certain applications, such as topology discovery by LLDP, exclude the native artifacts/ports. (This is a prescribed operational behavior.)

The integrated hybrid should support virtual interfaces (e.g., sharing a link down to the level of a VLAN tag). External/native features of any shared link (such as a ports supporting a VLAN trunk) should work across traffic from both domains (where the domains operate in parallel but do not cross-connect)[25]. Further, native interface features may be applied at the artifact (that connects the domains), but there is no assumption that they have to be supported. This behavior is vendor dependent, and support, consequences (unexpected behaviors), and ordering of these features need to be clearly defined by the vendor to their customers.

Conclusions

OpenFlow (and its accompanying standards organization, the ONF) is credited with starting the discussion of SDN and providing the first vestige of modern SDN control: a centralized point of control, a northbound API that exposes topology, path computation, and provisioning services to an application above the controller, as well as a standardized southbound protocol for instantiating forwarding state on a multivendor infrastructure.

Unfortunately, the OpenFlow architecture does not provide a standardized northbound API, nor does it provide a standardized east-west state distribution protocol that allows both application portability and controller vendor interoperability. Standardization may progress through the newly spawned Architecture Working Group, or even the new open source organization OpenDaylight Project.

OpenFlow provides a great deal of flow/traffic control for those platforms that can exploit the full set of OpenFlow primitives. The ONF has spawned a working group to address the description/discovery of the capabilities of vendor hardware implementations as they apply to the use of the primitive set to implement well-known network application models.

Even though there are questions about the level of abstraction implemented by OpenFlow and whether its eventual API represents a complete SDN API, there is interest in its application, and ongoing efforts around hybrid operation may make it easier to integrate its capability for matching/qualifying traffic in traditional/distributed networks or at the borders between OpenFlow domains and native domains.

---

25. Customers have requested the ability to use QoS on the physical port in a way that prevents VLANs from one or the other domain (native or OF) from consuming an inordinate amount of bandwidth on a shared link.

CHAPTER 4

SDN Controllers

Introduction

The three most resonant concepts of SDN are programmability, the separation of the control and data planes, and the management of ephemeral network state in a centralized control model, regardless of the degree of centralization. Ultimately, these concepts are embodied in an idealized SDN framework, much as we describe in detail later in Chapter 9. The SDN controller is the embodiment of the idealized SDN framework, and in most cases, is a reflection of the framework.

In theory, an SDN controller provides services that can realize a distributed control plane, as well as abet the concepts of ephemeral state management and centralization. In reality, any given instance of a controller will provide a slice or subset of this functionality, as well as its own take on these concepts. In this chapter, we will detail the most popular SDN controller offerings both from commercial vendors, as well as from the open source community. Throughout the chapter, we have included embedded graphics of the idealized controller/framework that was just mentioned as a means to compare and contrast the various implementations of controllers. We have also included text that compares the controller type in the text to that ideal vision of a controller.

 We would like to note that while it was our intention to be thorough in describing the most popular controllers, we likely missed a few. We also have detailed some commercial controller offerings, but likely missed some here too. Any of these omissions, if they exist, were not intentional, nor intended to indicate any preferences for one over the other.

General Concepts

An idealized controller is shown in Figure 4-1, which is an illustration replicated from Chapter 9, but is repeated here for ease of reference. We will refer back to this figure throughout the chapter in an effort to compare and contrast the different controller offerings with each other.

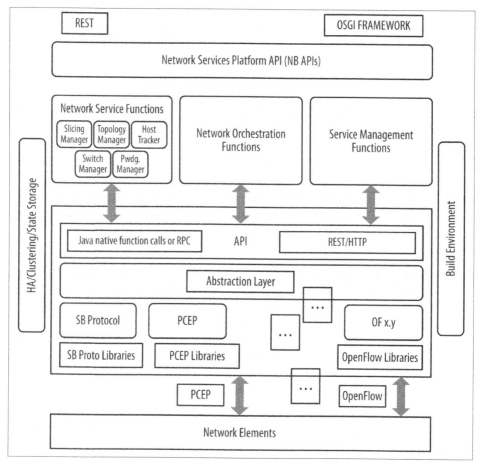

Figure 4-1. Idealized controller/framework

The general description of an SDN controller is a software system or collection of systems that together provides:

- Management of network state, and in some cases, the management and distribution of this state, may involve a database. These databases serve as a repository for information derived from the controlled network elements and related software as well as information controlled by SDN applications including network state, some ephemeral configuration information, learned topology, and control session information). In some cases, the controller may have multiple, purpose-driven data management processes (e.g., relational and nonrelational databases). In other cases, other in-memory database strategies can be employed, too.

- A high-level data model that captures the relationships between managed resources, policies and other services provided by the controller. In many cases, these data models are built using the Yang modeling language.

- A modern, often RESTful (representational state transfer) application programming interface (API) is provided that exposes the controller services to an application. This facilitates most of the controller-to-application interaction. This interface is ideally rendered from the data model that describes the services and features of the controller. In some cases, the controller and its API are part of a development environment that generates the API code from the model. Some systems go further and provide robust development environments that allow expansion of core capabilities and subsequent publishing of APIs for new modules, including those that support dynamic expansion of controller capabilities:

- A secure TCP control session between controller and the associated agents in the network elements

- A standards-based protocol for the provisioning of application-driven network state on network elements

- A device, topology, and service discovery mechanism; a path computation system; and potentially other network-centric or resource-centric information services

The current landscape of controllers includes the commercial products of VMware (vCloud/vSphere), Nicira (NVP), NEC (Trema), Big Switch Networks (Floodlight/BNC), and Juniper/Contrail. It also includes a number of open source controllers.[1]

Besides the use of OpenFlow and proprietary protocols, there are SDN controllers that leverage IP/MPLS network functionality to create MPLS VPNs as a layer 3-over-layer 3 tenant separation model for data center or MPLS LSPs for overlays in the WAN.

We cannot ignore the assertions that NETCONF-based controllers[2] can almost be indistinguishable from network management solutions, or that Radius/Diameter-based controllers such as PCRF and/or TDF, in mobile environments, are also SDN controllers. This is true particularly as their southbound protocols become more independent and capable of creating ephemeral network/configuration state.

---

1. Some vendors provide both open source and commercial products.

2. *http://www.uppersideconferences.com/sdnsummit2013/program-sdn-summit-2013.pdf*

As we discussed earlier in this book, the original SDN application of data center or-chestration spawned SDN controllers as part of an integrated solution. It was this use case that focused on the management of data center resources such as compute, storage, and virtual machine images, as well as network state. More recently, some SDN con-trollers began to emerge that specialized in the management of the network *abstrac-tion* and were coupled with the resource management required in data centers through the support of open source APIs (OpenStack, Cloudstack). The driver for this second wave of controllers is the potential expansion of SDN applications out of the data center and into other areas of the network where the management of virtual resources like processing and storage does not have to be so tightly coupled in a solution.

The growth in the data center sector of networking has also introduced a great number of new network elements centered on the hypervisor switch/router/bridge construct. This includes the network service virtualization explored in a later chapter. Network service virtualization, sometimes referred to as Network Functions Virtualization (NFV), will add even more of these elements to the next generation network architec-ture, further emphasizing the need for a controller to operate and manage these things. We will also discuss the interconnection or *chaining* of NFV.

Virtual switches or routers represent a lowest common denominator in the networking environment and are generally capable of a smaller number of forwarding entries than their dedicated, hardware-focused brethren. Although they may technically be able to support large tables in a service VM, their real limits are in behaviors *without* the service VM. In particular, that is the integrated table scale and management capability within the hypervisor that is often implemented in dedicated hardware present only in purpose-built routers or switches. The simpler hypervisor-based forwarding construct doesn't have room for the RIB/FIB combination present in a traditional purpose-built element. This is the case in the distributed control paradigm, which needs assistance to boil down the distributed network information to these few entries—either from a user-space agent that is constructed as part of the host build process and run as a service VM on the host, or from the SDN controller. In the latter case, this can be the SDN controller acting as a proxy in a distributed environment or as flow provisioning agent in an administratively dictated, centralized environment. In this way, the controller may front the management layer of a network, traditionally exposed by a network OSS.

For the software switches/routers on hosts in a data center, the SDN controller is a critical management interface. SDN controllers provide some management services (in addi-tion to provisioning and discovery), since they are responsible for associated state for their ephemeral network entities (via the agent) like analytics and event notification. In this aspect, SDN has the potential to revolutionize our view of network element man-agement (EMS).

VMware

VMware provides a data center orchestration solution with a proprietary SDN controller and agent implementation that has become a de facto standard. VMware was one of the genesis companies for cloud computing, founded in 1998.[3] VMware provides a suite of data-center–centric applications built around the ESX (ESXi for version 5.0 and beyond) hypervisor (and hypervisor switch, the vSphere Distributed Switch [VDS]). See Figure 4-2 for a rough sketch of VMware product relationships.

vSphere introduced the ESXi hypervisor (with version 5.x) to replace the older ESX hypervisor, making it lighter/smaller (according to marketing pronouncements; ESXi is 5% of the size of ESX) and operating-system independent. The change also adds a web interface to the existing ESX management options of CLI, client API, and vCenter visualization. It also eliminated a required guest VM (i.e., guest VM per host) for a service console for local administration.

VDS is an abstraction (as a single logical switch) of what was previously a collection of individual virtual switches (vSphere Standard Switch/es) from a management perspective—allowing vCenter Server to act as a management/control point for all VDS instances (separating the management and data planes of individual VSSs).

Within VDS, VMware has abstractions of the physical card (vmnic), link properties (e.g., teaming, failover, and load balancing—dvuplink), and networking attributes (e.g., VLAN assignment, traffic shaping, and security de facto dvportgroup) that are used by the administrator as reusable configuration templates.

Once provisioned, the components necessary for network operation (the ESXi vswitch) will continue to operate even if the vCenter Server fails/partitions from the network.[4] Much of the HA scheme is managed within organizational clusters wherein a single agent is elected as master of a fault domain and the others are slaves. This creates a very scalable VM health-monitoring system that tolerates management communication partition by using heartbeats through shared data stores.

---

3. *http://www.vmware.com*

4. vCenter Server can run on bare metal or in a VM. When run in a VM, vCenter can take advantage of vSphere high-availability features.

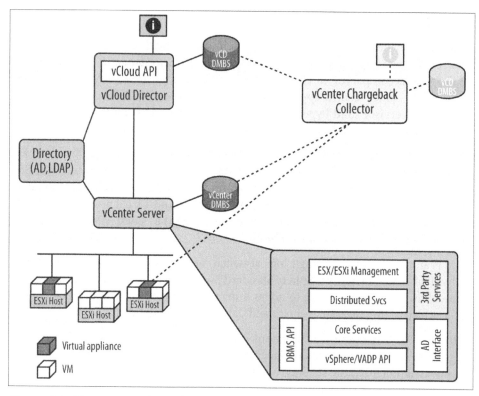

Figure 4-2. VMware product relationships (with vCenter Chargeback Collector as an example of how Operations Management Suite would connect)

The aforementioned VMware applications are available in different bundles, exemplified by the vSphere/vCloud/vCenter Suite designed for IaaS applications, which includes:

vSphere
> Manages what is labeled "virtualized infrastructure" by VMware. This includes managing the hypervisor integrated vswitch (from a networking perspective) as well as the other, basic IaaS components—compute, storage, images, and services. The suite uses an SQL Database (Microsoft or Oracle) for resource data storage.

vCloud Director and vCloud Connector
> Primary application for compute, storage, image resource management, and public cloud extension.

vCloud Networking and Security
> Self-descriptive applications.

vCloud Automation Center
> Provisioning assist for IT management.

vCenter Site Recovery Manager
  A replication manager for automated disaster recovery.

vCenter Operations Management Suite
  Application monitoring, VM host and vSphere configuration and change management, discovery, charging, analytic, and alerting.

vFabric Application Director for Provisioning
  Application management (primarily for multitiered applications, described in the definition of degree of tenancy, and managing the dependencies).

In 2011, VMware launched an open source PaaS system called Cloud Foundry,[5] which offers a hosted service that runs on VMware.

The virtual switch in the hypervisor is programmed to create VxLAN tunnel overlays (encapsulating layer 2 in layer 3), creating isolated tenant networks. VMware interacts with its own virtual vswitch infrastructure through its own vSphere API and publishes a vendor-consumable API that allows third-party infrastructure (routers, switches, and appliances) to react to vCenter parameterized event triggers (e.g., mapping the trigger and its parameters to a vendor-specific configuration change).

One of the strengths of VMware vSphere is the development environment that allows third parties to develop hypervisor and/or user space service VM applications (e.g., firewalls, and anti-virus agents) that integrate via the vSphere API.

The core of VMware solution is Java-centric, with the following features:

- HTTP REST-based API set oriented in expression toward the management of resources
- Spring-based component framework[6]
- Open Services Gateway Initiative (OSGI) module framework[7]
- Publish/subscribe message bus based on JMS
- Hibernate[8] DBMS interface (Hibernate is an object/relational mapping library that allows a Java developer to create/retrieve a relational store of objects).

The Spring development environment allows for the flexible creation and linking of objects (beans), declarative transaction and cache management and hooks to database services. Spring also provides for the creation of RESTful endpoints and thus an auto-API creation facility. Figure 4-3 shows the VMware/SpringSource relationship.

---

5. *http://cloudfoundry.com/*

6. The environment is provided through a subsidiary: SpringSource (*http://www.springsource.org*).

7. *http://www.osgi.org*

8. *http://www.hibernate.org*

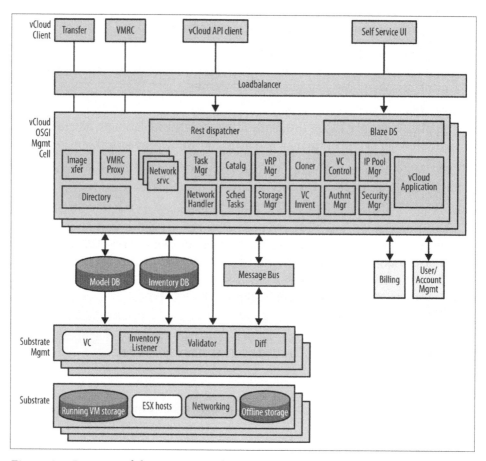

Figure 4-3. Drawing of the VMware vCloud/SpringSource software development architecture

When looking over the architecture just described, one of the first things that might be apparent is the focus on integrated data center resource management (e.g., image, storage, and compute). From a controller standpoint, it's important to note that the "controller" manages far more than just network state.

This is an important feature, as it can result in a unified and easy-to-operate solution; however, this approach has resulted in integration issues with other solution pieces such as data center switches, routers and appliances.

One of the primary detractions commonly cited with VMware is its cost.[9] This of course varies across customers, but open source offerings are (apparently) free by comparison. Even so-called enterprise versions of open source offerings are often less expensive than the equivalent offering. Other perhaps less immediately important considerations of this solution is its inherent scalability, which, like the price, is often something large-scale users complain about. The mapping and encapsulation data of the VxLAN overlay does not have a standardized control plane for state distribution, resulting in operations that resemble manual (or scripted) configuration and manipulation. Finally, the requirement to use multicast in the underlay to support flooding can be a problem, depending on what sort of underlay one deploys.

These points are not intended to imply that VMware has scaling problems, but rather that one of the facts of deploying commercial solutions is that you are more than likely going to have more than one server/controller, and the architecture has to either assume independence (i.e., a single monolith that operates as an autonomous unit) or support a federated model (i.e., clusters of servers working in conjunction to share state) in operation.

Table 4-1. VDS scalability (http://bit.ly/18RsNOC)[abc]

VDS Properties	5.0 Limit	5.1 Limit
Number of VDS per vCenter Server	32	128
Number of Static Port Groups per vCenter Server	5,000	10,000
Number of Distributed Ports per vCenter Server	30,000	60,000
Number of Hosts per VDS	350	500

[a] *http://www.vmware.com/pdf/vsphere5/r50/vsphere-50-configuration-maximums.pdf*

[b] *http://www.vmware.com/products/datacenter-virtualization/vsphere/distributed-switch.html*

[c] *https://www.vmware.com/pdf/vsphere5/r51/vsphere-51-configuration-maximums.pdf*

Nicira

Nicira was founded in 2007 and as such is considered a later arrival to the SDN marketplace than VMware. Nicira's network virtualization platform (NVP) was released in 2011 and it is not the suite of resource management applications that comprises VMware; instead, it is more of a classic network controller, that is, where network is the resource managed. NVP now works in conjunction with the other cloud virtualization services for compute, storage, and image management.

9. Licensing has had per socket and VRAM entitlement fees, with additional fees for applications like Site Recovery Manager. While this may be a "hearsay" observation, we have interviewed a large number of customers.

NVP works with Open vSwitch (OVS).[10] OVS is the hypervisor softswitch controlled by the NVP controller cluster. This is good news because OVS is supported in just about every hypervisor[11] and is actually the basis of the switching in some commercial network hardware. As a further advantage, OVS is shipping as part of the Linux 3.3 build.

Until the relatively recent introduction of NXP, which is considered the first step in merging VMware and Nicira functionality, Nicira required a helper VM called Nicira OVS vApp for the VMware ESXi hypervisor in order to operate correctly. This vApp is mated to each ESXi hypervisor instance when the instance is deployed.

Though Nicira is a founding ONF member and its principals have backgrounds in the development of OpenFlow, Nicira only uses OpenFlow to a small degree. This is unlike a number of the other original SDN controller offerings. Most of the programming of OVS is achieved with a database-like protocol called the Open vSwitch Data Base Management Protocol (OVSDB).[12] OVSDB provides a stronger management interface to the hypervisor switch/element for programming tunnels, QoS, and other deeper management tasks for which OpenFlow had no capability when open vswitch was developed.

OVSDB characteristics include the following:

- JSON used for schema format (OVSDB is schema-driven) and OVSDB wire protocol
- Transactional
- No-SQL
- Persistency
- Monitoring capability (alerting similar to pub-sub mechanisms)
- Stores both provisioning and operational state

The Nicira NVP controller (Figure 4-4) is a cluster of generally three servers that use database synchronization to share state. Nicira has a service node concept that is used to offload various processes from the hypervisor nodes. Broadcast, multicast, and unknown unicast traffic flow are processed via the service node (IPSec tunnel termination happens here as well). This construct can also be used for inter-hypervisor traffic handling and as a termination point for inter-domain (or multidomain) inter-connect.

---

10. *http://openvswitch.org*

11. ESX, ESXi, Xen, Xen Server, KVM, and HyperV.

12. *https://datatracker.ietf.org/doc/draft-pfaff-ovsdb-proto/*

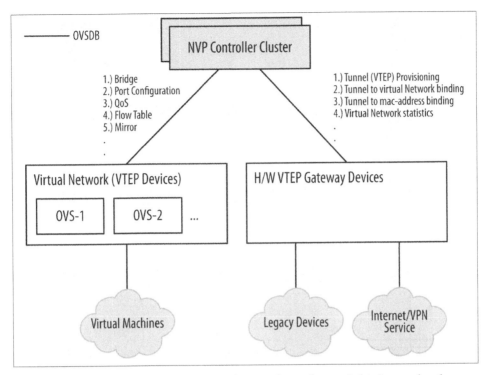

Figure 4-4. NVP OVSDB interactions with virtual switches and third-party hardware

A layer 2 or layer 3 gateway product converts Nicira STT tunnel overlays into VLANs (layer 2), layer 2-to-layer 2 connectivity (VLAN to VLAN), or provides NAT-like functionality to advertise a tenant network (a private network address space) into a public address space. See Figure 4-5 for a sketch of the NVP component relationships.

OVS, the gateways, and the service nodes support redundant controller connections for high availability. NVP Manager is the management server with a basic web interface used mainly to troubleshoot and verify connections. The web UI essentially uses all the REST API calls on the backend for everything you do within it manually. For application developers, NVP offers a RESTful API interface, albeit a proprietary one.

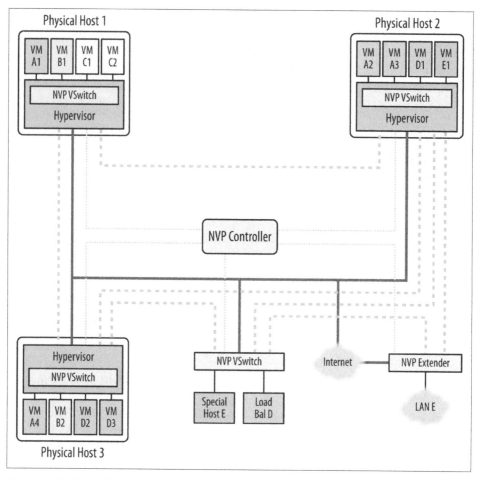

Figure 4-5. Nicira SDN Controller components

Relationship to the idealized SDN framework

Figure 4-6 illustrates the relationship of the VMware/Nicira controller's components to the idealized SDN framework. In particular, the Nicira controller provides a variety of RESTful northbound programmable APIs, network orchestration functions in the way of allowing a user to create a network overlay and link it to other management elements from vCenter/vCloudDirector, VxLAN, STT and OpenFlow southbound encapsulation capabilities, and OVSDB programmability in support of configuration of southbound OVS entities.

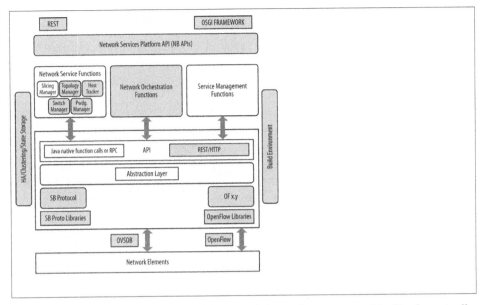

Figure 4-6. VMware/Nicira portfolio capabilities (against an idealized controller framework)

VMware/Nicira

Due to the acquisition of Nicira by VMware,[13] both of their products are now linked in discussion and in the marketplace. Though developed as separate products, they are merging[14] quickly into a seamless solution. Both Nicira and VMware products provide proprietary northbound application programming interfaces and use proprietary southbound interfaces/protocols that allow for direct interaction with network elements both real and virtual.

Nicira supports an OpenStack plug-in to broaden its capabilities in data center orchestration or resource management.

13. *http://blogs.vmware.com/console/2012/07/vmware-and-nicira-advancing-the-software-defined-datacenter.html*

14. VMware blends in Nicira SDN technology, reveals public cloud plans (*http://www.networkworld.com/news/2013/031313-vmware-sdn-public-cloud-267659.html?source=nww_rss*).

OpenFlow-Related

Most open source SDN controllers revolve around the OpenFlow protocol due to having roots in the Onix design (Figure 4-7),[15] while only some of the commercial products use the protocol exclusively. In fact, some use it in conjunction with other protocols.

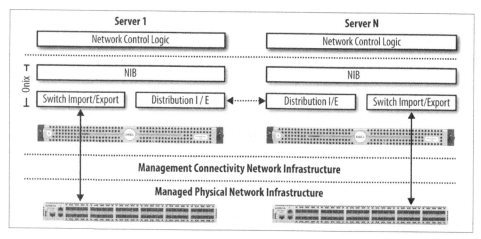

Figure 4-7. The Onix controller model

Unlike the VMware/Nicira solution or the L3VPN/PCE solutions that follow, OpenFlow solutions don't require any additional packet encapsulation or gateway. Although hybrid operation on some elements in the network will be required to interface OpenFlow and non-OpenFlow networks. This is in fact, growing to be a widely desired deployment model.

Unless otherwise stated, the open source OpenFlow controller solutions use memory resident or in-memory databases for state storage.

Relationship to the idealized SDN framework

Figure 4-7 illustrates the relationship of, generally, any open source controller's components to the idealized SDN framework. Since most controllers have been based on the Onix code and architecture, they all exhibit similar relationships to the idealized SDN framework. This is changing slowly as splinter projects evolve, but with the exception of the Floodlight controller that we will discuss later in the chapter, the premise that they all exhibit similar relationships still generally holds true.

The Onix controller model first relates to the idealized SDN framework in that it provides a variety of northbound RESTful interfaces. These can be used to program,

---

15. *http://static.usenix.org/events/osdi10/tech/full_papers/Koponen.pdf*

interrogate, and configure the controller's numerous functions, such as basic controller functionality, flow and forwarding entry programming, and topology. All of these controllers support some version of the OpenFlow protocol up to and including the latest 1.3 specification, as well as many extensions to the protocol in order to extend the basic capabilities of the protocol. Also note that while not called out directly, all Onix-based controllers utilize in-memory database concepts for state management. Figure 4-8 illustrates the relationship of the generalized open source OpenFlow controller's components to the idealized SDN framework.

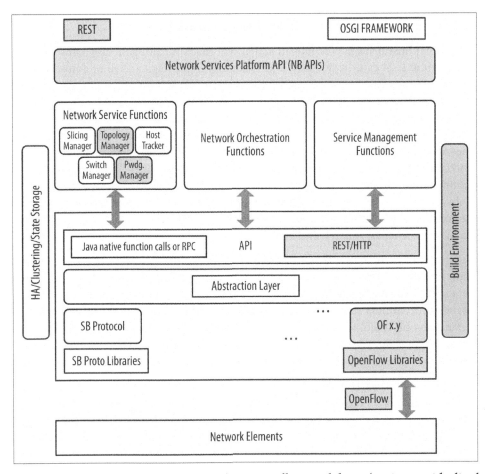

Figure 4-8. Figure Open Source OpenFlow controller capabilities (against an idealized controller framework).Onix capabilities (against an idealized controller framework)

Mininet

Before introducing some of the popular Onix-based SDN controllers, we should take some time to describe Mininet, which is a network emulator that simulates a collection of end-hosts, switches, routers, and links on a single Linux kernel. Each of these elements is referred to as a "host." It uses lightweight virtualization to make a single system look like a complete network, running the same kernel, system, and user code. Mininet is important to the open source SDN community as it is commonly used as a simulation, verification, testing tool, and resource. Mininet is an open source project hosted on GitHub. If you are interested in checking out the freely available source code, scripts, and documentation, refer to GitHub (*https://github.com/mininet*).

A Mininet host behaves just like an actual real machine and generally runs the same code—or at least can. In this way, a Mininet host represents a shell of a machine that arbitrary programs can be plugged into and run. These custom programs can send, receive, and process packets through what to the program appears to be a real Ethernet but is actually a virtual switch/interface. Packets are processed by virtual switches, which to the Mininet hosts appear to be a real Ethernet switch or router, depending on how they are configured. In fact, commercial versions of Mininet switches such as from Cisco and others are available that fairly accurately emulate key switch characteristics of their commercial, purpose-built switches such as queue depth, processing discipline, and policing processing. One very cool side effect of this approach is that the measured performance of a Mininet-hosted network often should approach that of actual (non-emulated) switches, routers, and hosts.

Figure 4-9 illustrates a simple Mininet network comprised of three hosts, a virtual Open-Flow switch, and an OpenFlow controller. All components are connected over virtual Ethernet links that are then assigned private net-10 IP addresses for reachability. As mentioned, Mininet supports very complex topologies of nearly arbitrary size and or-dering, so one could, for example, copy and paste the switch and its attached hosts in the configuration, rename them, and attach the new switch to the existing one, and quickly have a network comprised of two switches and six hosts, and so on.

One reason Mininet is widely used for experimentation is that it allows you to create custom topologies, many of which have been demonstrated as being quite complex and realistic, such as larger, Internet-like topologies that can be used for BGP research. Another cool feature of Mininet is that it allows for the full customization of packet forwarding. As mentioned, many examples exist of host programs that approximate commercially available switches. In addition to those, some new and innovative experiments have been performed using hosts that are programmable using the OpenFlow protocol. It is these that have been used with the Onix-based controllers we will now discuss.

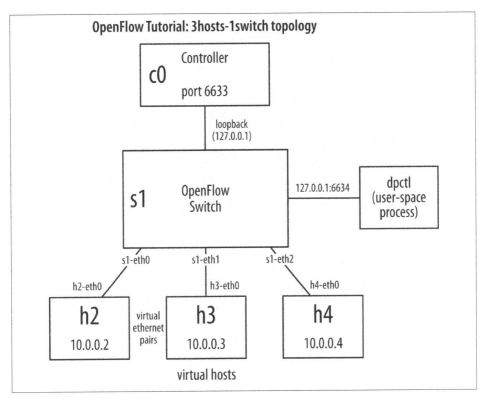

Figure 4-9. A simple example Mininet network

NOX/POX

According to the NOX/POX website,[16] NOX[17] was developed by Nicira and donated to the research community and hence becoming open source in 2008. This move in fact made it one of the first open source OpenFlow controllers. It was subsequently extended and supported via ON.LAB[18] activity at Stanford University with major contributions from UC Berkeley and ICSI. NOX provides a C++ API to OpenFlow (OF v1.0) and an asynchronous, event-based programming model.

NOX is both a primordial controller and a component-based framework for developing SDN applications. It provides support modules specific to OpenFlow but can and has been extended. The NOX core provides helper methods and APIs for interacting with OpenFlow switches, including a connection handler and event engine. Additional

---

16. *http://yuba.stanford.edu/~nickm/papers/p105-v38n3u-mckeownA4.pdf*

17. Both NOX and POX information can be accessed via *http://www.noxrepo.org/forum/*.

18. *http://onlab.us/tools.html*

components that leverage that API are available, including host tracking, routing, topology (LLDP), and a Python interface implemented as a wrapper for the component API, as shown in Figure 4-10.

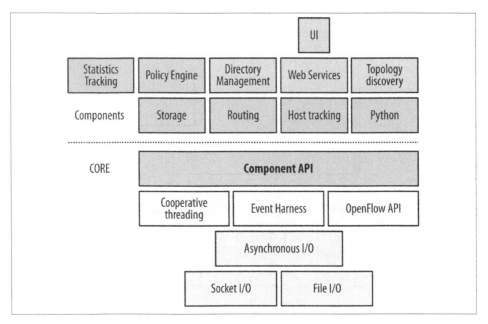

Figure 4-10. NOX architecture

NOX is often used in academic network research to develop SDN applications such as network protocol research. One really cool side effect of its widespread academic use is that example code is available for emulating a learning switch and a network-wide switch, which can be used as starter code for various programming projects and experimentation.

Some popular NOX applications are SANE and Ethane. SANE is an approach to representing the network as a filesystem. Ethane is a Stanford University research application for centralized, network-wide security at the level of a traditional access control list. Both demonstrated the efficiency of SDN by reducing the lines of code required significantly[19] to implement these functions that took significantly more code to implement similar functions in the past. Based on this success, researchers have been demonstrating MPLS-like applications on top of a NOX core.

---

19. *http://yuba.stanford.edu/~casado/nox-ccr-final.pdf*

POX is the newer, Python-based version of NOX (or NOX in Python). The idea behind its development was to return NOX to its C++ roots[20] and develop a separate Python-based platform (Python 2.7). It has a high-level SDN API including a query-able topology graph and support for virtualization.

POX claims the following advantages over NOX:

- POX has a Pythonic OpenFlow interface.
- POX has reusable sample components for path selection, topology discovery, and so on.
- POX runs anywhere and can be bundled with install-free PyPy runtime for easy deployment.
- POX specifically targets Linux, Mac OS, and Windows.
- POX supports the same GUI and visualization tools as NOX.
- POX performs well compared to NOX applications written in Python.

NOX and POX currently communicate with OpenFlow v1.0 switches and include special support for Open vSwitch.

Trema

Trema[21] is an OpenFlow programming framework for developing an OpenFlow controller that was originally developed (and supported) by NEC with subsequent open source contributions (under a GPLv2 scheme).

Unlike the more conventional OpenFlow-centric controllers that preceded it, the Trema model provides basic infrastructure services as part of its core modules that support (in turn) the development of user modules (Trema apps[22]). Developers can create their user modules in Ruby or C (the latter is recommended when speed of execution becomes a concern).

The main API the Trema core modules provide to an application is a simple, non-abstracted OpenFlow driver (an interface to handle all OpenFlow messages). Trema now supports OpenFlow version 1.3.X via a repository called TremaEdge.[23]

Trema does not offer a NETCONF driver that would enable support of of-config.

---

20. A new fork of NOX that is C++ only was created.

21. *http://trema.github.com/trema/*

22. *https://github.com/trema/apps*

23. *https://github.com/trema/trema-edge*

In essence, a Trema OpenFlow Controller is an extensible set of Ruby scripts. Developers can individualize or enhance the base controller functionality (class object) by defining their own controller subclass object and embellishing it with additional message handlers.

The base controller design is event-driven (dispatch via retrospection/naming convention) and is often (favorably by Trema advocates) compared to the explicit handler dispatch paradigm of other open source products.

In addition, the core modules provide a message bus (IPC mechanism via Messenger) that allows the applications/user_modules to communicate with each other and core modules (originally in a point-to-point fashion, but migrating to a publish/subscribe model), as shown in Figure 4-11.

Other core modules include timer and logging libraries, a packet parser library, and hash-table and linked-list structure libraries.

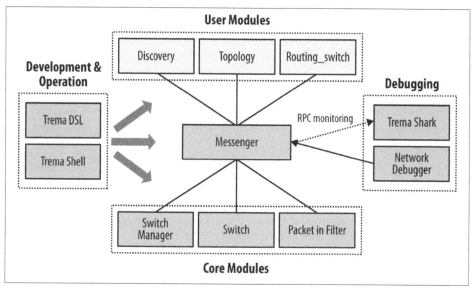

Figure 4-11. Trema core/user module relationships

The Trema core does not provide any state management or database storage structure (these are contained in the Trema apps and could be a default of memory-only storage using the data structure libraries).[24]

---

24. There was some discussion of an SQLite interface for Trema.

The infrastructure provides a command-line interface (CLI) and configuration filesystem for configuring and controlling applications (resolving dependencies at load-time), managing messaging and filters, and configuring virtual networks—via Network Domain Specific Language (DSL, a Trema-specific configuration language).

The appeal of Trema is that it is an all-in-one, simple, modular, rapid prototype and development environment that yields results with a smaller codebase. The development environment also includes network/host emulators and debugging tools (integrated unit testing, packet generation/Tremashark/Wireshark).[25] The Trema applications/ user_modules include a topology discovery/management unit (libtopology), a Flow/ Path management module (libpath), a load balancing switch module and a sliceable switch abstraction (that allows the management of multiple OpenFlow switches). There is also an OpenStack Quantum plug-in available for the sliceable switch abstraction.[26]

A Trema-based OpenFlow controller can interoperate with any element agent that supports OpenFlow (OF version compatibility aside) and doesn't require a specific agent, though one of the apps developed for Trema is a software OpenFlow switch (positioned in various presentations as simpler than OVS). Figure 4-12 illustrates the Trema architecture.

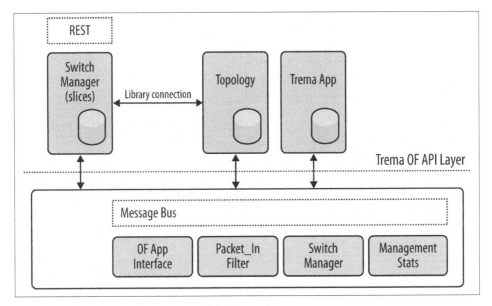

Figure 4-12. Trema architecture and API interfaces

25. The entire environment can be run on a laptop, including the emulated network/switches.

26. *https://github.com/nec-openstack/quantum-openflow-plugin*

The individual user modules (Trema applications) publish RESTful interfaces. The combination of modularity and per-module (or per-application service) APIs, make Trema more than a typical controller (with a monolithic API for all its services). Trema literature refers to Trema as a framework. This idea is expanded upon in a later chapter.

Ryu

Ryu[27] is a component-based, open source (supported by NTT Labs) framework implemented entirely in Python (Figure 4-13). The Ryu messaging service does support components developed in other languages.

Components include an OpenFlow wire protocol support (up through version 1.3 of OF-wire including Nicira extensions), event management, messaging, in-memory state management, application management, infrastructure services and a series of reusable libraries (e.g., NETCONF library, sFlow/Netflow library).

Additionally, applications like Snort, a layer 2 switch, GRE tunnel abstractions, VRRP, as well as services (e.g., topology and statistics) are available.

At the API layer, Ryu has an Openstack Quantum plug-in that supports both GRE based overlay and VLAN configurations.

Ryu also supports a REST interface to its OpenFlow operations.

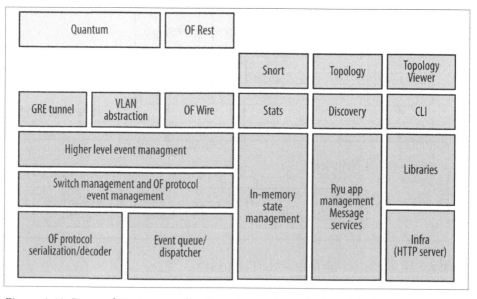

Figure 4-13. Ryu architecture, applications (non-exhaustive), and APIs

27. *http://www.osrg.net/ryu/*

A prototype component has been demonstrated that uses HBase for statistics storage, including visualization and analysis via the stats component tools.

While Ryu supports high availability via a Zookeeper component, it does not yet support a cooperative cluster of controllers.

Big Switch Networks/Floodlight

Floodlight[28] is a very popular SDN controller contribution from Big Switch Networks to the open source community. Floodlight is based on Beacon from Stanford University. Floodlight is an Apache-licensed, Java-based OpenFlow controller (non-OSGI). The architecture of Floodlight as well as the API interface is shared with Big Switch Network's commercial enterprise offering Big Network Controller (BNC).[29]

The Floodlight core architecture is modular, with components including topology management, device management (MAC and IP tracking), path computation, infrastructure for web access (management), counter store (OpenFlow counters), and a generalized storage abstraction for state storage (defaulted to memory at first, but developed into both SQL and NoSQL backend storage abstractions for a third-party open source storage solution).

These components are treated as loadable services with interfaces that export state. The controller itself presents a set of extensible REST APIs as well as an event notification system. The API allows applications to get and set this state of the controller, as well as to subscribe to events emitted from the controller using Java Event Listeners, as shown in Figure 4-14.[30] These are all made available to the application developer in the typical ways.[31]

---

28. *http://www.projectfloodlight.org/floodlight/*

29. While our focus is on the very familiar open source Floodlight, for the sake of comparison, the commercial BNC is also weighed. With BNC, BigSwitch offers virtualization applications and its BigTap application(s).

30. This is not an exhaustive list of BNS commercial applications (but critical ones to compare it to the idealized controller).

31. In their commercial offering, Big Switch Networks combines the support of a NoSQL distributed database, publish/subscribe support for state change notification, and other tooling to provide horizontal scaling and high availability. This is a fundamental difference between commercial and open source offerings (in general).

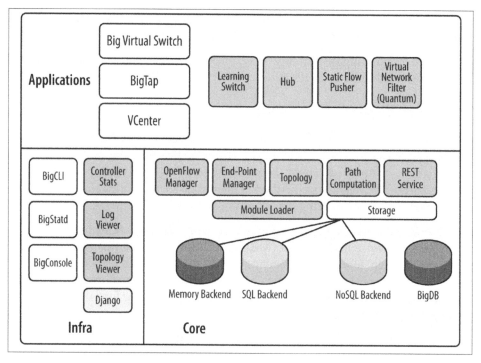

Figure 4-14. Floodlight/BNC combined architecture including open source components (non-colored items are in the commercial BNC product); the BNC version of the controller has enhancements to many of the core functions

The core module called the Floodlight Provider, handles I/O from switches and translates OpenFlow messages into Floodlight events, thus creating an event-driven, asynchronous application framework. Floodlight incorporates a threading model that allows modules to share threads with other modules. Event handling within this structure happens within the publishing module's thread context. Synchronized locks protect shared data. Component dependencies are resolved at load-time via configuration.

The topology manager uses LLDP (as does most OpenFlow switches) for the discovery of both OpenFlow and non-OF endpoints.

There are also sample applications that include a learning switch (this is the OpenFlow switch abstraction most developers customize or use in its native state), a hub application, and a static flow push application.

In addition, Floodlight offers an OpenStack Quantum plug-in.

The Floodlight OpenFlow controller can interoperate with any element agent that supports OpenFlow (OF version compatibility aside, at the time of writing, support for both of-config and version 1.3 of the wire protocol were roadmap items), but Big Switch also provides an open source agent (Indigo[32]) that has been incorporated into commercial products. In addition, Big Switch has also provided Loxi, an open source OpenFlow library generator, with multiple language support[33] to address the problems of multi-version support in OpenFlow.

As a development environment, Floodlight is Java/Jython (*www.jython.org*) centric. A rich development tool chain of build and debugging tools is available, including a packet streamer and the aforementioned static flow pusher. In addition, Mininet[34] can be used to do network emulation, as we described earlier.

Because the architecture uses restlets,[35] any module developed in this environment can expose further REST APIs through an IRestAPI service. Big Switch has been actively working on a data model compilation tool that converted Yang to REST, as an enhancement to the environment for both API publishing and data sharing. These enhancements can be used for a variety of new functions absent in the current controller, including state and configuration management.

Relationship to the idealized SDN framework

As we mentioned in the previous section, Floodlight is related to the base Onix controller code in many ways and thus possesses many architectural similarities. As mentioned earlier, most Onix-based controllers utilize in-memory database concepts for state management, but Floodlight is the exception. Floodlight is the one Onix-based controller today that offers a component called BigDB. BigDB is a NoSQL, Cassandra-based database that is used for storing a variety of things, including configuration and element state.

When we look at the commercial superset of Floodlight (BNC) and its applications, its coverage in comparison with the idealized controller rivals that of the VMware/Nicira combination (in Figure 4-5). The combination supports a single, non-proprietary southbound controller/agent (OpenFlow).

Layer 3 Centric

Controllers supporting L3VPN overlays such as Juniper Networks Contrail Systems Controller, and L2VPN overlays such as Alcatel Lucent's Nuage Controller[36] are coming to market that promote a virtual Provider Edge (vPE) concept. The virtualization of the

32. *http://indigo.openflowhub.org*

33. *http://www.projectfloodlight.org/blog/2012/10/02/preview-of-indigo-v2-0-and-loxi/*

34. *https://github.com/mininet*

35. *http://www.restlets.org*

36. *http://www.nuagenetworks.net/press-releases/nuage-networks-introduces-2nd-generation-sdn-solution-for-datacenter-networks-accelerating-the-move-to-business-cloud-services/*

PE function is an SDN application in its own right that creates both service or platform virtualization. The addition of a controller construct aids in the automation of service provisioning as well as providing centralized label distribution and other benefits that may ease the control protocol burden on the virtualized PE.

There are also path computation engine (PCE) servers that are emerging as a potential controllers or as enhancements to existing controllers for creating MPLS LSP overlays in MPLS-enabled networks. These can be used to enable overlay abstractions and source/destination routing in IP networks using MPLS labels without the need for the traditional label distribution and tunnel/path signaling protocols such as LDP and RSVP-TE.

L3VPN

The idea behind these offerings is that a VRF structure (familiar in L3VPN) can represent a tenant and that the traditional tooling for L3VPNs (with some twists) can be used to create overlays that use MPLS labels for the customer separation on the host, service elements, and data center gateways.

This solution has the added advantage of potentially being theoretically easier to stitch into existing customer VPNs at data center gateways—creating a convenient cloud bursting application. This leverages the strength of the solution—that state of the network primitives used to implement the VRF/tenant is carried in standard BGP address families.

In the case of Juniper Networks, which acquired its SDN controller technology from Contrail Systems, the offering involves a controller that appears to be a virtualized route reflector that supports an OpenStack API mapping to its internal service creation APIs. The Juniper approach involves a high-level data model (originally envisioned to be IF-MAP[37] based) that self-generates and presents a REST API to SDN applications such as the one shown in Figure 4-15. The figure demonstrates a data center orchestration application that can be used to provision virtual routers on hosts to bind together the overlay instances across the network underlay. A subset of the API overlaps the OpenStack Quantum API and is used to orchestrate the entire system.

The controller is a multi-Node design comprised of multiple subsystems. The motivation for this approach is to facilitate scalability, extensibility, and high availability. The system supports potentially separable modules that can operate as individual virtual machines in order to handle scale out server modules for analytics, configuration, and control. As a brief simplification:

Analytics
    Provides the query interface and storage interface for statistics/counter reporting

---

37. *http://www.trustedcomputinggroup.org/resources/tnc_ifmap_binding_for_soap_specification*

Configuration

Provides the compiler that uses the high-level data model to convert API requests for network actions into low-level data model for implementation via the control code

Control

The BGP speaker for horizontal scale distribution between controllers (or administrative domains) and the implementer of the low-level data model (L3VPN network primitives distributed via XMPP commands—VRFs, routes, policies/filters). This server also collects statistics and other management information from the agents it manages via the XMPP channel.

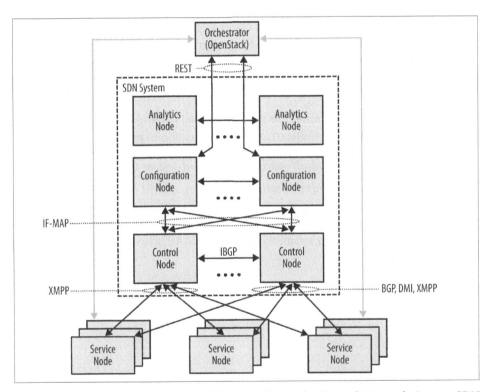

Figure 4-15. High-level operation of Juniper Networks Virtual Network System SDN controller system

The Control Node uses BGP to distribute network state, presenting a standardized protocol for horizontal scalability and the potential of multivendor interoperability. However, it's more useful in the short term for interoperability with existing BGP networks. The architecture synthesizes experiences from more recent, public architecture projects for handling large and volatile data stores and modular component communication.

The Contrail solution leverages open source solutions internal to the system that are proven. For example, for analytics data, most operational data, and the IF-MAP data store, Cassandra (*http://cassandra.apache.org/*)[38] was incorporated. Redis[39] was employed as a pub-sub capable messaging system between components/applications. It should be noted that Redis was originally sponsored by VMware. Zookeeper[40] is used in the discovery and management of elements via their agents.

Like all SDN controllers, the Juniper solution requires a paired agent in the network elements, regardless of whether they are real devices or virtualized versions operating in a VM. In the latter case, it's a hypervisor-resident vRouter combined with a user space VM (vRouter Agent).[41] In the case of the former, configuration via Netconf, XMPP, and the standard BGP protocol are used for communication.

The communication/messaging between Control Node and vRouter Agent is intended to be an open standard using XMPP as the bearer channel. The XMPP protocol is a standard, but only defines the transport of a "container" of information. The explicit messaging contained within this container needs to be fully documented to ensure interoperability in the future.

Several RFCs have been submitted for this operational paradigm. These cover how the systems operate for unicast, multicast, and the application of policy/ACLs:

- *http://tools.ietf.org/html/draft-marques-l3vpn-end-system-05*
- *http://tools.ietf.org/html/draft-marques-sdnp-flow-spec-01*
- *http://tools.ietf.org/html/draft-marques-l3vpn-mcast-edge-01*

An additional RFC has been submitted for the IF-MAP schema for transfer of non-operational state:

- *http://tools.ietf.org/html/draft-marques-sndp-l3vpn-schema-00*

---

38. Juniper doesn't insist on Cassandra as the NoSQL database in their architecture and publishes an API that allows substitution.

39. *http://redis.io/*

40. zookeeper.apache.org

41. Similar to the Nicira/VMware ESX situation prior to merge in recently announced NSX product.

The vRouter Agent converts XMPP control messages into VRF instantiations representing the tenants and programs the appropriate FIB entries for these entities in the hypervisor resident vRouter forwarding plane, illustrated in Figures 4-16 and 4-17.

The implementation uses IP unnumbered interface structures that leverage a loopback to identify the host physical IP address and to conserve IP addresses. This also provides multitenant isolation via MPLS labels supporting MPLS in GRE or MPLS in VxLAN encapsulations. The solution does not require support of MPLS switching in the transit network. Like the VMware/Nicira solution(s), this particular solution provides a software-based gateway to interface with devices that do not support their agent.

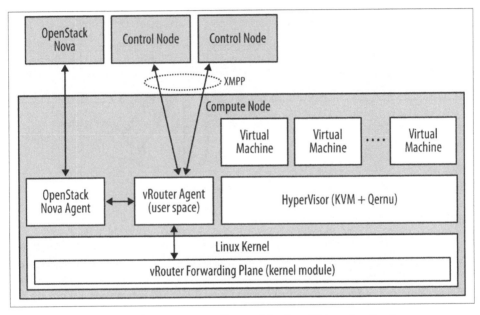

Figure 4-16. Interaction between controller and Juniper Networks vRouter

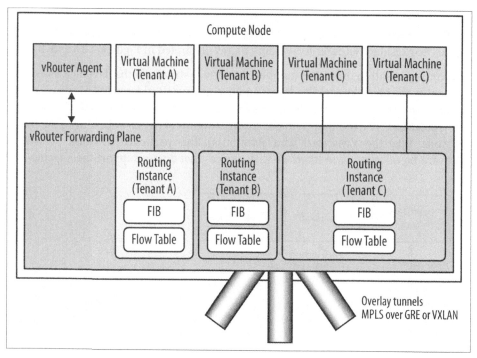

Figure 4-17. Multi-tenancy in Juniper Networks vRouter

Relationship to the idealized SDN framework

Figure 4-18 maps the relationship of the Juniper Contrail Controller's components to the idealized SDN framework, with the areas highlighted that the controller implements. In this case, the platform implements a RESTful northbound API that applications and orchestrators can program to, including the OpenStack API integration. There are also integrated HA/clustering and both in-memory and noSQL state storage capabilities. In terms of the southbound protocols, we mentioned that XMPP was used as a carrier channel between the controller and virtual routers, but additional south bound protocols such as BGP are implemented as well.

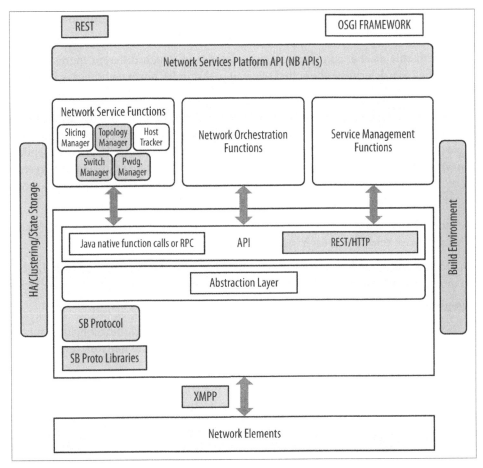

Figure 4-18. Contrail VNS capabilities (against an idealized controller framework)

Path Computation Element Server

RSVP-TE problem statement

In an RSVP-TE network, TE LSPs are signaled based on two criteria: desired bandwidth (and a few other constraints) and the available bandwidth at that instant in time the LSP is signaled within in the network.

The issue then is that when multiple LSPs (possibly originating at different LSRs in the network) signal TE LSPs simultaneously, each is vying for the same resource (i.e., a particular node, link, or fragment of bandwidth therein). When this happens, the LSP setup and hold priorities must be invoked to provide precedence to the LSPs. Otherwise, it would be solely first-come, first-served, making the signaling very nondeterministic.

Instead, when an LSP is signaled and others already exist, LSP preemption is used to preempt those existing LSPs in favor of more preferred ones.

Even with this mechanism in place, the sequence in which different ingress routers signal the LSPs determine the actual selected paths under normal and heavy load conditions.

Imagine two sets of LSPs, two with priority 1 (call them A and B) and two with priority 2 (call them C and D). Now imagine that enough bandwidth only exists for one LSP at a particular node. So if A and B are signaled, only one of A or B will be in place, depending on which went first. Now when C and D are signaled, the first one signaled will preempt A or B (whichever remained), but then the last one will remain. If we changed the order of which one signaled first, a different outcome would result.

What has happened is that the combination of LSP priorities and pre-emption are coupled with path selection at each ingress router.

In practice, this result is more or less as desired; however, this behavior makes it difficult to model the true behavior of a network *a priori* due to this nondeterministic behavior.

Bin-packing

A RSVP LSP gets signaled successfully if there is sufficient bandwidth along its complete path. Many times it is not possible to find such a path in the network, even though overall the network is not running hot.

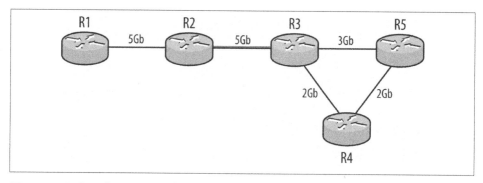

Figure 4-19. Simple TE network

In Figure 4-19, the numbers in Gb represent the bandwidth available on the links. If one wanted to setup a 4 Gb LSP from R1 to R5, then that setup would fail, because the link R3 to R5 has only 3 Gb available. However the sum of R3-R5 bandwidth and R3-R4-R5 bandwidth is 5Gb (3+2). Thus, there is bandwidth available in the network, but due to the nature of RSVP signaling, one cannot use that available bandwidth.

Thus, the bin-packing problem is "how do we maximally use the available network bandwidth?"

Deadlock

Additionally, deadlock or poor utilization can occur if LSP priorities are not used or if LSPs with the same priority collide. In Figure 4-19, if R1 tried to signal a 3 GB LSP to R5 (via R1-R2-R3-R5) and R2 tried to signal a 2GB LSP to R5 (via R2-R3-R5), then only one will succeed. If R2 succeeded, then R1 will be unable to find a path to R5.

The PCE Solution

Prior to the evolution of PCE, network operators addressed these problems through the use of complex planning tools to figure out the correct set of LSP priorities to get the network behavior they desired and managed the onerous task of coordinating the configuration of those LSPs. The other alternate was to over-provision the network and not worry about these complexities.

Path computation element (PCE) allows a network operator to delegate control of MPLS label switched paths (LSPs) to an external controller.

When combined with BGP-LS' active topology (discussed in Chapter 8), network operators can leverage those (previously mentioned) complex tools with a greatly simplified configuration step (via PCE) to address these problems (in near real time).

There are multiple components of the PCE environment: a PCE server, a PCE client (PCC), and the PCE Protocol that is the protocol for data exchange between the PCE server and PCC.

PCE has evolved through several phases in which:

- The server manages pre-configured LSPs in a stateless manner.
- The server manages pre-configured LSPs stateless fashion.
- The server manages pre-configured and dynamically created LSPs in a stateful way.

The PCE server provides three fundamental services: path computation, state maintenance, and infrastructure and protocol support. The PCE server uses the PCE Protocol in order to convey this information to network elements or PCCs. Ideally, the PCE server is a consumer of active topology. Active topology is derived at least in part from the BGP-TE/LS protocol, although as well as other sources such as routing protocol updates, the new I2RS general topology, and ALTO servers.

As PCE servers evolve, the algorithm for path computation should be loosely coupled to the provisioning agent through a core API, allowing users to substitute their own algorithms for those provided by vendors. This is an important advance because these replacement algorithms now can be driven by the business practices and requirements of individual customers, as well as be easily driven by third-party tools.

Relationship to the idealized SDN framework

The PCE server or *controller* takes a noticeably narrow slice of the idealized SDN framework, as shown in Figure 4-20. In doing so, it of course provides a RESTful northbound API offering a myriad of programmability options but generally only interfaces using a single southbound protocol (PCE-P). It is for this reason that we generally view the PCE controller as being an adjunct to existing controllers, which can potentially expand that base functionality greatly.

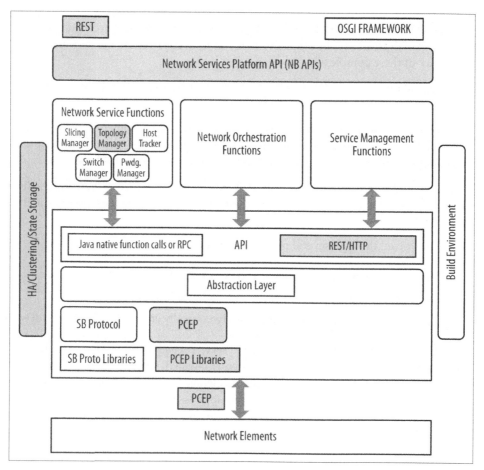

Figure 4-20. PCE server capabilities (against an idealized controller/framework)

The other components in this controller solution would be typical of an SDN controller and would include infrastructure for state management, visualization, component management, and a RESTful API for application interface, as shown in Figure 4-21. In terms of the APIs, these should include standard API conversions like an OpenStack Quantum plug-in to facilitate seamless integration with orchestration engines.

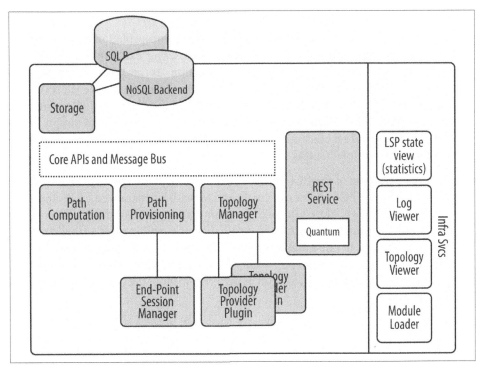

Figure 4-21. PCE server components (non-exhaustive/conceptual)

The original application of a PCE server was the creation of inter-area MPLS-TE tunnels with explicit paths. The motivation was simply to avoid the operational hurdles around inter-provider operational management, which even today, still remains as a big issue. The PCE server could act as an intermediate point that had sufficient visibility into each provider's networks to establish paths whose placement was more optimal than those established using routing protocols that only had local visibility within each component provider network. There are also compelling use cases in backbone bandwidth management, such as more optimal bin packing in existing MPLS LSPs, as well as potential use cases in access networks for things such as service management.

The MPLS Traffic Engineering Database (MPLS TED) was originally distributed as extensions to the IGP database in traditional IP/MPLS networks. Typically, this distribution terminates at area borders, meaning that multiarea tunnels are created with an explicit path only to the border of the area of the tunnel head end. At the border point, a loose hop is specified in the ERO, as exact path information is not available. Often this results in a suboptimal path. As a solution to this problem, BGP-TE/LS allows the export of the TED from an area to a central topology store via a specific BGP address family. The central topology store could merge the area TEDs, allowing an offline application with a more global view of the network topology to compute an explicit end-to-end path.

Because MPLS LSPs provide an overlay using the MPLS encapsulation that is then used to switch traffic based on the MPLS label, the PCE server can either by itself or in conjunction with other SDN technologies function as an SDN controller (see Figure 4-22). These MPLS LSPs are signaled from the "head end" node via RSVP-TE. In this way, this PCE-based solution can signal, establish, and manage LSP tunnels that cross administrative boundaries or just routing areas more optimally or simply differently based on individual constraints that might be unavailable to the operator due to the equipment not implementing it.

Another emerging use of the PCE server is related to segment routing.[42] In a segment routing scenario, the PCE server can create an LSP with a generalized ERO object that is a label stack. This is achieved through programmatic control of the PCE server. The PCC creates a forwarding entry for the destination that will impose a label stack that can be used to mimic the functionality of an MPLS overlay (i.e., a single label stack) or a traffic engineering (TE) tunnel (i.e., a multilabel stack) without creating any signaling state in the network. Specifically, this can be achieved without the use of either the RSVP-TE or LDP protocols.[43]

---

42. *http://datatracker.ietf.org/doc/draft-previdi-filsfils-isis-segment-routing/*

43. Arguably, the reduction of complexity in distributed control plane paradigms (at least session-oriented label distribution) is an SDN application.

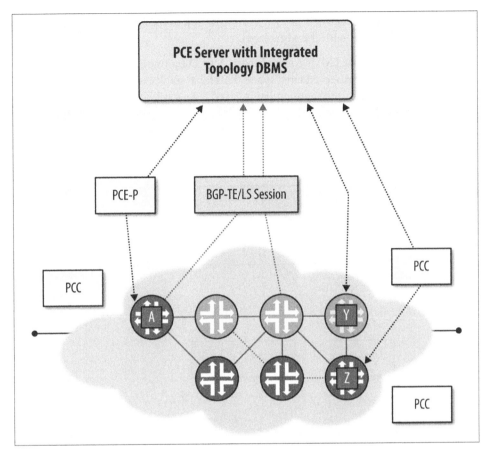

Figure 4-22. PCE Server manipulates ERO of LSP originating at A to change explicit path from terminating at Z to terminating at Y; BGP-TE/LS speakers provide redundant source of topology to PCE

Besides the obvious and compelling SDN application of this branch of PCE in network simplification in order to allow a network administrator to manipulate the network as an abstraction with less state being stored inside the core of the network, there is also some potential application of this technology in service chaining.

The association of a local label space with node addresses and adjacencies such as anycast loopback addresses drives the concept of service chaining using segment routing. These label bindings are distributed as an extension to the ISIS protocol:

- Node segments represent an ECMP-aware shortest path.
- Adjacency segments allow the operator to express any explicit path.

The PCE server can bind an action such as swap or pop to the label. Note that the default operation being "swap" with the same label.

In Figure 4-23, a simple LSP is formed from A to D by imposing label stack 100 that was allocated from the reserved label space. This label stack associates the label with D's loopback address—(i.e., the segment list is "100"). An explicit (RSVP-TE) path can be dictated through the use of an adjacency label (e.g., 500 to represent the adjacency B-F) in conjunction with the node label for D and B (e.g., 300) creating the segment list and its imposed label stack (i.e., "300 500 100").

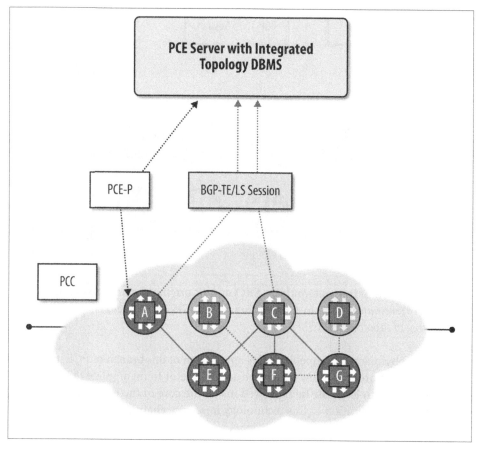

Figure 4-23. Segment routing using a PCE server as SDN controller

While extremely promising and interesting, this proposal is relatively new, and so several aspects remain to be clarified.[44]

It should be noted that PCE servers are already available from Cisco Systems, which acquired Cariden Technologies. Cariden announced a PCE server in 2012.[45] Other vendors with varying solutions for how to acquire topology, how to do path computation, and other technical aspects of the products are also working on PCE server solutions. In addition to these commercial offerings, a number of service providers, including Google, have indicated that they are likely to develop their own PCE servers independently or in conjunction with vendors in order to implement their own policies and path computation algorithms.

Plexxi

Plexxi Systems are based around the concept of affinity networking, offering a slightly different kind of controller—a tightly coupled proprietary forwarding optimization algorithm and distribution system.

The Plexxi controller's primary function is to gather information about affinities dynamically from external systems or statically via manually created policies and then translate this affinity information into forwarding topologies within the Plexxi network. See Figure 4-24 for a sketch of the Plexxi Systems architecture.

The Plexxi physical topology is ring based, and affinities are matched to ring identifiers, thus forming a tight bond between the overlay and underlay concepts. Some would say this tight bond is more of a hybrid, or blending into a single network layer.

---

44. *http://datatracker.ietf.org/doc/draft-gredler-rtgwg-igp-label-advertisement/*

   http://datatracker.ietf.org/doc/draft-gredler-isis-label-advertisement/

45. *http://www.sdncentral.com/sdn-blog/cardien-technologies-releases-service-provider-infrastructure-sdn-white-paper/2012/08/*

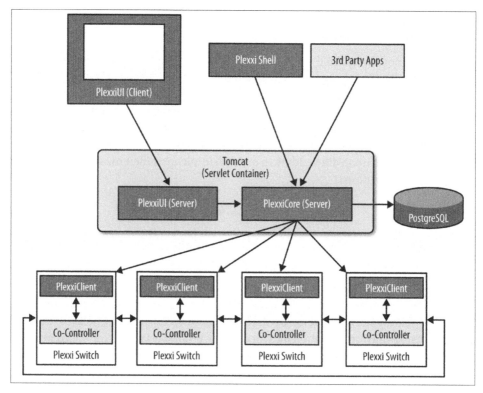

Figure 4-24. Plexxi Systems architecture (source: Plexxi Systems)

These topologies manifest as a collection of forwarding rules pushed across the switches within the controller's domain. There are additional mechanisms in place that preserve active topology on the switches if the controller(s) partition from the network.

The controller tasks are split between a controller and co-controller, where the central controller maintains central policy and performs administrative and the algorithmic fitting tasks, while the co-controller performs local forwarding table maintenance and fast repair.

In addition to learning about and creating affinities, the controller provides interfaces for operational and maintenance tasks. These interfaces include a REST API, a Jython shell, and a GUI. The Jython shell has numerous pre-shipped commands for working with the controller and the switches, however custom CLI commands can easily be created with a bit of Python coding. The GUI employs the JIT/GWT to auto-create interactive diagrams of the physical network and the affinities it supports.

The Plexxi topology and forwarding programming are part of a proprietary control protocol (PSCP). The forwarding programming uses ActiveMQ (*http://activemq.apache.org*) and the controller is based around PostgreSQL (*http://www.postgresql.org/*).[46]

The Plexxi control paradigm currently works only with Plexxi's LightRail optical switches.

Plexxi scale is up to 250 switches per ring per controller pair. Plexxi supports redundant and multiring topologies for scale and the separation of maintenance domains.[47]

The Plexxi relationship to the idealized controller would be the same as others with a proprietary southbound API (much like the Contrail VNS comparison in Figure 4-18), with the notable exception that the affinity algorithms provide differentiation in topology and forwarding.

Plexxi Affinity

An affinity consists of one or two affinity groups and an affinity link between them. An affinity group is a collection of endpoints, identified by MAC or IP address. An affinity link is a policy construct describing a desired forwarding behavior between two affinity groups or the forwarding behavior between endpoints within a single affinity group.

For instance, affinity group A can be a set of MAC addresses belonging to storage cluster members. Affinity group B can be a pair of redundant storage controllers. An affinity link between group A and group B can tell the controller to isolate this traffic in the network. Affinity information can be harvested from any type of infrastructure system through Plexxi connectors: IP PBXs, storage systems, WAN optimization systems, private cloud systems such as OpenStack, VMware deployments, and so on. In addition to these, affinities can be derived from flow-monitoring systems that store sFlow, netflow, or IPFIX data.

Cisco OnePK

The Cisco OnePK controller is a commercial controller that embodies the framework concept by integrating multiple southbound protocol plug-ins, including an unusual southbound protocol plug-in, the Cisco OnePK API.

The architecture is a Java-based OSGI framework that uses an in-memory state storage model and provides a bidirectional (authenticated) REST interface. Clustering is

---

46. Database replication will enable (on Plexxi roadmap for 2013) configuration and state replication in multi-controller or redundant environments.

47. Plexxi offers comprehensive network design guidance and has a roadmap for larger scale and more complex topologies.

supported using Infinispan and JBoss marshaling and transaction tools. See Figure 4-25 for a sketch of the Cisco OnePK controller concept.

Cisco claims the controller logic is capable of reconciling overlapping forwarding decisions from multiple applications and a service abstraction that allows troubleshooting as well as capability discovery and mapping.

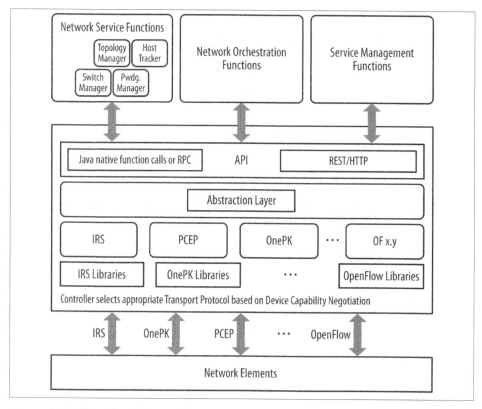

Figure 4-25. Cisco OnePK controller concept

While it's not unusual for the major network equipment vendors to offer their customers an SDK (a vendor-specific, network element programmability option that pre-dates SDN), the Cisco controller implements this as a plug-in in the generalized framework concept. This opens the door to the continued use of their SDK in an SDN solutions environment (e.g., blending the OnePK API with OpenFlow) in places where the SDK (or SDK apps on the controller) can add value.

Relationship to the Idealized SDN Framework

The Cisco OnePK controller appears to be the best mapping of functionality within a controller to the idealized SDN framework. It contains all aspects of the idealized controller in that it provides an extensible RESTful API, an integrated development environment, multiple computational engines, as well as different southbound protocols through which it can be used to interface to what is likely the widest variety of network devices real and virtual. The controller contains capabilities for both memory resident and offline, and distributed state management and configuration storage. It also contains provisions for horizontal controller-to-controller communication and coordination. Finally, in order to facilitate the Swiss Army knife of northbound and southbound protocols, the controller implements an abstraction layer that facilitates the many-to-many communication channels needed to program such a controller. It is this that really differentiates it from the other controllers discussed in that it can be further *extended* in the future with relative ease.

Based on these advantages, it is also no surprise that this controller is also used as the new gold standard for open source SDN controllers, as evidenced by it being the basis for the new OpenDaylight Project Linux Foundation consortium.

Conclusions

The term *SDN controller* can have many different meanings and thus exists in many different forms today. Much of the meaning is derived from the network domain in which the controller will operate, was derived from, and the strategy and protocol choices used in that domain.

The current state of the SDN controller market is that, while there is an expectation of standards-based behaviors whereby users often cite multivendor interoperability for provisioning as a compelling feature of SDN, this is not always the case. This fact remains, for better or worse. Vendors may use proprietary techniques and protocols that depend on the ubiquity of their products or the compelling nature of their applications to create markets for their products. The latter is true because applications were originally (and still are currently) closely bound to the controller in the SDN market through use of non-standardized APIs.

Because of the controller/agent relationship and the reality that not all existing network elements may support the agent daemon/process of the controller (that instantiates the protocol that delivers the network state required to create the aforementioned network abstractions), many controller product strategies also involve the use of host-based gateway solutions. In these gateways, the agents transform the tenant overlay networks into a common digestible format for non-controlled elements—typically turning the tenant overlay networks into VLANs. This strategy allows the interoperation of the old and the new networks with the caveats that the software-based gateway may be of lower packet processing capability—with a potential performance penalty.

The controllers surveyed[48] have the following general attributes when considered as a group:

- They provide various levels of development support—languages, tooling, etc.
- Commercial offerings tend to have proprietary interfaces but (as expected) offer more robust storage and scale traits today.
- The evolution of network-state specific controllers versus integrated data center solution controllers has led to new strategies for state storage in more recently developed products (e.g., the use of NoSQL databases by Big Switch Networks), messaging (e.g., Redis in the Juniper Networks solution), entity management (e.g., the use of Zookeeper). In the end, commercial offerings have to adopt a stance on state sharing (either atomic operation or federation).
- All SDN controller solutions today have a very limited view of topology. This is predominantly a single layer of the network or even only locally adjacent devices such as the case when using LLDP for layer 2, or in the case of PCE, the BGP traffic-engineering database.
- Few controllers support more than a single protocol driver for interaction with clients/agents. Some OpenFlow open source controllers don't support NETCONF and thus can't support of-config, for example.
- All controller solutions today have proprietary APIs for application interfaces. That is, no standard northbound interface exists in reality, although some are attempting to work on this problem such as the Open Daylight Project. Unfortunately the ONF has resisted working in this area until very recently, but other standards organizations such as the IETF and ETSI have begun work in this area. Also, the Open DayLight Project will be producing the open source code that will represent a useful and common implementation of such an interface, which may very well drive those standards.
- At best, the present SDN controllers address scalability by supporting multicontroller environments or with database synchronization and/or clustering strategies. These strategies hamper interoperability between vendors with the exception of the Juniper solution, which proposes the use of BGP for exchanging network state but still requires adoption by other vendors.

In the OpenFlow environment, the horizontal and vertical scalability of open source SDN controllers is questionable, since robust support of underlying DBMS backends is fairly new. Many were designed originally to run with memory resident data only.

---

48. This is not an exhaustive list and doesn't include all currently available or historic SDN controller offerings.

That is, they were not designed to share memory resident state between clustered controllers unless they are architected specifically. Big Switch Networks may be an exception, but many of their enhancements were reserved for their commercial offering.

Support for OpenFlow v1.3 is not yet universal. Most controllers and equipment vendors still only support OpenFlow 1.0. This can be an issue because a number of critical updates were made to the protocol by 1.3. Furthermore, along the lines of support for OpenFlow, many device vendors have implemented a number of vendor-proprietary extensions to the protocol that not all controllers support. This further puts a dent into interoperability of these solutions.

Most network-related discussions eventually come to the conclusion that networks are about applications. In the case of the SDN controller, application portability and the ecosystem that can be built around a controller strategy will ultimately decide on who the commercial victor(s) are. If none is sufficient when it comes to controllers, then an evolution in thinking about SDN and the controller paradigm may occur as well. This may be happening in how the Cisco OnePK (and the Open Daylight Project) controller has been created. Flexibility was absent from most controller architectures both in terms of southbound protocol support and northbound application programmability.

There are some notable technologies or thought processes in the surveyed SDN controllers regarding application development:

- The Trema model introduces the idea of a framework, in that it originally provided just a development core and each service module provided its own API that can then be implemented by more components or end-user applications.
- Big Switch Network's commercial product and potentially Floodlight, as well as the Spring-based environment for VMware accentuate API development tooling, in particular the ability to autogenerate APIs from modules or generate them from data models that the modules manipulate.
- Juniper Networks refines the idea with the idea of compilation by invoking the *SDN as network compiler* concept. This created high-level, user-friendly/app-friendly, data models that translate into lower-level network strategy/protocol specific primitives (e.g., L3VPN VRFs, routes, and policies).
- Several vendors have strategies that acknowledge the need for separate servers for basic functionality (even more so for long-term scalability) and potentially application-specific database strategies. As we get to more recent offerings, many are described as systems or clusters, which must define and address a consistency philosophy.

We've seen that, as we survey across time, the best of ideas like these are culled or evolve, and are then incorporated in new designs.

CHAPTER 5

Network Programmability

Introduction

The concept of *network programmability* lies at the heart of one of the key tenets of software-defined networks. The concept of programmability can exist in, or be a feature of, a number of network devices and software components—and this is not a new concept, as network management has existed since the beginning of time for networked devices. What differs now is in specifically how those devices—real or virtual—are not only managed, but also *interacted with*. Regardless of the type of target, the goal is to make it easily programmable and to facilitate a bidirectional channel of communication between it and the other piece of software communicating with it. This forms what we refer to as a tightly coupled *feedback loop* between these elements. This concept is in fact quite different from the traditional network management paradigm, where the manager and agent communicated in a relatively loose fashion with considerable lag between operations—including cases where essentially no feedback existed.

In order to realize this new paradigm of communication and interaction, tightly coupled, bidirectional programmatic interfaces are needed. These interfaces also need to be readily and rapidly implemented in software so as to encourage their use and ubiquitous deployment. These interfaces have been commonly referred to as *application friendly*. These interfaces also need to be developed by communities of developers in order to make them robust, secure, and widely used. This will lead to de facto standardization and ultimately proper standardization. Interfaces need to provide self-describing capabilities so that applications can easily and dynamically learn and understand the capabilities of a network element without having to be recompiled. The net effect then will be interfaces that one can safely code to and that are portable *across different* controller platforms.

We will describe programmatic interfaces in detail in this chapter, as well as explain how they can be instrumented in such a way as to facilitate this tightly coupled, bidirectional communications channel in order to form a feedback loop between the controller, the network devices it controls, and ultimately the applications that need to interact with both of these.

We should note that since the purpose of this chapter is to provide the reader with a survey of available technologies, we do not intend to go into great detail explaining each specific management interface. Instead, we will aim for a slightly higher-level view of the important pros and cons of any given protocol or approach in an effort to show the reader how it fits in (or doesn't) into the SDN model of the world. We will, however, provide the reader with references for further reading of such details.

The Management Interface

Management interfaces allow network operators to manage network devices in their networks. These interfaces generally provide the operator with a consistent operational view of a device, including its configuration and operational status. A management interface typically consists of two key elements: a protocol and a message format specification. In the case of the protocol, this describes the syntax and semantics associated with sending or receiving specific messages that either the manager or network element generates. These messages often contain commands, queries, or responses to earlier queries. In some cases, these messages can be emitted without a direct query—as is the case with events (notifications) that are emitted asynchronously in response to some event within the network element. The other key element of a management interface is the message format and the meaning of those messages. Some management interfaces define a data model that can be used as a directory of information available to the network operator. In some cases, these can also be used to describe how a manager might construct (or order) queries or commands between it and the device. The data model also typically describes the relationship between manageable objects within the system. For example, the system's name might be kept in an object called sysName and associated with another object called sysUpTime indicating the length of time the system has been running. Both of these objects would be related in that they are contained within the parent object called system, which represents the entire system.

The Application-Network Divide

Until recently, most modern network elements (e.g., routers, switches, or firewalls) supported a small set of traditional interfaces that were used to communicate with those elements. These typically included a proprietary command-line interface (CLI), SNMP, CORBA, and more recently, some form of NETCONF. These languages have a few key traits in common. First, they are, generally speaking, very static in nature and require a priori data model design and declaration. In practice, this means that code is often generated from these interfaces, which are built directly into the firmware images executing on the network elements, as well as the management software (or applications).

This meant that the interfaces used to converse with a network element had to be pre-programmed rather than being learned on-the-fly. Second, the syntax of the languages used to define the structure of messages and rules by which elements should handle messages (i.e., read-only and read-write) are somewhat purpose-built for those management interfaces. Third, these protocols often used binary encodings, meaning that while they were compact on the wire, they were difficult to program, debug, and otherwise represent. Finally, the common practices around writing the syntactic modules describing the schema of any one of these interfaces was often nonhierarchical, meaning that it was difficult to navigate not only for applications, but also for humans trying to find their way around the schema.

In most cases, an application that was allowed to have any sort of discourse with a network element or its services was required to either communicate using one of these protocols, or more commonly, had to communicate through a network management element management system (EMS). The EMS acted as a proxy between the network elements and the applications. Unfortunately, the EMS (or NMS) generally did not expose the network elements or the services they provided in any sort of application-friendly way, meaning that coding toward these interfaces and paradigms was cumbersome and ultimately resulted in long periods of time between an application signaling its desire to do something and that something actually happening. This is in fact what we call *the application-network divide*, illustrated in Figure 5-1.

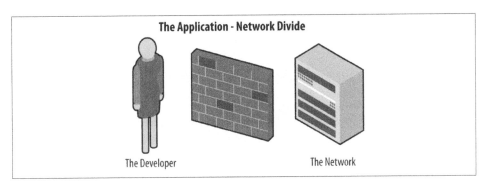

Figure 5-1. The application-network divide

To this end, one answer is to use interfaces that are application-friendly RESTful (representational state transfer) interfaces. It happens that these interfaces are generally defined using modern approaches such as JSON (JavaScript Object Notation). JSON solves many of the shortcomings just described because its schema is defined using human-readable XML, is self-referential, is hierarchical, and is something that is easily built into Java applications—the most common application programming language of the past decade. The code snippet here demonstrates a JSON example (other modern, application-friendly interfaces are Thrift and Google Buffers—we will describe these and a few others later in this chapter):

```html
<!DOCTYPE html>
<html>
<body>
<h2>
JSON Object Creation in JavaScript
</h2>
<p>

Name: <span id="jname"></span><br />

Age: <span id="jage"></span><br />

Address: <span id="jstreet"></span><br />

Phone: <span id="jphone"></span><br />
</p>
<script>

var JSONObject= {

"name":"John Johnson",

"street":"Oslo West 555",

"age":33,

"phone":"5551234567"};

document.getElementById("jname").innerHTML=JSONObject.name
document.getElementById("jage").innerHTML=JSONObject.age
document.getElementById("jstreet").innerHTML=JSONObject.street
document.getElementById("jphone").innerHTML=JSONObject.phone

</script>


</body>

</html>
```

Another of the key tenets of SDN technology is to facilitate a much more closely coupled interaction between applications and the network elements that support them. Specifically, the cycle of provisioning, analysis, and optimization represent three common and general actions that were often considered as independent in the past. We suggest that in an SDN approach, these be considered together. This is illustrated in Figure 5-2. The act of provisioning is that whereby an application indicates a desire to do something, change something, or generally affect the behavior of the network. The analysis phase is one of monitoring or gathering feedback from network elements as to their operational, fault, capacity, or otherwise well-being states. This includes, for example, statistics gathering or reception of status notifications. Finally, optimization is the last stage that is accomplished using the information gathered from the analysis phase and possibly causes another act of provisioning to take place (potentially through some embedded or external policy engine interaction) in order for the system to adjust itself in order to better operate. The tighter this feedback loop can be implemented, the quicker the entire system can potentially adjust itself to change and potentially operate more optimally.

Earlier, we described how older style interfaces promulgated application design patterns that often resulted in applications having to communicate with what was essentially a proxy or translator between it and the network elements. One often-overlooked side effect of this approach is that the feedback loop between an application and the network element is often measured in minutes, hours, or days! This rate of activity surely is insufficient if we are to do anything in near real time, such as some of the use cases we describe later in the book (e.g., bandwidth calendaring, which is covered in Chapter 12, or instantaneous CSPF, which is covered in Chapter 10).

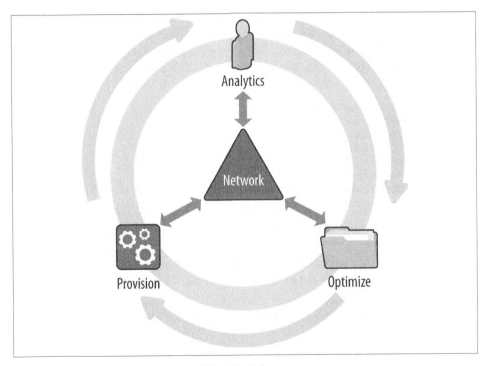

Figure 5-2. The application-network feedback loop

The Command-Line Interface

Each vendor since the beginning of time has had to provide some form of command-line interface (CLI) so that the operator could communicate with the device. The CLI is typically an ASCII character-based system that is intended to be used as the default and lowest common denominator management interface for any given device. The CLI is analogous to a UNIX shell prompt in many ways in that the CLI is effectively a syntax parser that takes some action based on a string of tokens as soon as the Return key is depressed.

Most devices support remote access to the CLI in the form of using a common protocol such as Telnet or Secure Shell (SSH). Since these protocols operate across a network, they are susceptible to network outages or other faults that could prevent a manager from communicating with a device. It is for this reason that most devices big and small still provide some form of hardwired attachment and supporting command set for local interaction (e.g., a hardwired USB or serial port).

In general, device manufacturers specify their command-line syntax as two parts: configuration and query, or monitoring. In the case of configuration, there is often a secure mode of operation that a manager enters in order to alter the running configuration of a device. Some devices allow an operator to store multiple copies of configurations in case they have different scenarios to configure or if a particular configuration happens to not work, they have another one to fall back to. This is shown in the brief snippet here:

```
RP/0/0/CPU0:ios#config t
RP/0/0/CPU0:ios(config)#interface
MgmtEth 0/0/CPU0/0
RP/0/0/CPU0:ios(config-if)#
RP/0/0/CPU0:ios#
RP/0/0/CPU0:ios#admin
RP/0/0/CPU0:ios(admin)#
```

The command-line syntax also typically provides a query mode, allowing a manager to interrogate the state or status of particular functions of a device. For instance, in the previous example, we used the system's name as one element that a manager could query in order to ensure they were about to configure the correct device. Another example is shown here, where we query the BGP protocol status of a device:

```
RP/0/0/CPU0:R2#show bgp summary
BGP router identifier 3.3.3.3, local AS number 1 BGP generic
  scan interval 60 secs

BGP table state: Active

Table ID: 0xe0000000
BGP main routing table version 561
BGP scan interval 60 secs
```

```
BGP is operating in STANDALONE mode.
Process Speaker Neighbor 20.0.101.1
RecvTblVerbRIB/RIB LabelVer ImportVer SendTblVer
StandbyVer 561 561 561 561 561 561
Spk AS MsgRcvdMsgSentTblVerInQOutQ Up/Down
St/PfxRcd 0 1 1068 1036 561 0 0 14:35:30 100
```

Unfortunately, the CLI syntax specified by any two vendors is typically different and incompatible, despite the fact that different CLIs might be used to manage the same conceptual elements. For example, a system's name might be allowed to be in mixed case on one system, while another might insist that it be in all capital letters (or disallow certain reserved characters). In an effort to focus on one de facto standard, many network equipment vendors have now copied the Cisco CLI as much is legally possible. While this has helped, these solutions are still hindered by the lack of semantic compatibility of operations, such as the one we just described. Despite this, no standard for CLI syntax exists. Some have tried to standardize it, but all have failed.

One early means of network programmability within the confines of the CLI that is still quite commonplace is to use UNIX scripting to interact with the device's CLI. Various tools exist to do this, including Perl, Expect scripts, UNIX shell commands, and Python. In these cases, scripts are programmed to connect to a device using a network transport and session protocols such as Telnet over UDP/IP or SSH. Once connected and perhaps authenticated, the scripts mechanically enter commands on the CLI as if a user were typing them. This is commonly referred to as "screen scraping" because one is not truly interacting with the system but instead acting as if one were washing windows with a window squeegee. This is unfortunately the most widely used approach for network programmability. The unfortunate feature of using these management robots is that their turnaround time between programming a device and then gathering statistics in order to adjust configuration or take actions is, relatively speaking, often quite long. Another unfortunate deficiency of this approach is that it is largely not application friendly. While some modern applications are written in Perl or Python, they generally are not written to understand the semantics and syntax of a particular vendor's CLI. Worse yet, in cases where multiple vendor devices are present in a network, the application must understand multiple ways in which to interact with a device, depending on its type, make, model, and firmware image. Most people familiar with this method of operation consider this requirement an inappropriate and undue burden on application programmers, who typically do not understand the details of programming a network device—nor should they!

NETCONF and NETMOD

The Network Configuration Protocol (NETCONF) is a network management (*http://bit.ly/1cdN29D*) protocol standardized by the IETF. It was developed and published in December 2006.[1] The IETF developed SNMP (*http://bit.ly/1aWEnoQ*) in the late 1980s, and it continues to prove itself to be a very popular network management (*http://bit.ly/1cdN29D*) protocol (*http://bit.ly/16jqaRH*) even today, at least for statistical monitoring. After about 10 years of deployment experience with SNMP, it unfortunately became apparent that in spite of what was originally intended, SNMP was not being used to configure network equipment but was mainly being used for network monitoring (*http://bit.ly/1aWEosO*). Around 2001, members of the IETF's network management community got together with network operators to discuss the situation. The results of this meeting are documented in RFC 3535 (*http://bit.ly/13mIZ66*),[2] but in summary it turned out that operators were primarily using proprietary command-line interfaces (*http://bit.ly/13ZqxQB*) (CLI) in order to configure their boxes instead of SNMP. The other important discovery that came out of this meeting was the reasoning behind this behavior. Some of the key points were that the CLI had a number of features that the operators liked, including the fact that it was text-based, as opposed to the BER-encoded (*http://bit.ly/1cdNepi*) (i.e., binary) SNMP. In addition, many equipment vendors did not provide the option to completely configure their devices via SNMP. Most had gotten the message earlier from operators and simply only allowed for read-only operation. Even still, those that implemented full read-write capability were on islands of their own in some regards because while the IETF provided standards-based MIB modules, each and every vendor still implemented its own proprietary MIB modules. It was often the case that other vendors did not implement these extensions. Finally, even with standards-based MIBs, some were designed using the semantics of one implementation that ultimately did not match that of another, making it even more difficult (or impossible) to use as a configuration vehicle.

As mentioned earlier, operators generally liked to write scripts to manage their network elements, but they uniformly found the CLI lacking in a number of ways. Most notably was the unpredictable nature of the output. The content and formatting of output was prone to change in unpredictable ways, including between firmware releases. While some provided written notification of changes, as well as documentation, others failed to provide this information, making a difficult situation worse.

Around this same time, Juniper Networks (*http://bit.ly/16jqiAP*) had been using an XML-based network management approach to communicate with its devices remotely (i.e., the protocol for the management interface) and as the native language in which to

---

1. RFC 4741 (*http://datatracker.ietf.org/doc/rfc4741/*) and RFC 6241 (*http://datatracker.ietf.org/doc/rfc6241/*)

2. RFC 3535 (*http://datatracker.ietf.org/doc/rfc3535/*)

specify the model for the CLI. This novel approach was brought to the IETF and shared with the broader community as a proposal for a more uniform and application-friendly management interface. This initial proposal and the meeting described in RFC3535 ultimately led to the creation of a new network management protocol by the IETF called NETCONF.

In short, NETCONF provides mechanisms to install, manipulate, and delete the configuration of network devices. Its operations are carried on top of a simple remote procedure call (RPC) layer (*http://bit.ly/166H6sF*). The NETCONF protocol uses data encoding based on the Extensible Markup Language [XML] (*http://bit.ly/17TB3cc*) for data as well as protocol messages. This in turn is realized on top of the transport protocol, which can be TCP, HTTP, or HTTPS. In general, the NETCONF protocol can be conceptually partitioned into four layers, as depicted in Figure 5-3. We will also describe each of these layers now.

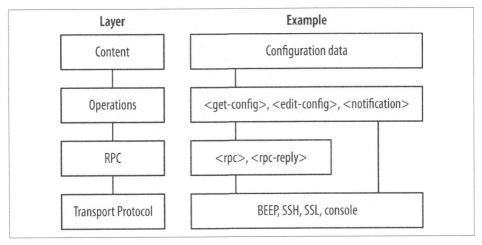

Figure 5-3. The four layers of NETCONF: content, operations, RPC, and transport protocol

Basic NETCONF Operations

The base protocol includes the following protocol operations: get, get-config, edit-config, copy-config, delete-config, lock, unlock, close-session, and kill-session.

Capabilities

The base NETCONF functionality can be extended by the definition of NETCONF capabilities. All additional protocol features that an implementation supports must be communicated between the server and the client during the capability exchange portion of session setup. Mandatory protocol features are not included in the capability exchange, since their support is assumed in all compliant implementations. Some optional capabilities (including :xpath and :validate) are defined in RFC 4741 (*http://tools.ietf.org/html/rfc4741*).

NETCONF also offers the ability to support subscribing and receiving asynchronous event notifications.[3] In particular, the `<create-subscription>` operation enables an operator to create real-time and replay subscriptions for notifications. Once emitted, notifications are then sent asynchronously using the `<notification>` construct.

One very important feature of NETCONF is that it supports the partial locking of the running configuration of a device.[4] This is critical because it allows multiple sessions to edit nonoverlapping subtrees within the running configuration. Without this capability, the only lock available is for the entire configuration, thus requiring an effective serialization of configuration entities that could slow down the entire configuration process.[5]

Finally, the NETCONF protocol can itself be monitored[6] and managed as a stand-alone entity. Elements such as datastores, sessions, locks, and statistics that facilitate the management of a NETCONF server are made available and can be used for important activities such as troubleshooting a server. But most importantly, a NETCONF server defines methods for NETCONF clients to discover data models supported by a NETCONF server and defines the `<get-schema>` operation to retrieve them. It is this capability that allows an application (or SDN controller) to dynamically discover the capabilities available of a device supporting NETCONF. It is this simple yet powerful feature that will facilitate dynamic and data-driven application code creation, including that inside of SDN controllers, which were discussed in Chapter 4.

SNMP

The Simple Network Management Protocol (SNMP) was designed by the IETF many years ago to be an easily implementable, basic network management tool that could be used to remotely manage network elements. The specifications that define SNMP specify a standard protocol, access methods, and a well-known format for representing managed data kept in network elements. Due to its longevity in the industry, SNMP has gone through a number of iterations in an effort to improve it over the years. Three versions of SNMP exist: V1, V2c, and V3. While the protocol itself still exists and is

---

3. RFC 5277 (*http://tools.ietf.org/html/rfc5277*), *http://datatracker.ietf.org/doc/rfc5277/*

4. RFC 5717 (*http://tools.ietf.org/html/rfc5717*), *http://datatracker.ietf.org/doc/rfc5717/*

5. The configuration lock/unlock cycle and the associated calling of daemons to validate the syntax of subblocks of the configuration that are invoked via the CLI configuration method (or scripting) are major stumbling blocks to provisioning in an SDN environment.

6. RFC 6022 (*http://tools.ietf.org/html/rfc6022*), *http://datatracker.ietf.org/doc/rfc6022/*

widely deployed, as already mentioned, it is primarily used for monitoring network elements, their status, and performance characteristics. Today, most production networks do indeed use SNMP as at least part of their element management strategy; however, most do not use it for configuration purposes.

The SNMP set of standards provides a framework for the definition of management information along with a protocol for the exchange of that information. The SNMP model assumes the existence of managers and agents, as shown in Figure 5-4.

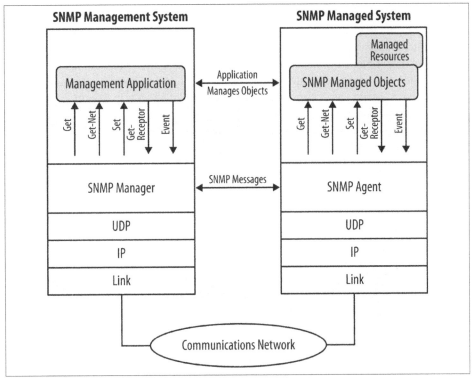

Figure 5-4. The basics of the SNMP Architecture are comprised of an SNMP Management system and an SNMP Managed System

In general, any application that wishes to query or configure network elements are called managers in SNMP parlance and thus contain a manager component. It is this component that communicates with an agent component that resides within a network element. The IETF SNMP Framework[7] defines a more generalized model of SNMP entities. The architecture of an SNMP entity is one that is more complex than the more simplistic

7. RFC 2571 (*http://datatracker.ietf.org/doc/rfc2571/*)

agent-manager relationship but still generally applies. Since the purpose of this chapter is to provide the reader with a survey of available technologies, we will not go into such details but instead aim for a slightly higher-level view of the important pros and cons of this protocol.

The SNMP agent

An SNMP agent is a software module in the network element responsible for maintaining local management information and delivering that information to a manager via the SNMP protocol. Typical implementations of network elements contain an agent. The agent manages the management information base (MIB) that is the conceptual data store within the device. Think of this as the collection of manageable objects within a device, such as the system's name, location, or date of last reboot. The agent also acts as a message dispatcher in that it intercepts, authenticates, and processes messages from the manager. A management information exchange can be initiated by the manager (via `get`, `get-next`, or `get-bulk` commands) or by the agent (via a trap or notification). The agent listens for requests and replies to them. When queried, an agent gathers information about the managed resource in response to the request from a manager. In doing so, it acts as a normalization layer between a manager and the device's internal implementation. For example, the internal system's name might be represented as two concatenated strings representing the system's first and last name, these strings must first be combined before responding to a manager's request to view the name. This is because the IETF standard defines the system's name as a single string of arbitrary length, but only as a single string. This is the normalization function that the SNMP MIB definitions provide, much like any management protocol's standard data model does.

The SNMP manager

The analogue to the SNMP agent is the manager. The manager represents what its name implies: an application whose job it is to manage a device. The term management can mean a variety of things and has evolved over time to encompass any application that is responsible for configuring, monitoring, or simply querying a network device in order to obtain some piece of information. The traditional picture of a network manager is that of a full-blown element or network management system such as CA's IM 2.0 or Alcatel's SAM product; however, it does not have to be. As we discussed earlier in the CLI section, a manager can be a simple Python application whose purpose it is to monitor a system's interface status. In this case, rather than the application having to SSH to a CLI, it would import an SNMP library and use the SNMP protocol as the communications channel between it and the agent/network element.

Manager and agent relationship

As mentioned earlier, SNMP facilitates communication between a managed device (a device with an SNMP agent—let's say a router) and an SNMP manager or management application. This basic relationship is illustrated in the Figure 5-5. Communication between these two entities is achieved via the SNMP Protocol. These messages are typically encapsulated in UDP packets, and four kinds of operations are permitted between managers and agents (managed device). These operations are:

Get

> The manager can perform a get (or read) to obtain information from the agent about an attribute of a managed object.

Get-Next

> The manager can perform a get-next to do the same for the next object in the tree of objects on the managed device.

Get-Bulk

> The manager can perform a get-bulk to obtain information about a group of data from the agent. This is not possible in the case of SNMP V1.

Set

> The manager can perform a set (or write) to set the value of an attribute of a managed object.

In addition to these messages, an agent may emit a trap or a notification that represents an asynchronous notification. These notifications are directed to one or more managers and are intended to indicate that some event on the managed device has occurred.

In more modern, highly scaled systems, the CPU burden created by the work of the SNMP agent (particularly when it interfaces with multiple managers) is often addressed by creating a local hierarchy that includes distributed proxies. Tweaks to the agent operation itself (such as the number of records fetched in each access of tabular data) and data management optimization techniques (such as local caching) are not uncommon.

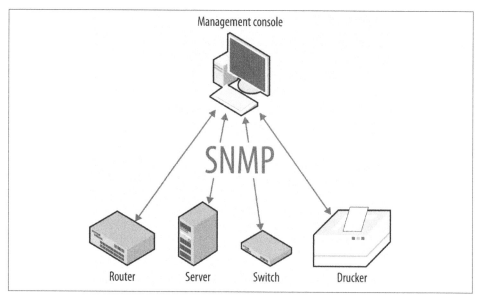

Figure 5-5. Basic SNMP manager and agent configuration; the manager is represented by the management console/PC, while agents can exist within just about any network-enabled entity including a router, switch, and the less obvious server or printer

The MIB (management information base)

SNMP specifies a scheme by which all of the objects and instances of those objects present within a system can be uniquely identified and specified. These items are called *object identifiers*, or OIDs. OIDs are specified as an ordered sequence of non-negative integers written from left-to-right and separated by a period (i.e., a dot). This is sometimes called dot notation. For example, the OID "2.1.0" represents a unique OID within some agent's MIB. OIDs are generally structured in the form of <object identifier>.<instance ID> in order to allow a manager to specify a specific instance of an object. Think of an object as a variable name and the instance as one or potentially many versions of that variable. OIDs can also indicate tabular objects and include indexes, or can indicate scalar objects. OIDs are arranged and organized in a hierarchical tree structure where the topmost levels in the tree are controlled by the ITU and ISO standards bodies in order to provide some order and structure to the standard tree. Subtrees within this structure are doled out to other organizations such as the IETF to manage, while subtrees within that structure are further distributed to organizations and corporations for experimental or private (i.e., proprietary MIB) use. Figure 5-6 demonstrates this arrangement.

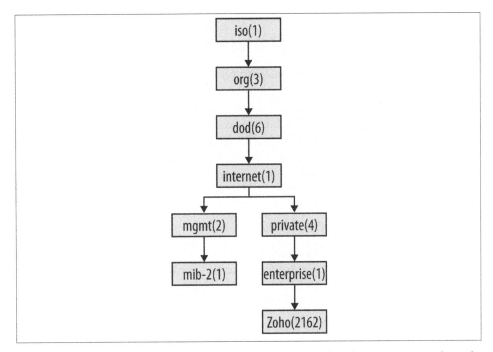

Figure 5-6. OIDs are arranged and organized in a hierarchical tree structure where the topmost levels in the tree are controlled by the ITU and ISO standards bodies

The SNMP manager or management application uses this well-defined OID naming syntax to indicate objects on which it intends to perform one of the aforementioned operations. To this end, every SNMP protocol message includes an OID and an operation to perform on that OID, as well as perhaps a value to set said OID to. The management information base, or MIB, is a conceptual store within a device containing all of the MIB *modules* that a device supports. This document is what specifies the syntax, and in some cases, semantic operational behaviors expected of any implementation of the module. MIB modules are created to manage specific functions such as protocols or features of a device. They are also designed to manage logical or physical entities such as interfaces and power supplies. For example, if a company wants to build new device and wants the BGP stack on that device to be remotely managed, it will write and implement a series of both standards-based and proprietary MIBs that will have information about that protocol.

Modern Programmatic Interfaces

Now that we have described the most common management interfaces, let's move the discussion to modern management interfaces and concepts. These new interfaces and concepts are those that enable and encourage network programmability in the best sense. To that end, these interfaces exhibit most if not all of the key attributes we spelled out in the introduction earlier: bidirectional, application-friendly, and self-describing. They also incorporate robust data models that can translate into data-driven behavior and rapid implementation, and of course are easily developed by communities of developers.

Publish and Subscribe Interfaces

Publish-Subscribe interfaces, or simply *pub-sub* as it is more commonly known, is a messaging pattern (*http://bit.ly/13veuag*) whereby senders of messages (*http://bit.ly/13mK1yM*) (called *publishers*) send messages to receivers (called *subscribers*). Senders do not program the messages to be sent directly to specific receivers but rather characterize published messages into classes. This is done without the expressed knowledge of what, if any, subscribers there may be at any point in time. In this model, subscribers express interest in one or more classes, and thereby only receive messages that are in the class of messages they are interested in. This is done without the knowledge of what, if any, publishers exist. In doing so, this implements what is called a messaging bus whereby messages are placed on the bus, and subscribers simply receive them. This pattern provides greater network scalability (*http://bit.ly/17i8yCL*) and a more dynamic network topology (*http://bit.ly/1aWF1Tb*) than a point-to-point system would due to properties such as lower state management requirements. Message buses can be reliable or unreliable and provide buffer queuing controls much like a virtual network would. In fact, the pub-sub paradigm is a sibling of the message queuing (*http://bit.ly/15vqDPH*) paradigm and so resembles many of the principles of networks. In order to handle the most robust set of use cases, most modern messaging systems support both the message queue and pub-sub models in their API (*http://bit.ly/14CLfBK*). One such example is the Java Message Service (*http://bit.ly/13zfsBB*) (JMS) that is very popular with Java applications programmers.

In the pub-sub model, subscribers typically receive only a subset of the total messages published. This is a very important feature, as it simultaneously lowers the burden of an application around message processing and lessens the overall system load of message delivery, maintenance, and accounting. The process of selecting messages for reception and processing is called *message filtering*. The two common forms of filtering are called *topic-based* and *content-based*.

A topic-based system publishes messages to topics that represent logical sets or are analogous to logical channels in a broadcast system. Subscribers in a topic-based system will receive all messages published to the topics to which they subscribe, but no others. All subscribers to a topic will receive the same messages and generally in the order in which they were published. Although certain messaging systems do account for message ordering, as well as buffering, others do not, and so this cannot be assumed for every system. In order for the messages to be understood by subscribers, it is important that the publisher first define the classes of messages to which subscribers can subscribe. If this is not done, then any messages that are not subscribed to are simply discarded (i.e., ignored) by all subscribers.

In contrast, a content-based system only delivers messages to a subscriber if the attributes or content of those messages match constraints defined by the subscriber. This is analogous to setting up search filters for email messages with matches on certain fields of a message. When messages are matched, they are placed in a special folder. This is the same in this case except that the message is delivered rather than ignored. Similar to the publisher in the topic-based approach, the subscriber is responsible for classifying the messages, or they are simply ignored.

It should be noted that many messaging systems support a hybrid of the two approaches in that publishers can post messages to a topic, and subscribers may simultaneously register content-based subscriptions to topics. In many pub-sub systems, subscribers register subscriptions with a broker, letting the broker perform the filtering. In this model, publishers post messages to an intermediary message broker or event bus (*http://bit.ly/1co7dQE*). The broker normally performs a store and forward (*http://bit.ly/14CLqwS*) function in order to buffer messages so that they are not lost in case of congestion. Once a message trickles up to the top of its queue, it is routed from publishers to subscribers. In addition, the broker may prioritize messages in a queue (*http://bit.ly/15vqI68*) before routing. Since a broker maintains all messages that are transmitted through the system, it can easily clone all messages so that they can be replayed at a later time. This is an important feature of such a system, as it can provide both a troubleshooting or diagnostic function, as well as a high-availability function if one imagines a broker replicating messages to a backup broker that can take over in case this broker somehow stops functioning.

One interesting part of this design pattern is that subscribers can register for specific messages at build time, initialization time, or runtime. It is this flexibility that makes this model so useful and widely adopted. Some frameworks and software products use XML configuration files to register subscribers, providing what we have been calling a *data-driven* approach that can dynamically adjust depending on system attributes, configuration, or local conditions.

Because publishers are loosely coupled (*http://bit.ly/1cdODMw*) to subscribers, they need not even know of their existence. This is an important attribute of this approach because it means that neither publishers nor subscribers need to keep track of the state, accounting, or other attributes around publishers or subscribers. This is the job of the broker, which while providing a single point of failure does have the benefit of centralizing these chores. This also means that publishers and subscribers remain unaware of system topology, meaning that there is essentially no configuration once a publisher or subscriber registers with a broker. This also means that no changes happen to publishers or subscribers as more subscribe or unsubscribe to topics, content, or the system as a whole. This also means that regardless of the state of all of the other publishers or subscribers, any given element can continue to operate normally.

Of course, if a publisher goes away (i.e., crashes, VM is paused, CPU is busy, etc.), messages from that publisher will cease to appear within the system or to subscribers. What is important is that the state of any given element is only loosely coupled to that of the others. This is in contrast to the traditional tightly coupled client-server paradigm (*http://bit.ly/15vqM5E*), whereby a client might not be able to post messages to the server while the server process is not running, nor can the server receive messages unless the client is running. One interesting implementation approach is that most pub-sub systems are capable of decoupling subscribers from publishers temporally. For example, a publisher might be disabled in order to allow subscribers to process a backlog of messages, thereby throttling the messaging bandwidth as well as processor usage of subscribers.

The pub-sub model provides the opportunity for better scalability (*http://bit.ly/17i8yCL*) than traditional tightly coupled client-server approaches in that parallel operation, message caching, and tree-based or network-based routing are possible within this system. Not only is there better scalability, there is also the potential for the system to be more highly available than the traditional ones.

For example, one approach would be to run two publishers in parallel, as described earlier, in order to afford the system some resiliency. In this case, one publisher could crash or be brought down for maintenance while the other continues without any loss of generality of the system. The pub-sub paradigm has proven its scalability to volumes far beyond those of a single data centers, providing Internet-wide distributed messaging through web syndication protocols such as RSS (*http://bit.ly/14imUZ8*), Atom (*http://bit.ly/1bJQjhB*), and XMPP. These syndication protocols accept higher latency as well as a reduction or outright loss of delivery guarantees in exchange for the ability to service massive numbers of subscribers.

One of most serious problems with the pub-sub approach is the decoupling of the publisher from the subscriber. The issue is that a broker in a pub-sub system may be designed to deliver messages for a specified time but then stop attempting delivery, whether or not it has received confirmation of successful receipt of the message by all subscribers. A pub-sub system so-designed cannot guarantee delivery of messages to any applications that might require such assured delivery. If publishers or subscribers are unaware of this limitation, then synchronization and other consistency issues might arise. One way to address such a limitation is, ironically, a tighter coupling of the designs of such a publisher and subscriber pair in order to overcome these limitations. This must be enforced outside of the pub-sub architecture to accomplish assured delivery, making this approach undesirable as it imposes additional burdens on the application programmer.

In terms of SDN systems that can benefit from the pub-sub model, both applications and controllers can be built with pub-sub constructs to enjoy the benefits described previously. In particular, a controller can use pub-sub to communicate with the elements it controls. This was illustrated in the Juniper Contrail controller/agent solution (based on XMPP—see the next section) in Chapter 4.

It is also a common inter-module communication scheme within the controller as exemplified in the CiscoOne controller (Chapter 4) and OpenDaylight Project (ODP) framework (Chapter 9).

Another example is for inter-controller communication to utilize a pub-sub model. Controllers can relay or convey status to one another using this loosely coupled approach, meaning that they can continue doing the work they need to do without blocking to process, send, or receive messages from other controllers. Finally, this can also be used in cases where many applications wish to interact with a controller. In order to enhance the scalability of the communications between the controller and applications, the pub-sub model can be implemented by installing a broker separately from the controller in order to mediate, process, and maintain communication between the controller and applications.

XMPP

As was just mentioned, the Extensible Messaging and Presence Protocol (XMPP) is an example of a pub-sub protocol and has been used to implement a number of publish-subscribe (*http://bit.ly/14inhTq*) systems. XMPP is a communications protocol (*http://bit.ly/16jqaRH*) based on XML [Extensible Markup Language] (*http://bit.ly/18RFKaW*) . The protocol can be used to provide near real-time (*http://bit.ly/132Kse2*) instant messaging (*http://bit.ly/18RFOYi*), presence information (*http://bit.ly/18MLJKF*), or just about any information really that needs to be extended to a subscription group. It was designed to be extensible (*http://bit.ly/1aWFKnr*), as its name suggests, and has in fact been extended a number of times over the years.

XMPP is an open protocol standardized at the IETF.[8] In addition to these core protocols standardized at the IETF, the XMPP Standards Foundation (*http://bit.ly/1bJRsFV*)

---

8. RFC 6120 (*http://tools.ietf.org/html/rfc6120*), *http://datatracker.ietf.org/doc/rfc6120/*; RFC 6121 (*http://tools.ietf.org/html/rfc6121*), *http://datatracker.ietf.org/doc/rfc6121/*; and RFC 6122 (*http://datatracker.ietf.org/doc/rfc6122/*)

(formerly the Jabber Software Foundation) is active in developing open XMPP extensions. Many implementations have been developed and distributed that are in use, such as Jabber, Google Talk, and Facebook Messenger

The architecture of XMPP is very decentralized and analogous to email in that anyone can run his or her own XMPP server and there is no central master server that everyone must connect to or authenticate with. Of course, private groups of publishers and subscribers can be implemented. This is the case, for example, in the controller and application example we just gave in the pub-sub section. The server itself acts like the message broker we described in the pub-sub section. It handles all of the registration and message passing required. Publishers and subscribers all register with the server using a topic-based approach in that they filter based on participating in what is effectively a group conversation. Servers can support multiple conversations. For example, many instant messenger servers support multiple private, multiway conversations among groups of users simultaneously.

The XMPP network uses a pub-sub client-server (*http://bit.ly/15vqM5E*) architecture in that clients do not talk directly to one another but instead register with a central server that acts effectively as the pub-sub broker function. This means that clients and servers are loosely coupled and enjoy all of the aforementioned benefits of such a relationship. The architecture is decentralized by design in that there is no global authoritative server, as there is with instant messaging services such as Facebook Messenger (*http://bit.ly/16jrOmm*) or Google Talk. This sometimes leads to confusion, as there is a public XMPP server being run at *jabber.org*, to which a large number of users subscribe. However, this is only for that community of users. Others may (and do) run their own XMPP server on their own domain, or now, as part of an application framework that has nothing to do with these public implementations.

In the XMPP architecture, every user in the system has a unique Jabber ID. We use the term user here loosely, as it really is either an application that acts as a publisher, subscriber, or both in the pub-sub paradigm. To avoid requiring a central server to maintain a list of IDs, the Jabber ID is typically structured like an email address (*http://bit.ly/1co8ze1*) with a username and a domain name (*http://bit.ly/12FpirM*) or an IP address (*http://bit.ly/13ZsgoY*). A further indication of the server where that user resides can be included by using an at sign (*http://bit.ly/1cdPMng*) (@) after the username, such as *username@example.com*. While common, this is not required and in fact might not suit frameworks that implement XMPP. In these cases, other localized naming schemes can very well be used.

The XMPP system has a notation of message priority. As we described earlier, some pub-sub systems employ queuing for message delivery. In this case, an ordered/priority queuing approach is employed. To this end, each resource may specify a numerical value called a priority when it registers with a server. Messages sent to that user will be treated with appropriate priority. The highest priority is specified using the largest numerical value. It should be noted that messages sent without a username are also valid in the XMPP system. These are used for system messages and control of special features on the server.

An important and interesting twist on the normal XMPP deployment model is the use of XMPP via HTTP and WebSocket transports. The original and native transport protocol for XMPP is the Transmission Control Protocol (*http://bit.ly/17ia6N9*) (TCP) over IP. This encoding used XML streams over long-lived TCP connections where the XML stream format was left up to the users to define and specify.

As an alternative to the TCP transport, the XMPP community has also developed an HTTP (*http://bit.ly/17iaawn*) transport for web clients and for users behind certain restricted firewalls (*http://bit.ly/14inC8G*). In the original specification, XMPP could use HTTP in two ways: either in polling mode or in a binding model. We will not consider the polling method, as it is deprecated. The binding method is implemented using bidirectional streams over synchronous HTTP. This method allows servers to push messages in an asynchronous manner to clients as soon as they are ready to be sent. This approach is far more efficient than the deprecated polling approach—hence its popularity. One other advantage to using an HTTP transport is that most firewalls allow clients to fetch and post messages without any issues related to port filtering or blocking. Using this approach, a server can simply listen on the normal HTTP or HTTPS ports and process XMPP-encapsulated traffic as it arrives.

Google's Protocol Buffers

Protocol buffers are Google's language-neutral, platform-neutral, extensible mechanism for serializing structured data. Google invented protocol buffers as a refinement to deficiencies their coders found in both XML and JSON.[9]

The major refinement of protocol buffers has been to make XML smaller and denser through the use of a binary encoding. One of the downsides to using XML is that while it is presented in a human-readable format, it is quite verbose in terms of the amount of characters that need to be transmitted to convey the same information that one would with a comparative binary format. This in fact was one of the arguments against using NETCONF (versus SNMP) in the early days of NETCONF. Recall that we discussed the relative merits of these earlier, and one of those was the speed at which SNMP could process requests due to its compact, binary format. While it was in a compact format, searching for which information to act on could take considerable time. Approaches such as those in protocol buffers do not necessarily suffer from either limitation. However, in general, the question one has to ask when comparing these approaches is

---

9. This section was not meant to be a full-blown description of Google protocol buffers; however, we did want to give a sufficient introduction to the material. For additional detailed information, see *https://developers.google.com/protocol-buffers/*.

whether or not the compactness outweighs the ability for humans to quickly inspect and understand the text. One way to help decide is whether or not the format will be used for internal or external APIs. In general, the consensus seems to be that it's a good idea to use binary-encoded APIs only for internally consumed APIs and use human-readable ones (i.e., XML, JSON, etc.) for public-facing ones.

There is a single way of defining a structured data format that then is exchanged and serialized in protocol buffers. This is done by defining a *buffer message type* in a *.proto* file. Each protocol buffer message then represents a logical record of information in this format. Each message then contains a series of name-value pairs using this syntax. Here is a very basic example of a *.proto* file that defines a message containing information for an address book entry:

```
message PersonalRecord {
  required string nameFirst = 1;
  required string nameLast = 2;
  required string streetAddress = 3;
  optional string emailAddress = 3;

  enum PhoneType {
    MOBILE = 0;
    HOME = 1;
    WORK = 2;
     HOME_OFFICE = 3;
  }
  message PhoneNumber {
    required string internationalNumber = 1;
    optional PhoneType type = 2 [default = MOBILE];
  }
  repeated PhoneNumber phone = 4;
}
```

As you can see, the message format is rather straightforward. Each message type has at least one uniquely numbered field, and each field has a name and a value type. Note that value types can be numbers (i.e., integer or floating-point), booleans, strings, raw bytes, or other protocol buffer message types (as in the previous example). These other types allow one to structure data hierarchically, in a manner that allows for customization and flexibility to suit the needs of the application. Optional fields, required fields, and repeated fields can be specified as well, and we showed that in the previous example with the repeated PhoneNumber portion indicating that four entries are repeated.

Once the data structure types and formats are defined, a number of protocol buffer compiler tools are available that can generate source code from these types in order to write and read these. These tools are available for a wide variety of data stream types as well as for a variety of languages, including Java, Python, Perl, and C++. Once messages have been defined, one of the protocol buffer compilers is run for a particular target language. This compiler is fed the *.proto* file or files as input, and that generates data access classes. Part of this process generates access functions for each field (i.e., query()

or set_query()) as well as methods to serialize or parse the already defined data structures to/from raw bytes—so, for instance, if your chosen language is C++, running the compiler on the earlier example will generate a class called PersonalRecord. You can then use this class in your application to populate, serialize, and send and retrieve Person protocol buffer messages.

One very cool feature of protocol buffers is that code that is generated for receiving messages will ignore structures with additional fields not defined in the version of the code compiled. This means that absolute compatibility between sides of the discussion need not be precise. This is allowed because its designers were concerned with server upgrades required as the APIs evolved rapidly and wanted to obviate the need to upgrade all of the servers at once. On a small scale, this might not seem like a big deal, but for a company like Google, upgrading tens of thousands of servers in a short period of time can definitely be an issue.

Getting back to the example, if you examine the newly generated C++ code, you can imagine populating these classes and using them to transmit a message such as the following:

```
PersonalRecord personalRec;
personalRec.set_name("David Blowfish");
personalRec.set_id(420420420420);
personalRec.set_email("blowfish@lovestogrowgrapes.com");
fstream output("someFile", ios::out | ios::binary);
personalRec.SerializeToOstream(&output);
```

To read the message, you would execute the following:

```
fstream input("someFile", ios::in | ios::binary);
PersonalRecord personalRec;
personalRec.ParseFromIstream(&input);
cout << "Name: " << personalRec.name() << endl;
cout << "E-mail: " << personalRec.email() << endl;
```

One of the interesting aspects of protocol buffers is that the format is self-describing—a very desirable feature of APIs used in SDN contexts. This is because those APIs not only can be used to generate code, but also to dynamically interpret the semantics or syntax. This also holds true if modified because the code is generated, meaning that an application can both detect incompatibility and modify itself based on asking about the updated API, and in doing so, suddenly become up to date. In addition to being used for short-lived Remote Procedure Call (RPC) requests, protocol buffers can also be used as a means of defining self-describing data persistent storage.

Protocol buffers are now the preferred choice for data formatting at companies such as Google and a number of other large data center providers where they are used both in RPC systems as well as for persistent storage of data.

Thrift

Thrift[10] is an interface definition language (*http://bit.ly/1cdRzbY*) that is used to define and create services (*http://bit.ly/18MMMdz*) for numerous languages.

Like protocol buffers, it too is used as a remote procedure call (*http://bit.ly/1eb7ep7*) (RPC) framework. Like protocol buffers, Thrift was developed to address the growing needs of a burgeoning application content service provider—Facebook. At the time of its creation, Facebook operated data centers on a massive scale and encountered issues similar to those Google ran into a number of years earlier. Thrift is written in C++, but its compiler can create code for a number of languages. Like protocol buffers, Thrift combines a code generation engine to build services with multiprogramming language support, although in the spirit of Facebook's much more flexible development environment, Thrift supports a very wide variety of generated languages including C++, Erlang, Go, Haskell, Perl, Cappuccino, Python, C#, Perl, Ruby, Smalltalk, Node.js, and PHP.

In April 2007, Facebook donated the project to the Apache Software Foundation, where it continues to be worked on and developed.

As mentioned earlier, Thrift includes a complete software library that can be used to create clients and servers, as well as an RPC mechanism between the two that facilitates communication.

Figure 5-7 shows the functional architecture of a Thrift client and server. The service client and read()/write() code is generated from the Thrift service definition file. This file is fed to the Thrift compiler that then generates client and processor code that is later incorporated into the client and server code. The protocol and transport layer shown in the figure are part of the runtime library that comes as a precompiled library included into the client and server base.

---

10. This section was not meant to be a full-blown description of Thrift; however, we did want to give a sufficient introduction to the material. For additional detailed information, see *http://thrift.apache.org/*.

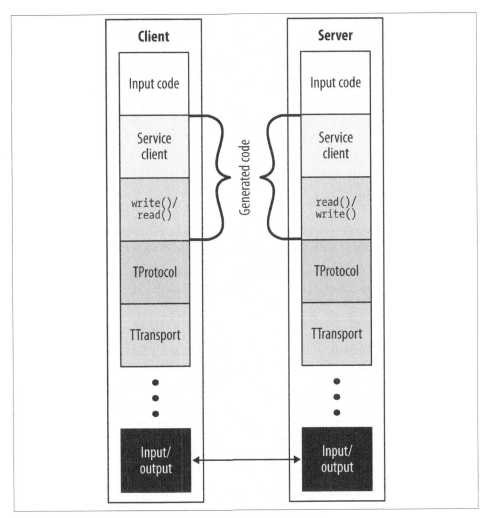

Figure 5-7. The Apache Thrift API client/server architecture

This standard Thrift library includes server infrastructure that is used to handle the underlying I/O calls.

As with Google protocol buffers, in Thrift it is possible to define a service and change the protocol and transport without recompiling the code. This is due to the fact that the code is generated from definition files, as well as the fact that unknown fields are ignored.

Thrift actually supports a number of protocols that can be used to satisfy various application requirements. For example, Thrift supports a protocol called TBinaryProtocol, which is a basic binary format that can be used in cases where the raw textual format is undesirable for performance reasons. Another is the TJSON Protocol that is used to include JSON encoding of data. There are numerous protocols supported (see the references for additional details on these).

This is an example of a Thrift service description file:

```
enum PhoneType {
  HOME,
  WORK,
  MOBILE
}
struct Phone {
  1: i32 id,
  2: string phoneNum,
  3: PhoneType type
}
```

As you can see, this code is quite similar to how structures would be defined in C++, which (for those familiar with that language) should be straightforward.

Thrift will generate the code out of this descriptive information. For instance, in Java, the PhoneType will be a simple enum inside the C++ class Phone.

JSON

JavaScript Object Notation, or JSON as it is more commonly known as, is a lightweight data-interchange format. One of the main appeals of JSON is that being based on XML, it is easy for humans to read and write. At the same time, it is relatively easy for machines to parse and generate. JSON is a text format that is completely language independent but uses conventions that are familiar to programmers of the C-family of languages, including C, C++, C#, Java, JavaScript, Perl, and Python. It is these properties that make JSON a very appealing data-interchange language and one that has proven to be excellent in use for constructing APIs for SDN controllers and applications.

JSON is based around the simple premise of the interaction of two structures: a collection of name/value pairs and an ordered list of values. In various languages this is realized as an *object*, *record*, or *struct*, among others. In most languages, an ordered list of values is treated as an *array*, or *list*. Most modern programming languages support these constructs, although the actual form varies from language to language.

It makes sense that a data format that is interchangeable with programming languages would also be based on these structures. In JSON, the data format takes on these forms.

An object is an unordered set of name/value pairs. An object begins with a { (left brace) and ends with a } (right brace). Each name is followed by a colon (:) and the name/value pairs are separated by a comma (,). The following is an example of a JSON definition:

```
{"menu": {
"header": "SVG Viewer",
"items": [
```

```
            {"id": "Open"},
            {"id": "OpenNew", "label": "Open New"},
            null,
            {"id": "ZoomIn", "label": "Zoom In"},
            {"id": "ZoomOut", "label": "Zoom Out"},
            {"id": "OriginalView", "label": "Original View"},
            null,
            {"id": "Quality"},
            {"id": "Pause"},
            {"id": "Mute"},
            null,
            {"id": "Find", "label": "Find..."},
            {"id": "FindAgain", "label": "Find Again"},
            {"id": "Copy"},
            {"id": "CopyAgain", "label": "Copy Again"},
            {"id": "CopySVG", "label": "Copy SVG"},
            {"id": "ViewSVG", "label": "View SVG"},
            {"id": "ViewSource", "label": "View Source"},
            {"id": "SaveAs", "label": "Save As"},
            null,
            {"id": "Help"},
            {"id": "About", "label": "About Adobe CVG Viewer..."}
        ]
    }}
```

I2RS

About two years ago, a group including Tom Nadeau, Ping Pan, Alia Atlas, and David Ward began thinking about how to standardize programmability concepts such as a northbound interface for a controller, (rapid) programming of devices, and network topology. These were all things that were at the heart of the SDN discussion, yet many definitions, descriptions, and implementations existed of these concepts. In some cases, partial standards existed or were in progress, while in others, the fate of the components lay in the hands of a not-so-open forum.

It was these motivations that hatched a plan to engage this work at the IETF, which was an organization well known for creating high quality and open standards. After much hard work, organizing and writing, we were able to lift the organization off the ground. It now exists at the IETF as the Interface to the Routing System (or I2RS in IETF short-hand lingo).

There are three key aspects at the head of the I2RSL:

- First, the interface is a modern programmatic interface much in the sense that we have been discussing in this chapter (meaning that it is asynchronous and offers fast, interactive access). It should be self-describing and easily consumed and/or manipulated by modern applications and programming methods.

- Second, the I2RS gives access to information and state that is not normally modeled or manipulated by existing implementations or configuration protocols. For example, this might be the active forwarding table of a device.
- Third, the I2RS gives applications the ability to learn additional, structured information, such as topology and events, from a device. This information will be offered in a manner that is filterable in order to support flexibility, scalability and ease of consumption by applications.

When I2RS started out, a survey and examination of existing mechanisms was done to determine feasibility and applicability to a number of use cases. The final contenders were SNMP and NETCONF because both allowed state to be written and read to and from devices but ultimately did not meet all of the key properties given in for I2RS.[11]

For example, the overhead of programming within the SNMP infrastructure is quite high and expensive for modern applications. In addition, many MIBs are not (in definition or practice) implemented in a read-only manner and thus are not suitable for configuration of a device's state.

In the case of NETCONF, it was determined that there is very limited capability to add new application-specific state to be distributed via the routing system. NETCONF possesses many useful traits such as configuration replay, rewind, and verification, but these are time-consuming and are thus not suitable for rapid configuration of devices that might have these things taken care of by an external SDN controller.

Given the nature of not only RIB data but also the potential for high transaction rates in SDN programmatic interfaces, the interface may need to also create ephemeral state in the target. This is a shortcoming in many existing interfaces, including NETCONF. To this end, proposals have come out of the I2RS effort that extend its capability to create and manage ephemeral state).

A few interesting use cases around I2RS are:

Route Control via Indirection
By enabling an application to install routes in the RIB, it is possible that when, for example, BGP resolves its IGP next-hop via the RIB, that could be to an application-installed route. In general, when a route is redistributed from one protocol to another, this is done via the RIB. Such a route could have been installed via the I2RS interface. This is very similar to the PCE-P server example in Chapter 4.

Policy-Based Routing of Unknown Traffic
A static route, installed into the RIB, could direct otherwise unrecognized traffic toward an application, through whatever appropriate tunnel was required, for further handling. Such a static route could be programmed with indirection so that its

---

11. *http://tools.ietf.org/html/draft-atlas-i2rs-problem-statement-00*

outgoing path is whatever is used by another particular route (e.g., to a particular server). This is very similar to the input-traffic detection and associated actions use cases described in Chapter 12.

Services with Fixed Hours

If an application were to provide services only during fixed time-periods, the application could install both a specific route on the local router in the RIB and advertise the associated prefix as being attached to the local router via the IGP. If the application knew the fixed hours, the state so installed could be temporal and automatically removed at approximately the correct time. This is very similar to the bandwidth calendaring example described in Chapter 10.

As we have discussed earlier in this chapter, a number of management interfaces exist today that allow for the indirect programming of the routing system. These include proprietary CLI, NETCONF, and SNMP. However, none of these mechanisms allows for the direct, rapid, and application-friendly programming of the routing system within a device. Such asynchronous interfaces are needed to support dynamic, time-based applications.

These interfaces should cater to how applications typically interact with other applications and network services rather than force them to use older mechanisms that are more complex to understand, implement, and operate. The interfaces should allow applications to have limited, filtered, or abstracted knowledge of the network.

Authorization and authentication are also critical so that the I2RS can be used by a network application that is not completely controlled by the network operator but is, nonetheless, given some access to I2RS.

The I2RS working group is developing standard data models with their associated semantics.

Whereas many routing protocols are standardized, associated data models for them are not yet available. Instead, each router uses different information, mechanisms, and CLI, which makes a standard interface for use by applications extremely cumbersome to develop and maintain.

Well-known data modeling languages, such as YANG,[12] exist, have some in-progress data models, and might be used for defining the necessary data models for I2RS; however, more investigation into alternatives is required. It is understood that some portion (hopefully a small subset) will remain as proprietary extensions; the data models must support future extensions and proprietary extensions.

Since the I2RS will need to support remote access between applications running on a host or server and routers in the network, at least one standard mechanism must be

12. IETF RFC 6020 (*http://datatracker.ietf.org/doc/rfc6020/*)

identified and defined to provide the transfer syntax, as defined by a protocol, used to communicate between the application and the routing system.

Common functionality that I2RS needs to support includes acknowledgements, notifications, and request-reserve-commit.

Work in the I2RS Working Group around defining appropriate candidate protocols is underway. Protocols that are chosen should ideally not require that applications understand and implement existing routing protocols to interact with I2RS. These interfaces should instead be based on lightweight, rapidly deployable approaches; technology approaches must be evaluated, but examples could include ReSTful web services, JSON, XMPP, and XML. These interfaces should possess self-describing attributes (e.g., a web services interface) so that applications can quickly query and learn about the active capabilities of a device. It may be desirable to also define the local syntax (e.g., programming language APIs) that applications running local to a router can use.

Since evolution is anticipated in I2RS over time, it is important that versioning and backward compatibility are basic supported functionality. Similarly, common, consistent error-handling and acknowledgement mechanisms are required that do not severely limit the scalability and responsiveness of these interfaces.

Since the I2RS effort is relatively nascent, we will only speculate that the effort has seen some success in rallying the community to begin to define the interfaces and other elements required to satisfy its lofty goals. Whether they are achievable or not, only time will tell.

Modern Orchestration

In recent years, the need to orchestrate a number of key elements of not only networks, but also data centers, has arisen. In particular, the need to motivate and monitor storage, compute, and storage within these deployment scenarios is a key requirement in order to achieve the fastest, cheapest, and most optimized deployments. In the past, these things were either done manually or with traditional management systems that were relatively slow and clunky. In order to achieve these things, a few rather parallel efforts have continued in order to define not only standards, but also more importantly *de facto* standards based on deployed, open source code that was used in production data center environments such as Yahoo, Bloomberg, Rackspace, and others.

From an SDN perspective, the network-activation APIs from these efforts represents a subset of the capabilities of the API of an SDN controller (largely because of their focus on a specific application).

OpenStack

OpenStack[13] is a global collaboration whose aim is to produce the open standard cloud operating system for both public and private clouds. OpenStack is a freely available, Apache-licensed software system that can be used to build massively scalable cloud environments.

OpenStack currently consists of many software projects (in addition to the Common Project that binds them)—see Figure 5-8: OpenStack Compute (code-named Nova), OpenStack Object Storage (code-named Swift and Cinder), OpenStack Networking (code-named Quantum), OpenStack Image Service (code-named Glance), OpenStack Identity (code-named Keystone), and OpenStack Dashboard (code-named Horizon).

These projects deliver a pluggable and extendable framework that forms an open source operating system for public and private clouds.

The OpenStack system has grown in popularity over the past year due to its tight integration with the most popular hypervisors in the industry. For example, support includes ESX, Hyper-V, KVM, LXC, QEMU, UML, Xen, and XenServer.

Nova is open source software designed to provision and manage large networks of virtual machines, creating a redundant and scalable cloud-computing platform. This project represents what most people envision when they imagine what Open Stack does. The software provides control panels and APIs required to orchestrate a cloud. This includes running virtual machine instances, managing networks, and accessing control for both users and groups (i.e., projects). OpenStack Compute is hardware and hypervisor agnostic in theory, although actual builds and support is limited largely to the most popular server platforms.

---

13. *http://www.openstack.org/*

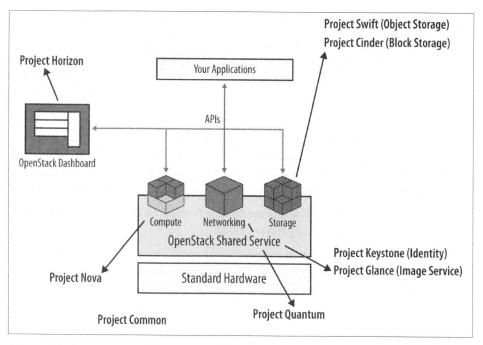

Figure 5-8. Components of the OpenStack architecture

Swift and Cinder is open source software for creating redundant, scalable data storage using clusters of standard servers to store multiple blocks of accessible data. It is not a filesystem or real-time data system, but rather a long-term storage system for large amounts of static data that can be retrieved or updated. Object Storage uses a distributed architecture in order to not have a central point of failure. This also affords the user greater flexibility of deployment options, as well as the obvious scalability, redundancy, and performance.

Glance provides discovery, registration, and delivery services for virtual disk images. The Image Service API server provides a well-defined RESTful web services interface for querying information about virtual disk images. These disk images may be stored in a variety of backend stores, including OpenStack Object Storage. Clients can register new virtual disk images with the Image Service, query for information on publicly available disk images, and use the Image Service's client library for streaming virtual disk images. These images can then be referenced later much in the way a menu of dishes can be made available to a diner in a restaurant.

Figures 5-9 and 5-10 demonstrate how each of the three components of OpenStack exists first before an image is launched (i.e., invoked via a hypervisor) and attached to virtual storage, and then later once an image is invoked.

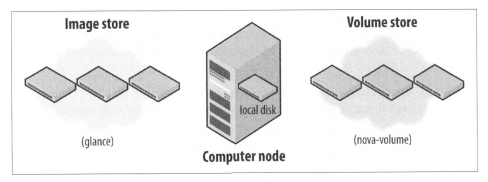

Figure 5-9. Each of the three major components of OpenStack representing storage, compute, and image management

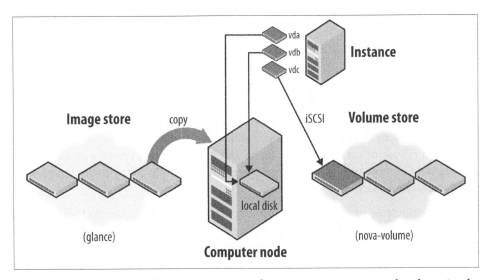

Figure 5-10. Each of the three components after an instance creation has been implemented using one of the cataloged images

Nova will not configure physical network interfaces but will automatically create all virtual network bridges (e.g., br100) and VM virtual interfaces (through the nova-network subset of functions).

Nova assigns a private IP address to each VM instance it deploys. This address is then attached to the Linux Bridge via the nova-network API and then (potentially) to a NAT function that allows the virtual interfaces to connect to the outside network through the physical interface. The network controller with nova-network provides virtual networks to enable compute servers to interact with one another and with the public network.

Currently, Nova (nova-network) supports three kinds of networks, implemented in three Network Manager types: Flat Network Manager, Flat DHCP Network Manager, and the VLAN Network Manager. The three kinds of networks can coexist in a cloud system.

Nova will automatically create all network bridges (i.e., br100) and VM virtual interfaces. All physical machines must have a public and internal network interface.

Quantum provides the API that builds required network connectivity between OpenStack physical nodes (i.e., between the vNICs managed by Openstack Nova—providing them network as a service functionality).

This makes the Quantum API most pertinent to the discussion of SDN and network programmability, though it should be noted that (because of its focus on the delivery of primitives required by a single application—orchestration) the Quantum API is a subset of the capabilities that could be exposed through the northbound API of most SDN controllers/frameworks/systems.

Quantum is targeted at the creation of advanced virtual topologies and services like the commonly used layer 2-in-layer 3 overlay that is used in larger deployments to skirt the limits of traditional VLAN-based deployments. That is, Quantum seeks to decouple *service specification APIs (what)* from *service implementation (how)*, exploiting a capabilities-rich, underlying topology consisting of virtual and physical systems. Openstack functionality is deployed via plug-ins that may be distributed as part of the public Quantum release or privately. The plug-in architecture allows vendors to support the standard API in the configuration of a network service while hiding their own backend implementation specifics.

The current release of the API (version 2.0) provides simple L2 connectivity via 7-10 plug-ins. The plug-ins follow a single-service/single-device model that makes supporting a multivendor vSwitch environment problematic. For example, separate plug-ins exist for Cisco Nexxus, OVS, and Linux Bridge. Similarly, separate plug-ins exist for both the Ryu and NEC OpenFlow controllers (and others, as shown in Chapter 4). Additionally, physical devices are typically managed manually, out of band (though a growing number of network element providers are providing their own plug-ins). In version 2.0, the term "network" has two implicit semantics: grouping of ports and service (layer 2 connectivity) and service given to ports (working on the assumption that the only reason to group ports was to provide them network layer 2 connectivity).

The elements of version 2.0 are network (connectivity service), subnet (policy) and port (tenant endpoint). Version 3.0 of the Quantum API (known as Grizzly) is in its proposal stage. Proposals include the addition of layer 3 network APIs (e.g., VPN), the addition of network service APIs (e.g., security, load balancing), and potentially a move toward a multiservice/multivendor plug-in model. See Figure 5-11 for a sketch of the differences between elements/relationships in Quantum version 2.0 and Quantum version 3.0.

Another 3.0 proposal decouples grouping and connectivity service semantics. The elements in 3.0 would include connectivity service (layer 2 domain, layer 3 domain), group, policy (subnet, securityPolicy, fIPPolicy, lbPolicy, and qosPolicy), rule(s) that define the policy, and a new endpoint abstraction that is either a consumer (or provider) endpoint or ports, VMs, and vApps.

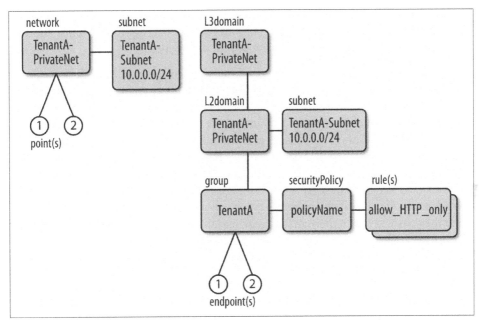

Figure 5-11. The elements and relationships of Quantum version 2.0 (left) and the proposed elements and relationships of Quantum version 3.0 (right)

CloudStack

CloudStack[14] is a Cloud Orchestration platform that pools computing resources to build public, private, and hybrid Infrastructure as a Service (IaaS) clouds. CloudStack is very similar to OpenStack in that it manages the network, storage, and compute nodes that make up a cloud infrastructure. A CloudStack cloud has a hierarchical structure that enables it to scale to manage large numbers of physical servers, all from a single management interface.

The CloudStack architecture is comprised of some basic elements: pods, clusters, and secondary and primary storage. A pod is hardware that has been configured to form clusters. A pod is most usually a data center rack containing one or more clusters and

---

14. *http://cloudstack.apache.org/*

connectivity to a layer 2 switch that is shared by all clusters in that pod. It is important in the CloudStack architecture that end users are unaware of and have no visibility of pods. This preserves the illusion of multitenancy and provides an element of security for both the hosting provider, as well as any other tenants in the data center. A cluster is a group of identical hosts running a common hypervisor. For example, a cluster could be a VMware cluster pre-configured in vCenter. Each cluster has a dedicated primary storage device. This storage device is where the virtual machine instances are hosted and launched from. With multiple hosts within a cluster, high availability and load balancing are standard features of a CloudStack deployment.

An availability zone is the largest organizational unit within a CloudStack environment and is shown in the Figure 5-12. A data center will usually contain a single zone but may contain more than one. By structuring CloudStack into geographical zones, virtual instances and data storage can be placed in specific locations in order to comply with an organization's data storage policies for performance or geographical optimization. This can also be utilized for regulatory compliance reasons where storage/compute must be kept within a certain geographical boundary. An availability zone consists of at least one pod and secondary storage, which is shared by all pods in the zone. Zones are visible to end users. This is important because this is how users are allowed to choose which zone they wish to create their virtual instances in. A public zone is visible to all users, but private zones can also be created that are then only available to members of a particular domain and its associated subdomains. This is in fact, how multitenancy can be implemented using CloudStack.

The secondary storage system is used to store virtual machine templates, ISO images, and snapshots. These are used later to launch instances of VMs. The storage is available to all pods in a zone. Storage can also be replicated between availability zones, thereby providing a common storage platform throughout the whole cloud. This can also be automated.

Primary storage is unique to each cluster and is used to host the virtual machine instances. Since primary storage is a critical component, it is often built on high-performance hardware with multiple high-speed disks that afford the system an element of both redundancy and higher-performance.

Secondary storage uses the Network File System (NFS). NFS is a widely deployed filesystem with built-in networking capabilities, thus any host in the zone can access CloudStack storage.

CloudStack is designed to work with all standards-compliant iSCSI and NFS Servers supported by any of the supported hypervisors.

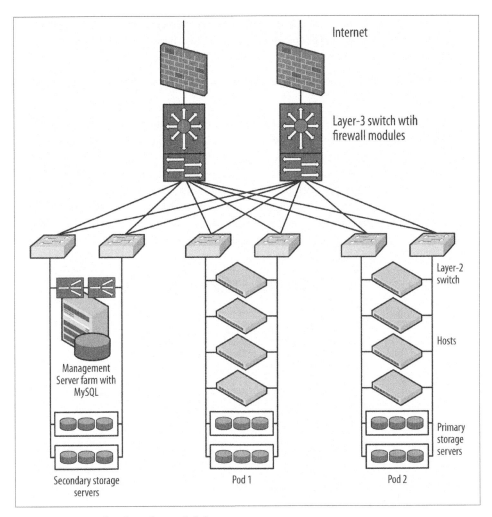

Figure 5-12. A CloudStack availability zone

Puppet

Puppet[15] is one of a group of IT automation software tools (commonly referred to as DevOps tools[16]) that help system administrators manage infrastructure throughout its lifecycle, from provisioning and configuration to patch management and compliance.

---

15. *https://puppetlabs.com/*

16. We chose Puppet to illustrate the capability of DevOps configuration tools in the discussion of network programmability. There are many other optional sources of software for the similar functionality, including Chef, Ganglia, and urban{code}. There is also an extended tool chain available (additional software modules from additional repositories), including applications for monitoring, logging and other functions.

See Figure 5-13 for a sketch of the Puppet DevOps management cycle. Puppet allows IT administrators to automate repetitive tasks, quickly deploy critical applications, and proactively manage change servers.

While Puppet is available as both open source, it is also available in a variety of commercial enterprise versions.

Puppet uses a declarative, model-based approach to IT automation. This language allows an IT administrator to easily define the desired state of the infrastructure's configuration using Puppet's declarative configuration language. It allows an administrator to simulate configuration changes before enforcing them. It enables the enforcement of the desired state of deployed infrastructure automatically. Administrators can use this to correcting any configuration changes as well. Finally, Puppet provides reports for an administrator that can then be used to detect differences between actual and desired states and any changes made to enforce the desired state of infrastructure.

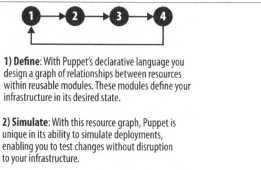

1) Define: With Puppet's declarative language you design a graph of relationships between resources within reusable modules. These modules define your infrastructure in its desired state.

2) Simulate: With this resource graph, Puppet is unique in its ability to simulate deployments, enabling you to test changes without disruption to your infrastructure.

3) Enforce: Puppet compares your system to the desired state as you define it, and automatically enforces it to the desired state ensuring your system is in compliance.

4) Report: Puppet Dashboard reports track relationships between components and all changes, allowing you to keep up with security and compliance mandates. And with the open API you can integrate Puppet with third party monitoring tools.

Figure 5-13. Puppet DevOps high-level management cycle

To define an infrastructure's desired state, one first selects from pre-built, freely downloadable configuration modules, or by building custom modules using Puppet's configuration language. Once defined, these configurations can be used across physical, virtual, and cloud environments as well as across operating systems to manage and orchestrate infrastructure components. It is also possible to combine or mix and match configuration modules in order to create complete application configuration stacks.

These stacks can be useful, for example, when integrated into infrastructure management applications, or in some cases, SDN controllers.

Once configured, the Puppet agent on each infrastructure node communicates regularly with the Puppet master server to automatically inform it of its state. The Puppet master can then choose to enforce the desired states of the nodes by instructing them to do so, or simply monitor and report their deviations from the expected configurations. The Puppet agent on the node sends what the Puppet architecture calls *facts* or data about the node's state back to the Puppet master server. This is done at regular intervals, or based on an event occurring. Using these facts, the Puppet master server compiles what is referred to as a *catalog*, or a detailed data set about how the node should be configured. This information is periodically sent back to the Puppet agent. See Figure 5-14 for a sketch of the Puppet configuration/provisioning cycle.

After making changes to return to the desired state, the Puppet agent sends a complete report back to the Puppet master. The reports are fully accessible via open APIs for integration with other IT systems. It should be noted that these reports could be executed in what is referred to as no-op mode, which allows an administrator to simulate changes without actually making changes to the network elements. This makes Puppet an important "what if?" scenario testing tool, as well as a planning tool.

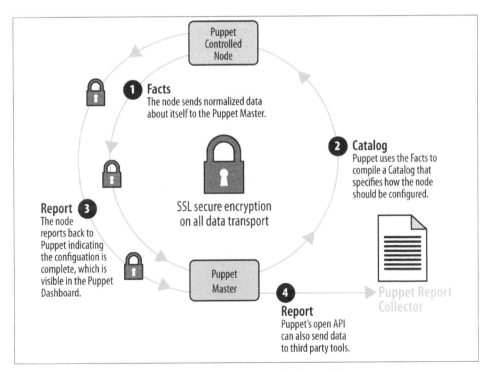

Figure 5-14. Puppet configuration/provisioning cycle (specific)

Conclusions

This chapter introduced the concept of *network programmability* as one of the key features or aspects of software-defined networks that truly differentiates it from what many might think of as just another form of network management.

We introduced the concept of programmability and showed how it can exist in network devices, controllers and software components as a key to how these elements interact with one another. Making a device easily programmable requires that we first create some sort of bidirectional communications channel between it and the other piece of software communicating with it—controllers or applications communicating with controllers.

We then introduced the concept of a tightly coupled feedback loop between these elements. We showed why this concept differs from the traditional network management paradigm that traditionally focused on a simple agent and manager model.

SDN thrives on having multiple managers, agents, and controllers, all interacting in a symphony of tightly coupled communication in order to achieve optimizations and abilities not possible with the old model.

In order to realize this new paradigm of communication and interaction, tightly coupled, bidirectional streaming interfaces are needed. We showed why these interfaces also need to be readily and rapidly implemented in software so as to encourage their use and ubiquitous deployment. These interfaces have been commonly referred to as *application friendly* and represent how modern applications are built today. Some of this was actually introduced in Chapter 4, but was expanded here to give fuller detail of how this is achieved. We'll take another look at it again in Chapter 9.

We then described a number of programmatic and streaming interfaces in detail, including JSON, Google buffers, Thrift, and more recently the work in the IETF's I2RS working group.

We concluded the chapter with a discussion of orchestration interfaces such as Open Stack, Open Cloud, and Puppet. These too are ultimately another form of programmability.

CHAPTER 6

Data Center Concepts and Constructs

Introduction

Prior to the existence of data centers, computing, storage, and the networks that interconnected them existed on the desktop PCs of enterprise users. As data storage grew, along with the need for collaboration, departmental servers were installed and served this purpose. However, they provided services that were dedicated only to local or limited use. As time went on, the departmental servers could not handle the growing load or the widespread collaborative needs of users and were migrated into a more centralized data center. Data centers facilitated an ease of hardware and software management and maintenance and could be more easily shared by *all* of the enterprise's users.

Modern data centers were originally created to physically separate traditional computing elements (e.g., PC servers), their associated storage (i.e., storage area networks or SANs) and the networks that interconnected them with client users. The computing power that existed in these types of data centers became focused on specific server functionality, such as running applications that included mail servers, database servers, or other enterprise IT applications.

It was around 10 years ago that an interesting transformation took place. A company called VMware had invented an interesting technology that allowed a host operating system, such as one of the popular Linux distributions, to execute one or more client operating systems (e.g., Windows) as if they were just another piece of software. What VMware did was to create a small program that created a virtual environment that synthesized a real computing environment (e.g., virtual NIC, BIOS, sound adapter, and video). It then marshaled real resources between the virtual machines. This supervisory program was called a *hypervisor*. This changed *everything* in the IT world, as it now meant that server software could be deployed in a very fluid manner and also could better utilize available hardware platforms instead of being dedicated to a single piece of hardware. This is shown in Figure 6-1.

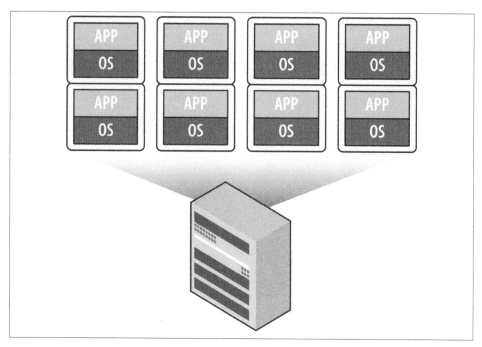

Figure 6-1. Virtualized applications running on a single bare-metal server as virtual machines

With further advances and increases in memory, computing, and storage, data center servers were increasingly capable of executing a variety of operating systems simultaneously in a virtual environment. Operating systems such as Windows Server that previously occupied an entire bare metal machine were now executed as virtual machines, each running whatever applications client users demanded. Moreover, network administrators now had the option to locate that computing power based not on physical machine availability. They could instead dynamically grow and shrink it as resource demands changed. Thus began the age of *elastic computing*.

Within the elastic computing environment, operations departments were able to move servers to any physical data center location simply by pausing a virtual machine and copying a file across their network to a new physical computing location (i.e., server). They could even spin up new virtual machines simply by cloning the same file and telling the hypervisor, either locally or on some distant machine, to execute it as a new instance of the same service, thus expanding that resource. If the resource was no longer needed or demand waned, server instances could be shut down or even just deleted. This flexibility allowed network operators to start optimizing the data center resource location and thus utilization based on metrics such as power and cooling. By using bin packing techniques, virtual machines could be tightly mapped onto physical machines, thus optimizing for different characteristics such as locality of network between these servers, or as a means of even shutting down unused physical machines to save on power or cooling. In fact, this is how many modern data centers optimize for virtual machine placement because their dominating cost factors are power and cooling. In these cases, an operator can turn down (or off) cooling an entire portion of a data center. Similarly, an operator could move or dynamically expand computing, storage, or network resources by geographical demand. Figure 6-2 shows a modern data center.

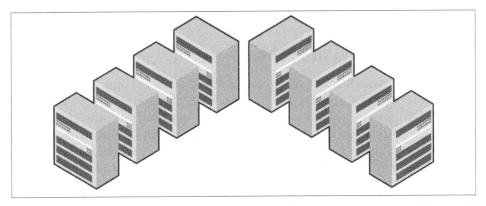

Figure 6-2. A modern data center comprised of compute, storage, and network resources

As with all advances in technology, this newly discovered flexibility in operational deployment of computing, storage, and networking resources brought about a new problem: one of operational efficiency both in terms of maximizing the utilization of storage and computing power and in terms of power and cooling. As mentioned earlier, network operators began to realize that computing power demand in general increased over time. To keep up with this demand, IT departments (which typically budget on a yearly basis) would order all the equipment they predicted would be needed for the following year. However, once this equipment arrived and was placed in racks, it would consume power, cooling and space resources—even if it was not used for many months.

The general consensus is that this was first discovered at Amazon. At the time, Amazon's business was growing at a break-neck rate—doubling every six to nine months. For a while its compute, storage, and network resources could not keep up with the growing demand placed on the company by its online ordering, warehouse, and internal IT systems. For a while, Amazon tried to get ahead of this demand using the old method of prepurchasing a lot of equipment, but ran into the same problems others did in that this equipment would have to be purchased so far in advance that it would in fact sit idle for a significant amount of time. At this point, Amazon realized that while growth had to stay ahead of demand for computing services, it needed to be tailored to be available just in time for their services to use. This is when the idea of Amazon Web

Services (AWS) was hatched. Basically the idea was to still preorder capacity in terms of storage, compute, and network, but instead of leaving it idle, the company realized that it could leverage elastic computing principles to sell unused resource pool so that it would be utilized at a rate closer to 100%. When internal resources needed more resources, they would simply push off retail users, and when they were not, retail compute users could use up the unused resources. Some call this elastic computing services —this book calls it *hyper virtualization* due to the fact that most large data centers do this on quite a massive scale and because the virtualization is so pervasive that this concept is used for storage, computing, and storage resources *simultaneously*.

The Multitenant Data Center

One key thing to notice in the Amazon AWS model is that not only is Amazon virtualizing its services, but in terms of access controls and resources management, it also now needs a different paradigm—by letting external users into its network, it has just created a *multitenant* data center environment. This of course created a new problem: how to separate potentially thousands of tenants, whose resources need to be spread arbitrarily across different physical data centers' virtual machines while giving them all ubiquitous and private Internet access to their slice of the AWS cloud? Figure 6-3 illustrates this concept.

Another way to observe this dilemma is to note that during the move to hyper virtualized environments, execution environments were generally run by a single enterprise or organization. That is, they typically owned and operated all of the computing and storage (although some rented co-location space) as if they were a single, flat, local area network (LAN) interconnecting a large number of virtual or physical machines and network attached storage. The exception was in financial institutions, where regulatory requirements mandated separation. However, the number of departments (or tenants) in these cases was relatively small—on the order of fewer than 100. These departments also were addressed using the same, private network IP address space. This was easily solved using existing tools at the time such as MPLS layer 2 or layer 3 VPNs. In both cases though, the network components that linked all of the computing and storage resources up until now were rather simplistic: it was generally a flat Ethernet LAN that connected all of the physical and virtual machines. Most of these environments assigned IP addresses to all of the devices (virtual or physical) in the network from a single network (perhaps with IP subnets), as a single enterprise owned the machines and needed access to them. This also meant that it was also generally not a problem moving virtual machines between different data centers located within that enterprise because, again, they all fell within the same routed domain and could reach each other regardless of physical location.

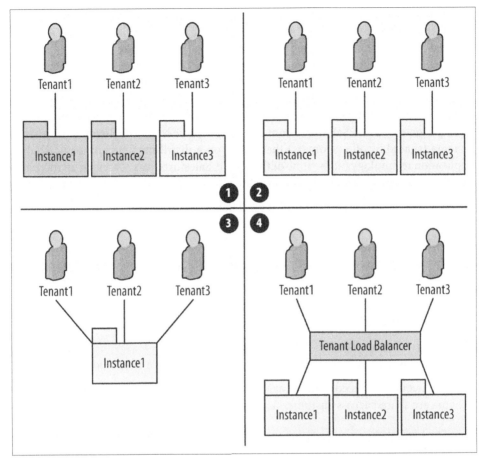

Figure 6-3. Multitenant data center concept; in multitenant data centers, users must have access to virtual slices of compute, storage, and network resources that are kept private from other tenants

The concept of a tenant can mean different things in different circumstances. In a service provider data center providing public cloud services, it means being a customer. In an enterprise data center implementing a private cloud solution, it can mean a department (which can be viewed as an internal customer). Multitenancy is different than multiuser or multienterprise, though not mutually exclusive of these terms. Tenancy occurs above the user or enterprise boundary. Multitenancy is common in both public and private clouds and not limited solely to Infrastructure as a Service (IaaS) data center offerings.

In 2008, when cloud computing was becoming a phenomenon, a blog by Phil Waine-wright[1] attempted to define the nuances within the term "multitenancy" as an architectural consideration established at the application layer. A tenant is a user of a shared application environment or (to the point of the blog) some subset of that environment. In the original posting, the differences in the definition of multitenancy were defined as the *degree of multitenancy*. This concept revolved around how much of the application is shared—down to the database, where the schema defines the database structure. The example given was of Salesforce.com (*http://salesforce.com*)'s deployment of a single schema (shared by all customers) that scaled on a distributed system using database replication technology (at the time of the article, Salesforce was achieving an incredible 1:5000 database instance-to-customer ratio[2]).

By 2012, this idea was revisited, and several notable cloud architects were mapping the degree to common data center application/service archetypes (see Figure 6-4):

Infrastructure as a service (IaaS)
Infrastructure (compute, storage, and network) are shared. Exemplified by Amazon.

Platform as a service (PaaS)
An application development environment is shared. Exemplified by Google Apps.

Software as a service (SaaS)
An application is shared. Exemplified by Salesforce.com (*http://salesforce.com*).

The architects introduced a second axis of multitenancy (other than the degree to which schema are shared across customers). In this model:

- The highest degree of multitenancy occurs in the IaaS and PaaS aspects of the data center service–offering hierarchy.

- The overall highest degree of multitenancy occurs when all three aspects of the service offering, including SaaS, are fully multitenant.

- A middle-degree of multitenancy may be seen when IaaS and PaaS are multitenant but SaaS is multitenant in physical clusters or for various subcomponents of SaaS.

- The lowest degree of multitenancy occurs when SaaS is single tenant.

These degrees describe the tightness of coupling application components and the network and security architectures required to support them—important dependencies related to movement of either a single VM or the distributed-but-dependent collection

---

1. *http://www.zdnet.com/blog/saas/many-degrees-of-multi-tenancy/533*

2. The schema-sharing degree comparison also included a second-degree example (Intaact, which had a 1:250 schema/customer ratio) and a lesser-degree example, which was the Oracle pod architecture (that the author labels "the abandonment of the shared schema principle").

of application/service components, that is, important to VM mobility—the poster child of SDN applications.

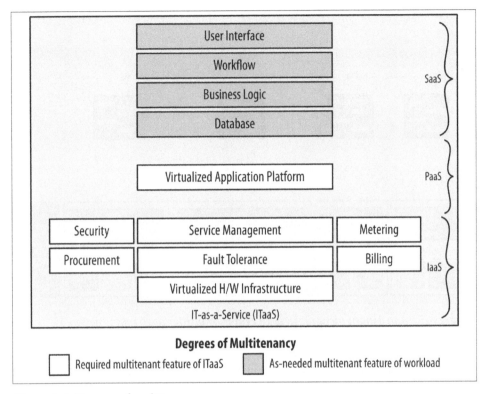

Figure 6-4. Degrees of multitenancy

In this chapter, we will explore the basic concepts behind the multitenant data center, associated architecture, and the potential control plane solutions vying to become standards for SDN in the data center.

The Virtualized Multitenant Data Center

The virtualized multitenant data center allows multiple tenants to be hosted in a data center while offering them private access to virtual slices of resources. The data center network may be a multitier network. Although the first designs started with a two-layer, spine-and-leaf design, additional growth has caused the appearance of a third, aggregation tier, as shown in Figure 6-5. The data center may also be a single-tier network (e.g., Juniper's Q-Fabric), as shown in Figure 6-6.

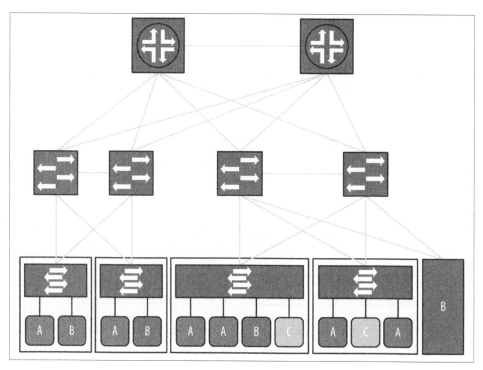

Figure 6-5. Multitenant virtualized data center (multitier data center network)

Generally, each tenant corresponds to a set of virtual machines, which are hosted on servers running hypervisors. The hypervisors contain virtual switches (vSwitches) to connect the virtual machines to the physical network and to one another. Applications may also run on a bare-metal server. That is, they are not run in a virtual machine but are instead executed on an entire machine dedicated to that application, as shown in the B server in the lower right corner of Figure 6-6.

Servers are interconnected using a physical network, which is typically a high-speed Ethernet network, although there exist variations where optical rings are used. In Figure 6-5, the network is depicted as a two-tier (access, core) layer 2 network. It could also be a three-tier (access, aggregation, core) layer 2 network, or a one-tier (e.g., Q-Fabric) layer 2 network. For overlay solutions, the data center network could also be a layer 3 network (IP, GRE, or MPLS).

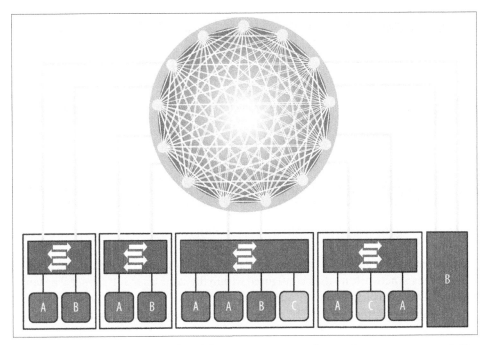

Figure 6-6. Multitenant virtualized data center as a single-tier data center network (Juniper's Q-Fabric)

Each tenant is assigned a private network, as shown in Figure 6-7. The tenant's network allows each service instance to communicate with all of the other instances of the same tenant, subject to policy restrictions. In reality, this means that each physical or virtual machine hosting the service must have network access either via layer 3 or layer 2 to the other machines in its logical tenant grouping. The tenant networks are isolated from one another: a virtual machine of one tenant is not able to communicate with a virtual machine of another tenant unless specifically allowed by policy.

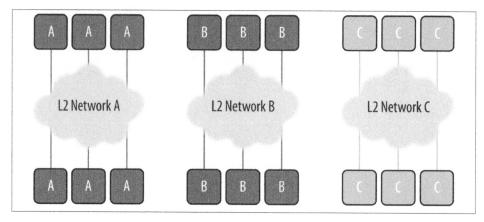

Figure 6-7. Logical network abstraction as presented to tenants

The tenant private networks are generally layer 2 networks, and all virtual machines on a given tenant network are then configured within the same layer 3 IP subnet. The tenant may be allowed to pick his own IP address for the VMs, or the cloud provider may assign the IP addresses. Either way, the IP addresses may not be unique across tenants (i.e., the same IP address may be used by two VMs of two different tenants). In these cases, some network address scheme (NAT) must be employed if those tenants are allowed to speak to each other or others outside of that network (such as public Internet access to the services).

A single tenant may have multiple networks, for example, for the purpose of implementing security zones, for combining multiple departments together such as in a case where IaaS is in use, or when multiple cloud providers are being utilized to host their services. Figure 6-8 illustrates how multiple cloud providers are attached to an enterprise's local data center in order to extend their data center, thereby providing elastic cloud services. The advantages of this configuration include redundancy, use of the cheapest cloud providers resources (much like consuming electricity from multiple providers is done), or simply to provide geographic coverage for services deployed over a wide geographic span.

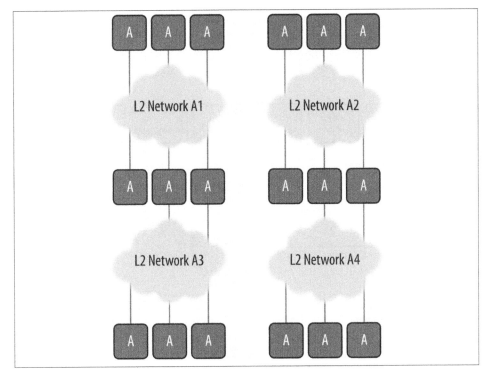

Figure 6-8. Multiple networks for a tenant enterprise; tenant cloud networks A1, A2, A3, and A4 span multiple geographic and logical service providers to weave together a consistent yet virtual service offering for customer A

Orchestration

One important aspect of a virtualized multitenant data center solution is *orchestration*. In order for a service provider to deploy and otherwise manage a multitenant data center solution, it must implement some form of logically centralized orchestration. Orchestration in a data center provides the logically centralized control and interaction point for network operators and is a central point of control of other network controllers. At a high level, the orchestration layer provides the capability of:

- Adding and removing tenants
- Billing system interface after provisioning operations are executed
- Workflow automation
- Adding and removing virtual machines to and from tenants
- Specifying the bandwidth, quality of service, and security attributes of a tenant network

This orchestration layer must cover all aspects of the data center that include interfacing with compute, storage, network, and storage systems or controllers. And it must do so at a high rate of change to support true elastic compute services, as demonstrated in Figure 6-9.

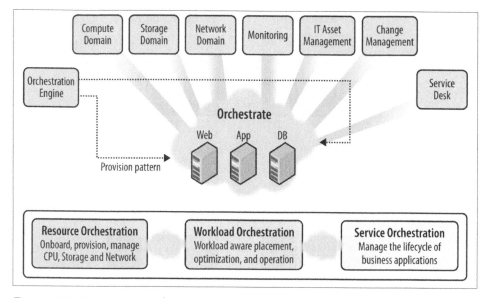

Figure 6-9. Data center orchestration engine example; orchestration in a data center provides the logically centralized control and interaction point for network operators and is a central point of control of other network controllers

Connecting a Tenant to the Internet/VPN

Data center tenants are typically connected to the Internet or the tenant's enterprise network via some VPN, as shown in Figure 6-10. The VPN can be a L3 MPLS VPN, a L2 MPLS VPN, an SSL VPN, an IPsec VPN, or some other type of VPN. The actual type of VPN has different pros and cons and also depends on which underlay network is employed in the data center (such as Ethernet, VLANs, stacked VLANs, VxLAN, and MPLS). The various types of underlays and network overlays will be discussed in detail later in this chapter.

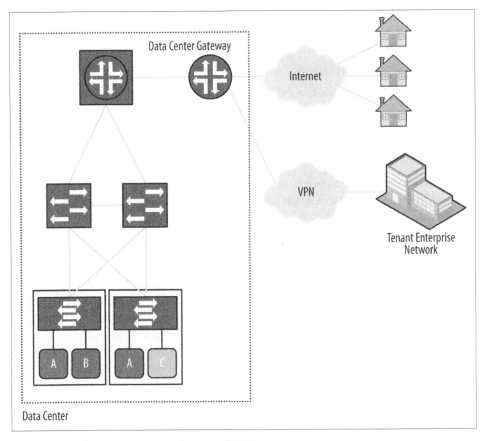

Figure 6-10. Connect tenant to Internet/VPN

The data center gateway function is responsible for connecting the tenant networks to the Internet, other VPN sites, or both, as shown in Figure 6-10. Note that multiple gateways may be employed, depending on the network architecture employed. While it is still typical to deploy physical devices as gateways, it is also perfectly viable to implement the gateway function in software as a virtualized service. We discuss this more in Chapter 7.

Virtual Machine Migration and Elasticity

Virtual machine (VM) migration is the act of moving a VM from one compute server to another server. This includes cases where it is running but can also include dormant, paused, or shutdown states of a VM. In most cases, the operation involves what ultimately is a file copy between servers or storage arrays close to the new computing resource (but proximity does not have to be the case).

The motivations for VM migration include:

- Data center maintenance
- Workload balance/rebalance/capacity expansion (including power management)
- Data center migration, consolidation or expansion
- Disaster avoidance/recovery
- Geographic locality (i.e., moving access to a service closer to users to improve their experience)

Given the earlier definition of tenancy and the concept of the degree of tenancy, the idea that migration is limited to a single server instance is the simplest case to illustrate. In some cases, the application may be multitier and represented by a tightly coupled ensemble of VMs and network elements. Migration of a single VM in this context could lead to performance and bandwidth problems. The operator and/or orchestration system needs to be aware of the dependencies of the ensemble. However, in other cases, where there is a loose coupling of the various layers of an application (i.e., compute, frontend load-balancer/web-services, and a backend distributed database), much as applications written to take advantage of Hadoop or other granular process distribution architectures, VM migration—or more commonly, destruction and creation, usually only has beneficial effects on the service. In these cases, live VM migration is typically not employed. The three-tiered architecture is shown in Figure 6-11. In the three-tiered architecture, a single VM is required to implement each of the three layers of the system, but more component VMs can be spun-up at any time to execute either locally on the same compute server or remotely in order to expand or contract computing resources. Seamless job process distribution is handled by technologies such as Hadoop, which enables this granular and elastic computing paradigm while seamless, easily scalable, and highly resilient backend database functionality is handled by technologies such as Cassandra.

There is still some debate about how frequently live migration might occur between data centers as a DCI use case. The reasoning is that in order for any migration to take place, a file copy of the active VM to a new compute server must be performed, and while a VM is being copied, it cannot be running, or the file would change out from under the copy operation. Hence this operation is becoming less and less common in practice. Instead, moving to a three-tiered application architecture where the norm is to create and destroy machines is far simpler (and safer).

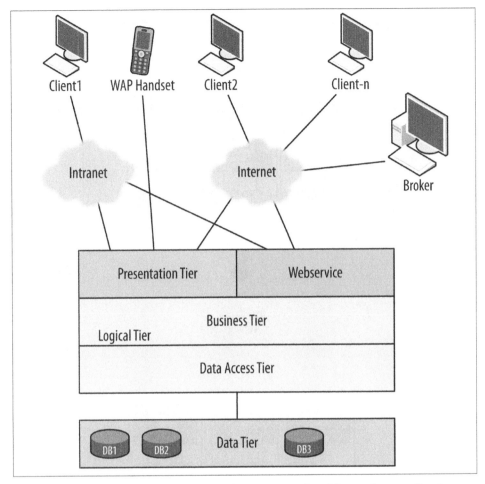

Figure 6-11. Three-tiered application architecture employed by modern applications

Figure 6-12 demonstrates a VM move between two compute servers. If the two servers are in the same data center, it is an *intra data center* VM migration requiring a simple point-to-point file copy of the VM file after pausing the VM. If the two servers are in different data centers, it is referred to as an *inter data center* VM migration and still requires a file copy between two IP end points but may require that file transfer to traverse a much more complex and lengthy network path. Based on this, and remembering the discussion regarding live VM moves, in order for the VM to remain live during the file transfer, the network must continue running throughout the migration, and all sessions (e.g., TCP connection) must remain up. This is a bit of wizardry handled by the hypervisor system that manages the VMs and the VM move.

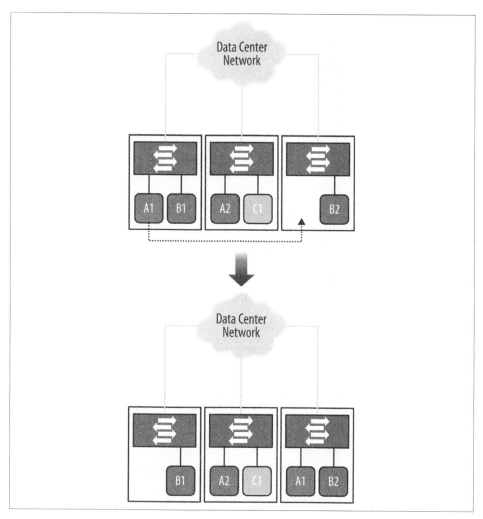

Figure 6-12. VM migration

Further complicating the situation is that in many cases, the MAC address *and* the IP address of the VM must remain unchanged, as well as any configuration state related to the VM, in order to facilitate a seamless move. This includes other network-related items such as QoS configuration, ACLs, firewall rules, and security policies. All of these things must be migrated to the new server and/or access switch. This also includes any runtime state inside the VM itself and in the vSwitch. In addition, the switches in the physical network must be promptly updated to reflect the new position of the VM. This includes MAC tables, ARP tables, and multicast group membership tables. It is for these complications that it is far easier to employ the three-tiered application design pattern and simply create and destroy component VMs.

The VM migration can be implemented in one of three ways:

Network Data-plane driven approach
VM migration can be detected through the supporting network devices monitoring network traffic to and from the VM (for example, detection of gratuitous ARP messages).

Hypervisor driven approach
The component inside the hypervisor (the vSwitch or the vGW) uses introspection to detect the VM migration. One way to do this is by virtue of the old hypervisor detecting that the VM is gone while the new hypervisor detects the VM has appeared.

Orchestrator driven approach
The VM migration is not detected at runtime a priori; instead, the orchestrator explicitly triggers the movement of runtime state before it performs the VM migration.

The runtime state can be updated in one of two ways:

Data-plane driven approach
The VM sends some traffic to force the runtime state to be updated. For example, the VM can broadcast a gratuitous ARP to force all MAC tables in the tenant network to be updated with the new location of the VM's MAC address.

Orchestrator or control-plane driven approach
The orchestrator uses a control-plane signaling protocol to explicitly update the runtime state in all places where it needs to be updated.

 The details of the specific method for detecting a VM migration and updating the runtime state are provided in the section "SDN Solutions for the Data Center Network" on page 184.

VM migration is implemented by copying the entire state (disk, memory, registers, etc.) from one server to another. This is generally accomplished by copying the VM's file that includes all of these things in a single file. During the initial phase, which can take several minutes, the copying process occurs in the background while the VM is still running on the original server. In the last fraction of a second, when the copying is almost complete, the original VM is suspended, the last remaining state is copied, and the VM is reanimated on the new server. This process requires high bandwidth and low latency between the two servers because the time it takes to replicate this last state equates to time that the service implemented by the VM is unresponsive.

An alternative approach is to take a snapshot of a VM, pause it, and then move the snapshot to another server, after which the hypervisor will un-pause the VM. This is a migration, but not a live migration.[3] There is an aspect related to storage in live migration, particularly if the two VMs use the shared storage model in which both VMs share a common logical volume on a common physical disk (array) and transfer a lock that allows I/O to continue during migration. Distance and latency allowed for this procedure varies with the disk access protocol (iSCSI, NFS, Fibre Channel). It is also possible to again split the application into multiple tiers whereby a common backend database is used to store state and other information. Just before the VM pauses before its move, that state is locked. When it reanimates elsewhere, it simply reconnects to this store and continues.

Scale and performance of VM moves will vary based on the type of service offering (IaaS, PaaS, or SaaS) and the degree of tenancy. A simple IaaS offering at a typical service provider with the current generation of Intel/ARM processor, c. 2012, might present the following rough scale numbers:

Number of data centers
    Multiples of tens (depends entirely on the geography of the offering; the example given would be for a country the size of Japan)

Number of servers per center
    Tens of thousands

Number of servers per cluster/pod
    1,000

Number of tenants per server
    Approximately 20 (current generation of processor, expected to double with next generation)

Number of VMs per tenant
    Approximately five

VM change rate
    Highly variable

VM change latency
    This is a target that varies by provider and application

---

3. Alternatives are available that use active/active synchronous data distribution between volumes, where distances supported are claimed to be up to 100 kilometers.

Data Center Interconnect (DCI)

Now that we have introduced the basic concepts of what a data center is and how one can be built, let's discuss how one or more data centers can be connected. In particular, for configurations where multiple data centers are required either for geographic diversity, disaster recovery, service, or cloud bursting, data centers are interconnected over some form of Wide Area Network (WAN). This is the case even if data centers are geographically down the street from one another; even in these cases, some metro access network is typically used to interconnect them. A variety of technological options exist that can achieve these interconnections. These include EVPN, VPLS, MPLS L3 or L2 VPNs, pseudowires, and even just plain old IP.

In cases where two or more data centers exist, then you must consider how to connect these data centers. For example, a tenant may have arbitrary numbers of virtual machines residing in each of these different data centers yet desires that they be at least logically connected. The Data Center Interconnect (DCI) (see Figure 6-13) puts all VMs of a given tenant across all data centers on the same L2 or L3 underlying (i.e., underlay) tenant network.[4] It turns out in order to interconnect data centers, you can treat data centers almost like Lego blocks that snap together, using one of the concepts extrapolated from the multitenant data center concept already discussed.

---

4. Another layer 2 network driver in Data Center networks is continual connectivity through VM motion. In general, during VM mobility, the source and destination server don't need to be on the same IP subnet, but to maintain IP connectivity, extending layer 2 connectivity may be attractive.

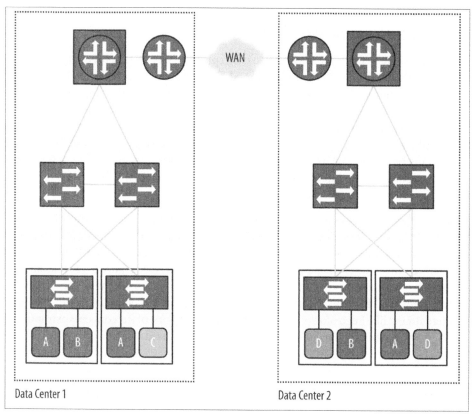

Figure 6-13. Data Center Interconnect (DCI)

As it turns out, interconnecting data centers is not necessarily a simple thing because there are a variety of concerns to keep in mind. But before jumping feet first into all the various ways in which DCI can be implemented, let's first examine some of the requirements of any good DCI solution, and more importantly, some of its fallacies.

Fallacies of Data Center Distributed Computing

When designing a data center and an architecture, or strategy, for interconnecting two or more data centers, one inevitably needs to list the requirements of the interconnection. These often start with a variety of assumptions, and we have found that in practice, many of these fall into a category of things that seem to make sense in theory, but in practice are impossible to guarantee or assume. These assumptions include the following:

- The network is reliable.
- Latency is zero.

- Bandwidth is infinite.
- The network is secure.
- Topology doesn't change.
- There is one administrator.
- Transport cost is zero.
- The network is homogeneous.

At first, these notions may seem quite reasonable, but in practice they are quite difficult (or impossible) to achieve. For example, the first four points make assumptions about the technology being employed and the equipment that implements it. No equipment is perfect or functions flawlessly, and so it is often a safer bet to assume the opposite of these first points. In terms of points four to six, these fall under administrative or personnel issues. All things equal, once your network is configured, it should continue operating that way until changed. And therein lies the rub: operational configuration errors (i.e., fat-finger errors) can be catastrophic from the perspective of the normal operation of the network and because they can also inadvertently introduce security holes. (There are statistics that have actually shown a *reduction* in network failures during holiday or vacation periods, when network operations staff is not operating networks.)

Data Center Distributed Computing Pitfalls to Consider

It turns out that the DCI must account for the fact that address spaces of tenants can overlap—for example, using L2 MPLS VPNs, L3 MPLS VPNs, GRE tunnels, SSL VPNs, or some other tunneling mechanism to keep the address spaces separate. Depending on the strategy chosen to manage addresses, these might fall into the issues just discussed under DCI fallacies. In particular, assuming that addresses overlap but are protected from one another can quickly unwind if an operational configuration misconfigures a new tenant that unexpectedly can see another tenant's VMs. So keep in mind that the choice of an addressing scheme goes beyond the obvious choice and should include consideration of operations and management verification and checking schemes.

There are performance criteria for the interconnection, too. Many of the constraints derive from the concept of live migration between data centers (including disk I/O, as previously mentioned), and there is a great deal of debate over whether live migration is really a use case to be considered in Data Center Interconnect design, given the hurdles that must be passed in order for that to function effectively. For example, discussions in the Broadband Forum on the topic of DCI assert that the VMware VMotion solution requires 622 Mbps minimum bandwidth between data centers and recommends less than 5 ms Round Trip Time (RTT) between source and destination servers (see Figure 6-14). This effectively sets physical limits on the distance between servers. In reality, the answer to how much bandwidth you need is derivable based on known data.

This data can be generalized, but is determined largely by the tenant service behavior and target constraints. DCI bandwidth is of a particular concern, as it is directly related to the change window duration and the amount of data to replicate. The RTT and thus, distance of data center separation, is also a constraint.[5] While a calculation could optimize for all constraints, the example just cited was for a three-hour change window for a particular data product with the bandwidth of the link set to a fixed value. Of course, these calculations can be performed for an atomic action or the aggregate of all operational actions, which will result in different values.

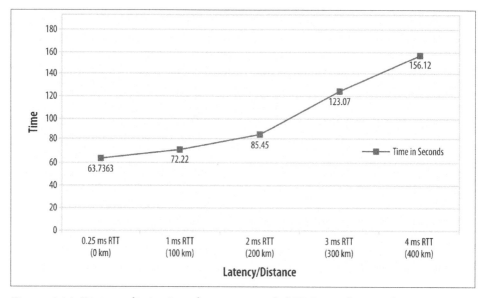

Figure 6-14. Distance limitations for recommended VMotion latency (at interconnect rate of 622 Mbps)

To review, the general scale concerns when designing the DCI include:

- MAC address scalability is an issue on the DC WAN edge for solutions that use L2 extension (e.g., 250k client MAC addresses in a single Service Provider data center multiplied across interconnected SP data centers and Enterprise data centers)
- Pseudowire scale (i.e., the number of directed LDP sessions, MAC learning)
- Control plane scale (i.e., whether or not an L2 control plane domain is extended between data centers)

---

5. The RTT/distance relationship is (for the most part) governed by the speed of light in fiber cables, so the 400 kilometer distance limitation comes from a rough calculation using .005ms/km as speed of propagation (and the fact that this is a round trip measurement, so the actual budget is 2.5 ms each way).

- Broadcast, unknown unicast, and multicast traffic handling (BUM)

In the end, a mixture of layer 2 extensions and IP interconnection may be required. The latter may be straightforward IP forwarding or L3VPN. The outstanding questions are around whether or not the control planes of the different centers are disjoint/separated.

DCI approaches

The common approaches for DCI that have been mentioned can be considered across a spectrum starting from the simplest to the most involved, placed into the following categories to better frame their pros and cons:

- VLAN Extension uses 802.1q trunking on the links between the data centers and is fraught with the same concerns of VLANs in the data center; MAC scalability, potential spanning tree loops, unpredictable amounts of BUM traffic and little control that allows effective load balancing over multiple links (traffic engineering).
- There are some proprietary solutions to the VLAN extension problem. For example, Cisco vPC (virtual port channel) suggests bonding inter-DC links and filtering STP BPDUs to avoid STP looping.
- VPLS uses MPLS to create a pseudowire overlay on the physical connection between the data centers. The MPLS requirement comes with an LDP and/or multiprotocol BGP requirement (for the control plane of the overlay) that may (to some operators) mean additional complexity, though this can be mitigated with technique like Auto-Discovery.[6]
- MPLS brings additional potentially desirable functionality: traffic engineering, fast reroute, multicast/broadcast replication, a degree of isolation between data centers allowing overlapping VLAN assignments and hiding topology, and fairly broad support and interoperability.

VLANs for DCI

The simplest solution for DCI is to simply use VLANs. In cases where there are fewer than about 4,000 tenants in any given data center, it is perfectly acceptable (and scalable) to use VLANs as a segregation mechanism. This mechanism is supported on most hardware from high-end routing and switching gear, all the way down to commodity switches. The advantages around using this mechanism are that basically they are dead simple to architect and initially inexpensive to operate. The disadvantages are that they are potentially complex to administer changes to later. That is, there are a potentially large number of points that will need VLAN/tag mappings modified in the future if changes are desired.

---

6. RFC 4761 (BGP-Based VPLS), RFC 4762 (LDP-Based VPLS), BGP Autodiscovery for LDP-Based VPLS RFCxxxx, Hierarchical VPLS option for LDP based VPLS

The VLAN solution for DCs is simply mapped to intra-DC IP or Ethernet paths that carry the tagged traffic between data center gateways, which forward the traffic down to the local data center.

VPLS for DCI

In cases where more than 4,000 tenants are desired, other solutions must be employed. One such option is Virtual Private LAN Service (VPLS). The basic operation of the VPLS solution is similar to that of the VLAN service except that MPLS (L2TPv3) and pseudowires are used to interconnect data centers, and VLANs (or stacked VLANs) are mapped to the pseudowires at the gateways, thus stitching together the data center VLAN-to-VM mappings. This is shown in Figure 6-15 where the CE represents either the gateway router/switch or the top of rack switch (ToR), depending on how far down into the network the architecture requires the VPLS to extend. In the case of the former, the VLAN-to-VPLS tunnel mapping happens at the gateway, while the mapping happens on the ToR in the latter case. Both cases have pros and cons in terms of scale, operations and management, and resilience to change, but in general the VPLS solution has the following characteristics:

- Flodding (Broadcast, Multicast, Unknown Unicast)
- Dynamic learning of Mac addresses
- Split-Horizon and full-mesh of PWs for loop-avoidance in core (no STP runs in the core, so the data center SPT domains are isolated)
- Sub-optimal multicast (though the emergence of Label Switched Multicast may provide relief)
- The VLAN to pseudowire mapping may place an artificial limit on the number of tenants supported per physical interface (4K)
- VLAN-based dual homing may require the use of virtual chassis techniques between the PE/DCI gateways and pseudowire redundancy (for active/active redundancy)
- Load balancing across equal cost paths can be only VLAN based (but not flow-based unless we introduce further enhancements like Entropy Labels or Flow Aware Transport (FAT) pseudowires)[7]

While VPLS is an improvement over a simple VLAN or stacked VLAN approach, it does still have issues. For example, the approach is still encumbered by MAC scaling problems[8] due to data plane learning, similar to the VLAN or stacked VLAN approaches. These issues will potentially result in issues at the CE points shown in Figure 6-15. Also,

---

7. RFC 6790 for Entropy Labels and RFC 6391 for FAT Pseudowires

8. One proposal to address the MAC issue is to use PBB/802.1ah with VPLS.

due to having to implement and deploy pseudowire tunnels between the PEs in the network configuration (i.e., either the gateway or the ToR, depending on the architecture) this also adds the potential for pseudowire scale and maintenance issues.

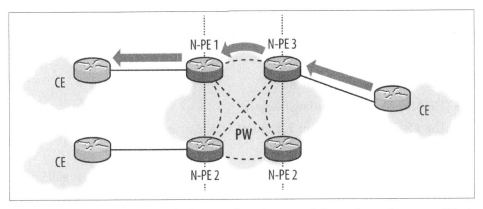

Figure 6-15. VPLS for DCI (split horizon has eliminated the paths to the target CE via N-PE2, NPE-4, and alternate LSPs on N-PE3)

EVPN for DCI. Another MPLS-based solution called Ethernet VPN (EVPN),[9] was developed to address some of the shortcomings of VPLS solutions. EVPN augments the data plane MAC learning paradigm with a control plane solution for automated MAC learning between data centers. EVPN creates a new address family for BGP by converting MAC addresses into routable addresses and then uses this to distribute MAC learning information between PEs in the network. Other optimizations to EVPN have also been made in order to further optimize MAC learning to enhance its scalability.

EVPN can use a number of different transport LSP types (P2P/P2MP/MP2MP)[10] and can provide some distribution advantages over VPLS:

- Flow-based load balancing and multipathing (layers 2, 3, and 4) in support of multihoming devices

---

9. EVPN (*http://datatracker.ietf.org/doc/draft-ietf-l2vpn-evpn*) can also be combined with PBB, propagating B-MAC addresses with EVPN. PEs perform PBB functionality just like PBB-VPLS C-MAC learning for traffic received from ACs and C-MAC/B-MAC association for traffic received from the core. Cisco OTV offers some of the characteristics of EVPN but is a Cisco-specific solution.

10. Because MPLS core networks may be problematic for some, IP/GRE tunnels can also be used to interconnect the MES(s). Fast convergence is based on local repair on MES-CE link failures.

   However, in this scenario, in a non-MPLS core, you obviously lose the potential for MPLS Fast Re-Route protection of the tunnels. IP-FRR *may*, depending on your topology, be an adequate substitute that would require you to run the LSPs over TE tunnels between the MES(s).

- The same flow-based or VLAN-based load balancing for multihomed networks (this can be based on auto-detection)
- Multicast optimization using MP2MP multicast distribution trees
- Geo-redundancy for PE/gateway nodes

EVPN introduces some new conceptual devices, which are further illustrated in Figure 6-16:

- The MES-MPLS Edge Switch
- The MFI-EVPN Forwarding Instance
- The ESI-Ethernet Segment Identifier (which is important in Link Aggregation scenarios)

Figure 6-16 illustrates how, within the data center, local MAC addresses are still learned through normal data plane learning in the EVPN model. MES(s) can learn local MACs through other mechanisms as well—management plane protocols or extensions to discovery protocols like LLDP—but still distribute these addresses to other PEs using split-horizon and other MAC bridging optimization approaches. The basic operation of EVPN also populates the table for the new address family in the MES and advertises it in BGP updates to neighboring MES(s) in order to distribute MAC routes. Furthermore, a MES injects the BGP learned MAC addresses into their layer 2 forwarding table along with the associated adjacency info. What differs from the typical VLAN approach described earlier is that this now can be done in a far more scalable manner. For example, WAN border routers may forward on the label only, and other MES points may only populate the forwarding plane for active MACs. This differs from having to have each end point learn every MAC address from each VLAN. Effectively, MAC addresses stay aggregated behind each MES much in the way BGP aggregates network addresses behind a network and only distributes reachability to those networks instead of the actual end point addresses.

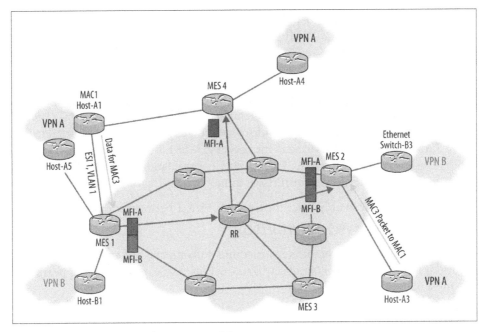

Figure 6-16. EVPN MAC-learning model

In addition to these advantages, EVPN does a lot to reduce ARP flooding, which can also lead to scalability issues. ARP storms can consume the forwarding bandwidth of switches very quickly. To this end, the MES performs proxy ARP, responds to ARP requests for IP addresses it represents, and doesn't forward ARP messages unless the BGP MAC routes carry a binding for the requested IP address.

EVPN also improves MAC learning and selective VLAN distribution through the implementation of BGP policies much in the same way BGP policies are used to enhance normal IP reachability. Route Targets (RTs) are used to define the membership of a EVPN and include MES(s) and Ethernet interfaces/VLANs connecting CEs (e.g., hosts, switches, and routers). RTs can be auto-derived from a VLAN ID, particularly if there is a one-to-one mapping between an EVPN and a VLAN. Each MES learns the ESI membership of all other MES in the VPNs in which it participates. This process enables designated forwarder election and split horizon for BUM traffic (for multihomed CEs).

The example in Figure 6-16 illustrates the capability of EVPN MES(s) to distribute different MFI to other MES that have members of the same VPNs. This is most often implemented employing a route reflector to further enhance scalability of the solution. BGP capabilities such as constrained distribution, Route Reflectors, and inter-AS are reused as well.

Also on Figure 6-16, both MES1 and MES4 advertise Ethernet Tag auto-discovery routes for <ESI1, VLAN1> along with MPLS label and VPNA RT. For example, MES1 advertises MAC Route in BGP:

```
<RD-1, MAC1, A1-VLAN, A1-ESI ID, MAC lbl L1, VPN A RT>
```

In the example, MES2 learns via BGP that MAC1 is dual-homed to MES1 and MES4. This still works despite the fact that MES4 might not yet have advertised MAC1 because MES2 knows via the Ethernet Tag auto-discovery routes that MES4 is connected to ESI1 and VLAN1. If MES2 decides to send the packet to MES1, it will use inner label <EVPN label advertised by MES1 for MAC1> and outer encapsulation as <MPLS Label for LSP to MES1> or <IP/GRE header for IP/GRE tunnel to MES1>.

MES2 can now safely load-balance the traffic to MAC1 between MES1 and MES4.

Summary comparison of VPLS and EVPN for DCI

As a summary, we think that it is instructional to compare and contrast the last two solutions for DCI given their similarity. Table 6-1 makes clear that EVPN appears to be the most optimal solution for DCI.

Table 6-1. Summary comparison of VPLS and EVPN for DCI

Desirable 1.2 extension attributes	VPLS	E-VPN
VM Mobility without renumbering L2 and L3 addresses	✓	✓
Ability to span VLANs across racks in different locations	✓	✓
Scale to few 100K hosts within and across multiple DCs	✓	✓
Policy-based flexible L2 topologies similar to L3 VPNs		✓
Multiple points of attachment with ability to load-balance VLANs across them	✓	✓
Active-Active points of attachment with ability to load-balance flows within a single VLAN		✓
Multi-tenant support (secure isolation, overlapping MAC, IP addresses)	✓	✓
Control-Plane Based Learning		✓
Minimize or eliminate flooding of unknown unicast		✓
Fast convergence from edge failures based on local repair		✓

SDN Solutions for the Data Center Network

In this section we consider SDN solutions for the modern data center. In particular, we will discuss how modern data centers that were just described are having SDN concepts applied to extend and expand their effectiveness, scale, and flexibility in hosting services. We should note that SDN solutions don't always mean standard solutions, and some of the solutions described are vendor proprietary in some form.

As described earlier, traditional data centers contain storage, compute (i.e., servers), and some network technology that binds these two together. Much in the way that servers and applications have been virtualized, so too have networks. In the traditional network deployment, VLANs were about as virtualized as a network got. In this sense, the VLANs were virtualizing the network paths between VMs. This was the first step in the virtualization of the network. As we introduced earlier in the DCI section, there are a number of protocols that can be used to not only form the network fabric of the data center, but as you will see, that can be used to also virtualize the fabric. In particular, we will introduce the notion of *network overlays* as a concept that allows for the virtualization of the underlying network fabric, or the *network underlay*.

The Network Underlay

The network underlay can be comprised of a number of technologies. Generally speaking, these can be divided up into layer 1, 2, or 3 solutions, but in all the cases, these solutions are designed to do basically one thing: transport traffic between servers in the data center. Figure 6-17 demonstrates how an overlay network creates a logical network over the physical underlay network. Typically the overlay network is created using virtual network elements such as virtual routers, switches, or logical tunnels. The underlay network is a typical network, such as an Ethernet, MPLS, or IP network.

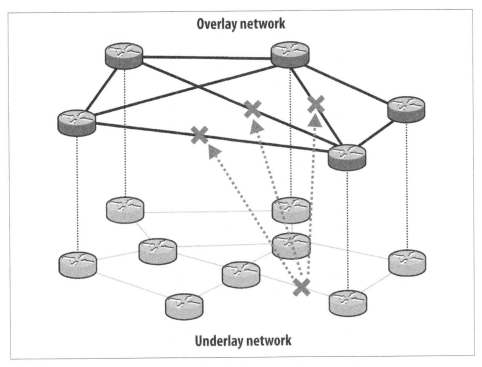

Figure 6-17. Data center overlay and underlay network relationships

Frankly speaking, all of the available solutions will work at providing an underlay network that carries an overlay. The question is one of how optimal each solution is at what it does, and how good it is at hosting a particular overlay technology. For example, while one solution might scale better for layer 2 MAC address learning, it may be terrible when one considers how this is used to handle VM moves or external cloud bursting. Another example might scale well for its speed of adapting to changes in the network, while another might require more time for semi-automated (or even manual) operator intervention. We will investigate all of these angles in the following section.

VLANs

This chapter is squarely focused on new SDN technologies, but do not lose sight that simplicity is king when operating a network. To this end, when tenancy of internal tenants is needed only, and that number does not exceed about 1,000, VLANS are still the simplest and most effective solution. This is a well-known approach, quite easy to operate, and is supported on the widest variety of hardware, so the simplest form of a network overlay is of course a flat IP network that rides over a VLAN substrate or underlay. This is in fact how data centers were originally constructed. There was no real need at the time to support multiple tenants, and when there's a need to segregate resources based on departmental access, VLANs were invented, but the overlay was still a relatively flatly addressed IP network. This approach even worked for a short while for external user access to data centers (remember the Amazon AWS case) until the number of tenants grew too large, address spaces had to overlap, and the general churn of these virtualized network elements required very fast (re)-programming of these resources. In these scenarios, the basic IP over Ethernet network sufficed for a single tenant and could be easily and unobtrusively extended to support up to about 4,000 tenants using VLANs.

Figure 6-18 illustrates how a basic VLAN approach can be used to implement a localized data center's overlay along with an IP overlay and implement a relatively simple DC interconnection. In the example, three 801.1q VLANs are created for each application (app, db, and management), and traffic is segregated using these VLANs across the network. In this approach, the same flat IP addressing space is used within the DCs in order to provide layer 3 access to the VMs hosting those services. The interface from the virtual machine to the hypervisor is an access interface. The hypervisor assigns this interface to the VLAN of the tenant. The server-to-access switch interface, as well as all switch-to-switch interfaces, are trunk interfaces.

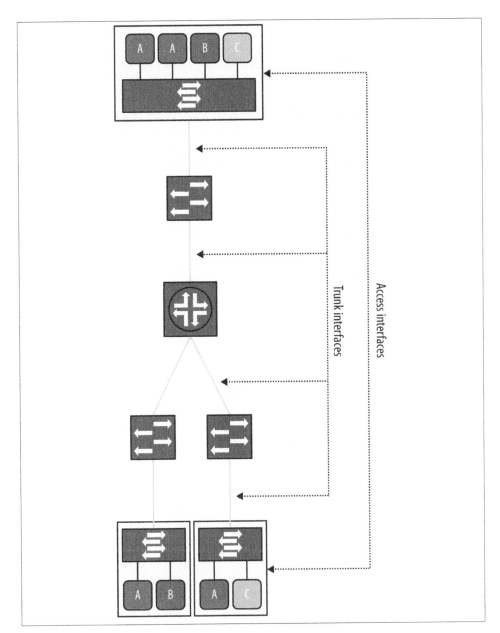

Figure 6-18. End-to-end tenant VLANs in the data center

While VLAN solutions are quite easy to implement, unless routing is inserted between VLANs, it has long been known that relying simply on bridging or the Spanning Tree Protocol (or its variants) does not scale well beyond around 300 hosts on any single VLAN. The problem with the protocol is that when the number of host MAC addresses becomes large, changes, moves or failures result in massive processing inside the network elements. During these highly busy periods, network elements could miss other failures or simply be overloaded to the point where they cannot adjust quickly enough. This can result in network loops or black holes. Early versions of Spanning Tree also suffered from the issue of wasting equal cost (i.e., parallel) links, in that the protocol effectively blocked all parallel links to the same bridge except one as its means of preventing loops. Even the latest versions of these protocols have limited ability to provide multipath capabilities. Finally, in most cases, bridges can suffer from a loss in forwarding of several seconds when they reestablish connectivity to other bridge links.

EVPN

Earlier we introduced EVPN as a DCI solution, and in doing so noted how the PE function could terminate at the DC gateway or the ToR. In the case of the former, we showed how VLANs (stacked, tagged, or flat) would then be used to form the underlay. We also pointed out that EVPN, as with VPLS, could be used to extend the number of tenants in a network beyond the 4,000 VLAN tag limit.

Figure 6-19 illustrates just how EVPN can be employed within a data center to carry traffic for tenants to other tenants. The general operation is simple in that traffic is transmitted as an MPLS encapsulated frame containing an Ethernet frame. MPLS tunnels terminate at the physical or virtual switch, which then de-capsulates traffic and delivers it as a layer 2 frame to the virtual or physical host, depending on the implementation. Similarly, transmission of layer 2 frames from the end stations are encapsulated into an MPLS tunnel and delivered to other end hosts. This behavior is identical to what was explained earlier.

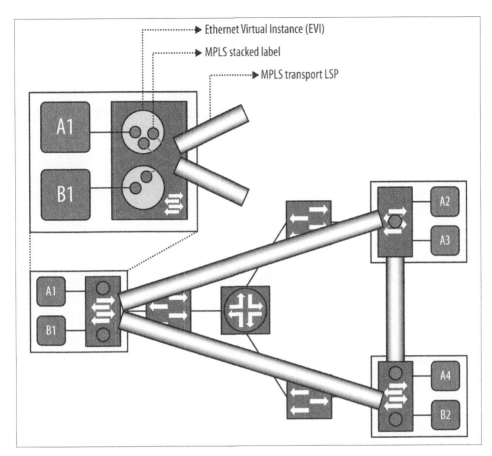

Figure 6-19. EVPN (data plane)

And Figure 6-20 demonstrates how the control plane establishes a full mesh of transport MPLS LSPs between the access and core switches using LDP or RSVP. The access switches run MP-IBGP to signal MAC learning reachability information in the same way described previously in the DCI section.

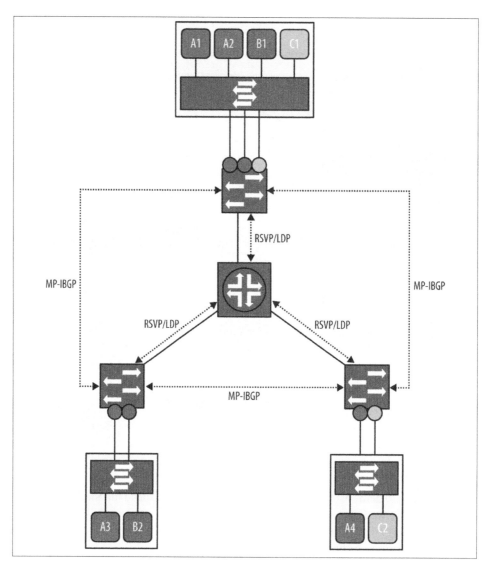

Figure 6-20. EVPN (control plane)

It is important to consider the scaling characteristics of this approach with other methods described earlier. In particular, since the physical network is a layer 3 (MPLS) network, it will scale and be operated in the same well-known ways that MPLS networks are. Similarly, all layer 2 traffic is tunneled across the network over MPLS, which is good for scaling because it avoids having large layer 2 domains and the associated scaling problems with them. Also comparing this approach to VxLAN or NVGRE, one must consider the number of actual tunnels that must be established and managed. In this case, there generally should be fewer than the VxLAN and NVGRE cases because stacked labels can be employed. Further extending the scale of this approach in terms of processing load on the switches is the use of BGP route reflectors in this scheme. These can enhance the solution very much. Finally, use of XMPP between the local switches (or vSwitches) and the MP-IBGP points in the architecture can potentially lighten the protocol configuration load on the end hosts.

Locator ID Split (LISP)

The current routing and addressing architecture employed within the Internet relies on a single namespace to express two functions about a network element: its network identity and how it is attached to the network. In essence, the problem is that we want to preserve the device's identity, regardless of which network or networks to which it is connected. The addressing scheme employed today was invented when network elements were relatively static, and the assumption was that the network-to-element ID binding was relatively static, too. Today we have to consider modern user behavior, where mobile elements rapidly move between base stations or radio access networks. That makes managing network connections, resources, and other things that should be pinned to a network element based on its identifier difficult because its entire address could change when it changes networks. Furthermore, in cases where network elements are multihomed, traffic engineering (TE) is needed, or address allocations are employed that prevent aggregation.

This problem has been exacerbated by two conditions. The first is IPv4 address space depletion, which has led to a finer and finer allocation of the IPv4 addresses space, which results in less aggregation potential. The second is the increasing occurrence of dual-stack routers supporting both IPv4 and IPv6 protocols. IPv6 did not change anything about the use of IP addresses and so still suffers from the same issues that IPv4 does.

A number of people at the IETF recognized these issues and sought to correct them by creating a new address and network element address split called Locator ID Split, or *LISP*, as it's now known. They created a network architecture and set of protocols that implemented a new semantic for IP addressing. In essence, LISP creates two namespaces and uses two IP addresses for each network device. The first is an Endpoint Identifier (EID) that is assigned to an end-host and always remains with the host regardless of which network it resides on. The second is a Routing Locator (RLOC) that is assigned to a network device (i.e., a router) that makes up the global routing system. It is the combination of these routers and the unique device identifier and the protocols used to manage them across the Internet that comprise the LISP system and allows it to function.

The separation of device identifier from its network identifier offers several advantages:

- Improved routing system scalability by using topologically-aggregated RLOCs.

- Improved traffic engineering for cases where multihoming of end-sites are employed.

- Provider independence for devices that are assigned an EID from a common EID space. This facilitates IP portability, which is an important feature, too.

- LISP is a simple, incremental, network-based implementation that is deployed primarily in network edge devices, therefore requiring no changes to host stacks, Domain Name Services, or the local network infrastructure used to support those hosts.

- IP mobility (EIDs can move without changing—only the RLOC changes!)

The concept of a location/ID separation has been under study by the IETF and various universities and researchers for more than 15 years. By splitting the device identity, its Endpoint Identifier, and Routing Locator into two different namespaces, improvements in scalability of the routing system can be achieved through greater aggregation of RLOCs.

LISP applies to data centers by providing the capability to segment traffic with minimal infrastructure impact, but with high scale and global scope. This is in fact a means by which virtualization/multitenancy support can be achieved—much in the way we have described VLANs or VPNs within DCs. This is accomplished when control and data plane traffic are segmented by mapping VRFs to LISP instance IDs, making this overlay solution highly flexible and highly scalable. This also has the potential for inherently low operational cost due to the mapping being done automatically by the DC network switches.

An additional benefit of this approach is that data center VM-Mobility can also provide location flexibility for IP endpoints not only within the data center network, but due to using the IP protocol, also across the Internet. In fact, VM hosts can freely move between data centers employing this scheme because the server identifiers, which are just EIDs, are separated from their location (RLOC) in the same way any other implementation of LISP would be. Thus this solution can bind IP endpoints to virtual machines and deploy them anywhere regardless of their IP addresses. Furthermore, support of VM mobility across data center racks, rows, pds, or even to separate locations is possible. This method can also be used to span organizations, supporting cloud-bursting capabilities of data centers.

VxLan

Virtual Extensible LAN (VxLAN) is a network virtualization (*http://bit.ly/1aWIn8P*) technology that attempts to ameliorate the scalability (*http://bit.ly/17i8yCL*) problems encountered with large cloud computing (*http://bit.ly/1codiwp*) deployments when using existing VLAN technology. VMware (*http://bit.ly/17TFDY7*) and Cisco (*http://bit.ly/15vtOXR*) originally created VxLAN as a means to solve problems encountered in these environments. Other backers of the technology currently include Juniper Networks, Arista Networks (*http://bit.ly/13mOZfa*), Broadcom (*http://bit.ly/166NRL1*), Citrix (*http://bit.ly/166NUXa*), and Red Hat (*http://bit.ly/18MOqMp*).

VxLAN employs a VLAN-like (*http://bit.ly/1b9tQqu*) encapsulation technique to encapsulate MAC-based (*http://bit.ly/1cdUr8F*) layer 2 Ethernet frames (*http://bit.ly/13Zw1uz*) within layer 3 UDP (*http://bit.ly/132NH5n*) packets. Using a MAC-in-UDP encapsulation, VxLAN provides a layer 2 abstraction to virtual machines (VMs) that is independent of where they are located for reasons similar to why LISP was invented. Figure 6-21 demonstrates the packet format employed by VxLAN. Note the inner and outer MAC/IP portions that provide the virtual tunneling capabilities of this approach.

Figure 6-21. VXLAN packet format

As mentioned earlier, the 802.1Q VLAN Identifier space is limited to only 12 bits, or about 4,000 entries. The VxLAN Identifier space is 24 bits, allowing the VxLAN Id space to increase by over 400,000 percent to handle over 16 million unique identifiers. This should provide sufficient room for expansion for years to come. Figure 6-21 also shows that VxLAN employs the Internet Protocol as the transport protocol between VxLAN hosts. It does this for both unicast and multicast operation. The use of IP as the transport is important as it allows the reach of a VxLAN segment to be extended far beyond the typical reach of VLANs using 802.1Q.

Fundamentally, VxLAN disconnects the VMs from their physical networks by allowing VMs to communicate with each other using a transparent overlay that is hosted over physical overlay networks. These overlay networks can also span layer 3 boundaries in order to support intra-DC scenarios. An important advantage to VxLAN is that the endpoint VMs are completely unaware of the physical network constraints because they only see the virtual layer 2 adjacencies. More importantly, this technology provides the capability to extend virtualization across traditional network boundaries in order to support portability and mobility of VM hosts. VxLAN allows for the separation of logical networks from one another much like the VLAN approach could, simplifying the implementation of true multitenancy, but extends it further by also exceeding the 4,000 VLAN limit with a much larger virtualization space.

The normal operation of VxLAN relies on Virtual Tunnel Endpoints (VTEPs) that contain all the functionality needed to provide Ethernet layer 2 services to connected end systems. VTEPs are located at the edges of the network. VTEPs typically connect an access switch to an IP transport network. Note that these switches can be virtual or physical. The general configuration of a VxLAN VTEP is shown in Figure 6-22.

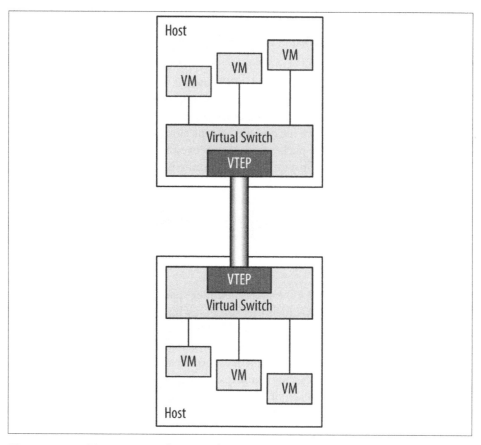

Figure 6-22. VTEP as part of a virtual (or physical) switch connecting VMs together across a data center infrastructure

Each end system connected to the same access switch communicates through the access switch in order to get its packets to other hosts. The access switch behaves in the same way a traditional learning bridge does. Specifically, it will flood packets out all ports except the one it arrived on when it doesn't know the destination MAC of an incoming packet and only transmits out a specific port when it has learned a forwarding destination's direction. Broadcast traffic is sent out all ports, as usual, and multicast is handled similarly. The access switch can support multiple bridge domains, which are typically identified as VLANs with an associated VLAN ID that is carried in the 802.1Q header on trunk ports. However, in the case of a VxLAN enabled switch, the bridge domain would instead by associated with a VxLAN ID.

Under normal operation, the VTEP examines the destination MAC address of frames it handles, looking up the IP address of the VTEP for that destination. The MAC-to-

OuterIP mapping table is populated by normal L2 bridge learning. When a VM wishes to communicate with another VM, it generally first sends a broadcast ARP, which its VTEP will send to the multicast group for its VNI. All of the other VTEPs will learn the Inner MAC address of the sending VM and Outer IP address of its VTEP from this packet. The destination VM will respond to the ARP via a unicast message back to the sender, which allows the original VTEP to learn the destination mapping as well.

When a MAC address moves to a different physical or virtual switch port (i.e., a VM is moved), the other VTEPs find its new location by employing the same learning process described previously whereby the first packet they see from its new VTEP triggers the learning action.

In terms of programmability, VxLAN excels by providing a single interface to authoritatively program a layer 2 logical network overlay. Within a virtualized environment, VxLAN has been integrated into VMware's vSphere DVS, vSwitch, and network IO controls to program and control VMs, as well as their associated bandwidth and security attributes.

NVGRE

The Network Virtualization using Generic Routing Encapsulation (NVGRE) protocol is a network virtualization (*http://bit.ly/1aWIn8P*) technology that was invented in order to overcome the scalability (*http://bit.ly/17i8yCL*) problems associated with large data center environments that suffer from the issues described earlier in the VLAN underlay option. Similar to VxLAN, it employs a packet tunneling scheme that encapsulates layer 2 information inside of a layer 3 packet. In particular, NVGRE employs the Generic Routing Encapsulation [GRE] (*http://bit.ly/17vBHdT*) to tunnel layer 2 (*http://bit.ly/1c7X394*) packets over layer 3 (*http://bit.ly/1c7X3WI*) networks. At its core, NVGRE is simply an encapsulation of an Ethernet layer 2 Frame that is carried in an IP packet. The result is that this enables the creation of virtualized L2 subnets that can span physical L3 IP networks. The first specification of the protocol was defined in the IETF in draft-sridharan-virtualization-nvgre-00. Its principal backer is Microsoft.

NVGRE enables the connection between two or more L3 networks and makes it appear to end hosts as if they share the same L2 subnet (Figure 6-23). Similarly to VxLAN, this allows inter-VM communications across L3 networks to appear to the end stations as if they were attached to the same L2 subnet. NVGRE is an L2 overlay scheme over an L3 network.

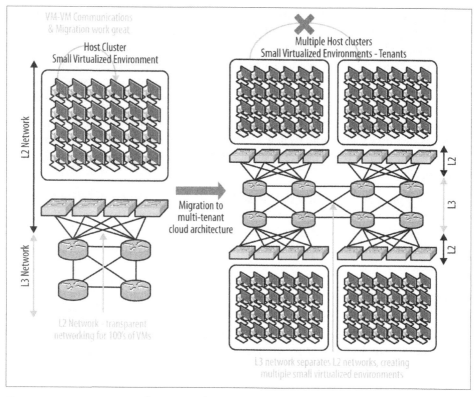

Figure 6-23. NVGRE overlay networks: enabling network scalability for a cloud infrastructure

NVGRE uses a unique 24-bit ID called a Tenant Network Identifier (TNI) that is added to the L2 Ethernet frame. The TNI is mapped on top of the lower 24 bits of the GRE Key field. This new 24-bit TNI now enables more than 16 million L2 (logical) networks to operate within the same administrative domain, a scalability improvement of many orders of magnitude over the 4,094 VLAN segment limit discussed before. The L2 frame with GRE encapsulation is then encapsulated with an outer IP header and finally an outer MAC address. A simplified representation of the NVGRE frame format and encapsulation is shown in Figure 6-24.

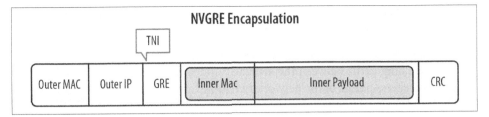

Figure 6-24. NVGRE packet format

NVGRE is a tunneling scheme that relies on the GRE routing protocol as defined by RFC 2784 as a basis but extends it as specified in RFC 2890. Each TNI is associated with an individual GRE tunnel and uniquely identifies, as its name suggests, a cloud tenant's unique virtual subnet. NVGRE thus isn't a new standard as such, since it uses the already established GRE protocol between hypervisors, but instead is a modification to an existing protocol. This has advantages in terms of operations and management, as well as in terms of understanding the other characterizes of the protocol.

The behavior of a server, switch, or physical NIC that encapsulates VM traffic using the NVGRE protocol is straightforward. For any traffic emanating from a VM, the 24-Bit TNI is added to the frame, and then it is sent through the appropriate GRE tunnel. At the destination, the endpoint de-encapsulates the incoming packet and forwards that to the destination VM as the original Ethernet L2 packet.

The inner IP address is called the Customer Address (CA). The outer IP address is called the Provider Address (PA). When an NVGRE endpoint needs to send a packet to the destination VM, it needs to know the PA of the destination NVGRE endpoint.

OpenFlow

We have described a number of underlay approaches that map loosely to variants of existing layer 2 network protocols. The one exception to this is the use of the OpenFlow protocol to establish and manage the underlay network over which, say, an IP network can be overlaid. In Chapter 3 and Chapter 10, we described the protocol's general operation, and so we will not repeat it here. However, it is useful to show how such an underlay would be constructed, and fortunately, it is quite simple.

Figure 6-25 demonstrates how an OpenFlow controller is setup in the canonical fashion to control a zone of a network's switches. Note that while we show the BigSwitch Floodlight controller in the figure, any OpenFlow controller can be swapped into this picture with basically identical operation. The switches in the figure are generally setup to be completely controlled by the controller, although as we described in Chapter 3, the hybrid mode of operation is also a distinct (and practical) possibility here. Each switch has an established control channel between it and the controller over which the OpenFlow protocol discourse takes place. Note that the switches that are controlled are shown as both virtual (vSwitch) and real (switch). It is important to understand that generally speaking, it does not matter whether the switch is virtual or real in this context.

The switches are generally constructed and configured by the controller to establish layer 2 switching paths between the switches, and will also incorporate layer 3 at the ingress and egress points of the network to handle things such as ARP or other layer 3 operations. We should note that it is possible to construct a true combined layer 2 and 3 underlay using this configuration, but the general consensus is that this is too difficult in terms of scale, resilience to failure, and general operational complexity if implemented this way. These issues were discussed in Chapter 4.

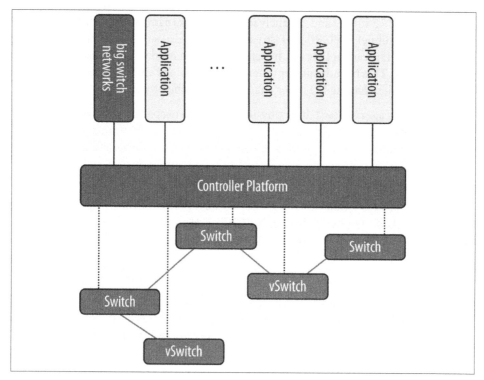

Figure 6-25. Creating a layer 2 network underlay using OpenFlow-controlled switches

Network Overlays

As mentioned earlier, while SDN has not invented the notion of logical network overlays, this is clearly one of the things that drives and motivates SDN today, especially in data center networks. Earlier in this chapter, we introduced the notation of a network underlay. The underlay is by and large the network infrastructure technologies employed by data center and other network operators today. With some exceptions, such as VxLAN and NGVRE, these basic technologies have been modified or augmented in order to support additional virtualization, user contexts, or entire virtual *slices* of the network itself. As with the variety of network underlays, a variety of network overlays exist. We will describe each of these, starting with the general concepts of where tunnels can be terminated that span between virtual machines.

Tunnels terminated at the vSwitch

Earlier in Chapter 4, we described virtual swtiches or vSwitches. A number of these exist both in the open source and commercial spaces today. Arguably, the most popular is the Open Virtual Switch, or OVS. We will generally refer to OVS in the rest of this chapter.

In this class of solution, you establish tunnels between vSwitches to carry the tenant traffic between other vSwitches. Since vSwitches generally reside within the hypervisor space, the vSwitch acts as a local termination and translation point for VMs. It also has the advantage of it not being modified in any way to participate in the overlay (or underlay for that matter). Instead, a VM is presented with an IP and MAC address, as they are in a non-overlay environment and happily exist. There are two subclasses of solutions when terminating tunnels at vSwitches: single and multitiered. The former solution is typical of many of the standards-based solutions that we will get into detail about a little later but generally depict a network comprised of multiple logical and physical tiers that when interconnected, form the underlying infrastructure that the overlay rides over. This approach is demonstrated in the Figure 6-26. In the figure, the VMs are shown as A and B boxes. The letters denote group membership of a particular overlay, or VPN. The larger boxes they reside in represent the physical host machine (server). The rectangle within this box represents the vSwitch. Observe how logical network tunnels are terminated and emanate from this point. This is the case regardless of the underlying network or *underlay*.

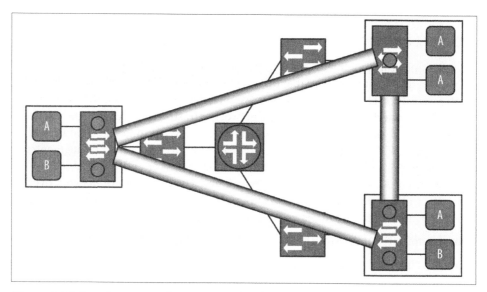

Figure 6-26. Overlays—tunnels terminated at the vSwitch for a multitier network

The other approach to overlays is a single-tiered approach. These are generally referred to as data center fabrics and most often are vertically integrated solutions that are largely proprietary, vendor-specific solutions. In these solutions, each overlay tunnel begins and ends in a vSwitch as they did in the multitiered solution, as shown in Figure 6-27. However, it differs from the multitiered solution in that these solutions generally establish a full mesh of tunnels among the vSwitches that establish a logical switching fabric. This potentially makes signaling and operations of this network simpler because the network operator (or their OSS) need not be involved in any special tunnel signaling, movement, or maintenance: instead, the fabric management system takes care of this and simply presents tunnels to the VMs as if they were plugged into a real network.

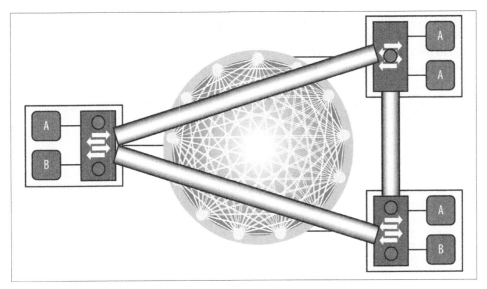

Figure 6-27. Overlays—tunnels terminated at the vSwitch using a single-tier network (a.k.a. a fabric)

Network Overlay Types

As mentioned earlier, network overlays exist that emulate different logical layers of the network. These include layers 2 and 3, and more recently one approach that tightly combines layer 1 with layer 2.

Layer 2 overlays

It can be argued that the majority of overlay tunneling protocols available encapsulate layer 2 tenant network traffic[11] over some layer 3 networks, although OpenFlow is the obvious variant in this case, where the usual approach is to construct a network out of entire layer 2 segments, as described earlier. The layer 3 network is typically IP, although as we have seen can be OpenFlow, GRE, or even MPLS, which is technically layer 2.5 but is counted here. The exact format of the tunnel header varies depending on the tunneling encapsulation, but the basic idea is approximately[12] the same for all encapsulations, as shown in Figure 6-28.

11. The option of tunneling layer 2 over layer 3 tenant network traffic is considered as a separate variation.

12. When MPLS is used, the outer IP header is replaced by an MPLS header, and the tunnel header is replaced by a stacked MPLS header.

The focus around layer 2 networking was historically driven by server clustering technologies[13] and storage synchronization, as well as the need for the network operator of OSS to have more freedom in binding IP addresses to VMs. However, these applications are no longer exclusively layer 2; we are seeing more and more migration to layer 3.

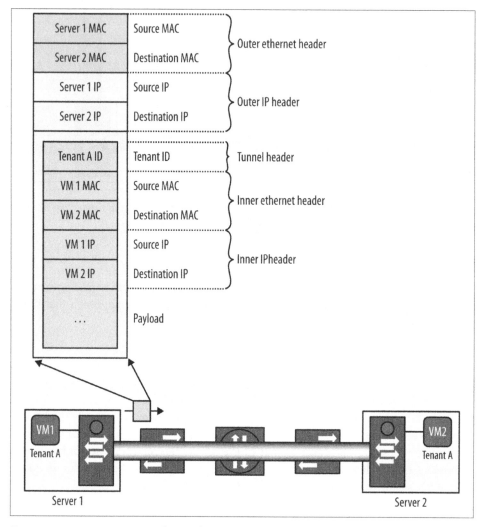

Figure 6-28. Layer 2 encapsulation for overlay tunnels

13. E.g., Microsoft MSCS, Veritas Cluster Server, Solaris Sun Cluster Enterprise, VMware Cluster, Oracle RAC (Real Appl.Cluster), HP MC/ServiceGuard, HP NonStop, HP Open VMS/TruCluster, IBM HACMP, EMS/ Legato Automated Availability Manager

All of the tunnel encapsulation used in these solutions uses some sort of tenant identifier field in the tunnel header to de-multiplex the packets received from the tunnel into the context of the right vswitch bridge, as shown in Figure 6-29:

- GRE uses the 32-bit GRE key [GRE-KEY-RFC] (*http://tools.ietf.org/html/rfc2890*) (32 bits).
- VxLAN uses the 24-bit VxLAN segment ID, also known as the VxLAN Network Identifier (VNI).
- NVGRE uses the 24-bit Virtual Subnet ID (VSID), which is part of the GRE key.
- VmWare/Nicera's STT uses the 64-bit Context ID.
- MPLS uses the 20-bit inner label.

The VNI in VxLAN, the VSID in NVGRE, and the context ID in STT have global scope across the data center. The inner label in MPLS has local scope within the vswitch, too.

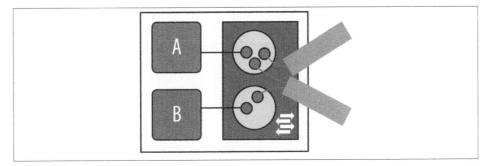

Figure 6-29. Using the tenant ID in the tunnel header to de-multiplex to the correct tenant

Layer 3 overlays

Another type of network overlay are layer 3 (i.e., IP) overlays. These overlays present IP-based overlays instead of layer 2 overlays. The difference between these overlays and layer 2 overlays is that instead of presenting a layer 2 logical topology between VMs, it presents a layer 3 network. The advantages of these approaches are analogous to existing layer 3 VPNs. In particular, private or public addressing can be mixed and matched easily, so things like cloud-bursting or external cloud attachment is easily done. Moves are also arguably easier. In this approach, rather than termination of a layer 2 tunnel at the vSwitch, a layer 3 tunnel is terminated at a vRouter. The vRouter's responsibilities are similar to those in a vSwitch except that it acts as a Provider Edge (PE) element in a layer 3 VPN. The most typical of these approaches proposed today is in fact a modified layer 3 MPLS approach that integrates with a vRouter inside of the hypervisor space.

Hybrid overlay-underlay approach

One approach that differs from the strictly layer 2 or strictly layer 3 approaches just described is one from a new startup called Plexxi. This solution is an underlay solution but at the same time provides a closely integrated overlay (Figure 6-30). We refer to this as a *hybrid overlay-underlay*. In the case of overlays, operators must still be conscious of network capacity, as this is a finite resource. Overlays are entirely unaware of the network, and as the entire overlay administrator knows, there is infinite bandwidth supporting them. In traditional network designs, including leaf/spine designs, capacity is statically structured. Studies have shown that much of the capacity in such a network remains idle. Plexxi's approach is to collapse the data center network into a single tier and to interconnect switches within this tier optically. This results in potentially fewer boxes and far less cabling and transceivers as part of this solution. When combined with dynamically maintained affinities, this means applications can have the capacity they require when they need it without structuring an abundance of otherwise unused capacity ahead of time.

In this approach, overlays are rendered into affinities, allowing capacity in the network to be managed dynamically, even though endpoints are hidden within the overlay. This is possible because the data required to do this is harvested from the overlay management system by a connector, which in turn pushes the data to the Plexxi controller via its API. The Plexxi controller is discussed in detail in Chapter 4, so it is not discussed further here.

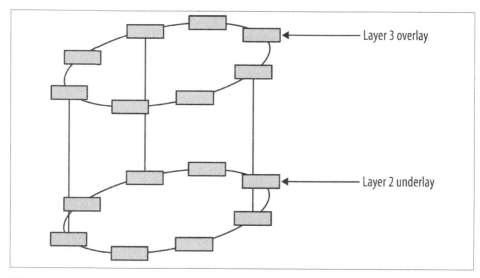

Figure 6-30. Plexxi's approach to a hybrid overlay and underlay

Conclusions

In this chapter, we presented a number of concepts and constructs that are used to create, run, maintain, and manage modern multitenant data centers. Some of these concepts are variations on an old theme, while some are new and driven from the SDN movement. In all cases, these solutions provide virtualized network access between virtual machines that wish to communicate privately from the other tenant VMs hosted in a data center operated by a single service provider. In some cases, these technologies can even be used to facilitate VMs that wish to communicate across data centers that span multiple providers. In some cases, the technologies explained allow these logical networks to span multiple data centers owned and operated by the same enterprise, or even multiple enterprises. Later in the book, we will consider some of the design implications of using one technology over another when implementing a data center.

CHAPTER 7

Network Function Virtualization

Introduction

Network Function Virtualization (NFV) builds on some of the key SDN topics introduced in prior chapters, including control/data plane separation, virtualization, SDN controllers, and data center concepts (particularly orchestration applications). Figure 7-1 illustrates the intersection of these topics.

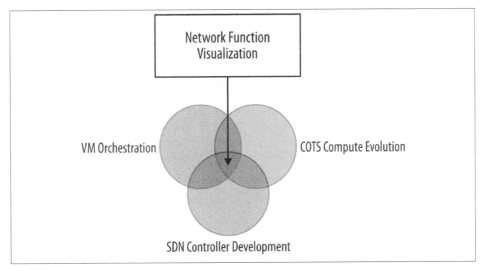

Figure 7-1. The intersection that makes Network Function Virtualization possible

Network Function Virtualization has its roots in several previously described network operations problems, particularly the implications of bundling services by network equipment manufacturers within their platform OS. NFV also applies to appliance vendors in a way that does not take advantage of the processing scale/innovation seen by many customers in their data centers.

Many large service providers had their own cloud offerings and thus an assumption of virtual machine orchestration in their operation. They were also tracking the I/O innovations by Intel in this space (VT-d, DDIO, DPDK, and SR-IOV support). These providers formally declared their desire for service virtualization and sponsorship of standards development around service virtualization through a paper published at a Layer123 SDN Conference (Darmstaad, Germany) in the fall of 2012.[1] This work ultimately ended up being sponsored within ETSI.[2] In addition to this paper, providers have repeatedly voted with their wallets in their moves toward commodity-priced, ODM-built, top-of-rack switches with off-the-shelf software. Behind the scenes, vendors were also already tracking the evolving I/O capabilities of COTS platforms and evaluating strategies for the next generation of service appliances and the future of dedicated network platforms that incorporate a large services component. These include the Broadband Network Gateway (BNG), its parallel in the cable space (CMTS), the node-B in the mobile space, and other service-oriented access and aggregation platforms.

What has evolved is a discussion of network services and functions into three general categories: simple virtualized services, service chaining, and services or platform virtualization. In all these discussions an SDN controller is involved, at least marginally in the case of simple virtualized services, and in others, it's arguably required.

Virtualization and Data Plane I/O

Virtualization of network services doesn't necessarily mean separate hypervisor partitioned VMs that contain each service instance; instead, it could also mean:

- Services implemented in a machine with multiple/compartmentalized OS(s)
- Services implemented within the hypervisor
- Services implemented as distributed or clustered as composites
- Services on bare metal machines
- Services implemented in Linux virtual containers

These methods may share state by using some form of Network Attached Storage (NAS) or other shared storage/memory architectures. See Figure 7-2 for a sketch illustrating these methods.

---

1. *http://www.tid.es/es/Documents/NFV_White_PaperV2.pdf;*   *http://www.lightreading.com/document.asp?doc_id=226204&*

2. ETSI is a SDO (Standards Development Organization). Access below the surface of the portal for NFV work (*http://portal.etsi.org/portal/server.pt/community/NFV/367*) requires ETSI membership.

Virtual machines provide tremendous advantages with respect to management[3] and are thus pursued as a primary vehicle for NFV. Linux containers have advantages in density (more instances per host) and performance but lack the management ecosystem and OS flexibility of virtual machines. Of course, bare metal machines trump both options when it comes to performance but are often considered behind the curve in terms of flexibility and management.

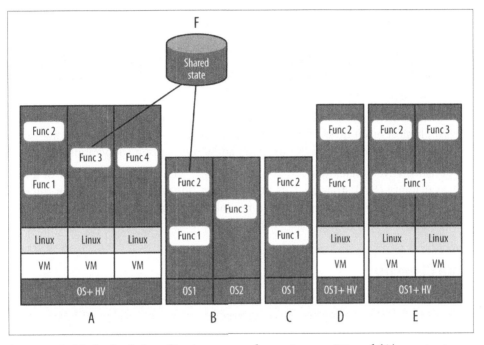

Figure 7-2. Methods of virtualization survey: hypervisor partitioned (A), compartmentalized OS (B), bare metal (C), hypervisor embedded (D), and distributed/clustered composite functions (E); two of these methods (A and B) also are depicted sharing state through shared storage (F)

Technologies like the Virtual Ethernet Port Extension (VEPA) port extension may also present an opportunity to provide per-VM services in a switch/router context using built-in or adjunct services.

Virtualization of network services will introduce reliability concerns that NFV practices and recommendations need to address:

3. A short list of management benefits (if you skipped Chapter 6): VM lifecycle management, storage management, VM placement optimization, VM snapshots, VM migration, disaster recovery, performance monitoring, compliance management, and capacity management.

- The introduction of the hypervisor and the potential of multiple virtualized services on the same physical hardware can lead to contention for physical resources, resulting in a potential degradation experienced by individual services/functions or a whole chain via that single component. Not only will the NFV orchestration system need to monitor for such degradation, it will need visibility into the hypervisor and host resources to troubleshoot and potentially isolate/mitigate the contention.

- The hypervisor itself introduces a potential single point of failure (SPOF) that can impact many concurrent VMs on a host and potentially many different service chains.

- The hypervisor virtual switch can congest while serving the multiple vNICs of the various VMs and needs to be able to identify and prioritize control traffic to avoid application and management failure.

- Additionally, the hypervisor can isolate the applications from awareness of changes in physical machine state like failure of a NIC port. This management awareness needs to be bridged by SDN controller and Orchestration cooperation.

- Finally, virtual machines can also be migrated while operating as part of a high availability (HA) strategy. This behavior can impact a service chain in different ways, and so this behavior is sometimes intentional or unintentional as part of this strategy insofar as being used for HA capabilities.

Data Plane I/O

Generally speaking, advances in data-plane I/O have been key enablers to running services on COTS hardware. Because the hypervisor vSwitch used in NFV/service virtualization methods adds an additional performance overhead for I/O simply because virtualization/abstraction is not free, there have been evolving penalty mitigation hardware and software strategies. I/O acceleration techniques that are software (OS or hypervisor) based include Virtio and SR-IOV:

- Virtio is the main platform for disk and network I/O virtualization in Linux, FreeBSD, and other operating systems. Virtio provides a layer of abstraction over devices in a para-virtualized[4] hypervisor/VMM and provides I/O benefits when compared to full virtualization.

- SR-IOV (PCI-SIG Single Root I/O Virtualization) works with the class of I/O hardware built around PCIe technology. This PCIe specification splits a device into multiple PCI Express Requester IDs (it splits physical functions into lighter-weight

---

4. Paravirtualization allows for the relocation of the execution of critical tasks from the virtual domain to the host domain by providing hooks that allow the guest and host OS to interact (for those tasks). Xen, VMware (external), and KVM (hypervisors) all use Virtio for I/O paravirtualization.

virtual functions), allowing the I/O MMU to distinguish between individual traffic streams, apply memory/interrupt translations, and perform delivery directly to a VM (each PCI Express virtual function, mapped to an ID, can be assigned to a VM). This bypasses the software switch layer and reduces the impact of software emulation on I/O. The mapping ratio of physical device to virtual device is 1:256.

The PCIE virtual functions appear to be hardware devices to the VM. All data packets flow directly between the specific guest OS and the virtual function through an independent memory space, interrupts, and DMA stream. I/O throughput, CPU utilization, and latency are all improved.

SR-IOV has both hardware (NIC) and software support requirements that translate into the BIOS as well as in the operating system instance or hypervisor.

Further acceleration of I/O can be bound in specific vendor hardware I/O enhancements (NIC and CPU).

Intel has been honing a series of I/O performance boosts for developers that have been progressing with the capabilities of their CPUs and NICs (those based on Intel architecture), including:

- Pure hardware design improvement—pipeline depth, direct cache access, integration of the memory controller, and integration of high bandwidth PCIe Gen3.[5]

- Intel Virtualization Technology (Intel VT)—VTx, c, and d.

- VT-x provides CPU-level hardware assist for VM migration and 32-bit guests (supported by VMware, Microsoft, Xen, KVM, Citrix, Red Hat, Novell, and Parallels).

- VT-d accelerates I/O virtualization by enabling direct assignment of an I/O device to a VM (requires BIOS support on OEM platforms, and a wide variety of hypervisor/VMM support).

- VT-c hardware assists in Intel Ethernet for network and storage connectivity, including VMDq and SR-IOV. Virtual Machine Device Queues (VMDq) refers to the sorting/grouping of network packets with multiple queues using LAN silicon instead of the VMM.

- Intel QuickAssist technology that enables Middleware for accelerated packet handling workloads (e.g., DPI, cryptography). Applications can integrate at different levels: program to the Intel QuickAssist technology API or program to open source framework (e.g., OpenSSL libcrypto, Linux kernel crypto API—scatterlist, and zlib) through patches/shims.

---

5. A quick mention for their (a bit more into the weeds for a surface treatment) AVX Extensions—a 256-bit Instruction Set Architecture (ISA) built on legacy 128-bit SIMD (SSEx—with enhancements) and 64-bit SIMD (MMX) ISA extensions; supported by GCC v4.6, Linux kernel 2.6.30, and the Intel C++ Compiler 12.1.

- Commercial integration partners (e.g., 6Wind[6] and Wind River[7]) offer scheduling and other enhancements that dedicate cores to packet I/O integrated via special packaging (e.g., Wind River Linux, and Wind River Hypervisor).

- Intel Data Direct I/O Technology (Intel DDIO)[8]—leverages integrated PCIe lanes on the CPU, reducing memory accesses and speeding up CPU data transfer, which is sometimes referred to as NIC core pinning.

- Intel DPDK[9]—Intel's most recent innovation in I/O virtualization improvements, Dataplane Development Kit (Figure 7-3), provides data plane libraries and optimized (poll-mode) NIC drivers (for Intel NICs) in Linux user space that provide advanced queue and buffer management, and flow classification through a simple API interface (supported via a standard tool chain—gcc/icc, gdb, and profiling tools).

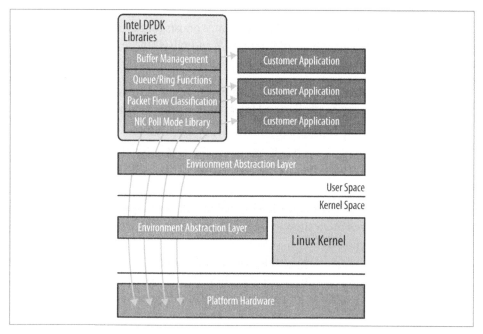

Figure 7-3. Intel DPDK

6. 6Wind (*http://www.6wind.com*) features a set of vEPC products for Intel hosts that features their dataplane I/O enhancements.

7. Intel acquired Wind River.

8. Introduced with Sandy Bridge CPU and Intel Ethernet PCIe I/O devices.

9. Intel has developed a DPDK-enhanced version of ovswitch for the public domain and works with major virtualiztion projects (KVM, Xen, UML, and xVM).

NIC vendors (other than Intel) are not without their own I/O acceleration tricks:

- RoCE (RDMA over Converged Ethernet) is potentially useful application of APIs for cluster computing between/among the virtualized network functions[10] (an I/O virtualization technique). Mellanox (*http://www.mellanox.com*) is a primary proponent of RoCE technology and its potential use in NFV. Their NICs accelerate RoCE support and provide dynamically linked, user-space libraries that offload network packet processing from the CPU by allowing applications to directly access the NIC.[11]

- Similarly, other specific, specialized virtual application acceleration (e.g., PCoIP—Teradici (*http://www.teradici.com*) offers NICs optimized for PCoIP) could potentially find applicability in the NFV virtual services space.[12]

There is a difference between (raw) data-plane I/O and data-plane processing (e.g., applying Access Control Lists or performing packet transformations at the vSwitch or bridge) that may have some bearing the efficacy of some virtualized functions/solutions. The history of routing/switching development has numerous examples of throughput fall-off in the presence of such operations (that were successfully optimized over time).

I/O Summary

While a number of details have been presented here, the net-net is that a great deal of scrutiny and effort is being applied to reducing interrupt density, context switching, and buffer memory copies (i.e., zero-copy strategies). This effort is primarily driven by the explosion in development of virtualized services and is quite appropriate due to their inherent I/O component and the need to improve overall performance and scale. Going forward, the most important goal for NFV will be to find optimization methods that the community deems acceptably open (i.e., not tied to a single vendor's hardware technology), unless an obvious de facto hardware standard evolves, potentially like the ones just described.

---

10. RDMA is possible in Infiniband networks, but these are less familiar outside of the data center environment.

11. The feasibility of RoCE assumes some of the attributes present in a DCB (Data Center Bridging) environment in which the separate priorities for different streams can be treated as separate pipes and latency can be lowered or bounded. In this environment, RDMA provides remote memory access API (an alternative to the Berkeley socket API) functionality that is bounded by an Ethernet broadcast domain (RoCE is a link layer protocol that requires some mapping between its GID system and the MAC).

12. PCoIP hasn't been proposed as a virtualization strategy for NFV (to date) and is used only to illustrate the potential of data plane optimizations in the NFV space.

Services Engineered Path

In 2010, a proposal to decouple the Service and Network infrastructure (plane) was proposed by Jim Guichard, then a principal architect in the CTO Office at Juniper Networks. The Service Engineered Path (SEP) concept (Figure 7-4) was introduced as a potentially new means of service delivery for the Service Provider community—a Juniper-specific solution, but one that solved the problem prior to any standardization of such a concept.

The problem statement addressed in SEP was that service providers were constrained in making new service offerings by the need to deploy the service appliances (or dedicated services blades) that would comprise the service offering. Service offerings included firewalls, Intrusion Detection Systems (IDS), Intrusion Prevention Systems (IPS), load balancers, and SSL off-loaders that were run within the edge routers that would serve their projected markets.

These constraints made service introduction laborious and disruptive to network operation and put a premium on predicting the markets for a service where you could have too few subscribers and you have stranded resources, or too many subscribers and then need to install more appliances/blades.

The motivation for the idea was manifold:

- Network devices that provide Service Enabling Technologies (SETs) would be transparent to the general network infrastructure.
- Changes/additions/upgrades to one or more service instances wouldn't affect routing in the network, providing a more stable service introduction environment.
- Provide flexible service SET and instance placement, and streamlined capacity planning of services.
- Faster time to market for services from a design, upgrade, testing, and deployment perspective.
- Edge routers need not be upgraded every time a new service is added or upgraded with new functionality.
- Providing the ability to link together services of differing types, thereby enabling new and innovative bundled services.

Basically, these providers could benefit both in cost and operations if these SETs could be pooled locally or remotely (the same basic appeal of host virtualization in data centers).

New services could be created by identifying qualifying flows at the edge and steering them through these SETs via a SEP (Service Engineered Path), which could be constructed using the overlay technologies available at the time: VLANs, MPLS, or IP tunnels.

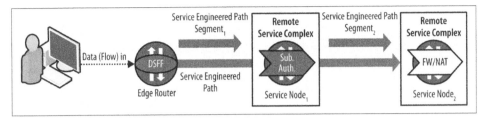

Figure 7-4. Basic SEP concept

The construction of service was a hierarchy of the following components:

Service
> A service function, application, or content used singularly or in collaboration with other SETs to enable a service.

SET Sequence
> Predetermined sequence of SETs that form the service.

Set Sequence Path
> As an instance of a SET may be available at multiple points in the network, there are potentially several combinations of Service Nodes that could form part of the SET sequence. The SET sequence path is a list of [Service Node, SET] combinations available that could be used to satisfy the service.

A service orchestration and registration service was envisioned to facilitate provisioning and ongoing management.

Traffic was originally identified and steered onto the path using Dynamic Service Flow Filters, and the paths themselves were controlled by MPLS encapsulation.

As time went by, SDN technologies—most notably PCE and OpenFlow—were introduced (Figure 7-5). The idea was refined, though there was some dabbling with the concept of using LDP label distribution as a potential way of creating the overlay abstraction/encapsulation.

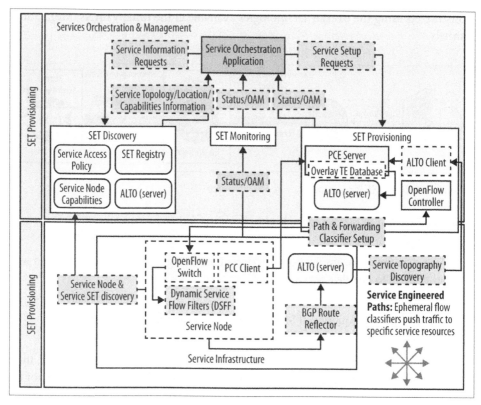

Figure 7-5. Evolved SEP concept with OpenFlow, ALTO (topology), and PCE

Virtualization techniques and virtual I/O improvements were just beginning to evolve when the SEP concept was introduced, so the wholesale virtualization of the service plane on COTS wasn't an integral part of the proposal as it is now with ETSI NFV. However, the genesis of the ideas of separating the service plane, network function virtualization, and service chaining can be traced back to this concept (as do some commercial products).

Ultimately (and unfortunately), network function virtualization became the superset terminology for earlier concepts like those introduced with SEP (as well as the name of the ETSI work group).

Service Locations and Chaining

The concept of service chaining shouldn't assume the service elements are located in a data center (or that all the service elements are virtualized), even though this may be a long-term goal of service providers for their edge/access deployments.[13]

Services may be naturally associated with network boundaries, for example, by attaching a security policy to a network boundary or by inserting a load balancer at a network boundary. As shown in Figure 7-6, this network boundary may be:

- The boundary between a tenant network and an external network (the Internet or the VPN to the enterprise network)
- The boundary between the network of one tenant and the network of another tenant
- The boundary between multiple networks of the same tenant

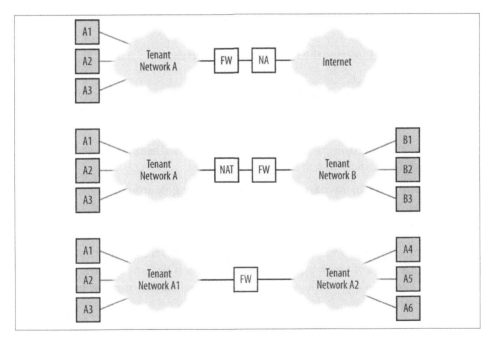

Figure 7-6. Services at network boundaries

Finally, services may be deployed in a more finely grained fashion and be attached to individual flows or groups of flows (i.e., aggregate flows), as shown in Figure 7-7. This

---

13. Many service providers already have distributed data centers to support mobile (infrastructure) and/or video caching (in either major metro centers or regional centers).

is the major model of interest for cloud service providers and in the Edge/Access network domain per-subscriber services.

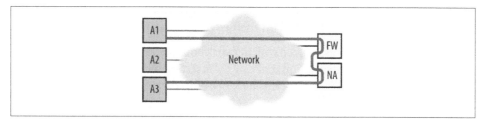

Figure 7-7. Services for flows

Applying services to flows of traffic involves several steps:

1. Defining the elements and the ordering and configurations required to implement a service. This definition includes the constraints on the placement of service elements.

2. Identifying and steering the flow of traffic to visit the service node or the sequence of service nodes.

3. Vendors have begun to label their current methodologies for doing service chaining. In the case of Cisco Systems, this is called vPath, and in the case of Juniper Networks, The Service Engineered Path (SEP).

4. Control plane signaling to the service nodes to inform them which services to apply to which flows, including the service parameters.

5. As we will see later, there are also optimizations possible around original placement of the service node and/or the ongoing placement of additional service instances to alleviate performance bottlenecks.

All of these tasks are well suited for an SDN controller. SDN controllers have domain/network-wide views of topology, hooks to orchestration systems (API), and the ability to manage/provision a network overlay (or the abstraction that might be used to match and direct traffic).

The use of an SDN controller may seem to be an obvious conclusion in the context of service chaining in the data center, but less so in the Edge/Access domains (where the added cost of a co-located controller may be prohibitive but the potential interaction delay between agent/controller may be problematic). This brings us back to the idea of an embedded controller, shown in Figure 7-8 (originally broached as an optimization to the control feedback loop in research studies on involving the identification of "mice and elephant" flows and forwarding table size management in OpenFlow controlled networks). Here, the data plane element that terminates the circuit at the edge where it has internal process acting as a slave subcontroller to a master controller, which would in turn interface with orchestration applications and simply provide state/rule and configuration updates.

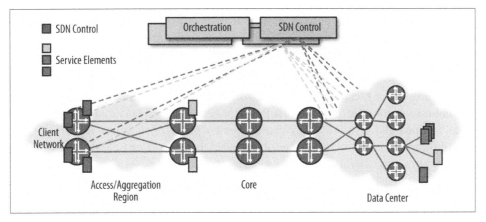

Figure 7-8. For non-data center regions of the network, embedded SDN control processes in network elements may be appropriate

In a mixed environment (i.e., virtualized and legacy service elements) or an entirely legacy environment, the elements may not support some of the tunnel encapsulations used in SDN overlays or a native agent that pairs well with the SDN controller. Thus, a mixture of VLANs and tunnel encapsulations, as well as configuration/control protocols between controller/controllers and network elements, may be required to create service chains.

Metadata

Outstanding questions remain regarding the standardization of the overlay encapsulation and the traffic matching protocol(s) used in creating service chains/paths. These questions are complicated by the consideration of whether some sort of metadata may need to be implanted in the flow.

This latter consideration comes both from knowledge of how service applications currently are designed in integrated systems that use metadata to pass clues from one processing block to another within the integrated system, as well as the potential (as envisioned in the ETSI NFV workgroups) of partial decomposition and virtualization of service functions (shown later in this chapter in Figure 7-13).

The answer to the question of whether metadata is required may depend on the vision of the role of the controller and its service chaining application, particularly whether they will be charged with creating a chain that precludes any inter-block knowledge. It may also depend on whether the virtualization vision limits function decomposition to the same virtual device or composite and thus separates an internal chain that uses some

IPC mechanism that allows internal embedded metadata from the external chain/overlay.

The most common examples used as an example requirement for metadata involving contexts that cannot be derived from the flow packet headers—e.g., subscriber-specific ad insertion in the treatment of a video flow (where some further clue is embedded that reflects geography, interests, or other triggers for the ad insertion).

Should there be a requirement for the passing of metadata between NFV functional blocks, and if the metadata was flow-associated versus per-packet association, there could be a role for a Metadata Access Point (MAP) in the overall architecture. Existing specifications like IF-MAP[14] may provide server/protocol solutions for creating and distributing metadata but need to be integrated in the flow set-up or SDN control phases of building service chains.

Metadata can be implicit (e.g., associated with an MPLS label) or explicit. The explicit alternative, to embed the metadata, may result in extensions or overhead in packets to pass metadata from one chain member to another that will almost certainly require standardization to promote an open environment and may bring on collateral concerns about transparency of such augmented flows to the existing network infrastructure.

An Application Level Approach

What if we're solving the service chaining aspect of NFV at the wrong level? Should we explore a solution using application-based protocols instead of network-based constructs? The network construct view requires tunneling because data flows have intrinsic routing that needs to be obscured (i.e., don't forward on destination address). This view assumes that network protocols can be manipulated to direct the flows as well as to manage metadata, with the aid of a controller.

The application construct view (Figure 7-9) treats data flows as application inputs and outputs. Applications run on servers (using discrete sockets), and those servers have resolvable names (DNS). That service instance name to IP address binding identifies the load balancer (or an anycast address for a bank of ADC/load balance capacity—the assumption of a load balancer is quite common) for a set of components that run the service and potentially multiple input and output ports representing different application personalities (i.e., configurations or behaviors). Bidirectional flows use two personalities.

14. http://www.trustedcomputinggroup.org/resources/tnc_ifmap_binding_for_soap_specification

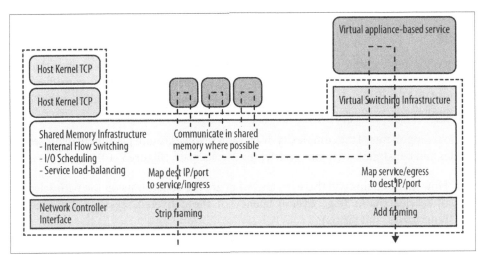

Figure 7-9. The application-level proposal for service chaining leverages an optimized stack to communicate with virtual appliances and allows a runtime environment for some virtualized network services that use shared memory to communicate (an optimization)

The service path specifies mapping from internal service ports to external transport ports for each service and connectivity between the transport ports.[15] These service paths are generated from a data model that expresses the relationships between a service component, services, and service paths, and propagated/applied from a management system to the service instances (through a yet-to-be-determined API). More explicitly, the model expresses relationships between service functions and internal port/socket to external port mappings, more general attributes like scaling/constraints and load balancing, and how the functions are interconnected to create a service.

While just in the idea/exploratory phase, this approach to chaining via a series of familiar application-keyed technologies (e.g., DNS and ADC/LB) in conjunction with some new application management technologies (e.g., controllers and their API) may be interesting if the number of chains (and thus tunnels) becomes overwhelming. As a benefit, one of the different ideas explored here is the idea that functional elements on the same device might use IPC mechanisms via shared memory to improve performance in cases where a mixture of application interaction via external protocol and internal IPC form the chain.

---

15. This is *not* a detailed description of the internal mapping to external mapping.

Scale

Even if the current state of SDN makes the network construct palatable, given that it is already an available entity with which we can experiment and build, considerations around scale and complexity can't be ignored. Scale and complexity also cannot drive the application-level approach conversation.

Major components of the complexity discussion revolve around placement of the service nodes and constraints that may restrict the service path (Figure 7-10):

- How many chains will there be, and what are the constraints on the path selection of service chains (e.g., overall latency of the delivered service, administrative boundaries, and tariffs)?
- How do those constraints affect the HA policy for a service (e.g., should individual SETs be added to or from the chain if their placement causes trombone flows in the network, or should the flow fail over to an entirely new chain)?
- How often will the chain topology change, and how dynamic/elastic is the loading of the elements in the chain?
- Is there a benefit to service placement algorithms that minimize the potential for network bottlenecks and contribution to overall delay in a serviced flow?
- What role does policy play in the service chain embedded within the chain as a decision/branch point or when expressed as multiple different chain topologies? When would packets be sent to a remote in-line service (i.e., not a proxy)?

Raw scale is also a factor in the complexity discussion:

- Number of subscribers/sessions
- Length/duration of sessions/flows and profile of packet lengths
- Packet throughput expectations, and both the capabilities of the overall chain and each individual element (e.g., load balancer)

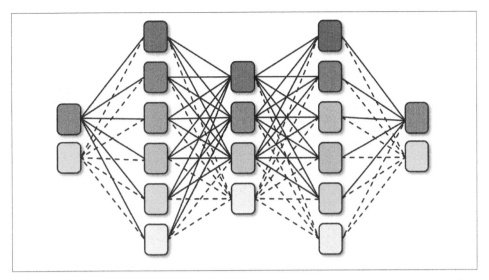

Figure 7-10. How complex will service chaining be? Load balancing and HA introduce a requirement for many tunnels to be set up between service nodes. Elasticity and dynamic paths require potentially large-scale tunnel creation/deletion.

Given the potential scale implications and overall service constraints, placement of virtual service functions and the resulting service chains are likely to be highly localized. The highest path diversity in the chain being potentially in the connectivity between an edge/access domain device and a centralized COTS resource bank (a data center)—with a failover to another such resource bank.

NFV at ETSI

NFV activity in ETSI hopes to address these and other questions about service virtualization. NFV in ETSI functions as an Industry Specification Group (ISG). The NFV workgroups (Figure 7-11) will not define standards. Instead, their goals are to define requirements, identify best practices, identify gaps in current standards, and make recommendations on how to fill those gaps. NFV has a main organizational body, a technical steering committee (TSC), and several subgroups with specific areas of focus. Vendors are invited to contribute to the discussions, but large service providers dominate the list of NFV officials by organizational design.[16] At the time this book was written, not all the groups had produced position papers, though early documentation has defined their interfaces and roles.

---

16. According to their current online list, only Huawei Technologies (UK), Hewlett Packard, and NEC (Europe) currently have "official" status in any subworkgroup.

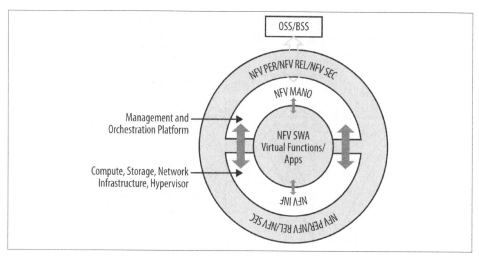

Figure 7-11. ETSI NFV work group organization/structure. Both MAN and INF have interfaces with NFV SWA as well as with each other. Cross-functional workgroups (PER, REL and SEC) don't have defined interfaces with MANO, INF and SWA, but work in conjunction with them. NFV SWA anticipates an interface to legacy OSS/BSS systems (not shown).

Management and Orchestration (MANO) defines a framework that can be used for the provisioning, configuration, and operation of virtualized network functions (VNF)—essentially defining an orchestrator that controls all the VNFs. The MANO Orchestrator has both an application (northbound) interface and element (southbound) interface. While the southbound interface is defined in another group (infrastructure), the northbound interface provides VNF lifecycle services (instantiation, operation, and monitoring), policing (usage controls), infrastructure monitoring (which would be somewhat of a pass-through function), and registration/topology.

MANO reinforces the concept that potentially new management tools may need to be added to the traditional OAM&P model to handle virtualized network services (the point was made earlier that the SDN controller may be uniquely positioned as a new management entity). In the MANO case, this is proposed as the NFV Orchestrator (NFVO), which will interface with legacy OSS/BSS.

It remains to be seen whether this implies that much of the management information that might have been collected by the SDN controller/agent mechanism is either represented by this application interface, other application interfaces, or some intrinsic interface at the SDN controller level to the legacy OSS/BSS. In the example of DC Orchestration, the MANO Orchestration platform can work in conjunction with a Cloud Management System, which is shown logically below the MANO Orchestration in some NFV documents.

Part of the MANO work will be to define data models (Yang, TMN) for these various tasks/interfaces and provide an open API. This work includes cloud and network models (in cooperation with NFV INF) that may allow the creation of a macro management application (a Manager of Managers?) for virtual infrastructure.

Somewhere in the orchestration function, there should be an ability to map functional capacity to demand and to potentially provide a service topology that includes both an API and visualization component. The SDN controller will need to manage the topology and endpoint mappings.

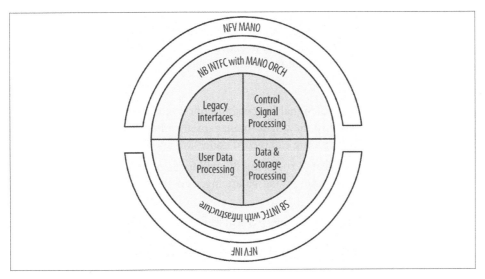

Figure 7-12. Interaction of ETSI MANO, INF and SWA work groups (SWA view with proposed inner functional groups)

Infrastructure—(NFV INF) defines common infrastructure for NFV. As shown in Figure 7-12, the intent is to include both hardware and software. This group has been very active in authoring documents and has already cataloged approximately 14 inter-domain interfaces in the NFV architecture. They are responsible for recommending the hypervisor-level architectures that streamline I/O and minimize context switching as well as the data model mentioned in the MANO section.

There has been a good discussion about which of the I/O optimization strategies common in the domain are best suited for NFV (e.g., DPDK versus SR-IOV) performance. This topic has a dependency on the proposed Reliability and Availability architecture, as the latter might include the concept of VM-motion, which may preclude an optimization strategy of SR-IOV. In discussion, the case has been made that SR-IOV is less friendly to VM-motion.[17]

Software Architecture—(NFV SWA) defines use cases and how solutions should be structured and possibly decomposed into functional blocks.

One of the interesting questions for NFV in general is what services can be virtualized and in what method. There is a spectrum of potential solutions, from the fully virtualized service running as a single VM through a multipart (a service comprised of functional sub-blocks), fully virtualized service to the service that must run on bare metal. Note that the latter could still benefit from orchestration from an operations perspective.

NFV SWA believes that the virtualized functions should be able to interact either directly with INF or indirectly through MANO to express operational requirements (e.g., compute, storage, security, QOS, memory resources, and support requirements (e.g., monitoring, metering, and billing).

- Their proposed Control Signal Processing Function Group will focus on authentication/authorization, policy, state management, mobility, and mobility-related support functions, including call record collection and lawful intercept.
- Their proposed User Data Processing FG will focus on packet forwarding, duplication, counting, processing, load balancing, and application layer steering (i.e., proxy).
- Their proposed Data and Storage FG will focus on data storage and management.

In SWA, NFV builds on the SEP concept of a SET (in NFV, now called a VNF), in that a SET or service function can be decomposed into component parts or functional blocks (assuming the set may be comprised of more than one functional block—e.g., signal processing, transaction management, and content processing).

If decomposed into more than one functional block, those blocks can then run in many possible arrangements. Thus, description is also required of the relationships and communication between the parts, operational behavior, and constraints (e.g., topology).

These function descriptors are similar to the policies attached to SDN applications, which will be expressed-to/imposed-on SDN controllers. Such policies specify each application's routing, security, performance, QoS, geofencing, access control, consistency, availability/disaster-recovery, and other operational expectations/parameters.

One very important task for the SWA is to define the descriptors in a way that allows flow-through provisioning. That is, while the orchestration system and SDN controller

---

17. While nothing has been decided at this point in time, this example is used more to point out the potential dependencies between NFV subgroups. There may be additional dependencies on outcomes from NFV PER testing.

can collaborate on placement, pathing and instantiation of the network functions, their individual and composite configurations can be quite complex—and are currently vendor-specific.

The Open Virtual Format (OVF) (currently the de facto standard for the packaging of virtual machines) is capable of expressing some configuration metadata today but is incapable of the potential configuration complexity of some of the envisioned services and thus needs to be extended or augmented.

The goal would be for the operator to not have to exit to separate configuration entities post-instantiation, avoiding retouching the collection of machines that comprise the individual or composite service.

One of the examples used is Evolved Packet Core (EPC) application (generically), which can be broken down into the following functions: policy/rule-set processing, user/session state management, layer 3 packet processing, layer 7 traffic steering function, and so on. This functional decomposition is illustrated in Figure 7-13.

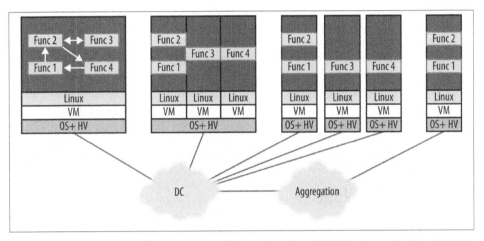

Figure 7-13. Functional decomposition. If a service (e.g., EPC) is virtualized, will all its subcomponents run in the same VM, in separate VMs on the same host, as separate VMs on different hosts in the same logical domain (e.g., data center), or as separate VMs on different hosts in multiple logical domains (e.g., data center and aggregation)?

Security (NFV SEC)
 Defining how to secure both infrastructure and the virtualized service functions (including the API). This would also include authentication, identity management, monitoring, detection, and mitigation of threats.

Performance and Scale (NFC PER)
 This is self-evident. The group will try and define practices that provide optimal performance, describe performance/scale/portability tradeoffs, and present

performance test data (several carriers have proposed tests including the impact on performance of the use of various vendor's NICs and different types of I/O mechanisms).

Reliability and Availability (NFV REL)

Defines deployment and management practices that assure reliability and availability. At this point, they've defined some useful terminology for the expression of application requirements and constraints: delay/traffic/disruption/fault tolerances, performance (e.g., QOS requirements), security (non-repudiation, confidentiality, authorization, etc.), and dependability/reliability.

This group has also touched on some interesting questions about in-chain failure (one element or function fails in the chain) and potential application involvement, the elimination of single points of failure (e.g., hypervisor), the need for heartbeat mechanisms between subcomponents, and the emulation of (hardware/software) watchdogs that might have been present in non-virtualized solutions.

NFV REL also will address some of the potential problems in a virtualized environment that need to be addressed for a carrier-grade deployment ("Virtualization and Data Plane I/O" on page 208).

Use cases documents seem to be coming from several groups besides the SWA. There is a Network Operations Council (NOC) that defines use cases, and the INF group has provided illustrative use cases as well. These are only limited by imagination and include specifics (e.g., WAN Optimization, Firewall, Router, IPTV Head-end, DPI, Residential Gateway/CPE, Mobile Base Station, and Mobile Packet Core) as well as more generic service descriptions (e.g., partial decomposition of a function, using purpose-built hardware, nd sharing compute between VNFs).

Non-ETSI NFV Work

The existence of the ETSI workgroup shouldn't imply that this is the only place service virtualization study and standards are being conducted or that production service virtualization offerings are not already coming to market. This is far from the case; for example:

- The academic community is beginning to study some of the questions around NFV as part of the burgeoning SDN research they are performing.

- Many existing controller/framework vendors are targeting service chaining as one of their applications and a few startups (e.g., LineRate, Embrane) are positioning controllers for layer 2 through layer 7 that work with their own virtualized services.

- Existing vendors of highly integrated network elements are investigating intermediate or total virtualization of their platform/solutions.

- Though it is too early for a complete section in this revision, the IETF has begun soliciting interest in the area of service chaining. A proposed work group (Network Service Chaining [NSC]) is currently collecting drafts in its BoF (birds of a feather) stage[18]. This includes drafts proposing formalized packet headers for expressing service context and metadata as well as the need for a standardized generic service control plane.

Middlebox Studies

In the academic community, recent studies have focused on optimization of Middlebox appliances,[19] which are essentially the virtual service appliances (or a subset) targeted by NFV studies. In particular, the studies focus on the ability to integrate, manage, and scale a complete Middlebox deployment, with the recognition that these could be more than one device—a service chain.

The University of Wisconsin has a progression of studies (Stratos,[20] which appears to progress as CloudMB[21]) that propose optimizing performance of such chains by monitoring serviced streams based on an application-reported performance metric and (using a greedy heuristic) spinning up or down instances of specific middleboxes to alleviate bottlenecks (triggered by significant change in performance over some time threshold) while maintaining a pre-determined level of application performance.

The study is also concerned with optimizations of the initial middlebox placement, the heuristic (scale) and in-flow assignment to the middleboxes such that inter-rack traffic was avoided (network-aware placement and flow distribution) as an additional bottleneck source.

There was also emphasis on not moving existing flows (no service interruption or make-before-break behavior) in the scale up/down phases (the scale down phase is an interesting inclusion because there could be cost savings during idle network periods).

There are interesting concepts in the research around the heuristic and some of the simplifying operations assumptions/assertions (in respect to service chaining):

---

18. The BOF (proposed for IETF 87) proposal and related papers are currently located online (*http://trac.tools.ietf.org/bof/trac/*) (though the documents may move to an archival status post-BOF).

19. These are publicly available and presented studies and not meant to be a complete listing of research on the topic.

20. *http://minds.wisconsin.edu/bitstream/handle/1793/61606/stratos_tech_report.pdf?sequence=3*

21. *http://www.opennetsummit.org/pdf/2013/research_track/poster_papers/final/ons2013-final28.pdf*

- The operator would prefer not to manually intervene at all (fully automated solution) and that the nature or function of the middlebox was somewhat irrelevant to the process (or could be made so by the process).

- The preferred solution to congestion in the service chain can be solved in place (relatively), without diverting or "trombone(ing)" traffic to an instance or chain segment in another location (i.e., minimizing branching).

- The assertion that monitoring can't be derived from traditional traffic counters in the infrastructure because of the nature of operation of some of the devices. Nor can the simple monitoring of resource consumption in the VMs be assumed to reflect end-to-end application performance. Thus, application involvement in monitoring is preferred.[22]

- The iterative heuristic was chosen over other strategies: scaling all middleboxes in the path, reliance on function-specific monitoring, reliance on packet processing time estimates, and monitoring CPU load on the service elements.

The solution uses a high-level topology abstraction for the definition of service chains, and a central controller to program forwarding (e.g., using an OpenFlow controller). The controller was augmented with a topology file that is populated with middlebox and application instances from which it can generate service-chain forwarding rules for the switching infrastructure (according to the abstracted topology chains). In a more generic sense, this augmentation alters the traditional (simple) topology and path computation of the controller to be service aware.

The system/process works in conjunction with a VM orchestration system to initially place the service VMs and to add/subtract instances as the heuristic spins up/down scale.

Slick[23] takes a different tack. While the semantics of SDN protocols have promised the ability to transmogrify a (v)switch into a network service appliance, limitations in both the protocol and existing implementations have prevented realization of that possibility. Slick navigates two broad areas: working around the limitations of the existing static semantics of flow matching in SDN and (maybe inadvertently) dynamic service chaining.

In this project, the specialized controller speaks to an agent (a Slick controller and agent) on a programmable device (e.g., a server, potentially with a programmable network element—FPGA, NPU, GPU) to dynamically load application functions and provide returning triggers to the controller from those functions.

---

22. This is not a unique perspective for overlay networks in particular (e.g., Resilient Overlay Networks (*http://nms.csail.mit.edu/ron/*)).

23. *http://www.opennetsummit.org/pdf/2013/research_track/poster_papers/final/ons2013-final51.pdf*

Applications interface with the controller to install functions in the network along with a matching set of flow specifications. The controller has responsibility for placement of the functions (a commonality with CloudMB) and to establish paths for the flows to the function.

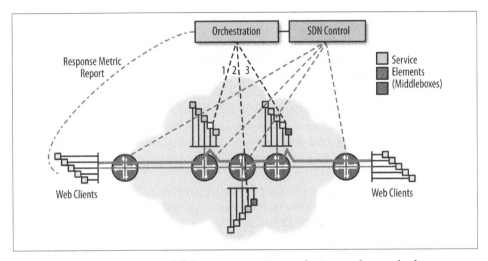

Figure 7-14. An iterative middlebox optimization technique; when web clients report out of specification response times, the orchestrator (in conjunction with the SDN controller) iteratively tries to add (localized) capacity to the different middleboxes in the service path to remove the bottleneck

The concept seems to break the vertical integration of middleboxes by removing the a priori assignment of functionality (e.g., the device is no longer a firewall per se, but could perform some of the functions of a firewall). So, Slick not only broaches service chaining in general but also the definition of a virtualized service.

Embrane/LineRate

While Embrane was not included in the book's controller survey chapter, it could be considered a very specialized SDN controller appropriate to the discussion of NFV. Embrane markets Heleos, a platform that enables the provisioning of virtual network services. Since it doesn't depend on any standardized SDN protocols and integrates the service management application directly into their application, the terms controller, orchestration and management system get a little blurry. (This is becoming a recurring theme in SDN in general!) Like some other SDN controller/agent architectures, Embrane's control processes (ESM—the Elastic Services Manager) only work with their devices (DVA—Distributed Virtual Appliances). A DVA is essentially a virtual service element for COTS compute. Embrane currently offers load balancing and firewall services.

One of the big questions with a solution like Embrane, and in fairness, with all SDN-like solutions coming to market, is whether it will develop an open ecosystem for the development and management of third-party applications or continue down a proprietary path. Should it choose the latter, whether customers will adopt the solution in numbers large enough to forge some sort of de facto standard is ultimately a fair question to ask of this solution.

LineRate Systems was acquired by F5 Networks.[24] LineRate spun up out of work at the University of Colorado and had one (public) product at the time, a virtual Load Balancer (LineRate Proxy). The virtual service was a full application layer proxy driven by external policy with traffic steering capabilities. This is very much a product relevant to the discussion of virtualized services/NFV. LineRate differs from Embrane in that it doesn't appear to have a separate controller/agent architecture or controller offering. Instead, it provides an external policy server. LineRate did have an interesting perspective on the definition of SDN and the decomposition of network functions:

- LineRate has what appears to be a DPI-like approach to SDN but claims to be different because it doesn't steer traffic based on packet-based matching/forwarding behaviors. Instead, it uses its ability to cache and replay application-level requests in combination with policies applied to the responses to do the steering. This allows the solution to potentially re-issue the request to a different source or an intermediary service, e.g., video optimization.

- LineRate points out in its marketing literature that perhaps as integrated network services (e.g., EPC) decompose, the LineRate solution is positioned to be even more effective as a control point.

NFV work in ETSI has contributions that also suggest that some mixture of low-touch control such as flow matching like that found in OpenFlow, and high-touch control such as full proxies, may be needed at different places in the flow. The low-touch control would be useful in flow setup and in doing some location steering, and the high-touch control would be used to split or aggregate traffic.

Embrane and Linerate both have advertised flexible licensing models including keyless, usage-based, and subscription options (each company uses different terminology for these models, but the ideas are the same). Since pricing/licensing can be fairly fluid, it can quickly become historic. But licensing is yet another important consideration in the discussion of NFV or service virtualization. For example, a usage-based pricing model would be more desirable with optimizations and automation like those presented by Stratos/CloudMB (or feedback loops like those shown in later use case chapters that optimize the traffic sent to service nodes).

---

24. *http://www.f5.com/about/news/press/2013/20130211/*

Platform Virtualization

Current service provider networks have evolved into a collection of purpose-designed, integrated elements or platforms. For example, the fundamental design of a core routing platform is to forward packets at an extremely high speed and low latency with packaging sensitive to physical footprint, power consumption, and associated heat. The placement of this platform at the network/provider edge, where a tradeoff may be required between forwarding rate, session state management, protocol session scale, and other services—may be difficult without an entirely different set of forwarding blades and service blades.

Over time, some vendors became specialists in packaging certain types of platforms. The most common examples are the Broadband Network Gateway and Evolved Packet Core components.[25]

As SDN began to be explored by network operators, competitors to the entrenched "big three or four" vendors of these platforms began to explore new packaging models that reduced cost and leveraged some of the principles of service virtualization.

The general designs put forward were to use an SDN Controller (e.g., an OpenFlow controller) to program forwarding state into a (much simpler and lower cost) switching element and create application specific state (protocol or user session state) on an associated server-based application. There are also the (previously mentioned) projects to replace or centralize the functions of the current generation of routers with cheaper components like RouteFlow (BGP and IGP on OpenFlow) or Flexinet (BGP on Open-Flow) and more recent work with IP Infusion[26] (ZebOS BGPD).

Traditional vendors are responding by virtualizing low-hanging fruit in traditional network operations like the BGP Route Reflector (vRR); Figure 7-15. These devices are purposely not in the data plane by design and thus are the most easily converted to running in a VM.

If the vRR has a standardized programming interface and standardized controller/agent control session, it becomes a potential SDN control centralization point. Then, existing Provider Edge deployments start to look like SDN deployments (even if they continue to leverage the existing distributed control plane for the most part), providing a bridge between present operations and a more virtualized future operation.

---

25. See *http://www.virtualization.net/5653-carrier-sdn-solutions-virtualized-epc/* or *http://www.huawei.com/en/about-huawei/newsroom/press-release/hw-196147-sdn.htm* (Huawei has also submitted vBNG as an NFV use case.)

26. *http://www.ipinfusion.com*

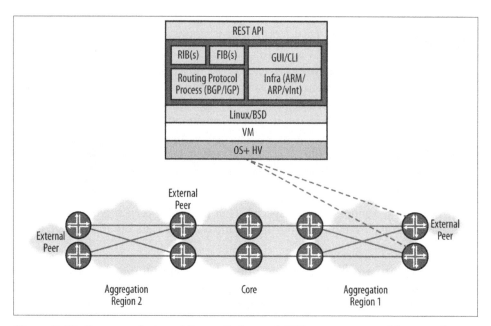

Figure 7-15. Conceptual virtual Route Reflector (vRR) as programmable control point for service provider network (e.g., injecting routes into aggregation network)

This model was explored in the Juniper Networks/Contrail and ALU/Nuage SDN controllers and is appearing in the presentations of other, traditional network element vendors. This is particularly easy to visualize in a data center context, where a virtual Provider Edge (vPE) manifests as a vRR and companion host-based agent (which programs a hypervisor-based routing entity for the data/forwarding plane) as a control plane and the tenant VMs appear as virtual Customer Edge (vCE) entities. However, the vCE could also be established as part of managed service offering for the Enterprise VPN market to centralize/optimize the processing for WaaS, IPSec, and other services (ostensibly by using tunneling of the flows). See Figure 7-16 for a conceptual drawing of a vCE proposal.

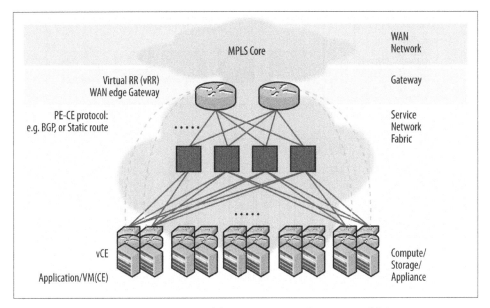

Figure 7-16. Fang/Bitar vCE proposal from MPLS & Ethernet World Congress 2013

There are also tactics that allow traditional network element vendors to incrementally separate their services portfolio from their hardware. For example, some vendors have programs that allow their services to run first on tethered servers (using extensions to their SDK/APIs that are used to chain services in the integrated platform) before ultimately virtualizing the service. This allows some interim scaling of the service on common compute while the chaining orchestration and protocols flesh out (Figure 7-17).

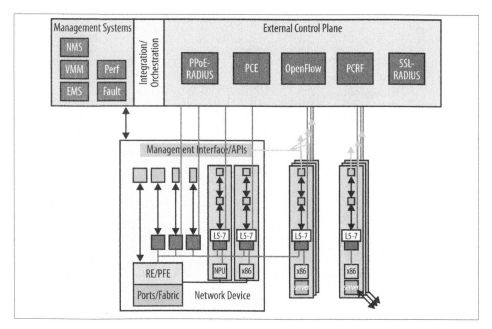

Figure 7-17. Transitional/integrated service virtualization strategies

Services can run on internal NPU or CPU blades, tethered COTS using API extensions that allow internal management and forwarding/chaining techniques to be used on the tethered compute and ultimately an independent entity controlled externally. This level of virtualization and chaining, though proprietary, does allow some scale out on COTS compute and can be combined with application-level load balancing and localized static routing to create new services (e.g., the mobile space's Service Delivery Gateway). In this model, however, the manager of the virtualized service could be the router/switch (particularly in the tethered-appliance model). Lacking any immediate standardization in service chaining protocols and encapsulation, the early market service chains could be created with GRE encapsulation and route-leaking techniques (Figure 7-18).

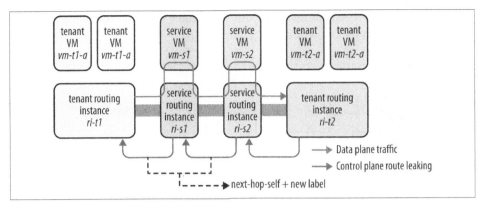

Figure 7-18. Service chaining using routing instances

Many public service providers (broadband aggregators) are also looking to move to a virtualized CPE device (vCPE). These explorations have folded back into ideas the traditional PE (Provider Edge) device for broadband aggregation (BNG/BRAS) might also be effective as a virtual entity (vPE). The motivation for vCPE for carriers was to enable the creation of new services, reduce costs, and reduce customer care calls by moving the functions of (an arguably exhausted) layer 3 CPE to a combination of layer 2 CPE and COTS hardware running layer 3 CPE basic services (e.g., NAT, DHCP, DNS) and possibly more advanced/future services (e.g., security, HTTP Proxy, etc.); see Figure 7-19.

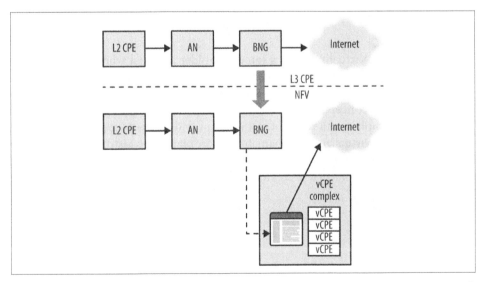

Figure 7-19. Network Function Virtualization applied to layer 3 CPE in service provider networks (proof of concept)

This work ultimately leads to investigations of whether the BNG functionality can be integrated with the vCPE functionality (Figure 7-20).

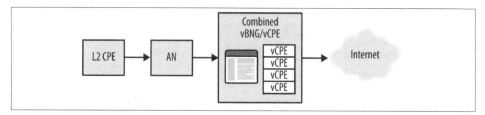

Figure 7-20. A broadband aggregation platform constructed by integrating and virtualizing the functions of both the BNG and the CPE

Work in this area (beyond proof of concept) includes studying performance implications of the placement of the virtualized functions (e.g., south or north of the BNG, colocated with the AN, etc.) and how the integrated functionality can be dissembled to create a horizontally scalable solution. This includes container strategies and I/O optimization strategies that are also being studied/discussed in ETSI NFV forums.

The currently integrated solutions (for the vCPE/vBNG example) have very low price points per subscriber that the new virtualized services will have to meet. Should these new virtual platform designs be technically feasible, it may only be at some point in the future that the cost per subscriber fits the business case (when the COTS price/performance curve crosses the appropriate thresholds).

Conclusions

Network Function Virtualization is a somewhat older idea that when first brought up was not really capable of being realized, but now with the advent of SDN, orchestration techniques and virtualization advances, is now being realized. Just as it does for the control plane, SDN concepts and constructs allow service providers and users to rethink the assumptions built into the current method of providing a service plane or delivering services using new virtualized and chainable service platform constructs. Virtualization alone does not solve all service deployment problems and actually introduces new reliability problem vectors that a service orchestration system or architecture has to mitigate.

While virtualization is the focus of this chapter and the NFV effort, the reality is that the orchestration and chaining involved need to have a scope that includes present and future fully integrated service platforms (at least up to the point where the I/O characteristics of fully virtualized solutions eclipse them and some "tail" period in which they would amortize).

It is unclear whether the data plane-processing overhead that exists today in the virtualization environment will make a great degree of multitenancy in virtual service hosts practical. One practical outcome of NFV will be the integration of orchestration and SDN for traffic steering and scale up/down on demand.

A great deal of research has begun into decomposing existing services into their functional elements and opinions vary on the granularity of this decomposition. Decomposition will ultimately influence service chaining resiliency and availability requirements for both the overall service as well as its individual elements. It further impacts scale and complexity of operation. The overall number of functional elements, service chains, and the constraints on how those chains are constructed and operate need to be defined and may only be known through trial deployments and experimentation. However, these chains will have to incorporate both virtual and non-virtual service elements.

 While service chaining is conflated with NFV, it remains to be seen if service providers will deploy service chains with a wide degree of variance in the physical location of elements or continue to build very linear/pipeline structures similar to those we see today without chaining,. The improvements of NFV leveraged being primarily in the scale up and down (in-situ) of services.

Even though the role of SDN in the control of service virtualization appears to be universally accepted, the type of control point is still debated. This is particularly true in the difference in approach between stateless and proxy control points.

Research like that in the University of Wisconsin[27], further underscores the role of topology in SDN (i.e., moving beyond a simple, single-layer representation) and in the types of abstractions we provide to or via applications (in this case the language to define

---

27. Academic research in general has been a great enabler of SDN and its applications—this is just a specific example.

service chains). This research also brings forward the (often forgotten) topic of troubleshooting in a new operational paradigm.[28]

Like troubleshooting, security currently lags in the top-of-mind conversation about service virtualization (as it does throughout the SDN conversation).[29] This may be one of the areas that the potential user community can bring the most insight/contribution/ enthusiasm (particularly those of you working in the deeper/darker halls of government and black-hat security expertise). Meanwhile, a market for virtualized services is already developing. Specialized SDN solution vendors like Embrane are providing turn-key solutions (that reinvent the load balancing and firewall service concept), and the more generalized controller/framework vendors now speak openly about service chaining being a target application for their platforms (some data center orchestration systems already include appliance recognition and placement in a domain-specific context).

Orchestration may allocate the service containers while SDN provides the connectivity in these NFV architectures or models, including some potential abstractions that hide some of the complexity that comes with elasticity. Both will have to work cooperatively to provide high availability and a single management/operations view. All the while, behind the scenes, traditional OSS/BSS is not really designed to manage the highly decomposed services of NFV, and the NFV Orchestration/SDN pairings will have to provide a transition. These systems will need to evolve and be adapted to the new future reality of virtualized network services that NFV promises.

In closing, it is clear that traditional vendors are pursuing low-hanging fruit transformations of their integrated service platforms via virtualization with an eye on when the price/performance characteristics of doing so may be feasible for more complex integrations at the Provider Edge (vCPE/vBNG/vPE). These will certainly include early offerings of virtualized firewall, DPI, and load balancing functions (since these are fundamental to almost every chain in production). Ultimately, Intrusion Detection Systems (IDS), Intrusion Prevention Systems (IPS), SSL off-loaders, caches, and WAN optimizers will be targeted (particularly for the Enterprise networking/tenant space). The burning question is whether or not these transformations will be soon enough to allow traditional hardware device vendors to keep pace with these trends, or if newer non-incumbents will be able to take a foothold.

---

28. There are currently drafts for creating an OAM-like functionality in VxLAN overlays, but generalized troubleshooting tools equivalent to OAM, ipsla, ping, traceroute (as they apply to the distributed control of the underlay) still need to mainstream in the multitude of overlay environments.

29. Though, to their credit, both the ETSI NFV forums and the ONF have started security subgroups (the former targets publication of a best practice recommendation in 2013).

CHAPTER 8

Network Topology and Topological Information Abstraction

Introduction

Topological information and its availability to applications that wish to utilize what amounts to rare gold in the networking world has long been available to a select few applications. These applications had to satisfy a few important criteria. First, they needed to be fluent in one of many routing protocols. And secondly, they had to be allowed to join in routing in the literal sense: they had to directly attach to a routing network—this took more than just racking up a server and plugging it into a network.

It often required the application to go through the same security and other quality assurance hurdles that any other piece of networking gear in that network had to. This often took literally *years* of testing to complete. And when that moment arrived when the application was allowed on the network, its grasp of network topology was then still limited to that of *active* topology—that which was used to actually route or steer traffic at that instant in time.

Inactive or *dormant* topological information is generally not required for routing calculations and thus is not carried in any routing protocol exchanges. This information *is* needed by some applications, as explained later in this chapter, and so in order to gain that information an application still had to manually locate it using out-of-band means such as the command-line interface or other management protocols.

One final downside to traditional approaches to topology was the format of the topology information itself. The information was, as one would expect, formatted such that a router could quickly gather and process the topology for the fastest routing computations, or if gathered using out-of-band methods, in yet another format suitable for a command-line interface, for example, but not for doing other calculations. Unfortunately, these formats were often suboptimal for other uses that these applications had, and thus required their further processing to make it useful—requiring further effort, expense, and kludges in order to make it work. Fortunately, recent and new approaches in the area of topological information, its discovery, retrieval, and processing, have been undertaken. It is in fact this new effort and approach to topology, how it is being made available to applications through the SDN controllers and frameworks, and what then can be done that we discuss in this book, and in detail throughout this chapter.

Network Topology

Before delving into the details of what it means to gather, construct, and maintain a modern network topology, especially for the purposes of SDN approaches, let's first step back and briefly give an introduction to network topology.

Network topology is the interconnection of, and relationship between, various elements of networks. Network topology boils down to two basic elements: nodes and links. Nodes represent any number of possible network devices, such as routers, switches, servers, phones, cameras, or laptops. Nodes can be *terminal* or *connecting*. In the case of terminal nodes, these exist at the ends of the graph and do not generally interconnect with other nodes in order to forward traffic between other nodes (e.g., laptops or iPhones). Connecting nodes do what the name implies: they connect other nodes together, such as routers or switches.

The topological structure of a network consists of nodes and links that are connected in one of two ways: *physically* or *logically*. Physical refers to just that—real network interfaces such as a physical cable (i.e., Ethernet) or fiber that is run between nodes. Logical, on the other hand, is a set of constructs that contains things such as virtual interfaces or network paths that are built on top of a physical infrastructure. For example, a layer 3 IP interface is merely a logical construct and encapsulation over a physical interface, such as a twisted pair category-5 Ethernet. Of course, distances between nodes, physical interconnections, or transmission rates of interfaces all may differ between two nodes regardless of whether or not the links are logical or physical.

An example of a topology that contains both logical and physical links and nodes is a simple Ethernet-based local area network (LAN) comprised of six nodes with physical or logical links between the nodes. In this case, each node would have at least a physical interface between each node, but then possibly a logical layer 3 IP interface stacked on top of that interface.

If one wished to display such a topology visually, it would look like one of a number of common geometric shapes such as those shown in Figure 8-1. One could then map the data flows between the physical or logical entities over this topology as a second layer of topological visualization over the (same) physical underlying topology.

In this way, you can see how topologies not only help keep track of actual entities such as nodes or links, but also how those things are used or which states they are in. For

---

example, one can imagine having a means of coloring the various elements in Figure 8-1 with red or green lights to indicate the operational state of those interfaces.

For completeness, there are seven basic topologies that are considered and shown in Figure 8-1:

- Ring or circular
- Mesh
- Star
- Fully connected
- A line or daisy chain
- Tree (acyclic or multidirectional)
- Bus

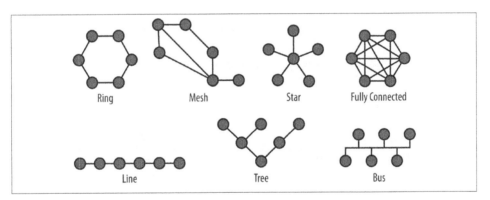

Figure 8-1. Classical network topologies

Of course, hybrids of the seven topologies can be constructed, and in fact, are very common in the real world.

Once a topology has been gathered and is considered stable, different representational modeling efforts can be undertaken in order to best represent the topology for consumption either internally by a management system, or for presentation to an external consumer of the information.

In most cases, *topological layering* is employed in order to join together and associate the various physical and conceptual layers of the topology. This concept is not one that was recently invented; rather, it has existed since the beginning of networks, although it has evolved over time to include more and more information. It should be noted that when considering multilayered topologies that layers 0 through 7 are considered here.

This therefore includes both physical optical topologies as well as virtual networks layered over this physical infrastructure, such as layer 3 MPLS VPNs.

Not only do typical topology diagrams now include the physical and virtual network components, but also they now include applications that consume, utilize, or otherwise occupy those links and nodes. It is important to represent these in the topology diagram as well, as in Figure 8-2, where not only is the logical layer 3 network represented, but two additional layers.

Representing these higher conceptual layers helps network planners and designers better monitor and adjust the network to changes both observed and foreseen in the future (i.e., predicted). This is particularly important in light of the discussion of NFV in Chapter 7.

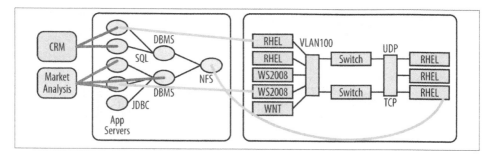

Figure 8-2. Conceptual diagram showing how a management station could represent a multilayered topology

Traditional Methods

Let's take a quick look at what maintaining, gathering, and discovering topology has meant in a real network prior to the advent of SDN.

Traditional approaches to topology include a few basic operations. These include initial discovery of a network's topology, keeping up with ongoing changes to the topology (i.e., rediscovery), and then the management and exposure of the topology once it has been gathered and deemed stable.

When gathering and interacting with the network topology, two largely different categories of approaches exist: a hodgepodge of screen scraping via a CLI; access to SNMP MIBs, or NETCONF; or joining routing.

In the first case, an application would generally rely on a network management station to gather their various topological information, and then consolidate, filter and abstract that information into a proprietary format that it would then expose for applications or other managed services to use. Once gathered, an application could search through the often-vast array of information finding the pieces and parts it needed, and then be on its way. In other cases, the management station would need to notify interested applications of changes to the existing topology. For instance, if a new node was discovered, it was important to notify applications in a timely fashion of the change.

When communicating with devices, a variety of approaches were used. These included CLI access, SNMP, NETCONF, or even ARP probing or IP ICMP ping discovery. This patchwork of approaches would return various information, including layer 2 or 3 reachability, attached neighbors, logical tunnels/paths, as well as basic status of each of these elements. Once gathered, this information is processed into a format that can then be dissected and abstracted, and ultimately made available for other applications to operate on and use.

Many successful companies were formed based on applications that performed the just described operations. Some, such as the original Cabletron Spectrum (now CA Infrastructure Manager) took topology discovery to new levels of sophistication. Not only did these applications discover active layer 3 topology, but they could also locate non-routed (i.e., layer 2) topology of devices such as HUBs and switches. Finally, they could also locate devices, links, or paths that were dormant, in a failed state, or simply not yet advertised in routing protocols. A screenshot of the CA Spectrum/IM product is shown in Figure 8-3. The figure shows how both physical and logical can be overlaid on a display in order to construct a more complete picture of the network for an operator.

Other companies have taken the approach of *joining routing* as a means of gathering most of their topological information, but as with the earlier approaches, they need to augment this information gathered from other management interfaces such as the CLI.

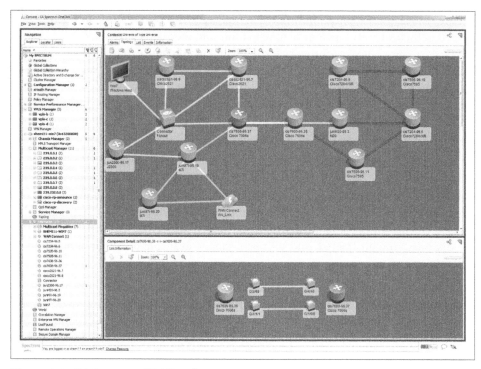

Figure 8-3. CA Spectrum/IM Topology

One such example of a product in this space is Packet Design's Route Explorer product. At its root, Route Explorer joins routing as a BGP, OSPF, or ISIS speaker and simply listens to routing exchanges. In doing so, it learns the network-wide topologies that are being advertised by routers within the network. Figure 8-4 illustrates how this works. The server where Route Explorer executes must have at least one interface (i.e., Ethernet port) from where it learns both IGP and BGP adjacencies.

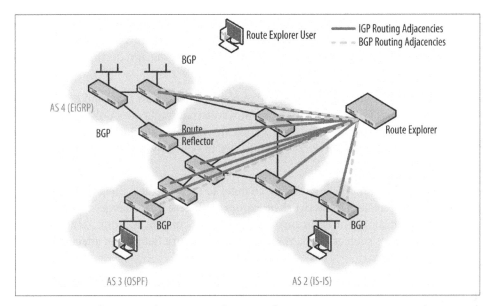

Figure 8-4. Packet Design's Route Explorer product joins active routing and masquerades as if it were a real router in order to listen to routing protocol updates in order to gather network topological information

Regardless of how the topology is gathered, once it is collected, it is the job of the topology management system to normalize the topology into a format that can be consumed by the rest of the system.

In the old days, the rest of the system consisted of other parts of the management application or operational support system (OSS). Since the vendor tightly coupled these elements, the format of the topology could be proprietary, or at least defined by the vendor and exposed as was necessary so that external applications might interact with it.

However, today's SDN controller architecture has a standardized northbound API as one of its key facets. Having this API alone is important, as it allows applications to be coded to interact with that controller; however, this is just the beginning. As we mentioned in Chapter 5, having this API defined as an industry standard allows and encourages *application portability*.

In the ever-growing world of SDN controllers, having a common API to program SDN applications to is not just theoretically important, but economically and operationally as well. It means a network operator can either buy or build a single application to accomplish a particular task, and then have it interact with all of the controllers deployed in his/her network.

One very interesting thing that can be done with network topology is called Network Change Modeling, or more colloquially, "what if?" scenario planning. This is one feature that can be used once a network topology has been gathered and deemed a stable topology.

Once a network topology is in hand, and one understands how that topology has been constructed (i.e., routing topology algorithms, constraints, network policies, link bandwidth utilization, interface status, etc.) one can view the topology as a very accurate model of the operational network. Not only this, but one now knows *how* that state was arrived at.

At this point, one can imagine making changes to see how they affect that model. For example, it is interesting for network operators to observe how changes to link metrics, bandwidth utilization, link addition or removal, back-up path addition, or any number of failure scenarios such as a link, node, or entire network failure can affect traffic patterns and behaviors.

Further, once a layered topology is achieved, as we showed, running applications, or the servers that host those applications and services, can be observed as well. Operations such as capacity future planning can also be imagined as a possibility.

One key SDN application that applies at this point is network function virtualization and service chaining of those virtualized functions to other real or virtual ones. One key to the success of these approaches is in fact the topological view of the services and how they are connected or *chained* (as already discussed in great detail in Chapter 7).

LLDP

Some of the early SDN controller and OpenFlow-enabled switch approaches described in Chapter 4 originally lacked a key component in their architectures: they needed to discover the network topology of the OpenFlow-controlled switches the controllers were in charge of.

This information was needed for the controller to plan, provision, and monitor the network paths between the switches, but it was unavailable because the switches did not have any paths set up until they were set up, and generally speaking, were waiting to be programmed by the controller in their initial state.

This represented a chicken-and-egg dilemma. To solve this, the LLDP protocol was enabled on the switch ports by default, but instead of only communicating directly with the remote switches with the discovery frames, the information was relayed to the SDN controller that would then collect this information into a centralized view of the network topology, and then forward it back to the neighbor switches. This worked well within the OpenFlow deployment architecture at the time.

The Link Layer Discovery Protocol (LLDP) is an industry-standard protocol that allows networked devices to discover and advertise capabilities and identity information onto a layer 2 LAN.

The layer 2 protocol that was standardized by the IEEE[1] replaces several proprietary protocols implemented by individual vendors for their equipment including the Cisco Discovery Protocol (CDP).

LLDP allows network devices that operate at the lower layers of a protocol stack (e.g., layer 2 bridges and switches) to learn some of the capabilities and characteristics of LAN devices available to higher layer protocols (e.g., IP addresses).

The information gathered through the LLDP operation is stored in a network device and can be queried using the SNMP protocol, the CLI, or NETCONF. A device's neighbor topology and associated information can also be gathered from this database.

Some of the information that can be gathered by LLDP includes the following:

- System name and description
- Port name and description
- VLAN name and identifier
- IP network management address
- Capabilities of the device (e.g., switch, router, or server)
- MAC address and physical layer information
- Power information

A device that is configured for LLDP operation sends PDUs on each of their interfaces where the protocol is enabled. The PDUs are sent at a fixed interval and are sent in the form of an Ethernet Frame or PDU. Each LLD PDU contains a sequence of type-length-value (TLV) structures that encode one of the aforementioned attributes.[2] These frames are sent to a special multicast address that is not forwarded. In this way, broadcast storms are prevented in cases of forwarding loops.

Figure 8-5 illustrates a basic network comprised of two switches, three phones, a PBX, and a PC. The LLDP neighbor discovery information is displayed as each switch receives it. Note the types and addresses that are shown for each neighbor in each switch's neighbor discovery table.

---

1. IEEE 802.1AB-2005

2. LLDP supports vendor extension/customization through TLV type 127.

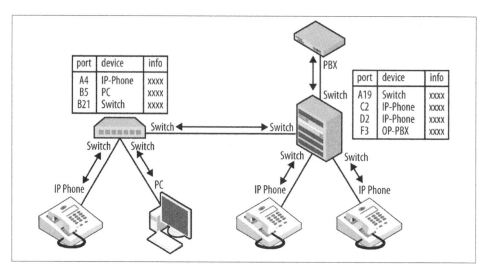

port	device	info
A4	IP-Phone	xxxx
B5	PC	xxxx
B21	Switch	xxxx

port	device	info
A19	Switch	xxxx
C2	IP-Phone	xxxx
D2	IP-Phone	xxxx
F3	OP-PBX	xxxx

Figure 8-5. LLDP Sample operation in a simple network containing two switches, three phones, a PBX, and a PC; the LLDP neighbor discovery information is displayed as each switch receives it

In an SDN context, LLDP can be leveraged as a switch discovery protocol. The information that is then gathered can be used to construct the network topology.

In the example shown in Figure 8-6, a very rudimentary network of two switches is shown that are under the control of the SDN controller at the top of the figure.

OpenFlow network discovery is achieved using *packet_in* and *packet_out* messages. As network ports advertise their discovery information as previously described, that information is punted to the SDN controller via the "packet in" rule and processed by the switch. It is then forwarded to the neighbor switches so they may learn the MAC address. But the salient point is that the network topology database is constructed.

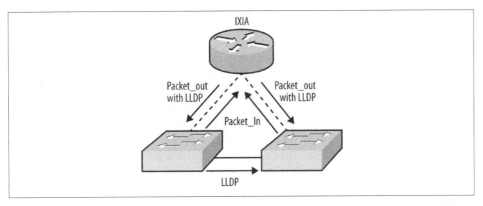

Figure 8-6. The use of LLDP as a switch port discovery protocol by an SDN controller

While the method for exchanging LLDP neighbor just described does solve the problem of neighbor switch topology discovery, there are issues with this approach.

First, the approach is limited to switches that speak LLDP. This is generally not a huge problem, but as with the other approaches that require speaking a specific routing (or now switching) protocol, these are things that are very unappealing to applications.

Second, the LLDP topology information is very localized to just the immediate layer 2 neighbors of the switch. If some ports are misconfigured (i.e., their initial configurations are incorrect), then no discovery is available on those ports.

Finally, topologies that span the zones of purely OpenFlow-controlled switches to those that are not, or hybrid zones, can have difficulty stitching this information together. The reason being that (as we described earlier with the northbound APIs of a controller) no standard for extension over these zones exists; therefore, the exchange of this information is still limited to applications or other controllers that understand a particular proprietary definition. And along those lines, the topology format itself and what it contains is proprietary.

Given these limitations, more work is needed toward a repository that allows individual approaches and datasets that can be merged to create a multilayer view (as per the earlier figure showing multilayered topology, Figure 8-2).

BGP-TE/LS

As we already mentioned, there are two basic ways of obtaining network topology information: management protocols or routing protocols. One new entrant into the latter category is BGP Link State, or BGP-LS, as it is more commonly known. One thing that we did not go into detail on in the earlier discussion around routing protocol-based approaches (but did mention) is that the routing protocols contain information suitable for routing calculations, which is not necessarily optimal for other computations needing topological information. BGP-LS sought to correct this deficiency.

BGP-LS is an extension to BGP that allows it to carry link-state information. This link state information is acquired from the IGP as is normally done with other state information, but in this case from the area's traffic engineering database (TED). This information can be aggregated from multiple areas and autonomous systems to perform interesting analyses of the state of the network.

Both the IGP's TED and the topological data gathered using BGP-LS should provide the same set of information. However, BGP-LS was invented specifically to leverage some properties of BGP that give it better scaling characteristics. These include TCP-based flow control and the strategic use of route reflector(s). It is for this reason that BGP-LS is also a more scalable choice when one needs to acquire multiarea topology information, which traditionally required one to gather it from each individual AS using more manual means.

A traffic engineering controller (e.g., an application of the PCE Server) will implement BGP-LS as a means to acquire the routing topology. In the context of SDN, this is (of course) just another SDN application/controller pairing. We in fact describe the controller in Chapter 4 and a use case in Chapter 12. BGP-LS also supports a policy mechanism whereby one can limit the exposure of certain nodes/links or sections of topologies as partitioned by the user. A TE controller will provide the requisite knobs to support this feature.

In the case where a topology change event such as a link/node going down occurs, the IGP flooding mechanism allows the topology information to be propagated to the TE controller much faster than as would be accomplished using BGP-LS. This is because BGP-LS has to wait for the local IGP on the routers in the network to update the TED before the BGP-LS signals this change event to its peers. This delay should not adversely affect the real time characteristics of the collection using BGP-LS.

So why was BGP-LS invented? What problem is it solving that wasn't already solved? As we just mentioned, there were already manual ways to obtain the network topology as well as joining routing to get routed link state information. There are several problems with the information contained within routing protocols for the purposes of topology. Let's investigate them now.

BGP-LS with PCE

We described earlier in Chapter 4 how a path computational element (PCE) can be used to compute MPLS-TE paths. When those paths were computed, they were done so within a domain such as an autonomous system (i.e., an IGP area), or computed across multiple ASs or area domains.

In these cases, we described how PCE could offer enhanced computational power through the use of COGS hardware in order to run the CSPF algorithm offline to routers that might have older or simply less powerful hardware. Additionally, alternative CSPF algorithms could be employed for custom computations that might not be available in some particular commercial hardware.

The problem is that in these cases, the lack of global topology (multidomain) might hamper the accuracy of these computations. For example, the wrong exit router for a particular path might be chosen, or the wrong transit node might be chosen. In other cases, simply non-optimal paths might be chosen.

In order to solve this problem, the PCE needs access to the overall or global, TED. Some previous solutions made the PCE a passive listener to the IGP much as we just described in the solutions that joined routing in order to glean the topology, but as we have discussed, this does not always provide the best format for this information. Figure 8-7 shows how a PCE can get its TED information by joining routing as well as leveraging BGP (BGP-LS).

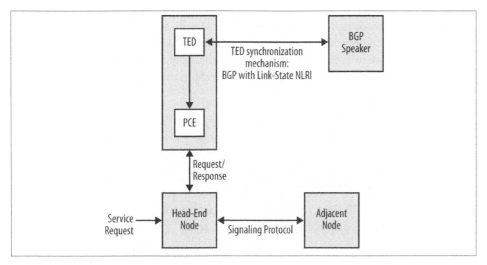

Figure 8-7. External PCE node using a TED synchronization mechanism

Going forward, the PCE server will be able to acquire a global topology through BGP-LS peering across multiple domains.

ALTO

One of the first efforts to standardize not only the format of topology information, but also making that standard format available to applications that do not interact directly with routing protocols was the Application-Layer Traffic Optimization (ALTO) Network Service. This is an important change, as modern applications are generally not written to do this. ALTO provides network information to applications, such as the network location, structure, and preferences of the network paths to various network services.

Currently, ALTO is aimed at providing these paths for content delivery networks (CDNs) and is also how it is being used in practice. The goal of providing this information is to inform applications such as those seeking the closest CDN server. In providing this information, applications such as this can improve application performance. An interesting side effect is that this service has the potential to further optimize network resource consumption patterns, which is very desirable for network operators.

The basic information an ALTO service provides is based on abstract or logical topology maps of a network. The maps can be constructed from physical or logical topology that is ingested by the ALTO server.

As we discussed earlier, network topologies can be physical or logical; in this case but not only logical but also at the level of network services.

In Figure 8-2, where we showed the layered topology, this is represented at the very top of the layers. The abstract topology maps provide an abstracted view of CDN nodes and the relative weights of paths between those nodes in the network. This has the effect of simplifying the topology scope down to a set that CDN-related applications are interested in. If they are interested in additional details, they are able to then consult other topological resources such as management interfaces or routing-based resources, as described earlier.

The ALTO server is a network service that is exposed to network-aware applications over a web services API. The ALTO protocol uses a RESTful design and encodes its requests and responses using JSON.[3] As indicated in Chapter 5, modern applications programmers choose this approach because of its flexibility and extensibility.

We also consider ALTO a precursor to the modern SDN movement and paradigm change. If viewed in this light, the ALTO server and protocol can be considered an early entrant into the SDN controller implementation space.

Figure 8-8 shows an example of an ALTO server and the network service it provides.

---

3. IETF RFC4627

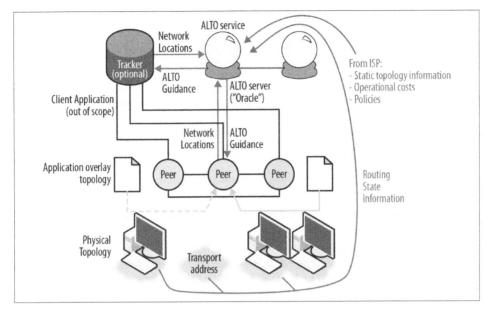

Figure 8-8. ALTO service architecture

BGP-LS and PCE Interaction with ALTO

As we described in the previous section, BGP-LS and PCE can be combined to form a more optimal solution for cross-AS path computation due to the faster, more consistent, and scalable acquisition of link state topology information.

We also described an ALTO server as an entity that generates an abstracted network topology and provides it to network-aware applications over a web service–based API. Example applications are p2p clients or trackers, or CDNs. The abstracted network topology comes in the form of two maps: a network map that specifies allocation of prefixes to PIDs, and a cost map that specifies the cost between PIDs listed in the network map. ALTO abstract network topologies can be autogenerated from the physical topology of the underlying network. The generation would typically be based on policies and rules set by the operator.

Both prefix and TE data are required: prefix data is required to generate ALTO network maps and TE (topology) data is required to generate ALTO cost maps. Prefix data is carried and originated in BGP, and TE data is originated and carried in an IGP.

While ALTO provides a single interface through which an ALTO server can retrieve all the necessary prefix and network topology data from the underlying network, an ALTO server can use other mechanisms to get network data (e.g., peering with multiple IGP and BGP speakers). Figure 8-9 shows how an ALTO server can get network topology information from the underlying network using the mechanism just described.

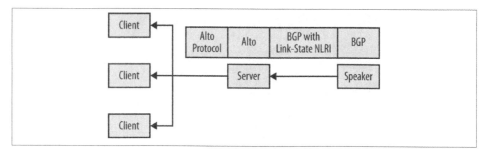

Figure 8-9. ALTO server using network topology information

While ALTO continues to be deployed and implemented, its applicability and use remains limited to that of CDNs. Some have ventured outside of this area, but there is
little traction in doing so. We conjecture that this is because, while the protocol and
architecture are indeed flexible enough to be used for other things, there seems to be a
perception that CDN is what ALTO should be used for.

I2RS Topology

As we mentioned in Chapter 4, an early effort called SDNP was hatched by a number
of people in an effort to standardize a few key components of what was (at the time)
canonical SDN architecture. This architecture was comprised of a logically centralized
controller that interacted with and/or controlled the data and control planes of a set of
network devices. The controller presented the services it implemented using a RESTful
web services API.

As we described, this effort was before its time and dwindled away. From those ashes
came a new effort at the IETF that was originally named the Interface to the Routing
System (IRS). Too many people objected to that name on the basis that it gave them
undue heartburn by reminding them of Uncle Sam, and so the name was changed
slightly to be the Interface to the Routing System, or I2RS.

Although still in its infancy, this effort now has strong support within the industry and
continues on a successful trajectory at the time of the writing of this chapter. We hope
this effort continues to blossom as it has the potential, at least, to solve some of the
stickier issues around SDN: the standardization of the northbound API (I2RS can both
read and write network state), and most apropos for this chapter, the standardization
of a generalized network topology service.

As we just described, ALTO was an early effort at the IETF to construct a standardized
topology collection and representation service consumable by applications using an
application-friendly API. Unfortunately this effort seems to be stuck on CDN. To that
end, generalized topology was added to the charter of the I2RS working group as one

---

of its key work items. Let's describe what this means and the current state of these affairs to better understand why this effort is important.

One key facet of the I2RS topology manager is the collection of topology (and topology related/co-incident) data from multiple sources, including network elements, routing protocols, inventory collection, and statistics collection.

It should be clear from the descriptions of the aforementioned topology efforts and approaches why collection from a diverse set of sources that include routing protocols is critical to form a complete and useful view of the network topology.

To this end, topology data sources may reside in multiple IGP areas, across multiple ASes and/or in multiple network layers (including administrative domains/systems within a single organization, like transport and routing). In addition to the usual links and nodes (both virtual and physical) that are provided by these sources, some other data sources such as some explicit node function (of a network service appliance), statistics, or physical inventory can be injected to augment the topology map.

This information might be used by the topology manager (e.g., in providing an operational map/view interface), but is likely to be even more interesting for applications such as network analytics, service location, and provisioning.

Ultimately, the topology manager's goal is the creation of global topology view. In practice this will be realized and presented to applications based on a common data model, used to normalized collected data and transform it into a standardized format that will be easily consumable and portable across applications. The topology view can ultimately span multiple network layers as well as multiple autonomous systems or entire networks, depending on how well different administrative domains will cooperate and share information.

It is important that the global view includes all network elements and resources existing in the infrastructure, whether they are actively used or not. An example consists of reconstructing the global view of the network, including router or switch ports that are available but not in use. Another may be constructing a global view of network, including router/switch ports and both used and unused underlying transport network elements. These are important for computing "what if?" scenarios.

This sort of operation is very difficult using the routing protocol-based approaches, for example, as the information is simply not present in any active routing updates (though the need has been exhibited through modifications to routing like the recent introduction of the SRLG concept in the MPLS-TE). It can only be done using additional means such as a proprietary CLI.

Once topology information has been gathered, it is important that it be presented in a format acceptable to modern applications. To this end, the topology manager will digest the information and normalize it using a standardized object model. This object model will also be used to generate the REST API that applications will use to gather this information.

At the top level, it all sounds fantastic until one realizes the sheer volume of information that might be present in a topology server. It is thus very important that the topology manager can create multiple (perhaps application-specific) views from its common global topology database. This (in a way) allows an application to specify a filter criterion for viewing information. For example, we just described an ALTO server. One could very well ask a topology server to only return CDN-tagged nodes and paths from the database, thus providing it with the CDN topology layer.

Topology information from network elements is relayed into the topology manager function via its southbound API, as shown in Figure 8-10. Sources of topology information may be network elements at different layers of the network, such as appliances, routers, Level 2 switches, optical transponders, optical switches, or monitoring, provisioning, and network analytics tools (such as statistics collection subsystems or an inventory subsystem).

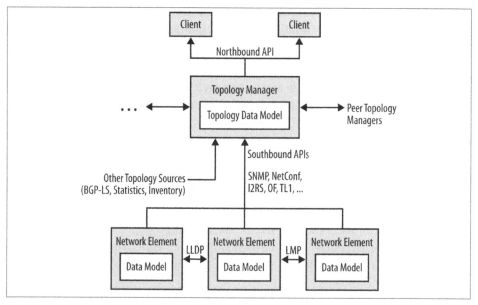

Figure 8-10. I2RS Topology Manager operational model

In terms of implementation, the topology manager function can be instantiated in a stand-alone server, be a part of a comprehensive orchestration, data collection, presentation framework, or even embedded in a routing element. A client can be an application or a function in an upper layer framework, such as a policy function. Depending on the data it collects, a topology manager may not have visibility into the entire network. In order to create a global topology, the topology manager may get complementary partial topology views from other topology managers via a peer topology manager API.

Conclusions

Topology is one of the critical pieces of information many applications require from the network. In this chapter, we have explored topology and tried to emphasize its criticality in the context of SDN.

While this book cannot capture all possible examples of SDN services—for example, policy could be its own section—topology is demonstrated here to illustrate a widely used example of an SDN. It is intended, in combination with Chapters 5 and 9, to illustrate SDN as a programming/development environment and how topology represents what we think is a critical component of this environment.

If a single SDN controller solution/architecture represents itself as the arbiter of SDN but has a limited view of topology, it limits the view of SDN to that subset of the network world. A current example of this conundrum is the OpenFlow controller paradigm, which currently only learns layer 2 topology via LLDP but is being augmented to understand at least an abstraction of the underlying transport network. This is a clear example of why generalized and abstracted topology is needed in order to form the most flexible and generally applicable solution.

Through the review of the limitations of historical OSS/topology interchanges, if they can be described as such, and the arc of management protocols, then LLDP, BGP-LS, ALTO, and finally the latest work in the IETF's I2RS Working Group, the requirements of topology as a service have been honed through experimentation, trial and real-life deployments. This evolution similarly tracks the evolution of SDN, from proprietary systems to service-oriented to (hopefully) open and modern northbound and southbound interfaces.

Related to the ongoing work in the network topology area are efforts to be done on storage architecture (tools and schema) of a multilayer topology and its artifacts. For example, we could devote a chapter to graph databases like Neo4j (*http:// www.neo4j.org/*), Titan (*https://github.com/thinkaurelius/titan/wiki*), Jung (*http:// jung.sourceforge.net/*), the TinkerPop toolkit (*http://www.tinkerpop.com/*), and the API that summarizes and/or joins the individual layer views.

In this chapter, we've hopefully developed the concept that topology is more than nodes and links. Instead, it's a rich set of surrounding information about or coincident with those nodes and links, as well as inactive or dormant network components. We have also hopefully impressed upon the reader here that access to this information needs to be done via modern, application-friendly interfaces such as the ones described in Chapter 5. For example, one clear mistake of the past has been to require that an application speak routing protocols in order to participate in network topology, or gain access to it via a proxy that does speak routing. We showed why this is clearly an unwanted and undesirable situation for modern applications programmers.

There is a lot of enthusiasm in this area, but still a lot of work to do. There is a significant task going forward for the area of network topology itself. Within the context of SDN, it will be defining the data models for the many topology sources that may exist in an SDN framework. This is needed to standardize and normalize the topology both on the wire and once it is extracted by an application, making these operations ubiquitous rather than laborious. We described this in the I2RS section and hope that we emphasized the relative importance of this effort to the wider SDN effort; without standardized topology upon which many other facets of SDN depend, the larger effort will not be as productive or impactful as it could be.

CHAPTER 9

Building an SDN Framework

Introduction

We can trace the history of the software-defined networks (SDN) concept reasonably well back to 2007–2008, when Nicira/VMware, NOX, and other related university efforts first appeared on the scene. Since that time, SDN as a technology has evolved and advanced, but has unfortunately still bounced between a variety of proprietary controller proposals with no firm plan for interoperability between these controllers. Worse still, this lack of interoperability between controllers—or how to communicate with them—prevents the applications that network operators, controller vendors, or third-party software houses build to function seamlessly across different controllers. Fast-forward to 2013, and a number of controllers and controller strategies exist but still none of them work together—at least easily. This certainly is a problem looking for a solution that we think can be solved by defining an *SDN framework* that is built upon an open source code foundation to ensure not only its syntactic correctness, but its semantic correctness, too. Then that framework and its ancillary components, such as protocols or protocol extensions, can be standardized at a standards organization such as the IETF.

In this chapter, we will introduce and describe just such an idealized SDN framework to which controllers might rally around. This framework first came from proof-of-concept work we did at Juniper, but now also appears in a slightly different form, as part of the Open Daylight Project's (ODP) controller framework. As part of the ODP framework, it will also find its way into the open source codebase to which ODP is building an industry standard SDN controller from. In this way, we believe definite progress is being made in the industry as solving one of the biggest challenges ahead for fulfilling the key promise of SDN: tighter integration between applications and the network.

Build Code First; Ask Questions Later...

To be fair, vendors built and still do build code and ask questions later in terms of interoperability. Some publicly distanced themselves from any standardization efforts, claiming that they would hamper innovation velocity or worse, produce controllers that were beholden to incumbent equipment vendors who really had no interest in supporting the brave new world of software-defined networks. What resulted is that no single vendor could deliver an open/multivendor standards-based northbound API for application development, or an open/multivendor standardized state distribution interface between controllers. This started to become problematic once controller offerings began to leave the test and qualification lab environments and be considered for real deployments. The fact that the controllers lacked the ability to manipulate the exact same type of state objects from multiple vendors (e.g., two OpenFlow controllers from different vendors) or across administrative domains (assuming the same vendor but two discrete databases) was an issue. Additionally, the lack of a definitive standards-based solution for southbound controller/agent protocols meant that the choice of any one controller required interoperability qualification testing with each and every deployed switch and also required subsequent testing if new switches were considered later. These problems came to a head when these controllers were considered for integration into operational support systems used by providers and enterprises to provision and control their overall networks. A final hurdle was the lack of application portability, a direct result of the failure to establish a standardized northbound SDN API. That is, those applications that relied on the controller to interact with the network, or network services, would need to be purpose-built based on the choice of controller. Suddenly the promises made by SDN for lower operational cost resulting from tighter interaction between operational software, software applications, and network elements were questioned.

To give some examples of why a standardized framework as well as a de facto codebase implementing that framework are important, consider how port management of OpenFlow-enabled switches is managed. In these situations, dilemmas can arise relating to port ownership, such as control delegation. Although this exists even within a monoculture of the southbound protocol that is prevalent in the generation of SDN controllers discussed in an earlier chapter, this difficulty can be worsened in cases where multiple controllers are desired.

For example, within the OpenFlow controller paradigm, if an operator were to choose vendor A because it had a preferable orchestration application to control ports in their data center switches, and then later choose vendor B because that one had a desirable virtual network tap application, how would they rectify control of the forwarding table between two controllers when both tried to program the same switch? Worse, since neither of the SDN controller vendors had settled on a standardized or even prearranged upon northbound API, the orchestration application from vendor A would likely be unable to communicate at least completely with vendor B's controller. The same would be true for the virtual tap application. In essence, this comes down to having no interoperable API for passing state or arbitrating control.[1]

Other fallout of the protocol monoculture is a somewhat stunted service set available on the controller, notably in the area of topology. This is true because most SDN controller/agent protocols obtain topology for the layer of abstraction the mono-culture provides—layer 2/MAC/FIB, layer 3/RIB/LDB, or layer 4+/service. The result is that a network-wide view is unavailable. Since this so critical for certain network control applications, such as the PCE server-based or segment-routing cases discussed in Chapter 4, those solutions simply will not function.

Finally, this lack of interoperability means that there is a limited ability to integrate SDN controllers into so-called *hybrid* operating environments without additional "glue" applications to arbitrate between the different ports. For example, the ability to stitch a VxLAN overlay driven by VMware/Nicira SDN systems to a subscriber VPN VRF instance at a data center gateway will require some automata—possibly via a NETCONF-based application or provisioning script.[2] Figure 9-1 demonstrates a similar scenario whereby a BigSwitch Networks Floodlight controller and a Trema OF controller both expose different northbound APIs that applications must interact with. Neither provides a consistent interface to which applications programmers can code to, nor do they provide the same network abstraction of the underlying switches or other services, such as topology, that they expose.

1. In fact, in the current OpenFlow paradigm, this is not supported. One of the applications in question would have to be rewritten to the other controller vendor's API.

2. For vendors with an established footprint, the solution is obvious—"support my agent and/or my API on your platforms". The question then becomes how many of these agents can reasonably be supported and whether the vendors of the network elements are willing and able to support this solution.

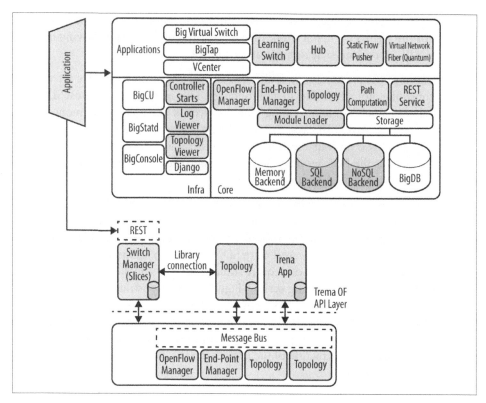

Figure 9-1. Big Switch Networks Floodlight controller and Trema OF controllers both expose different northbound APIs that applications must program to

Though some of the controller environments support modern development languages (e.g., Python) and coding methodologies (e.g., the Eclipse development environment), they also provide robust albeit proprietary frameworks that support and encourage application development. These environments include well-documented APIs to program to as well as debugging/test tools. In truth, most support some combination of these attributes. The question is: how do these controllers accommodate new or additional services, augmentation to what existing controller service apps provide, or cross-controller programming capabilities? After all, if SDN is really all about applications, then answering these questions is critical. Taking this a step further, one should then ask that if it is all about the applications, isn't there an argument in all these controller options for openness, interoperability, and modularity? This wouldn't be without precedent in the networking industry or even in the SDN solution space (e.g., OpenStack).

This view—that the SDN controller shouldn't be a protocol mono-protocol culture but should be open, modular, and focused on services provided to application developers —has led to the definition of SDN controllers as *network application development frameworks*. This is why we believe that this combination of elements will foster and result in the ultimate goal of rapid application development of applications that interact seamlessly, rapidly, and efficiently with the network and the services it provides.

Because some of the SDN controller services envisioned in the evolution of the framework concept are so demanding to support, the view of the controller has also migrated from a single device or even a simple federation of devices, to systems of devices and virtual machines hosting different components of those services. These components can then in-turn be federated through one of the system members, but also orchestrated as a single system through the network orchestration system. Let's investigate what it means to be an SDN framework and how one might evolve, keeping in mind that the concept of exactly what that framework looks like has been evolving with the other parts of the SDN technology it binds together.

The Juniper SDN Framework

In early 2011, prior to their acquisition of Contrail Systems in 2012, Juniper Networks put forward the idea that SDN should be more than a controller, but rather a framework that supports various service elements that when put *together* as a system, form a controller. More importantly, the goal of the project was to demonstrate how the system, when put together properly, could ultimately support a tight feedback loop between a network application and the network, thus supporting what we felt was the holy grail of SDN: *network programmability*.

Juniper Networks demonstrated a Java-based framework with a RESTful API that served as a rapid prototyping environment to aid in the development of new and useful network applications. A simple yet groovy scripting interface was provided that enhanced the API by blending it with an SDK concept. The fundamental concept was that the basic network application services components of the traditional controller (e.g., topology, path computation, and path provisioning) could have several sources. The service sources would provide their services through a plug-in architecture based on a common plug-in model definition that could be extended in the future to accommodate future applications. The generalized application services created would provide their own northbound APIs that abstract the capabilities of the southbound plug-ins. In this sense, these applications could recursively define new services that other services could consume or interact with.

The controller system doesn't have a storage interface and serves more like a service bus. The path computation service was provided with the actual Junos CSPF algorithm (after conversion into a Java applet) that was used in Junos devices. This algorithm was accessed through the plug-in infrastructure. The path provisioning service was provided through multiple southbound protocols and accessed via their associate plug-ins, as shown in Figure 9-2. These included NETCONF (via a NETCONF driver), path computation element (PCE) (via a Java-based PCE server), and OpenFlow (via a plug-in written for Big Switch Network's FloodLight controller). The topology service was also provided through multiple plug-ins, including BGP-TE/LS using a Java-based BGP-TE client, ALTO (both a client and server modules were available), and static file import capabilities to facilitate rapid and easy configuration capabilities of the system. There was also a topology acquisition plug-in for the OpenFlow controller, since it provides the required LLDP-based topology needed for OpenFlow-based control at the time.

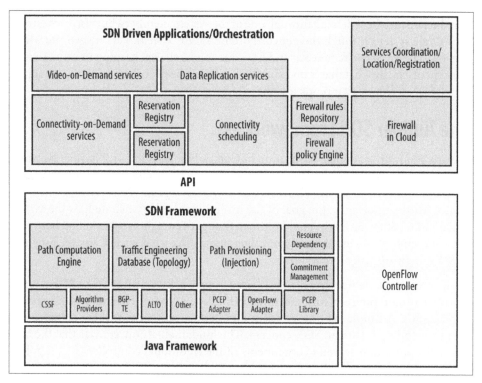

Figure 9-2. Juniper Networks proof-of-concept SDN framework

The proof-of-concept application that Juniper demonstrated was the so-called *bandwidth calendaring application* (BCA), which is explored in Chapter 10. The purpose of the BCA is self-descriptive—an application-based reservation of bandwidth through an example or relatively static network. These reservations can be based on a future reservation or immediate need and with or without a termination time (duration). This is a common application in research networks and in a few large Web 2.0 network service providers, too.

The application showed the framework modularity:

- The API made the application neutral to whether the elements in the selected path supported OpenFlow or a PCE manipulated MPLS LSP. This was done though the operator, or the application could specify a preference via the API.

- Active topology support via BCA used BGP-TE and OpenFlow to gather active topology information, although the topology that wasn't normalized. In an all-MPLS solution, where PCE provisioning in the network to accommodate flows was used, reservations were maintained within the distributed TED. The TED was updated through the BGP-TE/LS client whenever an LSP is updated or created. In a mixed network, the application has to manage the reservations on OpenFlow segments.

- The topology could be expanded through the use of OpenFlow configuration support and MPLS NETCONF/Yang models, albeit Juniper specific, that turn off/on MPLS or OpenFlow support in additional elements via a NETCONF plug-in.

The real point of the BCA application was the API that exposed the possibilities of *network programmability*. Two examples of the API were demonstrated. The first was a Guava-based visualization application acting like a traditional OSS-like console that presented the combined OpenFlow-only or PCE-only topology and the reservations in the system. The system would allow an application using the programmatic interface to program reservations as well as interrogate the state of the reservations and network paths. The second was via a Java applet that embeds the API that emulates a video on demand application. Other applications could then interact with this API.

In the latter stages of the concept period, this applet was moved from being runnable on a server that connected to various areas of the test topology to a port that became an Android app that was demonstrated on an Android tablet. This effectively demonstrated both a consumer use of the API and how network operators were moving toward using iPad and Android applications to manage and interact with their networks.

For this application, because the client is not as capable of handling large topologies, the ALTO client/server interaction was used to limit the topology that would need to be digested by the tablet app. In effect, the ALTO server would refine the search for a path to a best server, which was resolved in a first step ALTO query. This is congruent with the demands of most applications that would most often not want to view the entire network topology, but instead, an abstraction or otherwise filtered version. This is discussed in more detail in Chapter 8.

Some of the lessons learned in the exercise were:

- Topology is a fundamental data resource provided from network to application, and topology from multiple sources is hard to normalize from multiple sources, especially when representing multiple network layers. This is especially true if those layers are virtualized or require some sort of abstraction, as is the case when viewing layer 1 (i.e., optical) topology. These results in fact have allowed us to drive some of the IETF work in topology.

- Policy appears to be a fundamental application service, as it was embedded in every application generated.

- Structurally, the framework could have been better designed. For example, the APIs produced should be self-generating, which is what a number of other more recent approaches implement. This is incidentally called a *data-driven* approach and was discussed in detail in Chapter 5.

Unfortunately, for a variety of reasons, Juniper Networks never productized BCA or the framework it developed, although there has been talk of doing so in lieu of the Open Daylight Project as well as an application for the Contrail Controller.

The Juniper POC framework as well as the IETF frameworks that followed can be described as brokers. Conversely, many of the controller strategies position the concept of a *Network Operating System* (NOS) as a replacement for distributed routing protocols that oversees the data plane of the managed elements on behalf of applications that define network services. In the *broker model*, applications interact with the network via the broker so that they or the network can be more efficient, enforce target SLAs, or provide a more satisfactory end user experience. The obvious distinction between the models is in the type of application that the architecture is meant to service (the breadth of the solution).

IETF SDN Framework(s)

The fundamental framework concept began to manifest in IETF proposals for SDN work groups in 2012, particularly in the Application-Based Network Operations (AB-NO) and Software-Driven Network (Protocol), or SDN(P), proposals. To date, neither of these proposals has gotten much traction in the IETF, but they have translated into some efforts that have (e.g., the Interface to the Routing System, or I2RS). Also, these early efforts do illustrate some notable refinements to the Juniper POC framework that were enacted along the way.

SDN(P)

The Software-Driven Networks (Protocol)[3] effort was a proposed IETF Working Group that sought to explore and define protocols, architectures, and use cases[4] in the SDN problem space. In the architecture draft, the framework concept[5] just described is prominent, and captures the need for additional service components (e.g., policy) missing from the Juniper Networks framework. In fact, the framework of this effort was at least in part inspired by the Juniper SDN framework.

---

3. *http://tools.ietf.org/html/draft-nadeau-sdn-framework-01*

4. *http://tools.ietf.org/html/draft-nadeau-sdn-problem-statement-01*

5. *http://tools.ietf.org/html/draft-nadeau-sdn-framework-01*

The SDNP architecture (Figure 9-3) proposed the concept of an orchestrator as the point of control and coordination in the system. This was a bit different from the application in data center orchestration that plays the role of a controller of control planes (i.e., the OpenStack Orchestration System). This role was also a bit different from what at the time was a simple OpenFlow controller. This control point was software that acted as a hybrid external control plane with other protocol capabilities such as OpenFlow on the southbound side. In fact, much of this is what eventually turned into the hybrid OpenFlow mode at the ONF, but was later rejected. This entity was defined to manipulate the object models of the different plug-in southbound protocols, each of which was required to produce a self-describing object model that could also be used to generate a northbound API. These concepts were later common in the newer commercial controller offerings, including the use of a data/object model that self-produces an API, which was recently proposed for the Open Daylight Project controller.

Further, the proposal outlined a plan to rationalize or normalize communication between this controlling entity and the plug-ins that formed the essence of a plug-in contribution model. Finally, the proposal accounted for the federation or the horizontal communication between orchestrators, which is effectively a messaging bus concept that is still missing from most controllers today.

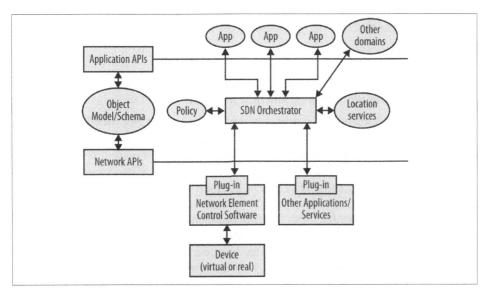

Figure 9-3. IETF SDNP framework straw man

Sadly, this effort was a bit ahead of its time for a variety of reasons. First, the IETF did not understand how to make heads or tails of SDN concepts and so could not figure out which one of the many areas—or collections of working groups—to put this into. Second, there was a lot of push back from the ONF, which was just formed and grabbing all of the SDN land it could, and so claimed it would handle these concepts. Unfortunately, this turned out to be largely optimistic. The IETF did ultimately find its way to form a working group that would work on the topology and programmatic and policy-based routing system programming, which are very important elements first discussed here. This group is now called the Interface to the Routing System (I2RS). Many of the other areas are being taken up by the Open Daylight Project.

ABNO

The Application-Based Network Operations (ABNO)[6] framework (Figure 9-4) first appeared in the Routing Area Workgroup as a proposal to extend the existing work items in the PCE working group, or perhaps even to form a separate working group. In the proposal, there is less focus on the suggested plumbing between the components than the SNDP proposal had made. Instead, the group took the tactic to focus on the roles of some of the components. In doing so, it avoided the term "SDN," which many at the IETF did not understand, and as such would avoid like the plague.

The framework reiterates the necessary role of policy in the framework. The proposal went beyond a simple PCE server in that it accommodates multiple southbound configuration/provisioning interfaces, including: PCE, OpenFlow, SNMP (as an interface with older OSS/BSS systems), NETCONF, and FORCEs. It also supports an interface similar to the one that is being proposed by the I2RS Working Group.

Some of the ABNO framework's unique ideas come from its PCE focus, in that:

- It includes the suggestion of the requirement for some troubleshooting, debugging, audit, or verification tools via an OAM Manager.
- In addition, it introduces a new component, the Virtual Network Topology Manager (VNTM—RFC5623). Because PCE can be used to create LSPs on both a layer 2 or layer 3 substrate, as well as an underlying optical transport system using G-MPLS mechanisms. The VNTM is used to normalize virtual topology between layers in the network and is a concept discussed earlier in Chapter 8.

The enhancement of topology with inventory information is other idea that is borrowed from I2RS. The ABNO Controller component handles request management from a traditional NMS/OSS and also arbitrates between PCEs in a hierarchical or inter-domain PCE arrangement. In this way, it allows for the federation and coordination of PCE controllers. It also forms a way in which they might be plugged into a larger orchestration system such as an OSS or even an OpenStack orchestrator.

---

6. *http://datatracker.ietf.org/doc/draft-farrkingel-pce-abno-architecture/*

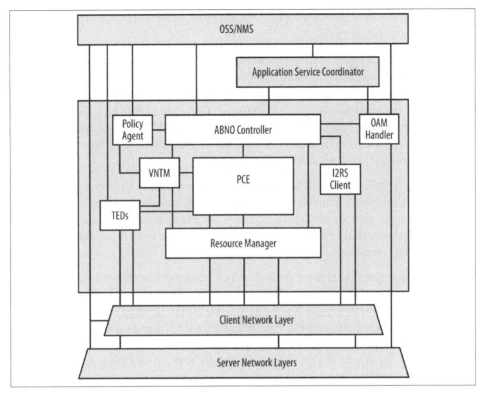

Figure 9-4. Generic ABNO architecture

Open Daylight Controller/Framework

In early 2013, the lack of a standard northbound SDN APIs for controllers, the lack of support for a hybrid mode of operation, and the proliferation of definitions as to what southbound protocols could define SDN beyond just OpenFlow came to a head with many prominent equipment and controller vendors in the industry. There had been a number of pushes to define these things in standards organizations such as the IETF, but those failed, and at the same time, ONF's reluctance to actual take on any of these issues in a serious manner simply pushed the industry to look in a different direction. It was at this time that a number of companies, including Cisco and IBM, discussed how forming an open source SDN controller project whose goals would be to create a common controller infrastructure as a vehicle to overcome the issues just mentioned was started. By February of 2013, the Open Daylight Project (ODP) consortium[7] was formed as a Linux Foundation project.[8]

Because the ultimate goal of this organization would be that of application portability, the organization was thus chartered to create a common SDN controller infrastructure that possessed a well-defined (and ultimately standards-based) northbound API, as well as support for a variety of southbound protocols. The result of the Open Daylight Project will be an open source controller/framework for SDN applications that creates a de facto northbound API standard that can then be used to program different southbound protocols, including OpenFlow, I2RS, and NETCONF.

This project is seeded with intellectual property, money, and engineering resources in the form of developers from multiple companies. It seeks to incorporate the lessons learned from the past controller and framework explorations into a state-of-the-art controller/framework that can be leveraged as the basis for what ultimately is enhanced network programmability.

Though it's anticipated that some vendors may continue to offer proprietary controllers, these are likely to standardize the infrastructure of these controllers on ODP's code much like Linux has achieved. Since any vendor is free to wrap its own proprietary/ value-added offerings around the core infrastructure either as a plug-in module, to digest and support the Open Daylight application API as immediate strategies for interoperability, or simply to add technical support in their own offering, a number of enterprise versions of the ODP controller are expected in the future. For the longer term, contributions may arise that standardize the east-west interface for the exchange of network operational state between Open Daylight and other controller solutions, as well as to enhance the interoperability of controller federation both within a single operational domain and across administrative domains.

Because it borrows from many of its immediate predecessors, the Open Daylight framework (Figure 9-5) is very modular, Java based (i.e., a pure JVM), and supports bidirectional REST and OSGI framework programming. This will support applications that run in the same address space as the controller application.[9]

At present, ODP is very focused on service. A service abstraction layer (SAL) maps both internal and external service requests to the appropriate southbound plug-in and provides basic service abstractions that higher-level services are built upon, depending on the capabilities of the plug-in(s).

---

7. http://www.opendaylight.org/announcements/2013/04/industry-leaders-collaborate-opendaylight-project-donate-key-technologies

8. The announcement was immediately followed by statements from the ONF that they too would be working on a standardized northbound (application) API.

9. http://www.osgi.org/Technology/WhatIsOSGi

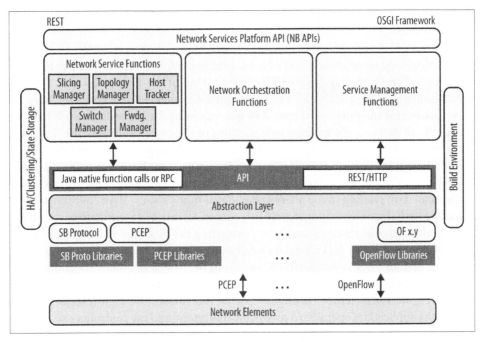

Figure 9-5. Open Daylight idealized framework/controller

An example of such a service would be the data packet handling service, which would allow an application like ARP handling to register interest for sending/receiving certain packet types without having to be aware of the methods or capabilities of the individual plug-ins that may provide or send these packets. Other interesting and important built-in services include topology abstraction and discovery, PCE-P (and CSPF), OpenFlow, I2RS (as it evolves), and NETCONF.

Though in its early stages, some of the proposed contributions already include advanced functions such as a virtualization management suite that can be used for building and tracking overlay networks. Another important proposed contribution is that of network function virtualization (i.e., service chaining) control. So, as you can see, the potential for building a very sophisticated and functional controller on which very sophisticated applications can be rapidly build is a very real possibility.

API

One of the architectural tasks in the Open Daylight Project is to make the northbound API match some reasonable subset of the southbound API, which will be populated by a variety of protocol plug-ins (see Figure 9-5). One of the proposed Open Daylight contributions is a high-level data model compilation scheme that is based on Yang and is to be used for the purpose of auto-API generation/update of code and will have the capability of dynamically grafting new portions of the object model on the fly. This is very cool functionality in that it will obviate the need to restart the controller. It also allows for dynamic service model discovery by applications both at the time they connect to the controller and on an ongoing basis, potentially allowing them to dynamically adjust based on reading in the altered or updated model. Some have envisioned applications even being able to autogenerate (or regenerate) much of their internal code based on the object model changes simply by reingesting the model as a change is detected. This current use of the data model does fall short of the proposal seen earlier in Chapter 4, in that an SDN controller/framework can be viewed as a network compiler, although it is very possible to modify the model in the future to function as a compiler generating network element configuration. In this model, the high-level data model allows the application/operator to simply express intent, and the controller executes this by compiling the intent into primitives (i.e., code) that it executes.

One of the attractions of that proposal is that reversing the compilation process should aid in troubleshooting. That is, if the compiled data model should transition intent to network state, it should be able to take in network state and flag any state that does not map back to intent through a reverse process, or potentially other problems that can be detected at compilation time, such as invalid configurations. This could also theoretically be a great policy enforcement and/or operations troubleshooting tool, as it allows an operator to visualize changes *before* they are pushed down to actual network configuration.

However, there may be performance implications in compiling every transaction between the high-level data model and a lower-level data model to implement the network primitives. In particular, if change sets occur too frequently, and the generation and subsequent programming of those changes into network elements takes too long, this could pose a problem. For example, if the system relies on implementation of the feedback loop between the applications, controller and network elements that we described earlier, the longer it takes to run through these phases, the longer it will take for the entire system to react to faults or other situations requiring adjustment.

The Open Daylight Project's use of data models is a bit simpler. Each module self-publishes its API when it is activated using the OSGI model. The new module's API might then be consumed by any other interested (i.e., already running) module. This implies that an API versioning scheme will be part of the overall framework, as API versions may change between load/unload cycles. It is hoped that the dynamically loading object model just described might help with this too. The ODP controller framework embodies the concept of a loosely coupled service bus approach to wiring internal modules together. In short, the design is such that not everything has to pass through storage to enhance performance. An example of this appropriate to the Java-based controller might be the use of publish/subscribe and a Java Message Service (JMS) provider service that supports the JMS API. In this case, JMS providers can support both publish and subscribe and asynchronous message domains. Ultimately, though, network state will have to be stored some place, which can be in memory or to permanent storage.

High Availability and State Storage

ODP implements a cluster-based, high availability model for state and event synchronization. In its original model, the controller stores everything in memory and uses JBOSS Infinispan for replication. One of the framework's projects is to create a framework backend that provides partition tolerant storage. This fundamental problem lies behind the database synchronization strategies of most (non-mem-cache-based) SDN controllers. More recent controller designs try to position nonrelational databases (i.e., NoSQL) for storage of network state as opposed to the mem-cached behaviors of the older, open source controllers or the use of relational stores in highly integrated orchestration-specific solutions. The trend in recent controller development has been to leverage Cassandra as a distributed key/value store for network state with support for a high transaction rate and Zookeeper for distributed element discovery/tracking/configuration management.

Nonrelational databases scale particularly well horizontally (i.e., elements of the data base—or shards—can be distributed to different processors and physical disk storage, while appearing consistent to the observer). In this way, NoSQL approaches can also be used in grid file systems. These approaches are particularly useful where the application is not concerned with transactional behavior but instead is interested in a consistency and available model. However, transaction processing can be supported through Zookeeper, which can also be leveraged as a locking service to support read/write coordination in Cassandra as a lock manager. Open source variants are available with the same relative performance as key-value stores but with the flexibility of relational databases.

Through the right parameterization, partition recovery can be implemented in a database like Cassandra and an eventual consistency model like the CAP Theorem.[10] Other applications may not be tolerant of an eventual consistency data store (like Cassandra) and may engender additional storage interfaces/contributions.

10. There are a number of good articles on open source database (particularly NoSQL database) experiences in startup application development. Some of these articles explore the tradeoffs in consistency, availability, and partition avoidance/recover expressed in CAP theory. An example: *http://ria101.wordpress.com/2010/02/24/hbase-vs-cassandra-why-we-moved/*.

Analytics

If the purpose of SDN is to expose network information to applications, then arguably the two most important network information pools to the application developer will be the information pertaining to certain utilization characteristics of network elements and services. For example, the canonical link and resource information can be used to gauge the expected or actual application performance across a network. When this information is combined with topology, some interesting and very powerful results can be obtained. For example, a combination of inventory, multiple layers of topology that can be cross referenced, and resource location on that topology—e.g., a service layer—when cross-referenced with certain performance data, can determine if network re-optimization might be needed.

Both the Open Daylight controller/framework and many other recent controllers acknowledge their roles in managing the virtualized infrastructure by incorporating statistics gathering and event notification into their management session data streams. They all attempt some sort of active topology discovery, albeit with limited layers of topological visibility, but the aim is still the same. Because it is an analytics data source, the controller/framework will need to provide an API to access this data store.

Stand-alone analytics applications have been gaining popularity and deployment, as they can help address some of the operational problems of network operators. Since this goal is well aligned with the goal and function of SDN, it's not surprising that many of the more recent SDN controller strategies propose an analytics service or application. These applications generally contain a collector, rules engine/processor, storage backend, visualization, and some sort of query interface. The management of information collection, particularly flow data, can create a scalability problem for the SDN controller in terms of creating limitations along various vectors; these include I/O, storage, and processing. Most of these lead to overall control session limits. Compression of flow data is normally a part of these systems, and an outstanding question is whether distributed processing in the form of grid computing (Figure 9-6) is applicable to this problem. How and where this would be integrated into a controller[11] is another interesting question.

Traditional relational databases are too slow for the high volume of data these systems generate. Newer NO-SQL databases haven't been universally applied in stand-alone applications but are showing promise in this regard as their scalability and performance seems acceptable for other large stores of data. Something important to observe is that this database technology transition has already taken place relative to network state storage in the newer generation of SDN controllers.

---

11. There are stand-alone, grid-based analytics systems available today from companies like Guavus.

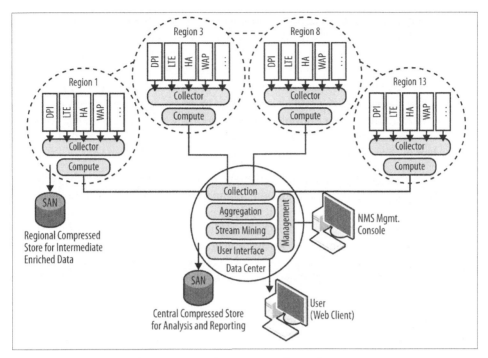

Figure 9-6. Guavus grid computing solution to analytics data compression

As we mentioned earlier, the requirement for analytics goes beyond basic packet counters or traditional statistics, which need to be synthesized into flow information in order to be useful. In particular, this information needs to be synthesized and correlated in certain ways in order to be useful when describing the virtualization or overlay layers an SDN controller might be managing. Traditional network element (i.e., router, firewall, switch, NIC, and so on) port packet counters can expose overall link utilization but not the source of that utilization unless somehow correlated back to a particular port and ultimately a VM. This is possible if the VM is relatable to a specific virtual port and a specific flow or set of flows, which is expected in the virtualized environment.

Resolution of flow data back to customer significance for the purposes of troubleshooting may require some callback/API to the orchestration system. The reason being that these routines are being incorporated in underlay elements as part of the sometimes exclusive API access arrangements between network equipment vendors and partner orchestration/SDN system vendors. Accomplishing this is more difficult for traditional network elements, which can export flow information via traditional means (Netflow, Jflow, IP-FIX), but these encapsulations are not granular enough to generally be associated with a VM, at least not easily.

The combination of utilization and topology could lead to powerful new applications, most of which leverage the provision/analyze/optimize feedback loop archetype common in SDN. An example combining this feedback loop with a BigData application is discussed as a use case in Chapter 10 where instant CSPF in the WAN is a potential application. At one point, there was research that suggested that tightening this loop might aid in the scalability problem created by imposing new flow tables on existing (less capable) hardware. For example, when OpenFlow was superimposed on hardware forwarding architectures that were not TCAM based, it was discovered that the controller had to carry much of the burden of fault detection and reaction.[12]

There is an ongoing association between analytics and big data insofar as the collection of data and its subsequent manipulation and analysis. For example, product Splunk[13] takes incoming stats data, massages it, and stores it in flat files called indexes. Splunk fosters many open source uses of their API, e.g. Shep, which allows streaming the Splunk data into a Hadoop environment to further boil down that data. Some analytics products provide trigger/response mechanisms that can be useful in applications like the mitigation of incast/microburst problems in the data center.

Incast occurs when a request for data or set of commands to multiple destinations results in a large burst of data/traffic back from each of those destinations to the requestor closely correlated in time (Figure 9-7). For the length of the overlapped burst, you get N:1 oversubscription, resulting in latency transients, tail drops, or simply packet loss along that path.

12. *http://conferences.sigcomm.org/sigcomm/2012/paper/hotsdn/p19.pdf* (and many others, some of which reference *http://www.sigcomm.org/ccr/papers/2012/January/2096149.2096152*, which is available by subscription).

13. *http://www.splunk.com/* and *http://blogs.splunk.com/2011/12/05/introducing-shep/*

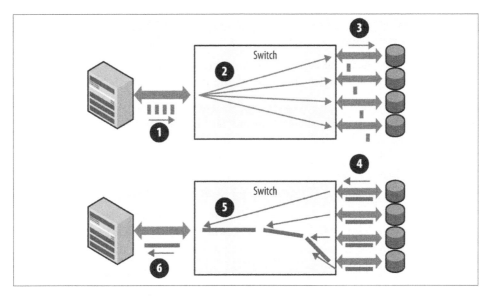

Figure 9-7. Incast/micro-burst

Policy

Analytics can also drive or aid in network policy control. In the evolution of frameworks, we have seen the recurring return to policy as a component that can be used to drive or manage operational behavior. While ODP is the closest to a complete framework available in what can be a commercial or open source offering, its early days architecture appears to be missing a policy component. Thankfully, with the modularity of the structure, this can be added to the service framework with relative ease and is likely something that we will propose in the near future.

Conclusions

The objective of this chapter was to illustrate the evolution in thinking about SDN control by illustrating a few frameworks, as well as to conclude with what the current thinking is for an ideal controller. We did not attempt to define controllers in depth, as Chapter 4 surveys the controller paradigm in detail. What we did intent to do is illustrate that behind a well-designed controller lies a well thought out framework on which it is not only based, but will continue to be built on in the future.

The SDN framework should act like an architectural blueprint for where the controller is and wants to be. To this end, we presented and defined such an idealized SDN framework that we hope will be used going forward by controller vendors and developers. We described the key elements of this framework including a north- and southbound API, a dynamic programming environment, and the importance of a state storage scheme. We described the elements of policy and analytics and how they play a key role in both a framework and a sound controller implementation.

We also discussed how the controller/framework evolution is also the evolution in thinking about the ideological purpose of the control entity: the NOS or broker/compiler.

There's also some unsettled debate about the nature of SDN that we touched upon. In particular, is it truly about bidirectional communication between the application and network or could it be an entirely reactive model as expressed in the mobility space through the use of policy?

We think it should be bidirectional (Figure 9-8). We think that one of the main tenets of SDN is the *feedback loop* between an application, the SDN controller, and the network elements that it controls. This touches on *network programmability*, or how the controller is programmed insofar as how it acts as a proxy between the network elements it controls and the application.

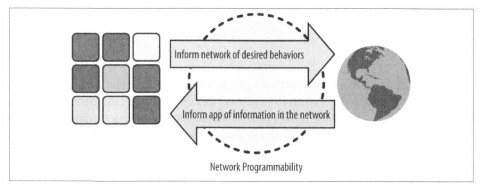

Figure 9-8. SDN as a bidirectional conduit between application and network

CHAPTER 10

Use Cases for Bandwidth Scheduling, Manipulation, and Calendaring

Introduction

Bandwidth calendaring is a category of use cases[1] that (at their heart) embody the concept of time-based bandwidth manipulation. In these cases, the manipulation refers to the addition, deletion, or modification of bandwidth in the network. The reasons, or *triggers*, that would cause one to perform bandwidth manipulation vary widely but include modification of bandwidth characteristics to more closely match traffic patterns, service demands and disruptions, or operational planning for future changes such as capacity. The common theme here is that these generally involve some sort of temporal cycle. In fact, not only is the bandwidth manipulated on some sort of timed schedule, but the causes for manipulating bandwidth are usually motivated by a need to do so based on some sort of schedule that otherwise would be (or is) performed manually. Let's explore.

And let's start simply. Figure 10-1 demonstrates a scenario where a service provider owns two data centers that are interconnected by some network links. One is located in Sunnyvale, California, and the other in Portsmouth, New Hampshire.

---

1. These examples are not meant to be "cookbooks" (each could spawn its own book at an appropriate/usable level of detail for that function), but rather a greater illustration of the use of SDN as applied to the WAN.

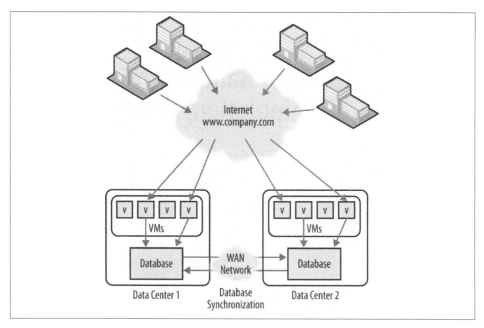

Figure 10-1. Data center interconnection example

The data centers are purposely geographically diverse to facilitate a lower-latency user experience and also to handle disaster recovery scenarios. To this end, each data center contains virtual machines that are used to host and operate the company's web-based music streaming service. Each data center contains, at stable points throughout the day, a copy of the other's customer records, music database, and other important information. Each data center is connected to the Internet, allowing proximity-based, low-latency access to the service, depending on the latency each user has between the music services.

In order for all of this structure to be kept transparent to the user and to make using the service as intuitive as possible, each VM is setup to appear as if it is the same service, even though it is logically servicing a partition of the superset of users. When users contact *www.TomsMusicStreaming.com*, they connect to the web server located closest to their current location (in reality this means of course that they connect to only one of the two aforementioned data centers). Well-understood web traffic load balancing (not discussed here) efficiently distributes user requests to one data center or the other. So conceptually, while the streaming music service appears to reside behind whichever service access point the user chooses, the reality is that this database is actually made up of two subsets of the same database at any given point in time. Both sides of the service implementation (therefore the VMs) could potentially serve the same user too, with one song coming out.

However, in our example, the user can stream music only from the database of songs housed in their particular data center. Since the overall database of information (say, user account billing information) that resides behind the web service actually is implemented as two logical partitions of the same logical database, both halves of the database must be periodically synchronized in order to keep it consistent. This is called *database replication*, or *synchronization*, and takes many forms, which are beyond the scope of this use case. But any kind of database synchronization requires some amount of network bandwidth in order for various pieces of the database—whether considered chunks of files, entire files, or the entire database, simply being copied as one large file—must be transferred over some network. It is this database replication and synchronization that is often performed at low-use or off hours. In many cases, these off hours can be correlated to daylight versus nighttime or diurnal usage patterns.

To continue with *TomsMusicStreaming.com*, let's say that the database is accessed mostly during the day, U.S. standard time, due to most of its customers being located in the United States. Let's also assume that at night, the majority of users do not use the service to stream music. Since it has also been determined that the music must be available regardless of locale, periodic synchronization of both customer records and music files must be done. It's safe to assume that both servers and network bandwidth between the data centers are underutilized during nighttime hours and that network operators would choose to synchronize the databases during these hours. It's easy to imagine an operator pushing a button on a console to trigger a nightly backup or synchronization activity, or have some job automation function trigger this at some fixed time.

In the past, a common approach to the algorithm just described was to simply set up bandwidth between both data centers that could handle the computed worst case for bandwidth demand between the two sites and call it a day.

Upon closer inspection, however, if one weighs the bandwidth versus the cost per bit and then compares that against the actual amount needed, during any given time of the day, this model is quite wasteful based on the diurnal example discussed. For example, let's assume the most bandwidth used is during the day, with peak demand requiring 85% of the network's resources, but that nighttime data replication duties require only 40%, so paying to provide similar bandwidth during nighttime hours is rather wasteful. Assuming TomsMusicStreaming.com has access to flexible pricing of bandwidth, it makes sense to be able to adjust bandwidth on a time-based demand model. Even for *fixed* priced bandwidth, being able to shut down or idle virtual machine or network equipment resources could be a significant optimization of power, lowering heating and cooling bills. To these ends, *calendaring*—making a forward reservation of path and bandwidth—is one such way to optimize our use case.

In a more global context, where large-scale transfers and their ensuing reservations may span multiple time zones (international), the overlapping diurnal usage patterns of the intervening network(s) may obscure a simple calendared reservation for an optimal direct transfer solution. And depending on the application and business operation tolerances, a *store-and-forward* path (a series of shorter distanced transactions) may exist that also provides significant economies.[2]

Because of the complex relationship between path availability, utilization information, and other mitigating factors (bandwidth cost, policy, and resource competition), it may be harder now for the reader to imagine the fictitious operator (manual) action, or even the job automation function trigger, providing the level of accuracy and responsiveness needed to realize the efficiencies promised in a bandwidth calendaring application.

Such an application will work with the controller or framework described in prior chapters to extract information from the network (active state), make an informed path computation for the transaction, manage the reservation, and when the time comes, provision the path linking application source and destination flows.

While it is possible for that same operator to have "push button" console control of a reservation through the application's GUI, the real power of the application is derived when the API calls made to trigger its services are embedded in the application themselves (or at very least through some broker or proxy). This programmatic interaction with the network is an example of the power of SDN.

Of course, behind the opportunity to gain new efficiencies through this interaction, many carriers or service providers may see an opportunity to sell new services that exploit the capability to schedule during low utilization periods.

Bandwidth Calendaring

Let's now look at a more detailed example of bandwidth calendaring, as shown in Figure 10-2, which is a real implementation of our conceptual *TomsMusicStreaming.com* example. See ya, Tom.

---

2. See *Inter-Datacenter Bulk Transfers with NetStitcher* (*http://www.cs.duke.edu/~msirivia/publications/netstitcher-sigcomm.pdf*) by Nikolaos Laoutaris, Michael Sirivianos, Xiaoyuan Yang, and Pablo Rodriguez; Telefonica Research.

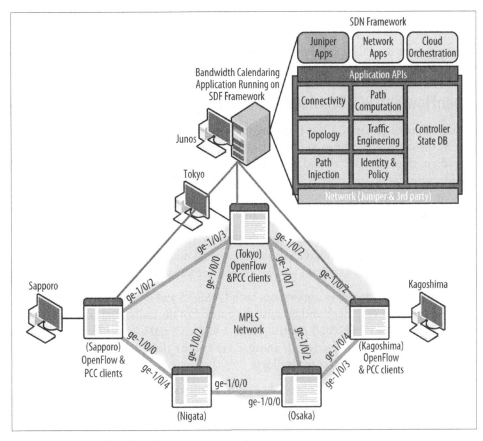

Figure 10-2. Bandwidth calendaring example

Base Topology and Fundamental Concepts

In Figure 10-2's topology, there are five routers located in Japan. Each router is positioned to support multiple sites for multiple tenants of the service provider. All five routers support both the OpenFlow protocol and MPLS/IP (to show how the solution may work with multiple different controller types).

Our Bandwidth Calendaring application runs on top of a conceptual SDN controller or framework of multiple, interchangeable controllers and other services.

Paths for reservations can be constructed (or signaled) using a variety of methods: the Open Flow protocol, MPLS Label Distribution Protocol (LDP), MPLS Traffic Engineered (RSVP-TE) paths computed by the routers, or PCE-P paths computed by a PCE-P application running on the controller. Let's focus on examples around OpenFlow and PCE.

In the case of OpenFlow, the application could reside above an OpenFlow controller (which provides layer 2-oriented topology, path computation, and provisioning services), whereas the PCE example would require more of a framework of services (since the PCE server does not have an integrated topology service component).

OpenFlow and PCE Topologies

A private management LAN is implemented allowing direct Ethernet connectivity between the controller and each device in the network. Though the OpenFlow control paradigm does support inband connectivity between the controller and network element, *out-of-band* connectivity is more common and less fraught with the concerns that may arise when mixing control and data traffic on the same link. Other controller types may not assume/require out-of-band connectivity.

In general, at the edges of our topology, there are Virtual LAN (VLAN) or raw Ethernet interfaces representative of a data center (of virtual machines, databases, and services needed by the tenant customer) and/or a customer/subscriber site network.

Assuming that our switches understand both IP/MPLS and Openflow (and can be configured as hybrid switches), and because the control of the individual ports is exclusive between the legacy MPLS/IP control plane and an OpenFlow controller, each edge router/switch is interconnected to another via two or three links (or in some cases, virtual links) to create our core topology.

For our specific examples, a subset of ports/links provide the infrastructure needed to construct a layer 2-only topology using Ethernet/VPLS encapsulation (which will be controlled via hop-by-hop OpenFlow flow entry mechanics).

Another subset provides the IP/MPLS topology (for the purpose of illustrating the example, these topologies may not completely overlap, allowing for layer 2-only sections of the network). To exploit the MPLS/IP path, an IGP-based underlay (on the MPLS/IP enabled links) is needed.

Nigata and Osaka are not configured/enabled for transit OpenFlow paths. All nodes are capable of MPLS/IP transit.

Because of specifics of the switch implementation of hybrid mode, the OpenFlow controlled ports are interconnected with the VPLS instances or MPLS LSPs by virtual tunnels (a virtual tunnel construct can have one logical end in a layer 2 forwarding instance and another in a layer 2 or layer 3 instance).

With this basic setup, paths can be established across the core of the network interconnecting the sites using a variety of methods, all of which technically can be considered SDN (given the fact that the control plane is being distributed from the data plane in this example).

Once baseline connectivity is established, reservations for specific client flows can be accepted by the calendaring application via its visualization interface or from clients passing through embedded API calls.

The most basic API call would be parameterized with a path preference (optional), a path provisioning method preference (optional), and flow information (resolvable source and destination address, flow sockets, or other match detail), bandwidth requested, flow duration, and start time (optional). Note that the default could be immediate, which would allow for the rule to be acted upon immediately after the command was consumed.

Our specific example will illustrate reservations/flows between Sapporo and Kagoshima. In particular, video client will be used on the (customer) subnet 3.3.3.0/24 in Sapporo to a video server (2.2.2.2) at the Kagoshima site. The reservation will be asymmetric (6.4 Mbps for high-definition video from the source to receiver and a 10 Kbps backchannel for video session maintenance from the receiver to the source).

 The supplementary files (*http://examples.oreilly.com/9781449342302-files/*) contain the complete configurations for this chapter's use case plus instructions on how to build a fully functioning working demo to explore.

Example Configuration

While the previous example is by no means an effort on our part to show that *only* Juniper Networks MX Series can be used to construct a bandwidth calendaring environment, this does happen to be a working, functional prototype we have built. In order to aid in the instructional nature of the example, we provide the actual configuration files for the example on this book's website with its publisher. The configurations are relatively brief and do work as is (with the exception of the obscured password strings) on Juniper MX80s running Junos 12.3I0. Note that the use of this configuration does require the use of the Juniper SDK. Signing up for the SDK will also provide you with the configuration files for the Bandwidth Calandering Application SDK application source code. This should give you a fully functional working demo to explore.

OpenFlow Provisioned Example

It is useful to remember how the OpenFlow configuration and flow provisioning model works. That is, TCP (secured via TLS) sessions are established between the controller and any OpenFlow-capable router, and subsequently Open Flow messages are exchanged over this control channel. Configuration messages establish the relationship of controller(s) to network elements (including flow retention behaviors, master/slave roles in the case of multiple controllers, port mapping to controller instance, and other basic configuration items). This configuration process leverages OpenFlow-specific Yang data models and the NETCONF protocol.[3]

In this example, the controller discovers topology using LLDP, but other mechanisms are possible, including Cisco Discovery Protocol (CDP), ICMP probing, or even static programming.

Wire protocol messages populate forwarding tables (on behalf of the application, in a proactive model) using messages that specify a table and a combination of packet header match/modification rules that include input port (on which to match) and either next_table or output port actions as specified in the OpenFlow wire protocol. As a simplification for our example, these rules indicate which traffic flows should be switched between one or more input and output ports.

Looking at the base configuration, the Kagoshima switch needs OpenFlow access to four ports: ge-1/0/5.0 (flow source/sink), logical tunnels lt-0/0/10.0 and lt-0/0/10.150 (providing access to the MPLS LSPs in layer 3 instance), and lt-1/0/10.0 (access to the VPLS instance interconnecting the OpenFlow transit routers).

The OpenFlow switch/controller sees these ports like this:

```
admin@Kagoshima> show openflow switch info 0
  1(ge-1/0/5.0): addr:64:87:88:5a:d2:5d, config: 0, state:0
  2(lt-0/0/10.0): addr:64:87:88:5a:d1:f8, config: 0, state:0
  3(lt-0/0/10.150): addr:64:87:88:5a:d1:f8, config: 0, state:0
  4(lt-1/0/10.0): addr:64:87:88:5a:d2:58, config: 0, state:0
  LOCAL(lo0.0): addr:64:87:88:5a:d2:f7, config: 0, state:0
```

When the client application is spawned off of Sapporo and requests a video flow from Kagoshima, there is an option to specify (in the applet and in the API) an OpenFlow only path. Selecting this option forces the flow through Tokyo.

Two uni-directional flows will be created.

Flow state in the path routers/switches (cut down outputs):

```
admin@Sapporo> show openflow switch statistics flows all
cookie=0xffffffffda6979c2, duration_sec=15s, duration_nsec=116000000ns,
  table_id=0, priority=32767,
  ip,in_port=1,nw_src=2.2.2.2,nw_dst=3.3.3.3,actions=output:4
cookie=0xa00000138ac0f2, duration_sec=15s, duration_nsec=116000000ns,
  table_id=0, priority=32767,
  ip,in_port=4,nw_src=3.3.3.3,nw_dst=2.2.2.2,actions=output:1

admin@Tokyo> show openflow switch statistics flows all
cookie=0xa000002d2dd7a5, duration_sec=56s, duration_nsec=116000000ns,
  table_id=0, priority=32767,
```

---

3. At the time this book was written, the ONF Configuration WG was working on a bootstrap routine to allow automatic configuration. Currently, *some* static configuration is required.

```
      ip,in_port=1,nw_src=3.3.3.3,nw_dst=2.2.2.2,actions=output:2
cookie=0xffffffffa31ecf59, duration_sec=56s, duration_nsec=116000000ns,
    table_id=0, priority=32767,
    ip,in_port=2,nw_src=2.2.2.2,nw_dst=3.3.3.3,actions=output:1

admin@Kagoshima> show openflow switch statistics flows all
cookie=0xa0000061b156c3, duration_sec=101s, duration_nsec=116000000ns,
    table_id=0, priority=32767,ip,in_port=4,nw_src=2.2.2.2,nw_dst=3.3.3.3,
    actions=output:1
cookie=0xa000006e97ed68, duration_sec=101s, duration_nsec=116000000ns,
    table_id=0, priority=32767,ip,in_port=1,nw_src=3.3.3.3,nw_dst=2.2.2.2,
    actions=output:4
```

Focusing on the Kagoshima outputs, mapping the outputs backwards to the port outputs is straightforward.

Note that while the duration of the flow requested maps to the duration of the flow entry from the controller, there is no way (in the flow entry) to express the bandwidth reservation. This would be tracked separately and is available through the visualization interface or analytics interface of the Bandwidth Calendaring application.

Enhancing the Controller

To further illustrate the utility of the controller, let's take a closer look at what components could comprise that controller. Figure 10-3 illustrates the details of what might comprise the innards of a basic controller that can be used to realize the previous example.

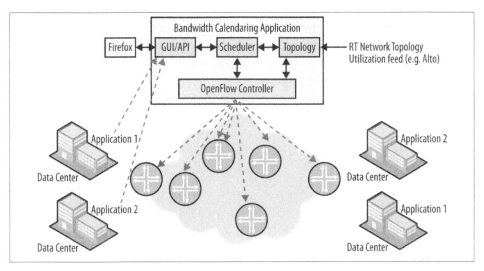

Figure 10-3. Breakout of Openflow controller

First, Figure 10-3 shows a RESTful API to the controller that can be used to communicate with it (therefore, create new LSPs, delete them or change the time-based scheduling of existing LSPs). This is illustrated with the Firefox icon communicating with the GUI. The addition of a RESTful interface to a controller is important, as it allows for fast, flexible interaction with the controller, and it also is a preferred application programming interface (API) used by modern application programmers such as those that create applications using Java, Python, or Perl.

Next, the RESTful interface manager communicates with the scheduler. This component does what you would expect: it is responsible for managing the schedule of programmed events for LSP creation, suspension, and tear-down. In reality, this can be as simple as a configuration file, or as complex as a multisharded SQL database. The scheduler then interacts with the topology manager component. It is responsible for managing and maintaining the topology. For the purposes of this example, let's assume that this is a repository of information gathered by LLDP, as discussed earlier. However, as noted, this database might be populated using a variety of mechanisms, including Cisco Discovery Protocol (CDP), ICMP probing, or even static programming. Finally, the scheduler interacts with the OpenFlow controller. This component in our example here is fairly straightforward and was built on the open source Floodlight controller, but you could easily replace it with most any of the open source controllers—or even roll your own.

Overlay Example Using PCE Provisioning

The more evocative example would be the use of stateful PCE, otherwise known as *PCE-P*. When you consider the use of external C-SPF algorithms that run on the controller, PCE-P is a very attractive option. PCE allows the application, via a PCE server, to manipulate the ERO of previously configured and delegated MPLS LSPs in the topology or dynamically create new LSPs (depending on the level of PCE support in the element software[4]). This is illustrated in Figure 10-4.

---

4. draft-crabbe-pce-pce-initiated-lsp-00 (*https://datatracker.ietf.org/doc/draft-crabbe-pce-pce-initiated-lsp/*) describes the ability to perform PCE-initiated LSP setup and builds on prior work for "stateful" PCE [draft-crabbe-pce-stateful-pce-mpls-te-00 (*https://datatracker.ietf.org/doc/draft-crabbe-pce-stateful-pce-mpls-te/*)].

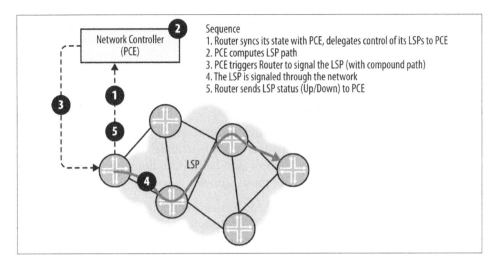

Figure 10-4. Conceptual PCE-P operation

The initial provisioning of the test bed can be automated in a similar method as the OpenFlow example (NETCONF/Yang).

Topology for PCE can be provided to the application via a static file (many tools can construct topologies from configurations or IGP database dumps), but to be useful, an active topology is preferred.[5]

The fact that we're using MPLS LSPs for our overlay brings forward several advantages:

- The provisioning happens only on the edge devices.
- There is potential for protection (reserving and provisioning both active and back-up paths).[6]
- The potential for dynamic LSP provisioning (our example allows the PCE to manipulate the ERO of an existing, pre-configured infrastructure LSP).[7]
- Natural affinity between existing path calculation algorithms (CSPF) and topology models like those provided by BGP-TE/LS.
- Active reservation management in the RSVP→BGP-TE/LS feedback cycle.

This last point can be either a blessing or a curse for the application developer, and is a distinction from the OpenFlow model. In the PCE model, the reservation requests (the

---

5. Options for active topology are discussed in Chapter 8.

6. draft-crabbe-pce-stateful-pce-protection-00 proposes the ability to create or manipulate path or local protection for created or delegated LSPs.

7. draft-crabbe-pce-pce-initiated-lsp-00 proposes the ability for a PCE to initiate LSPs on the PCC.

bandwidth reservation in the RSVP path request) are managed in the traffic engineering database (TED) and can *potentially* be constantly updated in the topology (if you choose BGP-TE/LS for topology learning). So, in the PCE model, the overall reservation of the system is a combination of the pending or future reservations (yet to be committed) and the existing active reservations. In the OpenFlow model, the reservations are managed solely as part of the application.

Both models need strategies for accounting for unreserved bandwidth. In the case of OpenFlow or PCE, this may be embodied in analytic updates. PCE has an option of mapping default traffic (unmatched) to an auto-bandwidth tunnel and capturing a periodic bandwidth utilization figure for those tunnels.

Unlike the OpenFlow-based example, the PCE-based example may require an on-ramp to map desired traffic onto the MPLS LSP. By default, the LSP FEC will be based on a destination IP prefix, so traffic maps to tunnels nearest the network node (next hop) advertising the destination prefix. Because this behavior may not provide fine enough control, most implementations of MPLS-TE support policy-based routing to load the tunnel. However, this option brings the burden of manipulating the policies (the vendor-specific syntax and lock/verify/commit behaviors), limited policy expression, and limited scale (in some implementations).

OpenFlow provides an interesting, dynamic, and open alternative for the on-ramp (traffic matching, filtering, and/or redirection) function. By using the matching capabilities of OpenFlow, you can map desired flows to the logical port represented by the MPLS-TE tunnel (LSP).

Other alternatives for on-ramp functionality may become viable in the future (e.g., via extensions to BGP Flowspec[8]).

Making the same request as in the prior example but not specifying an OpenFlow-only path causes our reservation to use an MPLS LSP manipulated by PCE.

Again, two uni-directional flows are created and (in this case) two uni-directional MPLS LSPs are manipulated to accommodate the reservation. Figure 10-5 illustrates how both can be achieved in a single network using a single controller.

---

8. draft-marques-sdnp-flow-spec-01 proposes the ability to extend flow classification to fields other than IP destination address in RFC5575 and draft-simpson-idr-flowspec-redirect-02.txt proposes changes to redirection rules in the same RFC (which will make it more useful as a policy-route on-ramp function).

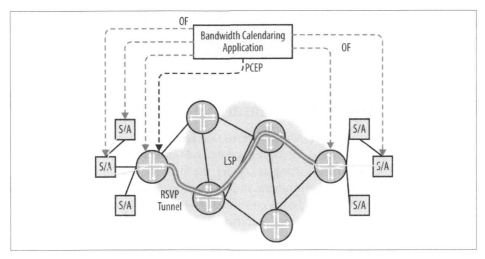

Figure 10-5. PCE-P and OpenFlow

Let's look at Kagoshima outputs.

Here, you expect to see the reservation of the named LSP Kagoshima_to_Sapporo manipulated (all the infrastructure LSPs were set up with a zero bandwidth reservation) and two flows created:

```
admin@Kagoshima> show mpls lsp extensive name Kag_to_Sap
Ingress LSP: 2 sessions
10.10.10.100
  From: 10.10.10.118, State: Up, ActiveRoute: 0, LSPname: Kag_to_Sap
  ActivePath: (primary)
  LSPtype: Externally controlled, Penultimate hop popping
  LSP Control Status: Externally controlled ← controlled by a PCE
  LoadBalance: Random
  Encoding type: Packet, Switching type: Packet, GPID: IPv4
 *Primary                    State: Up
    Priorities: 0 0
    Bandwidth: 6.30146Mbps ← up from original reservation of 10Kbps
    SmartOptimizeTimer: 180
        No computed ERO.
admin@Kagoshima> show openflow switch statistics flows all
cookie=0xa0000046ada2b3, duration_sec=42s, duration_nsec=883000000ns,
  table_id=0, priority=32767,
  ip,in_port=1,nw_src=2.2.2.2,nw_dst=3.3.3.3,actions=output:2
cookie=0xffffffffd2efad8b, duration_sec=42s, duration_nsec=994000000ns,
  table_id=0, priority=32767,
  ip,in_port=2,nw_src=3.3.3.3,nw_dst=2.2.2.2,actions=output:1
```

Similarly, you expect an MPLS LSP on Sapporo (Sapporo_to_Kagoshima) to have its reservation manipulated and dual flows to be entered in the OpenFlow table.

You shouldn't expect or see any OpenFlow state for this flow in any intermediary router, even if the LSP path transits an OpenFlow capable element.

Expanding Your Reach: Barbarians at the Gate

Let's return to the power of SDN applications that reside in the API (and the fact that SDN is about a programmatic interface) and extend our example to consumer applications (hence the barbarians at the gate). So far, the focus has been on high bandwidth flows in a relatively closed environment, indicative of internal applications on a somewhat closed network. Conversely, the consumer environment would be characterized by large numbers of somewhat lower bandwidth flows in a more open environment, with some required services added to our SDN controller/framework.

While there obviously are needs for security, policy, and potentially interfaces to OSS/BSS systems (e.g., billing), if the example is extended to an embedded API in a client browser (or client proxy) that is called when a client attempts to watch a certain class of videos, we can focus on the topology aspect to discuss the nature of the SDN API.

For computational and security reasons, you don't want to expose the entire topology database to such a client (which could be a smartphone or tablet), yet you need the API for topology to be scalable and customizable by policy. The ALTO[9] protocol offers examples of these API services.

Assuming an ALTO server is embedded as a topology provider in our SDN controller/ framework, when users attempt to download a high-definition version of a video, they would be prompted by an embedded applet (that calls the API using an ALTO client) to request a paid (the prompt is only needed for the consent, otherwise it may be unnecessary), prioritized, or guaranteed path for the flow. By using ALTO between client and server (controller/framework), you can limit the topology exposed to the client/ caller to something as simple as best path between source and destination or (to a proxy in the network making calls on behalf of the clients) a limited network view that consists of high-definition video source islands and usable video links.

---

9. *http://datatracker.ietf.org/wg/alto/* provides copious reading material on the IETF ALTO protocol.

Big Data and Application Hyper-Virtualization for Instant CSPF

Up to this point, the examples around the bandwith calendaring use case have required a simple set of services provided from the SDN controller/framework to the application. These focus primarily on topology, path computation, and path provisioning.

The topology is a layer 2 (OpenFlow) or layer 3/MPLS topology (PCE), and the path computation required is a relatively simple SPF (OpenFlow) or CSPF (PCE) with limited constraints (current network state, basic analytics in current flow stats and reservations, and a relatively simple, embedded policy).

The examples in the prior section are practical and demonstrable.[10] However, the example can be extended to a more complex application in which the reservation system of the bandwidth calendaring application is a component. This is illustrated in Figure 10-6.

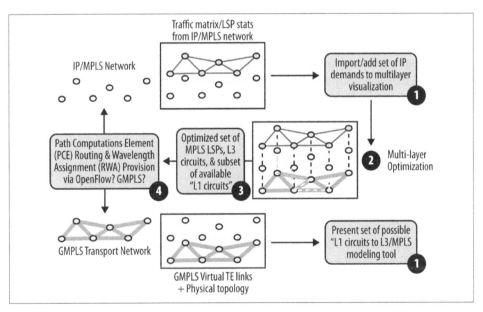

Figure 10-6. A predictive, multilayer topology network optimization workflow

Many network operators today perform periodic optimizations of their networks (or sections of their networks) using offline analytic and computation engines. These efforts are largely manual (with some potential for automation) and are limited by both the

---

10. The Ofelia research project, OESSS (OES3) software and Juniper Network's BCA demo application have all demonstrated Bandwidth Calendaring in 2012.

capability of the tools used and the static provisioning model (that we were working around in the bandwidth calendaring application). Because these operations predate the advent of OpenFlow and SDN-driven overlay solutions, they commonly use MPLS-TE LSPs to steer traffic (with the same loading/on-ramping limitations mentioned in the earlier PCE example).[11]

The working paradigm is to ingest a static topology (depending on the tool vendor, from element configurations or routing protocol database dumps), flow data, and user-defined policies or constraints (e.g., maximum path delay or avoidance of Shared Risk Link Groups) and optimize it for the most efficient network utilization (normally in both an active and limited hypothetical failure scenarios). The result of an analytical run is normally in the form of a recommendation that's exportable to a spreadsheet that is then converted to vendor-specific tunnel creation syntax/semantics, and provisioned during a maintenance window. Potentially rerouting traffic during live operation is problematic for both the time the static provisioning model requires and the fact that it is impossible to orchestrate the changes in a near-simultaneous fashion in that provisioning model (which could lead to undesirable interim inefficiencies).

The strength of current offline tools is in the variety of their parameters and policies they can incorporate and the complexity of the mathematical algorithms they use to divine a result. But, depending on the complexity and scale of the network itself (or the flow data), they currently can run for a very long period of time.

Operators would like to take advantage of the provision-analyze-optimize cycle inherent in the network control SDN promises to implement in a more dynamic/automated workflow.

In this workflow, the path computation component could optimize based on:

Current utilization
Commonly from a flow data repository

Historical utilization
Generally a less specific graph of utilization based on historical flow data to indicate a diurnal pattern of network use (this diurnal pattern can be updated with a sliding window of historical data if there is a distinct variance in the trend)

Future reservations
Managed by the Bandwidth Calendaring reservation system

These inputs will probably not be exclusive, and the real power in prognostication is derived from their combination.

---

11. Though incremental, progress has been made on several of the problems in this area through drafts like those that allow for sub-LSPs.

Though only a potential application, SDN and big data techniques may provide viable solutions for this network optimization application, and the range of potential service demands between bandwidth calendaring and this automated network optimization ("fly-by-wire") application accentuates the need for modularity in components and (again) flexibility in the service APIs exposed.

While the BCA application and its underlying controller(s)/framework provide a template with which to solve this problem, the path computation component will need a serious upgrade. Also, a more robust analytics module must be incorporated to capture, format, and (potentially) summarize relevant flow data.

Several commercial tool vendors are addressing the computational complexity of both the analytics management and path computation problems using big data techniques —for example, grid computing for customized distributed summarization of analytical data and Hadoop to farm the computational exercise, and interfacing their results to a PCE server for provisioning.

 The recent IETF draft draft-farrkingel-pce-abno-architecture-02 (*https://datatracker.ietf.org/doc/draft-farrkingel-pce-abno-architecture/*) proposes a PCE-based architecture that may propel such an application.

Expanding Topology

This use case chapter has focused on dynamic network path creation and network optimization. Now let's circle back again to topology as a service of the SDN controller/framework. It should be evidently clear now that network topology is quite an important aspect and service of the SDN framework because it pertains to both the practical bandwidth calendaring application and the futuristic network optimization application.

In both examples, the topology exposed is limited by what is configured and seen in either the layer 2 or layer 3/MPLS topologies.

Some operators' business models require them to optimize by network exit point, and in some cases, potentially in conjunction with link utilization policies. This often creates a challenge because most active topology sources include resolution of external prefix reachability using configured, and therefore distributed, route policy and the BGP best-path algorithm. This represents only a subset of the true peering points advertising that prefix. Though enhancements to BGP allow for multiple potential best paths,[12] this may

---

12. draft-ietf-idr-add-paths-08 (*https://datatracker.ietf.org/doc/draft-ietf-idr-add-paths/*) describes BGP add-path operation to expose multiple paths (augmenting best-path) and draft-ietf-idr-add-paths-guidelines-04 (*https://datatracker.ietf.org/doc/draft-ietf-idr-add-paths-guidelines/*) provides guidelines around the use of this enhancement.

burden the network with an additional active state, especially if you are going to tunnel traffic to the exit point—and that means that all the intermediary nodes do not need to be aware of this state. The solution to this problem is to merge route-server-like state with the active topology in the SDN controller/framework topology repository. Tools to collect this information nonintrusively are under development.

Still others would enhance the topology with dark resources that can be used as part of the path computation solution (where adding additional capacity to handle bursts is a more preferred policy than rerouting traffic or is used in conjunction with rerouting). It is important to note that dark resources result from connected but unprovisioned (at layer 2 or layer 3) ports on network elements. Of particular interest is additional link capacity at layer 0 (optical paths) that may be made available on demand. The vision here is that the optical network provider, or the operator of the layer 2/layer 3 network (if the operator *is* the transport provider), provides a configurable partition of its optical network that provides potential paths to the upper layer operator.

Currently, tool vendors (referred to in our prior section) allow the merge of layer 0 topology with upper layer topologies, but this is not yet automated, nor is the data format standardized. Nonetheless, this topology is available to the path computation engine, and existing combinations of PCE-GMPLS and proposed extensions to OpenFlow (Transport WorkGroup) make these paths dynamically provisionable.

Conclusions

This chapter demonstrated a few simple yet important use cases for SDN. In particular, it showed how one can use an SDN controller in a centralized manner to control network paths, scheduling those paths at certain times of day or under certain other conditions. It also showed how a centralized controller on its own provides little value without additional smarts, such as stateful PCE and offline analytics tools. For instance, the Openflow protocol section demonstrated that simple path placement using such a tool, although interesting and instructional as an example, is not particularly useful in real networks without additional tools that augment the control plane function. This is a fruitful and interesting area in the SDN space. As additional reading for the reader, there are a number of interesting advances in the SDN arena around these use cases that we recommend exploring included in the companion web site. Also, the configurations for the devices are available on the companion website (*http://examples.oreilly.com/9781449342302-files/*) for you to take into the lab or elsewhere.

Use Cases for Data Center Overlays, Big Data, and Network Function Virtualization

Introduction

Use cases[1] for data centers can be as varied as the applications that reside in the data center. To tie together some of the concepts from earlier chapters, we'll look at examples that demonstrate:

- A hierarchical application with a low degree of multitenancy in an orchestrated overlay

- A DevOps alternative to overlay orchestration

- SDN in a big data application (application-driven network control)

- NFV/service chaining both in and outside the data center

Data Center Orchestration

The roles played by data center infrastructure can be pure IaaS, PaaS, SaaS, or any combination of these services.

A typical vertical industry service center that primarily provides SaaS services (a data center for specialized information management, for example, medical records management, human resources outsourcing, etc.[2]) might envision several client types, with

---

1. These examples are not meant to be "cookbooks" (each would spawn its own book at an appropriate/usable level of detail for that function), but rather a greater illustration of the use of SDN in Data Center applications.

2. Our specific use case comes from the health care vertical and the clients can be doctors' offices or other service providers both care and business related (e.g., imaging, pharmacy, billing collection, etc.).

varying levels of commonality (the variance comes in how they might connect to the outside).

Their client's commonality comes from the fact that all assume some level of public/Internet access to the SaaS service and that access will always traverse an ADC (the ADC does some fundamental security, and load balancing).

The operator's primary concerns are scale, ease of operations, and security. In the case of the latter, all the systems are to be protected from worms, viruses, malware, and other types of intrusion.

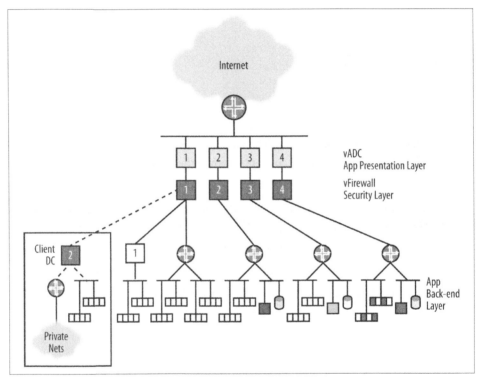

Figure 11-1. A conceptual specialized service center (data center). Tenant type 1 is completely virtualized with two VM pools, the service app (yellow) and their own app (white). Tenant type 2 has off-premise instances of the app as well as private network connectivity. They also have their own non-virtual apps and DBMS hosted in the DC (blue). Tenant type 3 has the service app (virtual) and its own non-virtual app and DBMS (orange), which are only accessible via the Internet. Tenant type 4 is using the DC for infrastructure (IaaS) only (dark red).

As shown in Figure 11-1, the first client type has multiple virtual networks within the data center. The first serves the primary service center application/data management function, and the others are outsourced networks for other purposes (thus, the client subscribes to a combination of IaaS, PaaS, and SaaS within the data center). The client also manages its own VMs inside its own network, which can attach to the data center.

Addressing from the client network is extended into the service center. This fits the VPN client model.

There are four discrete flow types:

- Server-to-server within a segment.
- Server-to-server between segments (via the gateway)
- User traffic from the outside via the vADC and vFirewall (the firewall can be inside or outside the gateway)
- Server-to-server from the client network VMs within the service center to the tenant network VMs, traversing one or more (local and/or remote) firewalls.

The second client type shown in Figure 11-1 extends the service center application (SaaS) to its site and may also have a combination of virtual and physical assets in the data center (the virtual assets are managed via the SDN/Orchestration system). In this scenario, the virtual machine management extends to the tenant's own facility.

This mode of operation could fit the cloud-bursting model.

The flow types include #1 and #3 from the former scenario (except for true cloudburst, the flow in #3 would first use the client site VMs before overflowing into DC VMs). Flow #2 is slightly modified because it is between a VM and a physical device (which many not be managed by the VM orchestration system). Flow #4 varies slightly in that it can be between local and remote VMs, but the DC provider manages them all.

This second scenario introduces two new flows:

- From tenant VMs in the service center to the machines/VMs in their private network (an extra gateway traversal)
- From remote-but-managed VMs to remote machines in the private network

The third scenario in Figure 11-1 is Internet-access-only, whether for IaaS, PaaS, or the service center specific applications (SaaS).

And finally, the fourth scenario shown in Figure 11-1 is like the second; only the private network is not on a client premise, but rather within the service center (an extra-net connection). Management of that network may be partitioned from the service center operator or provided by the operator.

What this actually looks like in a data center is a lot less idealized. There could be separate storage, host, management (both out-of-band monitoring and image load/stand-up), and vMotion networks. To realize the benefits of pooling, the network will become an overlay-heavy physical infrastructure (which is hard to depict in a small picture like Figure 11-2), as clients get more randomized on that infrastructure.

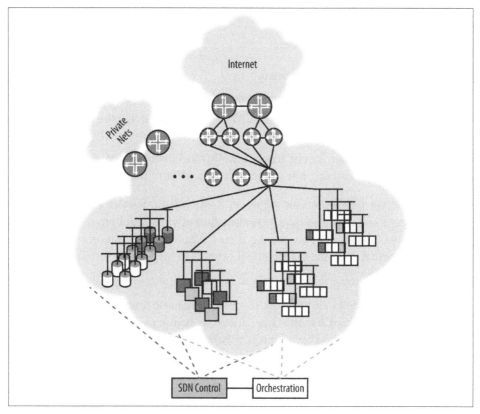

Figure 11-2. What the service center actually looks like—interspersing of physical, virtual, and storage placements enabled by overlay virtualization (hard to depict here, but each color would be a spiderweb of overlay tunnels)

Creating Tenant and Virtual Machine State

In any of the overlay approaches, when the first virtual machine of a given tenant is instantiated on a server, the following steps need to take place (as shown in Figure 11-3):

1. A new virtual machine is instantiated.

2. A logical bridge for the tenant is created in the vSwitch.

3. The new virtual machine is attached to the logical bridge using a virtual Ethernet interface.

4. If it doesn't already exist, a tunnel is instantiated from the server to each of the other servers in the data center that has at least one virtual machine for the same tenant.

5. A virtual Ethernet interface is created on top of each tunnel to represent the tenant ID and attached to the logical bridge (see Chapter 6 for per-encapsulation specifics on how the tenant ID is transmitted/expressed).

6. Apply services to the virtual interface of the VM such as QoS, firewall policies, access lists, etc.

 When an additional virtual machine for the same tenant is instantiated on that same server, only steps 1, 3, 5, and 6 need to take place.

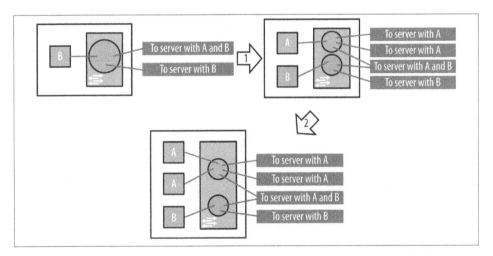

Figure 11-3. Adding a virtual machine for a tenant on a server; add first VM for tenant (1); add additional VMs (2)

It is the responsibility of the SDN controller to create the logical bridge, to create the tunnels, to create the virtual Ethernet interfaces, and to attach the virtual Ethernet interfaces to logical bridges. There needs to be some sort of signaling protocol between the SDN controller and the server to signal these operations, as shown in Figure 11-4. We discuss this in detail in Chapter 4. In general, the SDN controller is only responsible for the network aspect of the data center. It performs the low-level network operations based on high-level instructions from the orchestrator. The orchestrator is responsible for the overall operation of the data center, not just the network but also compute, storage, and services.

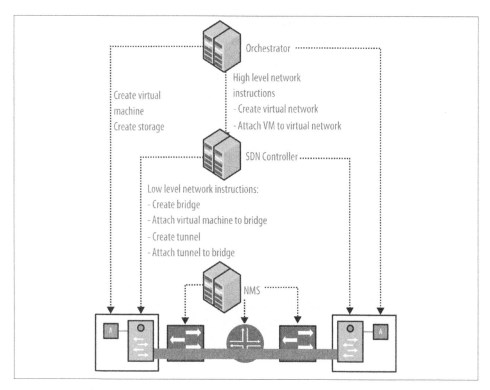

Figure 11-4. The role of the orchestrator, the SDN controller, and the NMS

One important observation is that neither the orchestrator nor the SDN controllers touch the physical network; they only touch the servers. In the overlay model, adding a tenant or adding a virtual machine to a tenant does not involve any changes to the physical network. It is the responsibility of the Network Management System (NMS) to manage the physical network. The NMS needs to interact with the physical network when switches are added or when servers are added, but not when tenants are added or virtual machines are added. This is clearly an advantage of the overlay model. The physical network is very stable and as a result more reliable; all the dynamic changes related to tenants are dealt with in the virtualized network.

Forwarding State

In addition to the state related to tenants and VMs (namely tunnels, bridges, and interfaces), there also needs to be forwarding state on the servers for each tenant, including:

- A MAC address table for each tenant bridge in the vSwitch
- An ARP table for each VM

This is illustrated in Figure 11-5.

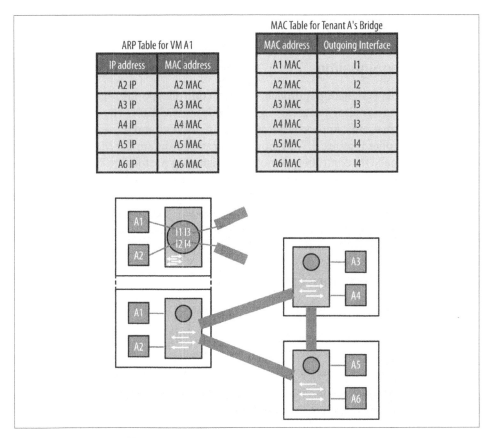

Figure 11-5. MAC table in the vSwitch bridge

The MAC table can be filled in two ways: data-driven learning or control-plane signaling.

Data-Driven Learning

The data-driven learning approach uses the same mechanism as normal (i.e., non-overlay) switched networks. Frames with an unknown destination MAC address are flooded across the entire tenant network. By observing the source MAC address and incoming interface of Ethernet frames, the switch creates the MAC address table. It also creates an ARP table. The ARP table that is used to map IP addresses to the MAC addresses is created through the broadcast of an ARP request across the entire tenant network. The data-driven learning approach has scaling and stability problems. The need for STP can be eliminated or reduced by using split-horizon on the tunnel interfaces (never forward a frame received over a tunnel to another tunnel). The data-driven learning approach has challenges dealing with VM mobility in that it must be implemented in such a way that can react quickly enough to VM moves to reprogram all of the information just described.

Control-Plane Signaling

In the control-plane signaling approach, the SDN controller populates the MAC address table using some signaling protocol (e.g., OpenFlow or XMPP). The controller has all necessary information: it knows the location, MAC address, and IP address of each VM. The SDN controller is aware of VM moves and can reprogram the MAC address table accordingly. The SDN controller cannot use a signaling protocol to fill the ARP table in the VM because the VM runs application software and cannot be assumed to contain a signaling agent to communicate with the SDN controller. One option is to use the normal ARP resolution process and accept the flooded ARP requests. Another option is to implement an ARP proxy in the vSwitch, which intercepts the ARP requests and tunnels them to the SDN controller.

Scaling and Performance Considerations

Reviewing the basic advantages of the overlay approach (from Chapter 6):

- No tenant state in the physical switches. Specifically, the physical switches do not contain any MAC addresses of tenant virtual machines. In the absence of overlays, the core switches contain all MAC address of all VMs of all tenants.

- If overlay solution uses layer 2 over layer 3 tunneling, there is the option of making the physical network a layer 3 routed network instead of a layer 2 switched network. This improves bandwidth utilization and performance (natural multipath support). A layer 2 physical network uses STP and needs a protocol like TRILL to support multipath.[3]

By terminating the tunnel in the hypervisor (e.g., versus using VEPA on the ToR), tunnel state is distributed among the hosts and their hypervisors. A DC provider presented the following metrics that we can use in discussing the implications of overlays on tunnel state:

- Most examples of widely used ToRs today will support 48 hosts.
- Each host currently supports an average of 20 virtual machines.
- The typical tenant will have four or five VMs.

---

3. Arguably, routing protocols are inherently more scalable and stable than switching control protocols such as STP.

A tenant may also need to interface with an appliance (e.g., firewall) and/or a gateway, as in our example.

Assuming some level of redundancy of the appliance/gateway and a worst-case VM distribution for the tenant, where every VM on the host is unique, a quick calculation of the number of potential tunnels would be in the low hundreds (about 160—8 tunnels per VM, 4 tunnels to other hosts in the group, 2 to redundant firewalls, and 2 to gateways, 20 VMs). The number of flows mapping onto those tunnels can be an additional but currently manageable scale multiplier (not always a 1:1 correspondence).

As you add VMs per tenant and create a very highly meshed fabric that is further complicated with technologies like LAG and attempt to exploit that fabric through multipath, the number of tunnels/links per host can scale quickly. Of course, this worst-case scenario is also based on the assumption that the hosts were capable of (and desired) full mesh connectivity.

In our specific case, many of the flows must first traverse a firewall or gateway because there are fewer intra-segment flows anticipated. This is particularly true of the third tenant type in our service center example (see Figure 11-1), where Internet access may be only for the service center application. In these cases, the total tunnels in the host hypervisor approach the number of VMs on the host with some small multiplier for redundancy scenarios (similarly, the mapping of flows to these tunnels would scale as noted previously).

Either way, the worst-case scale for this provider's average tenant size and flows is supportable on the current generation of COTS hosts. On the other hand, the tunnel state could be at least order of magnitude larger (potentially 48X) if we originate the overlay from the ToR switch. This tunnel scale is achievable in some network silicon, but at a cost.[4]

It remains to be seen if the next generation of servers/CPUs and its accompanying increase in VMs supported will fit into the forwarding space of the hypervisors, but the expectation is that it should be manageable. The bound would not be processing power, which continues to grow every day, but instead process space *within* the hypervisor.

---

4. Recall that we are exploring overlays to avoid hop-by-hop flow (e.g. OpenFlow) provisioning. In such a scenario, the per-port flow scale would be in the hundreds, and internal (spine/aggregation) switches would see a similar multiplication (48 times or larger) in flow state. This "second-effect" flow scale is problematic on today's commercial silicon and may require the application of summarization to be manageable.

Puppet (DevOps Solution)

If the number of client types and the scale is not overly large (where "large" is objective), the operator may not need an orchestration-driven SDN solution. The DevOps option of using a template-based, build-out tool like Puppet, Chef, Cobbler, or Ganglia, may be appropriate.

The strengths of these tools developed around image/role and server management, including address assignment and network configuration (for both bare metal and virtual hosts). For example, when using Puppet, the role of the Puppet Master is to assign nodes (devices) into classes (e.g., web server, database server, etc.). Each class definition describes the catalog of resources needed on device (e.g., Apache, MySQL, etc.). The resources describe what to do, not how to do it.

Applying this concept to networking, the resources would be interfaces, VLANs, and so on. If the operating system of a traditional network element supports a Puppet client/agent, interesting solutions can emerge. For example, if the scale of the data center operation was small enough to fit within the scope of VLAN separation (not requiring an overlay), then extensions to Puppet can be used to configure VLANs on ports and trunks appropriate to such an architecture.

Juniper Networks and Arista Networks have both extended Puppet to support agents in their respective OS(s).[5] In our example shown in Figure 11-6, the (Juniper Networks) solution consists of two files:

- The first, */netdevops/netdev_stdlib*, includes Puppet type definitions for netdev resources. Netdev is a vendor-neutral network abstraction framework created by Juniper Networks and made freely available on GitHub (*https://github.com/NetdevOps/puppet-netdev-stdlib*).[6]

- The second file, *juniper/netdev_stdlib_junos*, uses Junos OS-specific code that implements each of the types defined by `netdevop/netdev_stdlib`.

This latter file is necessarily vendor-specific, working around the current lack of common data models for these services.[7]

---

5. Arista Networks supports both Puppet and Chef (*https://github.com/opscode/eos-cookbooks*).

6. This file should (ultimately) move to PuppetForge.

7. One of the themes in this book is the need for the development of standard data models. The VLAN model is very simplistic, but there is nothing preventing the modeling of overlay encapsulations and other networking abstractions for both network elements and the hypervisor vswitch.

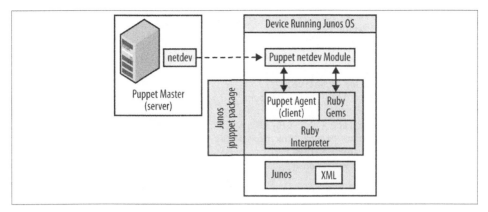

Figure 11-6. Network element support for Puppet netdev

This combination supports the following types:

netdev_device
  Models the properties of the network device.

netdev_interface
  Models the properties for a physical interface. The properties for a physical interface are managed separately from the services on the interface.

netdev_l2_interface
  Models the properties for layer 2 switching services on an interface. The services for a layer 2 interface are managed separately from the physical interface.

netdev_lag
  Models the properties for a link aggregation group (LAG). The properties for a LAG are managed separately from the physical member links and services on the interface.

netdev_vlan
  Models the properties for a VLAN resource.

For a user of Puppet, assignment of VLANs to a host would mean editing the netdev section of the manifest for a host. The Puppet master will compile the manifest and the changed code can be (periodically) downloaded by the host/element (via SSL).

For example, deploying application foo on switch fooswitch1 in bar.com (assigning foo to a port and a trunk with VLAN 100 to talk to other foo-like servers) would look something like:

```
node "fooswitch1.bar.com" {
    netdev_device { $hostname: }
    netdev_vlan { "Foo-net":
      vlan_id => 100,
```

```
    }
netdev_vlan { "Native":
    vlan_id => 103,
}
    netdev_l2_interface { 'ge-0/0/19':
        untagged_vlan => Native,
      description=>"local foo host port"
    }
    netdev_l2_interface { 'ge-0/0/20':
        description => "trunk Link from local ToR",
        untagged_vlan => Native,
        tagged_vlans => [ Foo ],
    }
}
```

Though this example is relatively static, most DevOps template/script languages are highly parameterized and can use class definitions. The Puppet framework enables large-scale changes to devices by simply changing the class definition on the Puppet master.

Our example with variable definition might be as follows:

```
$vlans = {
    'Foo'    => { vlan_id => 100, description => "This is a foo vlan, just updated" },
    'Native' => { vlan_id => 103, description => "This is a native vlan" },
}
```

And this might be its corresponding class definition:

```
class foo_switch {
    netdev_device { $hostname: }
    create_resources( netdev_vlan, $vlans )
    $db_port_desc = "This is for foo-ap"
    $db_ports = {
        "ge-0/0/0"  => { description => "${db_port_desc} ge0" },
        "ge-0/0/1"  => { description => "${db_port_desc} ge1" },
}
    $db_port_settings = {
        untagged_vlan => Native,
        tagged_vlans => [Foo]
    }
    create_resources(netdev_l2_interface,$db_ports,$db_port_settings )
}
```

And its corresponding invocation call might look something like this:

```
node "fooswitch1.bar.com" {
    include foo_switch
}
```

While this example is limited by the vendor contributed library extensions in Puppet to layer 2 operations, there are no real limitations on the functionality that could be exposed in the future. It should be noted that similar functionality limitations exist for alternatives like OpenStack Quantum, though this should be addressed in a subsequent release of the API. That is, it's just a question of the effort the vendor puts in to support and expand the API over time to enable layer 3 services, overlays, or services.

Network Function Virtualization (NFV)

In "Data Center Orchestration" on page 299, the operator offers services that include the use of virtual appliances (e.g., firewall). In general, the use of these appliances can be orchestrated in a way that allows for simple traversal of a pipeline of operations where logical interfaces representing both an ingress and egress from the tenant network create a simple traffic flow pattern. This is in fact at the heart of *network function virtualization* (NFV) and how those functions are chained together using a concept called *service chaining* (Figure 11-7).

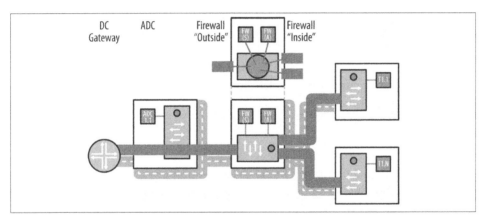

Figure 11-7. Our data center service chain; there could be additional complexity in the overlay derived from the high availability strategy (active and standby VMs shown, but active/standby devices are more likely from a throughput standpoint)

The meta concept around NFV is that in the definition of the service for all the tenants in our example is one fundamental service chain: ADC-Firewall for all traffic ingress from the Internet.[8] It is actually two, in the case of the VPN/private network cases. The actions by the appliance are either forward, modify-and-forward, or drop. No additional logic is required. No metadata is necessarily passed from one service element to another. There is no significant branching logic in the chain.

Service chains are generally constructed by some controlling or orchestration entity (i.e., an SDN controller). This entity is responsible for the provisioning (i.e., placement)

---

8. The return flows, for the most part, traverse a single device (firewall, and even that may not be necessary).

of the services, and then the chaining of them together. The actual per-tenant configuration of the services such as firewall and gateway can vary but need to be maintained by the NFV controller or orchestrator. The transparency of the provisioning effort at this point in time may depend on the orchestration vendor selected and the firewall product deployed. If they are from the same vendor, there is a good chance that flow through provisioning (transparent) is possible. If they are not, some degree of transparency could be maintained through a higher-level broker (OSS) that interfaces with both the SDN controller and the firewall vendor EMS/provisioning entity. The same could be said about *any* appliance/service-chain relationship (today).

The complexity in the chain in this example will be derived from high availability and/or a load balancing use case that we will discuss later in the book (creating the bowtie seen in Figure 7-10 in Chapter 7). We should note too that this is not meant to imply that all data center service chaining is fundamentally simple, as some configurations can be quite complex to not only provision correctly, but to maintain over time.

NFV in Mobility

Much more complex chains may evolve, particularly outside the data center in the decomposition of integrated network platforms, particularly those that deal with broadband subscription or mobility (e.g., EPC). Of course, it's the vision that many of these services will move into the DC.

The reasons behind this are the per-subscriber nature of the service customization:

- For a typical mobile subscriber, there can be multiple chains: HTTP traffic (L4 filtering, ADC, Media Optimization, Caching, CGN, FW—stateful and stateless), Peer-to-Peer (DPI, CGN, FW—stateful), VoIP and others—some of which may require session proxy. (Ad hoc analysis of current mobile service providers potential use cases has shown an average of 7 to 10 possible service chains.)

- Service chain characteristics depend on business aspects (e.g., sponsored charging for traffic toward a specific application server) and not on network characteristics.

- Service chains are dynamic and personalized.

- Because of the per-subscriber nature of traffic treatment, some metadata or context may need to be associated with the chain OR

What is typically referred to as the Gi LAN (based on the 3GPP interface nomenclature) or service LAN is currently a series of value-added services with traffic steering based on VLAN. This is originally set by APN matching and subsequently reset through DPI action—advised by policy interaction (Figure 11-8).

One of the reconfiguration options for this service would be to send the traffic to a next generation proxy. However, WiFi tethering is increasing in the mobile space, so a lot of laptop traffic is going through the proxy, which is inefficient, costly, and adds latency.

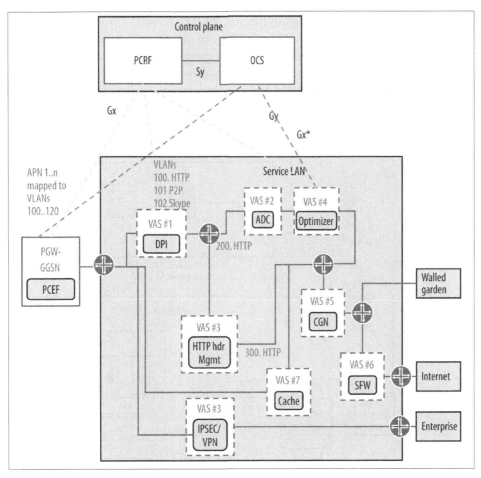

Figure 11-8. Typical mobile service LAN with a collection of value-added services (VAS). The different APNs are mapped to VLANs. Further remapping may result from DPI (e.g., VLAN 200, 300 branches).

Traffic steering (in the SDN sense, given current tools) is layer 3, making options like steering based on URL impossible. Yet, this is the granularity required to differentiate which VAS different customers might traverse.

A reasonably scalable solution might be a PCC-controlled subscriber binding to a service chain. In the case of OpenFlow control, a combination of VLAN ID per service chain for local/legacy VAS, and data center VAS with additional MAC rewrite in the encapsulation to direct to a Next Hop (in WAN and data center)—all done through flow mods directed by the URL/IP to service chain mapping in orchestration (Figure 11-9). This can be extended/scaled to a VxLAN or GRE encapsulation by replacing the more intricate (and potentially limiting) VLAN/NH-MAP flow modifications of OpenFlow with a routable tunnel encapsulation (flow to VNID to service chain mapping). Some legacy VAS may still require VLAN mappings to and from the tunnel overlay via a vendor-specific gateway or within the network element (acting as a gateway on behalf of the overlay orchestration). The TDF function allows the provider to leverage existing application-based charging systems and dynamic policy- or business-related service adjustments.

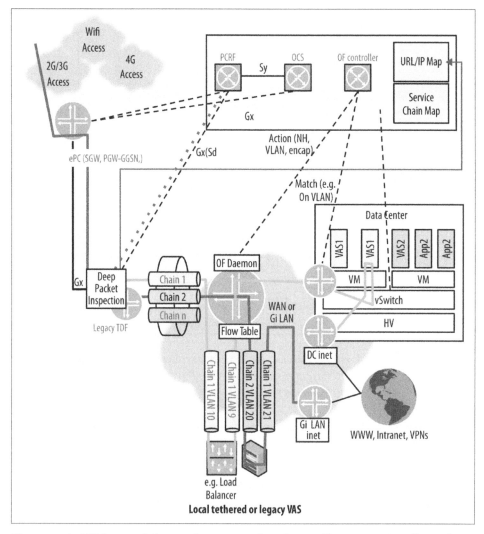

Figure 11-9. SDN control that performs per-subscriber traffic steering. Traffic is identified by TDF (DPI) function. Local/legacy (doesn't understand tunnels) VAS chained via VLAN, otherwise VAS steering via tunnel overlay.

It also represents a philosophical shift away from the bidirectional conversation between application and network. In this model, the network control reacts to what it is presented with via the policy engine and the DPI sniffer.

Optimized Big Data

The label "big data" represents transition in high performance computing from purpose-built computing (i.e., SUN microsystems, CRAY, etc.) to an approach that takes advantage of the economics of COTS hardware through the use of smaller, cheaper devices that can be clustered together. This is accomplished using divide-and-conquer approaches that dissect computational problems into small chunks both in terms of data and actual computation, and spreads that across those smaller, less powerful but significantly less expensive hardware. It should be noted that adopters of big data techniques have noticed the natural affinity between the topological view and central control of SDN and some big data applications.

In general, big data is not normally a virtualized environment because the hypervisor overhead is unnecessary. Hadoop is one of the most popular of a class of cluster computing architectures for big data that uses an application controller to manage job requests.[9] Hadoop is used for a class of applications called *Map/Reduces*, which process tremendous amounts of data by breaking the problem (i.e., the data set) into a number of sections/blocks, spread across a number of machines for parallel processing. This system also takes advantage of Hadoop's distributed filesystem—HDFS.

The main overhead in the application is in distributing the sectioned file, storing and then collecting the results. This is magnified by a redundancy strategy that causes several copies of the same block to be distributed in case one of the compute nodes fails—replication is a hierarchical operation.

The Hadoop architecture has three functional components: clients, masters, and slaves (Figure 11-10). The client is the ultimate end user of the cluster, submitting a job request with a file to manipulate with instructions on how to manipulate/process it and collecting results. The master node in Hadoop has overall responsibility for file distribution and managing the processing nodes. It depends and interacts with two other nodes: the name node and the job tracker. The name node is responsible for the distribution/storage, and the job tracker coordinates the compute.[10]

---

9. HBase, Dryad, Spark (*http://www.ibm.com/developerworks/library/os-spark/*)

10. The Name node and Job Tracker functions can run on the same device, depending on the scale of the cluster.

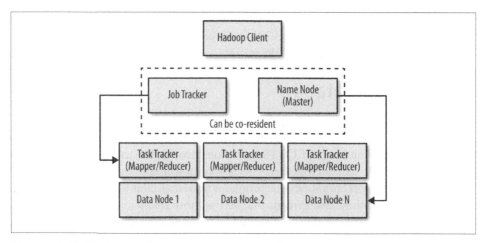

Figure 11-10. Hadoop architecture

The slaves are called the mappers and take the blocks and process them. The reducers collect and aggregate the results. The job tracker controls the task tracker process and also processes and coordinates jobs submitted by clients. The job tracker talks to the name node to determine the location of the data being processed. The job tracker is also responsible for submitted work to the task tracker nodes that have been chosen to do the work. As a means of redundancy and high availability of the system, the task tracker nodes must ping the job tracker at periodic intervals. If these heartbeat signals are not received after some period of time, the job tracker decides to resubmit the job elsewhere, can blacklist the task tracker, or just remember that this particular node's performance characteristics for the future because it may only be a temporary condition. It could also denote the start of a host/server failure.

The name node keeps a map of where the file is and to which machines the blocks are distributed. It has some level of topology awareness on its own, in that it understands the relative position of hosts by a manually configured rack number associated with the host by the administrator. The name node then works using algorithms that try to optimally distribute the data to cut down on inter-rack transfers but still maintain separation of the replicates so that redundancy/replication can work.[11]

The problem with this is the manual nature of the configuration (particularly in a large and continually growing/adapting data center) and the less than dynamic nature of the algorithm (there are assumptions about the relative performance in-rack that may not always be true, particularly in the presence of other traffic).

---

11. Hadoop is also a layer 3 aware filesystem, so it works in a routable network, allowing the architect to limit the size of layer 2 network domains and to potentially use Hadoop across larger areas. While WAN is possible, there are practical limits. The reference is more to the point of being able to use the entire footprint of the Data Center (to the limits of the spine and or aggregation switch bandwidth).

Using an SDN (OpenFlow) controller and a modified version of Hadoop (a modified job tracker and task), an alternative more dynamic version of Hadoop can be realized in a traditional switched/shared Ethernet-based topology (Figure 11-11). For example, a recent study that optimizes the shuffle phase where mappers send results to reducers by using OpenFlow-driven QoS so that the shuffle traffic can consume more link bandwidth has shown promising results.[12]

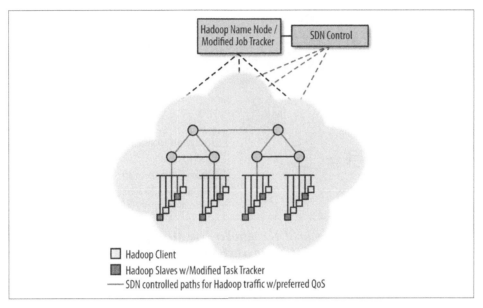

Figure 11-11. Modified Hadoop with SDN control giving Hadoop traffic favorable QoS treatment (in a generic, Ethernet-switched data center architecture)

This solution can be even more attractive when the switching infrastructure is programmable optics. In this case, optimized topology configuration can be implemented as OpenFlow rules in an electro-optical network (Figure 11-12).[13]

12. SCC Proceedings of the 2012 SC Companion: High Performance Computing, Networking Storage and Analysis (*http://dl.acm.org/citation.cfm?id=2476992*)

13. The depiction depends on the nature of the OCS. If it is optical-electrical and hosts are Ethernet attached, flow matching could be used to mux the traffic onto a dedicated lamba. In an all-optical switch, individual lambdas could be used through the network of switches and muxed at the end node or muxed per-hop. There were a lot of choices.

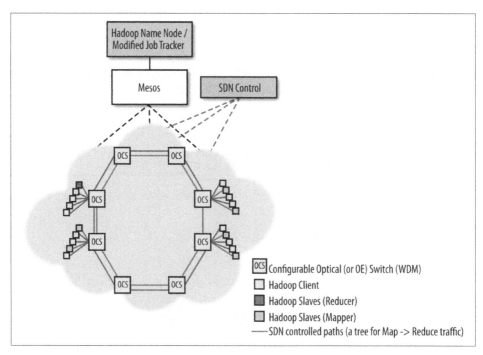

Figure 11-12. Hadoop using an SDN controller (via Mesos, if desired) to create a tree topology for mapper-to-reducer traffic in a network of configurable optical switches

Another recent study[14] in this area shows the flexibility of the combination. Range was derived from multiple tree topologies where reducers were closer to the root than their associated mappers. This information was then used to reduce multihop transfers in very scalable Torus or Hypercube network shapes that were ultimately enabled by changes in the data shuffling strategy.

A further expansion of both of these ideas is suggested by binding the controller to a dynamic resource manager for clusters (e.g., Mesos,[15] which we incorporated in Figure 11-2). By using a manager, the operator can run multiple frameworks in the same cluster to control utilization (particularly for storage) and potentially share data (as opposed to static partitioning).

What we have essentially created is a network-aware application that will attempt to optimize its functions placement or influence their interconnection/plumbing based on network knowledge. This differs in philosophy from optimizations based on network

14. *http://www.cs.rice.edu/~eugeneng/papers/HotSDN12.pdf*

15. *http://dl.acm.org/citation.cfm?id=2476992*

level analytics—application-aware networks (e.g., Plexxi, Helios,[16] OSA[17]) or the previous TDF-enabled mobility NFV example.

Solutions like Plexxi can work both ways, as the Hadoop job tracker/name node could be modified to export the list of nodes in a manner that can be imported as an affinity-map (static) by the Plexxi controller.

Conclusions

Our health services-related data center has multiple target customer scenarios and multiple resulting potential flows (and issues), with some customizable but recognizable service elements (load balancing, firewall, and network gateway).

But data center orchestration doesn't always have to mean complex, nor does it have to incorporate SDN. To that end, we incorporated a DevOps example appropriate for a simpler, VLAN-based data center deployment.

We ended by focusing on a specific application class—big data. In addition to introducing how SDN can influence big data, we open (and purposely leave open) the discussion about the role of SDN—whether it is to enable applications to be network aware, the reverse, or (potentially) both.

In this chapter, we have attempted to illustrate some common yet useful data center and NFV-related use cases. These topics had to be combined in the examples, as it is hard to separate these topics today. While seemingly theoretical, the use cases are based on real, albeit purposely anonymous, deployments, and public research. Data center orchestration is the poster child application of the SDN effort, and given its tenure in the spotlight, it's hard to introduce a new use case, so we've shown and discussed some more typical deployments. The future is bright for SDN, and the data center will be one of the areas in which it will flourish going forward. We recommend you check back here often for changes and advances, as they are rapid and continuous.

---

16. *http://cseweb.ucsd.edu/~vahdat/papers/helios-sigcomm10.pdf*

17. *https://www.usenix.org/sites/default/files/conference/protected-files/osa-nsdi12_.pdf*

CHAPTER 12

Use Cases for Input Traffic Monitoring, Classification, and Triggered Actions

Introduction

One category of use cases[1] that seems to recur frequently is a variation on the theme of input traffic monitoring or classification, and then taking some sort of triggered action (or actions). The general premise is one of interception or detection of some traffic pattern somewhere in the network—often at the edge or access point—that then results in one or more triggered actions. The action or actions can vary and be quite robust: from as simple as dropping incoming packets or as complex as triggering a query to a radius server or an HTTP redirection. Once those actions are triggered, the system can either return to its original state and simply process traffic as if it had never happened, or alter its actions to do something else either implicitly, or as a consequence of receiving a response from a query such as a radius request. Let's investigate a few canonical examples to help illustrate how this all might work, starting with the most basic input traffic interception mechanism available: the firewall.

The Firewall

At its heart, a firewall is a system comprised of an input traffic pattern-matching engine populated with a set of classification rules to match input traffic on. Classification rules range in capability from quite simplistic and primitive, to complex regular expressions. In all cases, each classification rule has a corresponding action that is taken by the engine based on a positive match of the classification rule. Thus, the basic function of a firewall

---

1. These examples are not meant to be "cookbooks" (each would spawn its own book at an appropriate/usable level of detail for that function), but rather a greater illustration of the use of SDN in basic traffic monitoring application(s).

is to pattern match input traffic, and take an action. The action, incidentally, can be as input to another rule, which might result in recursive or iterative rule triggers and processing. In effect, the firewall rules become almost their own programming language. This is, in fact, how the most sophisticated firewalls operate today in order to handle the myriad of rules needed to protect and control a modern corporate or service provider network.

As an aside, another similar and often equivalent concept is called access control lists (ACLs). These were the precursors to firewall rules and are often still limited to fairly rudimentary matching rules. The advantage is that most high-performance routing platforms implement the matching logic in hardware and can do the processing at quite high rates, which is something that many firewall devices still cannot do. ACLs are features you might encounter as a feature of most network routing and switching devices, not to mention the most inexpensive wireless routers you have at home.

Let's investigate how firewall classification rules can be specified, as well as the resulting actions. As mentioned earlier, at their heart, firewall rules are a 2-tuple consisting of {<input pattern>, <action>}. A firewall typically stores the rules in an array format, numbering each rule sequentially. Figure 12-1 illustrates this basic concept.

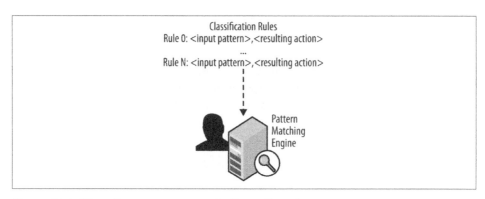

Figure 12-1. The salient components of a firewall service

The match-action rule can be something as simple as "allow all" or "deny from any interface <n>" which would either forward any matching traffic or drop all incoming traffic on interface *n*, respectively. Or they can be as complex as matching multiple pattern fields within incoming packets, such as filtering on TCP port ranges, "drop from any ipv4 TCP PORT 61000:65095". Match-action rules can be then chained together to form more complex actions, too. For example, you could jump to a matching rule group if input traffic matched a certain pattern as in, "ACCEPT from 192.168.1.0/24 to Interface eth0 –j GOOD-DMZ". In that example, you would jump to another set of rules defined in the "GOOD-DMZ" rule group. To put these concepts together, let's look at some sample output from the Mac OS X pfctl firewall:

```
Firewall
#
# anchor ruleset for the Adaptive Firewall
# anchor name: 400.AdaptiveFirewall
# see afctl(8), pfctl(8), pf.conf(5)
#
block in quick from 122.110.1.78 to any
```

In this example, traffic from a specific host (122.110.1.78) is explicitly blocked. This is achieved by specifying an explicit classifier match pattern in the last line. If the firewall matches input traffic coming from that IPv4 source address, the resulting action is to block or discard the traffic.

As mentioned, rules can be chained to form more complex rule sets that give network operators the ability to narrow down traffic patterns based on input conditions, or to allow subsequent match rules to be fired only based on certain, possibly dynamic, input conditions to exist. For example, input traffic rate limiting or *input traffic shaping*, as it's more well known, is really an action function triggered by receiving traffic above a certain threshold. The resulting action is to drop or sometimes *selectively* drop (i.e., shape), input traffic matching those criteria.

It should be noted that firewall pattern matching can be quite sophisticated. Until now, the discussion has centered on simple rules such as "allow" or "drop," but there are other possibilities, too, such as "rewrite" which instructs the firewall to modify parts of the packet upon matching. For example, it is possible to do *network port mapping* within the firewall. That is, when a pattern is matched, say, receiving a packet from any host on any externally facing interface, it translates some port to one that is internally used. This is a function that can be used to map a variety of services accessible externally to internal hosts behind a Network Address Translation (NAT) gateway. For example, you could define a rule set such as:

| From any | *.*.*.* | port | 22 | interface wan0 | rewrite dest | 192.168.1.45 | port | 22000 |
| From any | *.*.*.* | port | 23 | interface wan0 | rewrite dest | 192.168.1.46 | port | 23000 |

The first rule would match traffic from any host that arrives on the device's "wan" or externally facing interface with IPv4 port 22 and rewrite the ipv4 destination address to 192.168.1.45 and the port to 22000. This could be used to map the normal secure shell (SSH) traffic that comes to this network to a special gateway host that is configured as the server with special authentication capabilities. The second rule similarly rewrites traffic coming to this device with port 23 to port 23000 and sends it to host 192.168.1.46. This effectively rewrites that traffic stream's port to a special incoming one and sends it to another special host. Figure 12-2 illustrates how these input rules could be applied to a firewall device.

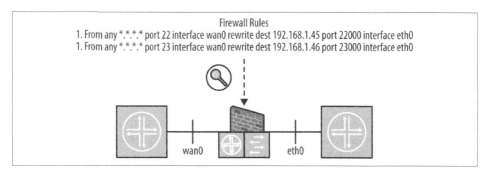

Figure 12-2. A basic firewall

Firewalls as a Service

So far, the discussion has been about the capabilities of just about any firewall you will encounter in a network today. Traditionally, these functions were implemented in system software that ran on physical devices that were dedicated to that specific function. In fact, many of these devices were built with hardware that was optimized for these functions, including optimized input pattern matching hardware interfaces and switching fabrics that connected the input port(s) to the output port(s) of the firewall.

So the question is: why virtualize this function? The answer is simple: flexibility and cost. Firstly, the flexibility of taking the software out of a custom designed device and running it on commodity hardware—let's call it Intel x86—is very appealing. It allows network operators to have a variety of options about how they assemble their network, or more importantly, change it later. The other option they have is to also shut that software off and run something else in its place! If you imagine the requirements to physically move a firewall—both physical and those of the operational support system (OSS)—it should be clear that it is cheaper and *far* faster to move the firewall software rather than its hardware. The flexibility of placement also lends itself to *service chaining*, as we discussed earlier in Chapter 7, as a potential use for chaining together physical and virtual services; a firewall, virtual or otherwise, is considered a network service.

It should be noted that running commodity hardware is not a new idea, and in fact, many of the firewall devices that you will encounter *are* and *have been* running on x86-based devices for quite some time. That is, the control plane software (the software responsible for maintaining the rule sets and the general control configuration, user interface, etc.) has been executing on an x86 CPU for quite some time. That CPU did not actually process user packets; instead, special switch fabrics and purpose-built port processors were created to connect the input and output ports, with special pattern matching hardware that was then essentially statically programed to look for specific patterns and ultimately forward, drop, or modify a packet. The instructions (i.e., rules) were programmed in that hardware by the system software or control plane that ran on the CPU. In effect, you had a split system with the brains residing in the x86 CPU, and the brawn doing the heavy lifting of the packets down in purpose-built hardware.

What is new in the modern hardware scene is that off-the-shelf network interfaces that were once woefully inadequate are now approaching the packet processing performance characteristic of custom-designed hardware. Furthermore, modern CPUs can handle a great deal of pattern matching capabilities, especially when optimized for packet processing such as been done by the Intel Data Plane Development Kit (DPDK) system.

Given the great improvements in packet processing with cheap, off-the-shelf hardware, we now can not only imagine but actually run virtual firewall instances. While not at 100% the same processing performance as dedicateed hardware, when you attach the virtual firewall instance to a single CPU and network interface, you can attach the problem using a divide-and-conquer approach and achieve nominally the same approach, albeit with more moving parts to manage. That is, if you spread a copy of the virtual firewall instance to a number of x86 CPUs, all with their own network interfaces, and appropriately steer input traffic to them to handle a subset of the overall input traffic, you have effectively sliced the input traffic workload among many devices rather than relying on one big (and expensive) piece of custom hardware.

This leads to the second advantage: price. There is a break-even point for spreading workloads across commodity hardware that differs depending on the actual product in question, so let's not attempt a guess at the actual point here. However, since many network operators are moving to generic x86-based data centers for other computational tasks, one can imagine that they have spare capacity available for firewall processing. Being able to use the same hardware for multiple purposes is a clear optimization of the overall equipment cost.

Figure 12-3 demonstrates how this scenario could be set up. Notice the mixture of real and virtual firewall services deployed in the network. One note is that the operator must understand that the virtual machine's placement within the network is critical, as is its connection to the actual network, because this will affect its packet processing rate, as well as the delay the packets it processes experience. For example, poor placement of the virtual machine, geographically, will result in additional hops of forwarding, thereby adding delay to the packet's journey through the network. Also, placement of a virtual firewall on a physical system that is already well-loaded, either in terms of CPU processing or packet processing on its input interfaces, can also result in delay or even packet loss.

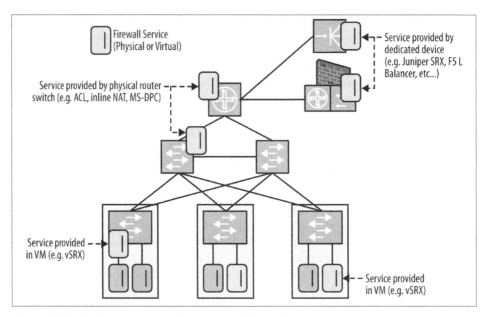

Figure 12-3. Deploying physical and virtual firewall network services

A final twist on the virtualization of firewall services is to add centralized control of the firewall service itself. This can be implemented as a combination of centralized control of not only the service (and the virtual machine in which it lives), but also the actual firewall rules that are used to drive the pattern matching function of the firewall. If you look at the instances of firewalls both virtual and real in the previous example, you can imagine how a centralized controller could control and orchestrate the network of firewalls from a centralized point, as well as from a distributed approach. In the case of the former, a network operator would have the advantage of a single point of control (logically centralized) from which to enact changes to the configuration state of any firewall in the network. In the second decentralized case, the operator would have to first understand which control point controlled which subset of firewalls before then adjusting the configuration.

Network Access Control Replacement

Network Access Control (NAC) might be considered a derivative or simplified case of firewall as a service. NAC is commonly achieved through the use of switch/router Access Control Lists (typical of fixed port ownership relationships like those exhibited in an Enterprise VPN environment) and/or policy-based solutions hinging on radius/diameter interaction between a policy server and the switch/router (typical of per-subscriber sessions on shared access infrastructure).

These solutions have their limitations. Critically, most implementations allow for a pre-compiled (i.e., statically programmed) ACL that is less suitable for a dynamic (fast-changing) environment. That is, the rules are pushed down to every switch in a network via a provisioning system, effectively reconfiguring every switch. For most devices, this is rather time-consuming because configuration operations take on the order of minutes to tens of minutes. Some early adopters of SDN technology want to use the more dynamic nature of SDN as a NAC replacement strategy.

To illustrate Network Access Control with a centralized SDN controller, let's use an OpenFlow-based example. It should be noted that you can use other mechanisms to implement this use case, but OpenFlow has characteristics that make it particularly appealing for solving this problem, such as the completeness of the solution compared to alternatives (at the time this book was written). Also in particular, OpenFlow allows matching across a wide swath of the datagram header, while alternatives like BGP flow-spec (IETF RFC5575), though more dynamic than the static ACL, lack this range and are currently limited in universal address family support and IP prefix related filters.[2] Further, if the vendor implementation of OpenFlow rules does not reuse the ACL or firewall filter structures effectively, implementing OpenFlow as a true forwarding table entry rather than a feature phase of forwarding, you can avoid the compilation dilemma of typical ACLs. That is, you can achieve rather painless and dynamic adjustment of NAC rules.

Of course, this would normally relegate the privilege of first lookup to the OpenFlow table as a tradeoff.[3] In cases where the implementation does not reuse the ACL or firewall structures, the implementation will suffer from a variety of performance and scalability penalties. In particular, a naïve implementation will attempt to literally program each OpenFlow rule verbatim without the benefit of rule compilation. Rule compilation effectively compresses and optimizes the rules down to their salient components and effectively shrinks down the number and complexity of the actual rules used to program the hardware. This not only means less space needed to store the rules in hardware, but potentially more optimal processing by avoiding unnecessary look-ups or recycling of rules.

Using the central controller, we will attempt to address what at first seems like a relatively simple problem. That is, constraining the use of the corporate IMS/SIP subsystems to approved desk or wireless IP phones and restricting access to the corporate network to registered devices in a rapidly evolving bring-your-own-device (BYOD) environment.

---

2. See prior chapter for references that extend flowspec to make it more usable for this and other purposes.

3. The authors have seen customer RFP requests to treat OpenFlow rules as if they were dynamic ACLs, maintaining "first forwarding lookup" in the default IP forwarding tables. But, to our knowledge, this has not been implemented.

Let's preface the discussion first with some background information. Though the IT department originally considered using 802.1X manufacturer identification, the truth is that not all devices support 802.1X, and the brand of IP phone selected for their offices falls into this category. Furthermore, after examining a multivendor solution, the IT department also noticed a number of incompatibilities between devices. So in an effort to not get hemmed in to a single vendor for their enterprise Ethernet switches, this example was constructed.

The building blocks of the solution are illustrated in Figure 12-4. The approach of the solution is straightforward and involves the use of a simple radius glue-logic application that resides above an OpenFlow controller to verify the registration of the each device entering the network. The capability of an OpenFlow (v1.0) enabled device (i.e., the access switches) is only required to match traffic based on source MAC address and perform PACKET_IN and PACKET_OUT functions. Switches must also be able to punt packets matching a rule to the controller, or shunt the traffic to a VLAN. It needs to be noted that the underlying network uses IP/MPLS forwarding to provide layer 2/IP infrastructure for packet delivery from edge to edge.

The combination functions as an OpenFlow hybrid network.[4] The connection between the two functional sides of the hybrid can be made using an Integrated Route-Bridge instance in the OpenFlow domain and OpenFlow NORMAL functionality, or by using a logical port structure (e.g., logical tunnel) that has ends in the OpenFlow domain and a layer 3 routing instance (a RIB association) as the incoming/outgoing port in Open-Flow rules.

When a client device sends its first packet, a lookup is done to see if a rule matching that specific source MAC exists already in the switch. If this fails, the packet is sent using a PACKET_IN operation to the active controller. This same controller is responsible for creating rules for the virtual switch inside the access switch. This switch is also where the controller delegates the ingress port.

In order to avoid wasting cycles in the authentication glue logic on the controller, a cache is maintained of recently authorized flows on that same controller. This is the case even if the flows are inactive on a particular switch. Since the IT network users are expected to be mobile, they conceivably could change wireless access points resulting in a potential change in their association with a physical access point at the edge of the network. If a rule exists, the controller will populate the switch with that rule and perform PACK ET_OUT, which will return the original packet to the pipeline for forwarding.

---

4. The operation of the network edge as an OpenFlow hybrid is optional. One could argue that NAC is implicit in a pure OpenFlow network.

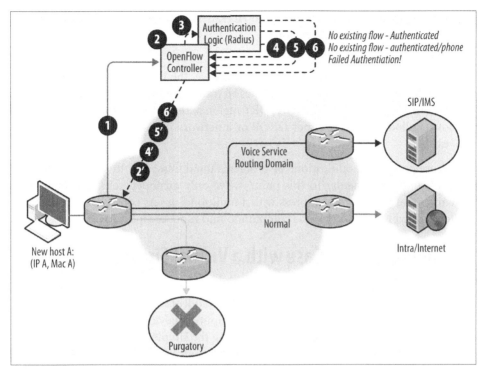

Figure 12-4. Simple network access control using OpenFlow in a hybrid network

The authentication lookup can result in one of the following:

AUTHENTICATED_MAC_PHONE

The MAC is a registered MAC and it is an approved phone type for the IMS/SIP subsystem. In this case, the flow modification sent to the switch will indicate that all traffic matching that MAC will be allowed to access the IMS/SIP region of the network. This would be expressed simply in an outgoing port action for that match of the logical port that connects to that infrastructure (be it layer 2 or layer 3). Depending on the underlying network plumbing (for example, if a logical tunnel doesn't represent this access, but a shared layer 3 construct and the NORMAL action does) the rule may need further embellishment to specifically match on the IP prefix(es) assigned to the IMS/SIP system as destination IP.

AUTHENTICATED_MAC

The MAC is a registered MAC, but not a phone. In this case, the flow modification sent to the switch will indicate that all traffic matching that MAC will be allowed to access the intra/internet regions of the network. This could be done by matching a fairly generic flow rule based on the source MAC with an outgoing port connected to that region of the network, with similar caveats about the underlying plumbing (in the case of a shared layer 3 construct and NORMAL operation, additional match rules would explicitly deny access to NORMAL for flows with a destination IP in the prefix of the SIP/IMS region).

AUTHENTICATION_FAILED

The MAC isn't a registered MAC. In this case, the flow modification sent to the switch will indicate a rule that matches all traffic from that MAC with an outgoing port that represents the PURGATORY region of the network (this is the customer's own colloquialism for either DROP or a network on which a registration server exists0.

There are potential modifications or problems unaddressed by this example that will lead to some refinements. To this point, we've only exhibited some minimal policy dynamics that were hard to express with a traditional access control list on the access switch. [5] In typical networks, it is common to find more complex ACLs.

Extending the Use Case with a Virtual Firewall

The limits to the model, and where we depart from simple Network Access Control, are seen when supporting any authenticated MAC address. This opens up the realm of possibilities from just VoIP devices to any computing device that could be attached to the corporate IT network. Further complicating the simple scenario might be treating the traffic from both a desk phone and the laptop softphone or media application with higher quality of service (e.g., by marking the packets in the flow with a special DiffServ Code Point (DSCP) that results in that traffic being honored as a higher class of service in infrastructure forwarding devices).[6]

The unfortunate truth is that a simple flow-matching rule won't work here for a variety of reasons. First, most media applications use RTP in UDP encapsulations. These in turn use amorphous ports for the sender and receiver once flows are established. The flows are established by a separate control protocol. This is typically SIP, but in some evolving services, the control channel may be encrypted, potentially making signature detection much less efficient. The alternative of not using the firewall at all and simply treating all unknown UDP packets preferentially is considered too easy to exploit by

---

5. SDN is also used in this example to normalize the deployment of access control and to deploy in a vendor-independent manner—free of the ACL syntax/semantics specific to any particular vendor (which is one of the fundamental appeals of the use of standardized SDN protocols as provisioning tools).

6. There are other options when using OpenFlow (to achieve QoS treatment on a node-by-node basis—assuming all the nodes are controlled by OpenFlow). For example, the "optional" Set-Queue action in OpenFlow could assign the packet to a queue, assuming that the switch supports queue and queue property discovery (configuration of the queue parameters MIN/MAX rates and an EXPERIMENTER field to communicate information are supported in OpenFlow version 1.2 and beyond). This could be combined with the "optional" Meter structure of OpenFlow 1.3 to affect many different QoS actions. However, because these are recent, optional, and the actual queue configuration is still separate from the OpenFlow wire protocol, a simpler example is used that relies on external (non-OpenFlow) QoS treatment.

end users. At this point we are going to need the services found traditionally in the firewall to detect these flows through an application signature, requiring the firewall to monitor a certain percentage of traffic or a flow sample that can then be used for detection of an application signature.

This approach has two potential solutions. First, build the firewall-like application on top of the controller,[7] or second, identify the traffic using a firewall (real or virtual) somewhere in the flow. This application would then perform appropriate QoS treatment. To build the application on top of the OpenFlow controller, you would have to use the PACKET_IN capability of the OpenFlow switch/controller combination or create a tap rule.

To avoid overloading the firewall application, you can use proactive flow rules limiting the PACKET_IN traffic to unknown UDP ports. In this case, you have to be both careful and aware of the changes in this mechanism in the different versions of OpenFlow. If our controller and switch don't support OpenFlow 1.3, then the PACKET_IN mechanism has to use the TCP control session between controller and agent. Because the agent is maintaining the sequence number for the TCP session, it's difficult (if not impossible) to remove it from the packet path[8] or do any sort of performance enhancement for the packet processing, making this approach to a firewall application infeasible. It should be noted that with the advent of OpenFlow 1.3, a UDP flow can be used for PACK ET_IN, which could make the application on top of the controller more palatable.[9]

Another way to build an application on top of the controller is to create a tap rule that mirrors the traffic to the firewall app. The rule will duplicate outputs to two separate ports as the action on matching the unknown UDP flow.[10] In this scenario, the application would sink/drop the matching traffic and send back flow modifications via the controller API when the application senses the media applications and identifies the ports for specific flows.

---

7. "On top" does not imply the firewall application Virtual Machine is co-resident with the controller, since the northbound API for OpenFlow controllers is normally RESTful. But you do need to be mindful of any latency pushing the packet from the controller to the application may introduce and that impact on the apparent "responsiveness" of the application. For this application, if the media flow is a video (particularly a video chat) the flow is expected to be large and of reasonable length (assuming the function is more like a meeting and average meeting times are measured in 15 minute increments). If the media flows were all VoIP, the responsiveness of the application may be more critical, since the flow length may be relatively short (by the time the flow entries are in place to enable QOS treatment, the flow may have ceased).

8. This pathway is the traditional "slow" path for routers and switches (lower packet throughput, more CPU usage for the agent process on the switch/router).

9. At the time this book was written, there is little (if any) experience with using the UDP-based PACKET_IN functionality.

10. Incidentally, the Virtual Tap application is a specific application for an OpenFlow controller that uses this same mechanism to mirror traffic to a monitoring device.

An example of this approach is seen in the FortNox[11]/FRESCO[12] combination (SRI), which combines a conflict mitigation module (making sure flow rules from multiple sources follow policy) and a scripting/development framework that can allow plug-in type modules to reflect/scan/affect traffic forwarding.

Since the appeal of the on-top and the tap solutions may be limited, you could try an alternative solution that uses an in-line firewall but manipulates the UDP traffic in a way that reduces the burden on the firewall (Figure 12-5).

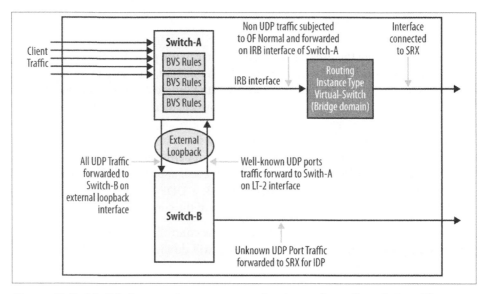

Figure 12-5. Modified network access control using a firewall and OpenFlow in a hybrid network

The particulars of the sample design include:

- There is one IRB (or logical tunnel) interface for forwarding all "non-UDP traffic" to routing instance using OpenFlow action "Normal". This IRB (or logical tunnel) interface is configured as an OF port in OpenFlow configuration stanza(s) on the switch/router.

- Two logical switching constructs are used to create a loop for the unknown UDP traffic to be treated (by the firewall) for QoS. The logical switches allow for some rule partitioning for administrative reasons. The external loopback could be created physically via the firewall (versus between the logical switches). There was some

11. *http://www.csl.sri.com/users/vinod/papers/fortnox.pdf*

12. *http://www.openflowsec.org/OpenFlow_Security/Publications.html*

thinking that the switch port resource was less expensive than the firewall resource at the time of this design.

- A port-to-port OpenFlow rule in Switch B pushes all traffic returning from the firewall, including the (potentially) treated unknown UDP through the loopback toward Switch-A. A port-to-port rule in Switch A then pushes the traffic from the loopback to the IRB (and a static associated QoS policy).

Feedback and Optimization

Both the firewall application on the controller and in line within the firewall will have a common optimization goal: minimize the traffic sent through the firewall. This is based on the assumption that the firewall resource introduces additional hardware or operational costs that are defrayed by managing the scale of the solution. Once a specific media flow, including the amorphous ports, has been identified by the application, a feedback mechanism that puts in place a specific flow rule should pipeline this traffic to the egress port.

However, in our OpenFlow example, QoS treatment requires the controller/switch to support either the optional SET QUEUE primitive as mentioned in previous footnote with an associated dependency on the support of messaging to discover port queue assignments and properties, or the optional ability to set DSCP of a packet directly. The latter will rely on the externally configured QoS policy on the egress port. The minimum version required for either of these capabilities is OpenFlow 1.2.

The ability to create feedback between network elements, services, and a logical point in the network is critical in order to optimize the use of network resources, and it is fundamental to many examples, regardless of the SDN control scheme or protocol used. More to the point, although we have used an OpenFlow example in this section, it is fundamental to enable and facilitate the feedback loop between network control and network resources. Such feedback loop principles are discussed in the example that follows.

Intrusion Detection/Threat Mitigation

The Intrusion Detection/Threat Mitigation System (IDS) illustrated in Figure 12-6 uses a similar strategy to minimize the load on the network service element (a real or virtual IDS system) by deploying an interior perimeter of rules:

- Generic rules that do flow forwarding based on IP source and destination prefixes.
- More granular (i.e., longer match and higher preference) for specific and approved flows between these sources and destinations.

- A rule handling flow misses (UNKNOWN traffic) with a rule that will create a copy of the packet using an action set like that of the tap application, and forward a miss to the IDS. The IDS software can be doing device profiling flow signature matching and other tasks.

- Depending on the outcome of the analysis, a specific flow entry allowing passage of the traffic can be installed via an API call to the OpenFlow controller at the interception point or a specific flow entry. The action would be to DROP the flow. This rule can be installed on the ingress switch(es).

In either case, the flow will not continue to traverse the IDS/UTM.

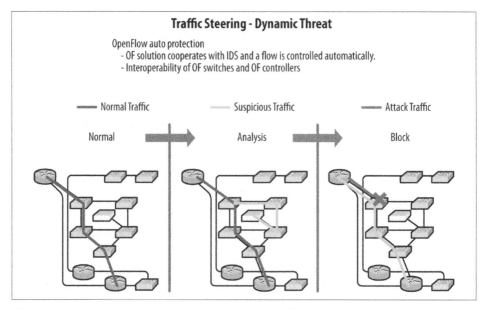

Figure 12-6. Dynamic threat mitigation using OpenFlow

Optimally, this feedback loop would create a learning system wherever possible. It needs to do this so that default rules and policies are incremented to capture these learned behaviors. Some of the more logic-driven aspects of intrusion detection and threat mitigation such as the logic that tracks changes in expected behavior or profiles—like when a known print device begins to initiate flows associated with a compute device, up to and including network mapping or port scanning—may be too difficult to capture in a small set of rules and thus defeat learning. However, some degree of learning could be expected with this particular example.

If you consider service chaining as an SDN application,[13] not only will feedback loop optimizations be applicable, but also triggered behaviors (e.g., based on DPI inspection and policy rules) will make flow paths even more dynamic. This further limits the capability to learn a larger permanent flow rule set.

Other examples of such a feedback loop abound, and in particular, the recently added 3GPP Traffic Direction Function (TDF) in the mobile domain, as shown in Figure 12-7, shows similar functionality.

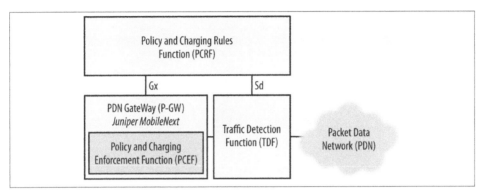

Figure 12-7. Traffic Detection Function

The TDF (normally a DPI device) is instructed by the PCRF (via the Sd interface) to look for specific application flows, and the TDF uses the same interface to alert the PCRF when they are detected. In turn, the PCRF may then instruct the PCEF to install a change rule using the Gx interface.

Conclusions

This chapter has demonstrated use cases for ingress traffic detection. Its examples showed how input traffic could be classified using simple firewall rules or access control lists (ACLs), and corresponding actions taken. These included the canonical firewall device and the virtualized firewall device. It then expanded from these simplified examples to demonstrate how the Network Access Control (NAC) protocol could be replaced using two key tenants of SDN: logically centralized control and ingress traffic detection. It then demonstrated how this could be further adapted to implement dynamic threat mitigation. Along the way, we discussed why it is important to enable another key tenet of software-defined networks: the application-controller feedback loop, and specifically, why certain optimizations could not be achieved without it.

---

13. We have been dealing with NAC and its derivative examples in this chapter, but have migrated the example into the territory of service virtualization, even though we haven't explicitly shown a chain.

CHAPTER 13

Final Thoughts and Conclusions

What Is True About SDN?

Most of the ideas that motivate the exploration of SDN start from revolutionary ideas but often normalize through experience. This happens through the natural evolution of prototype construction, lab trial studies, and early deployments. All of these eventually lead to evolving our perspectives and (hopefully) help make our networks better at delivering services more efficiently. This can be visualized in Figure 13-1, which shows how concepts move the present method of operation for networks to some different/new future method of operation.

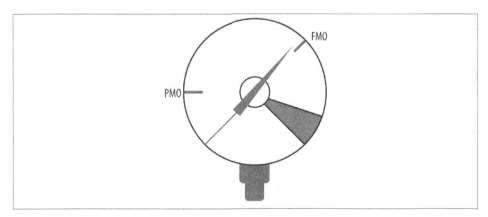

Figure 13-1. SDN will change our present method of operation (PMO) to a more optimized future mode of operation (FMO), which may not be as drastic as originally claimed (the red zone)

Though it's too early to pick a winning technology, or even a winning definition of SDN, one thing remains true—the *explorations into* SDN will change our present method of operation. The question is: will it be for the better?

There *is* something going on here, but it might not be obvious because it's under the surface in many cases.

We can't forget that there is an operator need driving SDN research and development. By 2010, the operation of large network providers had reached a stagnation point of innovation. The combination of OSS/BSS systems required to support a myriad of services in a large-scale multivendor environment was a drag on innovation. Worse, it was a drag on the bottom lines of service providers. Data growth from the influx of new video-enabled, "always on" mobile devices, as well as fundamental shifts in the way content is consumed (i.e., now streamed) was triggering staggering infrastructure demands for growth. In short, the very model of the Internet was morphing into a quickly changing, content-centric interrelationship between providers, versus the hierarchical, slowly changing access paradigm of the past. Evidence to this was the fact that new network services, enabled by new features in existing vendor software offerings or new vendor hardware offerings, could take at a *minimum*, 18 months to develop, integrate, and deploy. Meanwhile, new service providers such as Google, Amazon, and Facebook had found a genuinely better way.

The following fundamental ideas will endure because they in some way address both the chaos and stagnation of the present:

- Uncouple our provisioning from vendor-specific semantic dependencies.
- Virtualize the networking elements to some degree to allow greater scale and lower cost through flexibility in pooling and dynamic relocation.
- Abstract network topology as a service in ways that free a networked application from needing to know the arcana of network protocols or drink an ocean of data.
- And generally promote the open exchange of information between the application and the network.

SDN may actually redefine our assumptions and expectations around network management. For the rapidly growing number of virtualized network elements such as hypervisor switches, routers, and bridges, SDN controllers will function in ways that remind us veru much of the EMS/NMS/OSS of yester year, by providing provisioning, event management and analytics streams.

What we've attempted in this book is to illustrate the broad arc of SDN:

- The friction between distributed and centralized control models.
- How OpenFlow fits into the discussion of SDN, but in reality does not define or even dominate it any longer.

- How controller designs have evolved over time to become clustered/federated systems from the single entity practical only in trials and research. They have evolved to support multiple protocols and adopted considerable infrastructure to support application development and design considerations around state consistency.
- The impact of virtualization technologies and the major applications enabled by SDN when it mixes with virtualization and how this mixture moves the SDN controller into a future role in network management: data center orchestration (today), network function virtualization (near future), and fully integrated virtualized compute, storage and network with service chaining (future).
- The underlying goal of programmability, the need for openness and standards (which are implied in concept but incomplete in reality), and the evolution of controllers into development frameworks that provide robust, network-centric application services.

Mundane details often derail seemingly good ideas like SDN. With SDN, these details are tied up in management, which to most is likely not exciting; however, the reality is that hard work and sometimes mundane efforts are necessary to operationalize a new paradigm, as well as to optimize its and economics. This is the journey SDN has begun, but we predict is not even close to finishing.

Economics

Various bloggers have stated that the virtualization and SDN combination is, in the best case, an economically a zero-sum proposition for the consumer. In the worst case, it is actually a negative proposition. Personal experience has shown us that this is *currently* true. Research firms (e.g., IDC) also show the same in their recent data. In fact, one such study shows an 80% increase in IT management costs in data centers that can be attributed to the rise of virtualization. But this does not mean we should stop here; there is much work to do to get us past this point into the realm where SDN can actually provide a net gain or benefit for the network operator.

Evidence of this is the introduction of an open source SDN controller called The Open Daylight Project that might address and further optimize the needs of commercial deployments. With this step, the market is essentially acknowledging that the value in SDN is in the applications, and no longer as much in the SDN controller or even the hypervisor.

Consumers still want and need SDN (particularly if they have embraced virtualization).

The economic result of SDN for the short term may be a shift in the component cost of solutions that creates an even larger software component (both in new business apps and new/requisite management apps) of the solution sum.

This is not threatening to the existing ecosystem of network element (hardware) vendors —as long as it is their own software sales that are pulling through sales of their own hardware (i.e., they keep most or all of the sum). Some vendors are even claiming gains in their high-end hardware by adopting SDN concepts.

Embedded network element vendors are actively doing the math on the costs and benefits of virtualization of their embedded platforms (e.g., BNG), and when they do, their calculations have to take into account optimizations that new entrants might make (e.g., discarding unnecessary functionality that clutters the code base, dissembling the components in more cost-effective configurations), and currently see the packaging (power in W/Gbps and footprint) and silicon cost/performance having advantages over the current generation of Intel/ARM processing (with IO optimizations).

Whether this will always be the case remains to be seen, but they have already begun the refactoring of services to comply with customer desires and create new, optimized versions of these platform solutions that include x86 compute for some parts.

So, while direct economic impacts of SDN are harder to find, the indirect consequences have already begun to manifest.

SDN Is Really About Operations and Management

We're probably not done spending on or exploring the management aspect of SDN yet, as a new generation of BSS/OSS is still evolving to be able to keep up with a more virtual/programmable/nimble network.

Traditional B/OSS vendors like BMC, Amdocs, CA, and others are struggling against IPsoft, Tail-f, and ServiceNow in the Cloud OSS market as the evolution of a real-time OSS for these environments (in some cases, incorporating advanced capabilities like integrated policy engines and embedded analytics) has begun.

This environment also opens opportunities for traditional network equipment vendors (e.g., Cisco, ALU) to participate more fully in the next generation of OSS/BSS (as well as venerable SDN heavyweights like VMware).

In the end, one of the main thrusts and motivations of SDN is about optimizing operations. Earlier in the text, we talked about the network-application divide. It is this analogy that forms the basis for much of what SDN is out to solve—or at least make better, both for the network user and the network operator.

Multiple Definitions of SDN

SDN is still evolving an operational level of abstraction. There are different general definitions of what SDN is that have a correlation to the amount of the distributed control plane that is maintained (Figure 13-2).

The ONF offers a forwarding plane SDN definition (a.k.a. clean slate), in which there is no real vestige of the distributed control plane (arguably, there is a necessary thin layer of distributed control plane in the high-frequency loop applications like OAM and BFD) and the layer of abstraction is hop-by-hop forwarding entries to construct a flow path (versus the overlay SDN model, which would only program the tunnel heads and tails on the periphery of the network).

The overlay SDN definition focuses on creating a flexible overlay of tunnels to create virtual networks and presumes that the distributed control plane exists in the underlay and is actually helpful. For example, ISIS is very good at element discovery, very stable, and thus helpful with the "bootstrap the network" problem for the underlying network. The underlying distributed control plane is assumed to be somewhat optimized (e.g., it supports a high degree of ECMP). And, while this mode assumes the reuse of the existing distributed control paradigm, it is a more simplified distributed control in comparison with the control plane SDN in that it doesn't presume the use of MPLS or higher level processes like BGP. Rather, the simpler distributed control paradigm is combined with a controller for managing the bulk of external state (which may have been carried in BGP address families in the control plane SDN model).

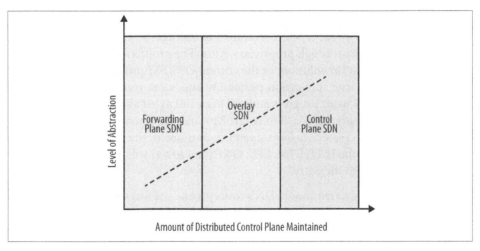

Figure 13-2. The many classifications of SDN (abstraction and control plane)

Traditional network equipment manufacturers put forth a control plane SDN definition in which the programmability of the existing IP/MPLS RIB (and attending routing and security policies) is the focus. This mode assumes the reuse of the existing distributed paradigm (with some potential simplifications). This higher level of abstraction relieves the controller of some of the requisite knowledge of element hardware forwarding capability attendant in the forwarding plane SDN definition:

- In control plane SDN, there is room for some logical centralization, particularly for a centralized proxy that distills the necessary set of forwarding entries applicable for a specific application on a smaller/weaker forwarding entity (e.g., a hypervisor based switch).

- In control plane SDN, there is room for simplification (e.g., eliminating the distribution of labels via LDP or RSVP with segment routing or eliminating the need for extensive configuration to create and populate VRFs with XMPP).

- In control plane SDN, it will be possible to do source/destination-based routing with segment routing in combination with programmability extensions to a centralized PCE server (without the creation of an overlay mesh of LSPs).

For all modes of SDN, the mantra of logically centralized but physically distributed (which was coined to address the reality of highly available geo-dispersed deployments) is *still* distributed at its heart, where the problems with state consensus have just moved to another distribution mechanism.

Are We Making Progress Yet?

In writing this book, we see repeated examples of excellent application ideas bound to proprietary controllers through proprietary APIs. The proliferation of a different type of silo mentality is not the solution for the current OSS/BSS problems SDN has set out to address. Without true application portability and some reasonable expectation of interoperability, SDN won't progress and will fizzle out as yet another fad. It remains to be seen if the framework approach to controllers and the Open Daylight Project open source initiative will create a *de facto* standard, or if one of the longer-winding standardization roads like the IETF, ETSI, ITU, ONF (and so on) will bring a solution or just add more confusion to the party.

While it's good to be excited about SDN's concepts and the ways in which it's taking us, it is easy to get caught up in the tales of unicorn sightings. To this end, we believe there is still much research and plain hard work to be done in areas like troubleshooting (overlays are more difficult than underlays to troubleshoot because forwarding is the concert of all flow operations and we need a potentially new toolset), security, verification, and policy (much of which is being addressed in academia today and slowly entering standards and consortia consideration). Many of these areas will remind of us hard work we did years ago in the operational areas around other new technologies, such as MPLS or IP in order to optimize their use for commercial networks. This often mundane work remains ahead in the SDN area. So with this in mind, the duck on the cover of this book does form an appropriate analogy for the state of SDN today and its future: there is lots of work going on under the surface that may not be visible, or obvious. But if it continues, it can very well propel that duck towards its goal.

Index

We'd like to hear your suggestions for improving our indexes. Send email to index@oreilly.com.

routing information base (RIB), 12
Routing Locator (RLOC), 191
Routing System Working Group (IETF), ix
RSVP-TE networks, 101
Ryu, 92

S

scalability
    of centralized control planes, 38
    in data center orchestration, 306
    of VMware, 79
    in OpenFlow environment, 115
    of pub-sub model, 134
    of routing/switching system, 22
    and SDN controllers, 115
    and service chaining, 222
schema sharing, 162
SDN controllers
    attributes in common, 114
    Big Switch Networks/Floodlight, 93, 115, 115
    Cisco OnePK, 111, 115
    functionality of, 8
    general concepts of, 72
    idealized controller/framework, 72
    layer 3 centric, 96–109
    Mininet, 86
    as network application development frameworks, 265
    as new management entities, 224
    Nicira, 79
    NOX/POX, 87
    OpenFlow-related, 84
    Plexxi Systems, 109
    products available, 73
    and proprietary techniques, 113
    Ryu, 92
    services provided by, 71, 72
    Trema, 89, 115
    varied meaning of, 113
    VMware, 75–79
    VMware/Nicira portfolio, 82
SDN frameworks
    bidirectional communication in, 280
    IETF framework(s), 268
    interoperability and, 262
    Juniper Networks, 265
    Open Daylight controller/framework, 272–278

standardization of, 261
SDN(P) (Software-Driven Network Protocol), 268
segment routing, 106
service abstraction layer (SAL), 272
service chaining, 217–223, 236, 239, 311, 324
Service Enabling Technologies (SETs), 214
Service Engineered Path (SEP), 214
service-oriented architecture (SOA), history of, xi
Ships in the Night (SIN) model, 64
Simple Network Management Protocol (SNMP), 124, 127–131, 245
slow path lookups, 16
software as a service (SaaS), 162
software paths, 16
software-defined networking (SDN)
    benefits of, xiii
    control point controversy, 239
    control/data plane separation, 9, 20
    definition of, xii, xviii, 8, 48, 341
    economic result of, 339
    effect on future mode of operation (FMO), 337
    evolution of, 5
    future of, 342
    history of, ix, xii
    prerequisites to learning, xix
    service chains and, 238
    tight feedback loop in, 121
software-driven networks, 6
southbound interface
    definition of, xxi
    Open Daylight Project and, 274
Spanning Tree Protocol, 188
Spring development environment, 77
SR-IOV, 211
standardization, 117
state storage, 275
stateful PCE (PCE-P), 290
stateless control points, 239
store-and-forward path, 284
subscribers, 132
Swift and Cinder, 148
switched virtual circuits (SVCs), 39
switches
    dual function, 65
    OSI model layer of, xx
syndication protocols, 134

About the Authors

Thomas D. Nadeau is a distinguished engineer in the PSD CTO Office at Juniper Networks, where he is responsible for leading all aspects of software-defined networks and network programmability. Thomas received his BSCS from The University of New Hampshire and a Master of Science from the University of Massachusetts in Lowell, where he has been an adjunct professor of computer science since 2000 and teaches courses on the topic of data communications. He is also on the technical committee of several prominent networking conferences, where he provides technical guidance on their content and frequently presents.

Ken Gray is a distinguished engineer at Juniper Networks responsible for technical strategy and innovation for Juniper Network's Platform Systems Division, and focuses on core routing and the evolving area of software-defined/driven networks. Prior to his current role, Ken worked at Cisco Systems from 1995 to 2011 in a variety of roles, ultimately as a principal engineer working on the development and deployment of high-end routing platforms and operating systems. From 1984 to 1995, Ken was a network geek responsible for designing large public and private networks at a company that ultimately became Verizon. Ken has his MSEE (telecommunications) from the University of Maryland.

Colophon

The animal on the cover of *SDN: Software Defined Networks* is the goosander duck (*Mergus merganser*), also known as the common merganser. These large ducks can be found in rivers and lakes across Europe, Asia, and North America, near forested habitat.

These birds are nicknamed "sawbills" for the serrations on their beaks that help them grip fish, their primary source of food. They will also eat mollusks, crustaceans, amphibians, and other aquatic prey. Their usual hunting technique is to drift some distance on the water and then fish their way back upstream, diving repeatedly along the way. They are powerful swimmers, and find most of their food by sight.

Male and female goosanders have different plumage; the male is white with a dark green iridescent head and back, while females are a more subdued gray with a reddish-brown head. They prefer to build nests in tree cavities, but will also use nest boxes or rock crevices, depending on their surroundings. In early spring, the female lays 9–12 eggs, which she incubates for about a month. Within a day or two of hatching, the ducklings head for the water and soon learn to feed themselves with fish larvae and insects.

These ducks are social and live in small groups—in the winter, they occasionally come together in "floating flocks" of several thousand. Each goosander eats an average of 10–20 ounces of fish a day, which can cause conflicts with the commercial fishing industry.

The cover image is from *Riverside Natural History*. The cover font is Adobe ITC Garamond. The text font is Adobe Minion Pro; the heading font is Adobe Myriad Condensed; and the code font is Dalton Maag's Ubuntu Mono.

Get even more for your money.

Join the O'Reilly Community, and register the O'Reilly books you own. It's free, and you'll get:

- $4.99 ebook upgrade offer
- 40% upgrade offer on O'Reilly print books
- Membership discounts on books and events
- Free lifetime updates to ebooks and videos
- Multiple ebook formats, DRM FREE
- Participation in the O'Reilly community
- Newsletters
- Account management
- 100% Satisfaction Guarantee

Signing up is easy:

1. **Go to: oreilly.com/go/register**
2. **Create an O'Reilly login.**
3. **Provide your address.**
4. **Register your books.**

Note: English-language books only

To order books online:
oreilly.com/store

For questions about products or an order:
orders@oreilly.com

To sign up to get topic-specific email announcements and/or news about upcoming books, conferences, special offers, and new technologies:
elists@oreilly.com

For technical questions about book content:
booktech@oreilly.com

To submit new book proposals to our editors:
proposals@oreilly.com

O'Reilly books are available in multiple DRM-free ebook formats. For more information:
oreilly.com/ebooks

Spreading the knowledge of innovators   oreilly.com

CPSIA information can be obtained at www.ICGtesting.com
Printed in the USA
BVOW10s1535230813

329296BV00001B/1/P